Small Group and Team Communication

Small Group and Team Communication

THIRD EDITION

Thomas E. Harris
University of Alabama

John C. Sherblom
University of Maine

Boston ■ New York ■ San Francisco
Mexico City ■ Montreal ■ Toronto ■ London ■ Madrid ■ Munich ■ Paris
Hong Kong ■ Singapore ■ Tokyo ■ Cape Town ■ Sydney

Series Editor: Brian Wheel
Executive Editor: Karon Bowers
Editorial Assistant: Jennifer Trebby
Marketing Manager: Mandee Eckersley
Editorial Production Service: Whitney Acres Editorial
Manufacturing Buyer: JoAnne Sweeney
Cover Administrator: Joel Gendron
Electronic Composition: Omegatype Typography, Inc.

For related titles and support materials, visit our online catalog at www.ablongman.com.

Between the time Website information is gathered and then published, some sites may have closed. Also, the transcription of URLs can result in typographical errors. The publisher would appreciate being notified of any problems with URLs so that they may be corrected in subsequent editions.

Library of Congress Cataloging-in-Publication Data

Harris, Thomas E.
      Small group and team communication / Thomas E. Harris, John C. Sherblom. — 3rd ed.
         p.   cm.
      Includes bibliographical references and index.
      ISBN 0-205-41491-5 (paperback)
      1. Teams in the workplace.   2. Communication in organizations.   3. Small groups.
   I. Sherblom, John, 1949–   II. Title.

   HD66.H3746   2005
   658.4'036—dc22   2004050367

Printed in the United States of America
   10 9 8 7 6 5 4 3   09 08 07 06 05

Contents

Preface

We have worked to ground this text in the scholarly research of communication while integrating real-world examples and hypothetical situations into the discussion of each chapter's topic to make them readable, interesting, and relevant. The book uses systems theory as a basic orientation to describe small group communication as open and complex systems. In addition, it presents several perspectives for understanding group communication within this systems framework, including a focus on diversity, creativity, and teams. Diversity is treated in a chapter and then integrated into topics throughout the book, connecting diversity to communication in small groups and presenting a functional model that focuses on how diversity can strengthen a group and its ability to perform tasks. Creativity is connected to being a group member and presented with a set of problem-solving tools that are useful to facilitating creativity in small groups. The Team chapter relates group communication to the business world, showing the importance of groups and teams beyond the classroom and school through the use of multiple examples. This edition has been fully updated to reflect changes in the 21st century.

Special Features

Each chapter begins with a short quotation or vignette and ends with a discussion exercise. The quotations and vignettes introduce the chapter topics in thought-provoking ways, to engage the reader and stimulate a lively classroom discussion. Whether it poses Stewart Brand's question to Gregory Bateson about the color of a chameleon on a mirror to introduce the concept of systems of interaction (Chapter 2), Abbott and Costello's "Who's on First?" routine to introduce listening (Chapter 7), or Thoreau's famous telling of the ants' battle in *Walden* to introduce conflict management (Chapter 12), the vignettes, quotations, and other examples introduce the chapters' concepts and provide entry points for discussion. At the end of each chapter, exercises such as "the new truck" exercise that works with group norms and roles (Chapter 3), the "diversity and living together" exercise that examines diversity of living habits (Chapter 5), and the "to catch a spy" exercise that looks at verbal and nonverbal communication (Chapter 6) are designed to move beyond the reading, in an enjoyable and engaging way, into an application and experience of the concepts presented.

The Chapters

Chapter 1 starts with The Rolling Stones' 1997, $89.3 million Bridges to Babylon tour to introduce the concepts of the power of groups—symbolic behavior, shared meaning, interpersonal attraction, attitude similarity, need complementarity, need for affiliation, and commitment to group goals and activities. The chapter looks at the founding of the Sony Corporation and of Hewlett-Packard Corporation, and ends with exercises including an example of the invention of the light bulb to stimulate a discussion of what constitutes a group and how many people's work goes into a single invention or creation.

Chapter 2 begins with Stewart Brand's posing of a riddle to Gregory Bateson about the color of a chameleon placed on a mirror. It uses this example to introduce the concepts of systems of interaction, of general systems theory's conceptions of open systems (wholeness, synergy, openness, transformation, interdependence, feedback, entropy, equifinality) and complex systems theory (quantum change, double-loop learning, sensitivity to initial conditions, strange attractors, phase space, bifurcation points, irreversibility). The chapter ends with exercises and a discussion of the systems principles involved in training elephants at the San Diego Zoo.

Chapter 3 introduces the concepts of group norms, roles, cohesiveness, and groupthink through an example of a surgical nurse working in a hospital. It ends with exercises and a role-play in which participants collectively decide who gets a new company truck.

Chapter 4 introduces the common phases (forming, storming, norming, performing, and finally terminating) that groups typically go through, with an example of an international consulting team and their accomplishment of a project in South America. It concludes with exercises including one in which groups form a small consulting firm that must define itself and its vision through the development of a name, logo, and slogan that all work together and project a coherent image.

Chapter 5 deals with diversity in groups and begins with a quotation from *Finite and Infinite Games* on the relationship of the individual to the community. It ends with a query and discussion of common everyday-living decisions that people make and an inquiry into the reasons behind those decisions to show that diversity of perspective is more than just thinking differently. It is based in the different experiences in life. Several exercises allow the reader to apply the concepts.

Chapter 6 starts with a joke and investigates the verbal and nonverbal aspects of communication. What makes things funny? What gives meaning to communication and to its interpretation? It ends with group exercises including "to catch a spy," in which participants make judgments about others based on their verbal and nonverbal communication in a way that all can see the accuracy and inaccuracy of those predictions, as well as the aspects of that communication that are interpreted in a way that leads to those predictions.

Chapter 7 introduces listening and feedback with the Abbott and Costello routine "Who's on First?," then moves on to topics of active listening, the barriers to active listening, and ways of providing constructive feedback. It ends with several exercises including a "nondebate" exercise in which participants choose one side of an issue and develop their argument, but then must listen carefully and paraphrase the other side of that issue.

Chapter 8 describes the evolution of groups into teams. It begins with Bill Russell's description of magical periods of basketball during which the game evolves from more than a game, more than a competition, to really playing. This chapter describes the importance of teams, their qualities, the limitations to quality circles, and the development of self-managing work teams. It ends with exercises on group evolution.

Chapter 9 begins with a simple decision to drink a cup of French vanilla coffee with a fly in it and moves through the stages of decision making and problem solving, examining brainstorming, group process, and concurrence seeking. It ends with several exercises designed to work through the critical and creative stages of decision making.

Chapter 10 investigates creativity, beginning with an interesting story from Lewis Thomas's *Lives of a Cell* about a methodical but noncreative wasp. It defines creativity and its importance in small group discussion, decision making, and problem solving. It discusses the barriers and facilitators of creative processes, and ends with an exercise designed to explore ways in which groups can develop their creative interactions. Exercises applying these concepts conclude the chapter.

Chapter 11 introduces group process and presentational techniques. Starting with Rod Serling's story about the selling of a Sherman tank, it moves through brainstorming, creative decision-making techniques (focus groups, nominal group technique, delphi technique, synectics, buzz sessions, idea writing, and listening teams), problem-solving tools (flowcharts, fishbone diagrams, Pareto's principle), risk and performance evaluation techniques (RISK, PERT), and small group presentation formats (forum, panel, colloquium, symposium). Exercises at the end involve practicing these techniques.

Chapter 12 moves from a destructive ant war to constructive conflict management among humans. It deals with productive conflict management within systems of interaction, patterns of effective conflict resolution, and power within that context. It ends with a mediation exercise designed to highlight and illustrate the application of these concepts. Additional exercises are presented.

Chapter 13 introduces leadership as vision, credibility, and competence; provides a brief history of leadership theories, the characteristics, tasks, influences, and problems of leadership; and ends with an exercise of taking on leadership roles. Exercises are offered at the end.

Chapter 14 uses March's quip about a U.S. Senator proposing to end the Vietnam War by having the army "declare a victory and come home" to introduce the need for observing and evaluating small group communication and process. It ends with sample evaluation forms and an exercise for using them.

Chapter 15 connects the small group process with computer mediated group communication (CMC). It explains the key CMC uses and the benefits and limitations. The chapter ends with exercises that assist in understanding CMC.

Each chapter in this book is designed to focus on one aspect of communication in small groups in a way that builds on and is integrated with the other chapters.

We could not have produced the present book alone, and we'd like to thank the people who have made it possible. We thank our spouses Shelia Harris and Liz Sherblom, who have provided social and emotional support, listening ears, and who helped with important decision-making suggestions throughout the process. They were engaged in seemingly endless reading and editing, and they even contributed to parts of the book. And we thank the reviewers: Carolyn L. Clark, Salt Lake City Community College; John Meyer, University of Southern Mississippi; and C. Thomas Preston, Jr., University of Missouri–St Louis. All made helpful comments and suggestions for the direction and development of the third edition of this book. Our goal has been to write an interesting and informative (as well as instructional) book that is fun to use with small groups. We hope that you enjoy it.

1

Small Groups: Power, Definition, and Attraction

CHAPTER OUTLINE

The Power of Groups

Defining Small Group Communication
Transactional Process
Symbolic Behavior
Shared Meaning

Why Join a Group?
Interpersonal Attraction
Need for Affiliation
Commitment to Group Goals and Activities
Assignment by Someone Else

Ethical Behavior

Characteristics of Small Groups
Interdependence and Interactivity
Exponential Number of Interactions
Synergy

Characteristics of Small Group Communication
Complex Transactions
Interactive Complexities

Types of Small Groups

Groups in Organizations
Examples from the Automotive Industry
Meetings

Meeting Effectiveness

Summary

Discussion Questions

Exercises

References

CHAPTER OBJECTIVES

- Understand the power of groups.
- Understand the reasons for joining groups.
- Explain the basis for interpersonal attraction.
- Outline the essential characteristics of small groups.
- Explain synergy.
- Map the small group communication process.
- Introduce the types of groups.
- Demonstrate the role of small groups in organizations.

KEY TERMS

Attitude similarity
Complex communication
  characteristics
Conference groups
Educational or learning groups
Exponential interactions
Interactive
Interdependence
Interpersonal attraction
Mediated communication
  groups

Meetings
Need complementarity
Organizational groups
Physical proximity
Primary groups
Problem-solving groups
Quality circles
Self-managing work groups
Shared meaning
Simultaneous sending
  and receiving

Social and casual groups
Substance, pattern and
  process
Symbolic behavior
Synergy
Therapeutic groups
Transactional Process
Work groups

When The Rolling Stones finished their worldwide Voodoo Lounge tour in 1994, they had made over $300 million (Lander, 1994). Their 1997 Bridges to Babylon tour in the United States alone generated another $89.3 million ("Rolling Stones top," 1998). The Rolling Stones had broken up in the 1980s, but Mick Jagger and Keith Richards quickly discovered that they needed the group synergy to produce their best-selling recordings. Now, as a group, they make more money than any of them could expect to make on their own (Davis, 2001). Michael P. Stone, on the other hand, earned $20 an hour as a member of a self-managed work team in an electronics company until he was fired because his team decided that he detracted from their productivity and they could perform better without him. Not many of us will ever have the opportunity to earn $300 million as part of a rock group, but most of us have to work effectively in groups to do ordinary, less glamorous, and less profitable jobs in today's work world.

Group work can be exciting, ego-enhancing, and creative. It can also be boring, demeaning, and extremely frustrating. The key to successful, satisfying groups is effective communication. This book is about developing communication strategies that help make group work more satisfying, effective, and successful—strategies that help produce groups that are fun to work in and that generate useful, sometimes even outstanding, results.

The information you will learn will apply equally well to teams, which have become a cornerstone for many organizations. Xerox, a corporate name so familiar that it includes an activity called xeroxing, champions "rugged groupism." It has a firm belief that "a diverse group of people—using their own creativity, innovation, judgment, intuition, and brainpower, can do a better job in today's world of constant change" than traditional management ("Beyond Quality," 1992, p. 24). Using diverse groups to make decisions wisely takes advantage of the importance of different opinions, perspectives, and insights. Although we are more likely to be emotionally comfortable with a homogenous or similar group or team, a heterogeneous or diverse group or team improves performance in terms of decision quality (Jackson, May, & Whitney, 1995). The more we function in diverse groups, the greater the likelihood we will learn to profit from expanded perspectives. Organizations view a diverse work force as both the right thing to do and a competitive advantage in terms of problem solving and attracting employees (Mehta, 2000).

Few of us will engage in occupations as challenging as Formula One automobile racing. Frank Williams, head of one of the most successful Formula Race teams of all times, concludes: "Teamwork is an essential ingredient on and off the race track" ("The team," 1998, p. 24). Brushing aside a near fatal car accident in 1986 that left him confined to a wheelchair, Williams's crew has outperformed the other 11 international teams that compete in the approximately 16 Formula One races held globally. His first priority is an "emphasis on communication" with every team member. At Suburban Hospital in Bethesda, Maryland, teams are credited "with reducing errors, shortening the amount of time patients spend in its twelve bed ICU (intensive care unit) and improving communication between families and medical staff" (Appleby & Davis, 2001, p. B1). Appleby and Davis (2001) add "one reason that teamwork is so vital in modern medicine is the speed at which advances are being made" (p. B2). Teams keep the members up to date. Like the ICU, "in high-pressure workplaces, such as nuclear plants, aircraft cockpits, or the military, teamwork is essential to survival" (Appleby & Davis, 2001, p. B2). Teams, like groups, come in many shapes and sizes. Motorola, Ritz-Carlton Hotels, Boeing, Federal Express, and Texas Instruments all see teams as critical but use different types and configurations.

Learning to be a useful and effective team member is important to our careers. Survey results titled "Unwanted: Solo Artists" report what 150 executives told Accutemps, a staffing firm, would more likely hurt a person's chances for getting ahead. Poor team player skills received 57% of the responses, complacency received 21%, excessive complaining received 14%, and defensiveness received 6% ("By the numbers," 1995). Seventy-eight percent of all U.S. companies of 100 or more employees have employees working in teams. "Teams are a favorite way to organize employees, to get work done, and to facilitate workplace learning" ("1995 Industry Report," 1995). We will offer additional examples of the power of groups and teams throughout.

The Power of Groups

In 1945 in a bombed-out department store in Tokyo, Masaru Ibuka met with seven other former store employees and committed his total personal savings of $1,600 to start a company. They had no product and no immediate plans or ideas, so the group sat together in conference in those depressing surroundings for several weeks, brainstorming about what kind of business the new company should enter. The result of that group process was the company known today as the Sony Corporation (Collins & Porras, 2002).

When Bill Hewlett and Dave Packard founded their company in the late 1930s, they had no specific product in mind and no goals or plans, but they did trust each other's abilities, and they knew how to use the small group communication process to develop their expertise into what became the Hewlett-Packard Corporation. Over time that corporation grew so large and had so many levels of management that eventually it moved too slowly to maintain its competitive edge, and Hewlett-Packard began heading for extinction (Belasco, 1990). In 1989, however, Hewlett-Packard again drew on the creative power of small groups and transformed itself from an organization that took years to make a decision into one that could act in weeks or days to resolve important issues (Hof, 1992). Hewlett-Packard got its start through the synergistic power of small group communication, grew into an organization dependent on bureaucratic rules and top-down decision making, and finally returned to its roots in small group decision making to reinvigorate itself and become successful once again.

These are not isolated examples. Groups are the fundamental building blocks of any organization. Marriott, Motorola, Honda, Disney, Wal-Mart, Nordstrom, Merck, and Procter & Gamble all began with a small group of motivated and gifted individuals meeting on a regular basis. These and many more great companies can trace their beginnings to small group decision-making processes. Not all of their first attempts succeeded, but they believed in the importance of group effort and ultimately developed highly successful companies based upon the effective work of small groups (Collins & Porras, 2002).

Defining Small Group Communication

We define communication, in general, as a transaction between and among people, whereby all the parties are continually and simultaneously sending and receiving information. A small group is a collection of at least three and ordinarily fewer than 20 individuals, who are interdependent, influence each other over some period of time, share a common goal or purpose, assume specialized roles, have a sense of mutual belonging, maintain norms and standards for group membership, and engage in interactive communication. *Small group communication is the transactional process of using symbolic behavior to achieve shared meaning among group members over a period of time.* There are three key concepts in this definition: transactional process, symbolic behavior, and shared meaning.

Transactional Process

Communication is more than merely exchanging messages or transferring information from one person to another. Early models of communication focused on senders putting their messages into words and gestures and sending them through channels to the receiver. The conscientious sender tried to make the message as clear as possible so that the receiver could take the information and act as expected. When that did not occur, it was considered a failed communication.

This one-way, linear flow of messages was criticized for neglecting the receiver's influence. This led to the development of interactional models of communication. Feedback was added, and the importance of reciprocal message exchanges between the sender and receiver was recognized. While an important improvement, these models still envisioned communication as a sophisticated Ping-Pong match where the sender serves and the receiver is expected to return the serve. When the receiver failed to return the serve as expected, these models attributed the results to a communication breakdown.

Neither of these approaches adequately describe communication failures or help facilitate better communication. While there is a certain appeal to the simplistic notion that human communication breaks down along straightforward lines, this concept tends to ignore the interactive dynamic of the communication process itself. In small group communication, all group members are both senders and receivers, *simultaneously sending and receiving both verbal and nonverbal messages.* No one can *not* communicate (Watzlawick, Beavin, & Jackson, 1967). While the communication may not be what we intend to communicate, we nevertheless communicate something. Remaining silent during an important meeting is as much a communication as speaking. Standing someone up for an appointment or a date is a message, whether we intend it that way or not.

It is often interesting to note how we adapt our own behaviors and speech patterns to accommodate those of others in a group. An intriguing test of this concept is to sit in a small group and, when another person is speaking, make eye contact with that person and scratch your nose. Notice what that person does. We are frequently unaware of the extent to which we modify our behaviors or what we are saying, in response to the behaviors and reactions of other group members. This adaptation is often not conscious, but it has an important effect on the group process.

Once we accept the impossibility of not communicating, we can begin to understand why actions we may take, and to which we attribute little or no importance, may have an impact in a small group out of all proportion to what we intended. How often we attend meetings, whether we arrive on time or late, where we sit, how often and when we speak, our tone of voice, and our other nonverbal behaviors are all communicating something. These transactions impact our role in the group process and affect the overall group dynamic as much as the content of what we say.

Symbolic Behavior

For many observers, our most important defining characteristic as human beings is our capacity to use and respond to a system of significant symbols (Duncan, 1962). The meanings of both verbal and nonverbal communication exist in the symbolic significance we attribute to the words and the nonverbal behaviors. The meanings exist in us as individuals, not in the words themselves. We will develop a discussion of verbal and nonverbal communication later in this book, but consider for a moment how different people respond to the nation's flag, to obscene words, to public displays of affection, or to one's own school colors. While the symbols are real, our reactions are based on the symbolic importance we, as individuals or social groups, have attached to them. The use and abuse of symbols is an inherently human activity (Wood, 2000).

Shared Meaning

Because we each assign different symbolic significance to verbal and nonverbal expressions, arriving at common or "shared" meanings can be difficult. If I am in the mood to listen to music and someone tells me to "buy CDs," I am likely to think in terms of music CDs, rather than the certificates of deposit (CDs) that person may have had in mind. The development of shared meaning is, however, an essential goal of small group communication, and an ideal for small group meetings is to end with everyone arriving at a more or less shared understanding of the meaning of the ongoing communication. This is difficult to achieve in actual fact because we are all deeply influenced by our own sets of experiences and assumptions, but it is an ideal nonetheless.

Why Join a Group?

We join groups for many reasons. Four of the most common are: interpersonal attraction, personal need for affiliation, meaning, or identity, commitment to group goals and activities, and assignment to the group by someone else (see Figure 1.1). Working with other people can be gratifying and it can be frustrating. As social beings, we seek opportunities to join with others who share our interests or meet our needs. Groups can help us define, clarify, or understand important issues through discussion and the sharing of multiple perspectives. Groups can also help us develop our leadership skills and facilitate our understanding of particular topics. By working with and explaining things to others, we clarify our understanding of a given topic, strengthen our ability to organize our thoughts, develop our ability to think through problems, and learn to better articulate that thinking process to others. By adapting ethical approaches to group work we can achieve even greater success (see Figure 1.2).

Interpersonal Attraction

The three major influences contributing to interpersonal attraction as a reason for joining groups are physical proximity, attitude similarity, and need complementarity (Miller, 1990).

Physical Proximity.   Physical proximity refers to the amount of interaction with other group members in the same physical location. When we all work for the same organization, go to the same university, or live in the same community, we see each other on a regular basis, and it becomes easier to establish a relationship or develop a friendship. While long-distance relationships are possible, the dis-

FIGURE 1.1

Interpersonal Attraction   Need for Affiliation

Physical Proximity
Attitude Similarity
Need Complementarity

┌─────────────────────────────────┐
│   │
│   *Why Join a Group?*   │
│   │
└─────────────────────────────────┘

Commitment to Group   Assignment by
Goals and Activities   Someone Else

tance itself usually places a stressor on the relationship, making it more difficult to maintain (McShane & Von Glinow, 2003). However, proximity alone does not mean that we will want to interact with a particular person. That desire depends on at least two other issues: attitude similarity and need complementarity.

Attitude Similarity. Attitude similarity accounts for one of the reasons we find some people more appealing to interact with than others. When others have similar economic, political, and social views, for example, we are more likely to enjoy interacting with them (Cohen, Fink, Gadon, & Willits, 2001). Although we don't have to agree with each and every attitude someone holds, we do usually need to feel some basic attitude similarities, particularly in areas that are likely to arise in our interactions. However, studies suggest that a congenial conversation with someone we disagree with can ease initial feelings that we simply "do not get along" with that person because of his or her views (Miller, 1990). Alternately, getting into a "heated disagreement" over one's attitude can put a strain on even the best relationship.

Need Complementarity. Need complementarity suggests that we are drawn to other individuals because of some psychological fit. Although we do not always fully agree with another's attitude or perspective, we may share complementary needs. For example, if I like taking charge, am well organized, and am willing to do more than "my fair share of the work," I may work well with people who are looking for a leader and, similarly, they may find me an attractive member of their group. In addition, we are drawn to people we admire or from whom we believe we can learn something. We may also find some group members more directly useful for accomplishing the group's goals than others. To the degree that each member brings a different set of needed skills to the group, there is, within the group, a need complementarity being fulfilled.

Thus, interpersonal attraction, as evidenced by proximity, attitude similarity, and need complementarity, is one of the reasons we join and remain in groups. Our group affiliations are not confined to our attraction to good looks or popularity, but extend to affiliation with those who share similar views or who, while being quite different from us, complement our abilities and fulfill a personal or group need.

Need for Affiliation

Groucho Marx is credited with the line, "I would not want to be a member of any club that would accept me as a member." Most of us, however, need some amount of social contact and frequently find this need met in the relationships formed in groups and clubs (Shaw & Gouran, 1990). Being a member of student government, a motorcycle riding club, a model train society, a sorority or fraternity, an intra-mural volleyball team, or a skydiving club adds a further dimension to our personal identities. Belonging to groups helps us develop and refine our interests, enhances the way we spend our time, and cultivates the types of activities we enjoy.

Many individuals find their work satisfying in part because it provides them with affiliation and identity in work groups. Since most of us spend more time working than we do pursuing any other individual activity, it makes sense that we come to identify a part of ourselves with it and enjoy it. Organizations expend a great deal of time and energy trying to align our identity with their group goals and objectives (Schein, 1985; Harris, 2002). Groups, whether social or work related, offer affiliation, meaning, and identity to our lives.

Commitment to Group Goals and Activities

Groups, as a whole, also have reasons, purposes, and goals for existing that draw us to them. These can range from saving the world, to changing the grading system, to finding a new method for marketing a product. The old expression that "Politics makes strange bedfellows" highlights the notion that people with very different personalities and from different backgrounds may share a common goal and, therefore, can often find themselves members of the same group. You might, for example, work out three times a week at a gym and find that you are more motivated to maintain a regular workout schedule because you work out as part of a group. The three or four people you join during those workouts might have little in common with you outside the gym, but you become a tight-knit group with feelings of interconnectivity within the gym context. If the gym's management tried to close the facility during the hours that your group normally works out, you would probably band together to achieve a mutually important goal of maintaining an open facility during those hours.

FIGURE 1.2   Ethical Behavior

Underlying all group and team success is a commitment by members to ethical behavior. "Ethics concerns the rights and responsibilities, privileges and obligations of our conduct within and between" group or team relationships (Anderson & Englehardt, 2001, p. 7). They are our standards of moral conduct or judgments about whether our actions, values, or decisions are right or wrong (Harris, 2002). Ethics focuses on what we actually do when we are part of a group. The following guidelines are not intended to cover all possible situations but they will lead to greater group and individual effectiveness.

✓ Allow others choices rather than forcing them

✓ Follow-through with group related obligations

✓ Be sensitive to individual group members' needs

✓ Maintain confidentiality

✓ Honesty, keeping promises, fulfilling commitments

✓ Fairness in work assignment, dealing with others, and treatment of others

✓ Strive for full participation by all members

✓ Concern for the group or team

✓ Tolerance of other members' ideas, strengths, and weakenesses

✓ Focus on success for all group members not just ourselves

✓ Seek the greatest good for the group members

Sources: Anderson & Englehardt (2001), Hackman & Johnson (2000), Harris (2002).

Assignment by Someone Else

We do not always have the option of deciding for ourselves which groups we will join. In almost any organization, there are necessary—sometimes arbitrary—assignments to groups. Frequently, we find ourselves in groups that are important to us but that we did not identify or select for ourselves. We were assigned to them by someone else. Even so, participation in these groups can be fulfilling and fun (see Figure 1.2).

Characteristics of Small Groups

Three principal characteristics define small groups. These characteristics are interdependence and interactivity, the number of possible interactions among group members, and the possibility of synergy in the group's efforts and results.

Interdependence and Interactivity

Simply meeting and talking with each other is not enough to constitute a small group. If the associated collection of people are primarily interested in individual accomplishments, have little or nothing vested in the activities of each other, or if they are frequently absent from meetings, this collection of people will not be considered a small group in this discussion. It becomes a small group when the members are interdependent and interactive to the point of each being impacted by the group process.

This interdependent group can be a pick-up basketball team or the board of directors of a large corporation. A family sitting around the dinner table discussing family matters, reviewing the day's activities, and resolving important family issues constitutes a small group because of their communication interaction. On the other hand, a disengaged set of family members sitting together in silence in front of the television set may not constitute such a group. An accidental or momentary meeting with friends at a local restaurant might qualify as a small group in terms of their small group communication, if they experience an interdependence, a common goal, or a sense of purpose, and if they engage in interactive communication roles. Many important decisions are made by groups of friends, business associates, and public officials meeting over coffee and talking informally about key issues and concerns. Thus, small group communication can take place in casual, informal settings, as well as in more formal business, community, social, sports, and school settings. The key to identifying small group communication is not the setting but the interaction of the group and the quality of the communication.

Exponential Number of Interactions

Another characteristic of small groups is the dynamic resulting from the exponential number of interactions among the members. As we add members to our small group, we increase the number of potential interactions, and we alter the possibilities for communication among members. As shown in the following chart, the potential number of inputs and alternative viewpoints increases exponentially as each new person is added. This can be seen simultaneously as one of the major benefits and one of the major drawbacks of small group communication.

People and Interactions							
Number of people in group	2	3	4	5	6	7	8
Interactions possible	2	9	28	75	186	441	1,016

Each of these interactions requires attention, and as the number of interactions grows, a group needs an increased sensitivity to and understanding of background issues. Increased numbers of interactions create a more complex decision-making process as the number and diversity of relationships within the group must be taken into account. Outcomes, however, also have an opportunity of being more sophisticated as the diversity of perspectives that must be taken into account and addressed increases.

Synergy

Synergy comes from the Greek word *sunergos* which means "working together" (Morris, 1981). Synergy results from two or more people working together, sharing ideas with open minds and mutual respect, and managing conflict in ways that empower all members. Synergy is defined as "the action of two or more . . . to achieve an effect of which each is individually incapable" (Morris, 1981). This is the advantage of working in a group: The whole of the group is greater than the sum of its parts. The group process creates an outcome that is different from and often superior to what any of the group members might have generated on their own. Something happens as a group allows one person's ideas to stimulate another's thoughts during the discussion, causing a third person to think of something totally new. This new idea is refined by the first person, incorporated within a new idea by the second, extended further by the third. As the group process continues, something emerges that is new, creative, and unique to this particular group and interaction. In such an interactive building process, it becomes impossible and irrelevant to attribute the final solution or even any set of ideas to a particular individual. The outcome is a new whole, no longer easily separable into its component parts (Wite, 1999).

The effectiveness of small groups lies in the dynamics of the decision-making process. Because members bounce ideas off each other and parts of many ideas may be recombined, coalescing to form new and different ideas, the result is frequently something entirely new and unexpected. This process of small group decision making is similar to the chemical reaction that produces water from hydrogen and oxygen. The water is an entirely new substance, having properties not easily explained by the characteristics of hydrogen and oxygen molecules alone. This synergistic reaction is what makes small groups such a potentially powerful decision-making tool. A review of 50 years of studies on cooperative decision making found that problem solving is more effective when done by groups over the work of individuals (Berko, 1996).

Characteristics of Small
Group Communication

Each of us, as group members, brings our own definition, interpretation, personal history, and judgment concerning the appropriateness of any particular group activity. This response, in and of itself, creates an ongoing, continuous modification of that activity. Therefore, while a small group is communicating, it is nearly impossible to freeze-frame a given moment. That moment is defined by the continuity of all that has gone on before, during, and even after that moment. It represents a complex transaction occurring between and influenced by each of the participants and their perceptions of those events. Group members, individually and collectively, provide a continual defining and redefining of the group: the member relationships; topics open for discussion; and group norms, rules, and roles. If, for instance, a group member suddenly gets angry at a particular point being made, that anger may trigger a group response. That one person's reaction may redefine the group discussion, even if only temporarily. This sense of a wholeness in a group's communication can also be seen in the experience of something that strikes the group as hysterically funny. Relating the humor of that incident to someone else who was not present often becomes impossible. "You really had to be there" to appreciate the humor within the process and context of the group.

Complex Transactions

Complex group transactions involve three elements: substance, pattern, and process. The *substance* consists of the content of the group interaction—the issues around which the group is formed and communicates. The *pattern* consists of the relationships and interactions between the group members (Watzlawick, Beavin, & Jackson, 1967). The *process* is the intermediary action between the substance and the pattern; it is the catalyst that gives "life" to the group interaction.

If I say, "Let's meet at 7:30 on the Mall," the statement has a literal content meaning but it also contains a relational, interactive element—an assumption of a pattern in our relationship. It assumes that it is appropriate for me to suggest the time and place of the meeting and that those to whom I am speaking are expected to show up. The way each of us interprets and reacts to this statement indicates our relational process. If a group member shows up for the meeting at 7:35, is she or he late? Has he or she violated a group "timeliness norm"? Has he kept everyone waiting? Is she being rude or simply applying appropriate group expectations for behavior? Likewise, if I tell a joke in the middle of a serious group discussion, am I fulfilling an important group communication function of "lightening things up," engaging in inappropriate behavior of "wasting the group's time," or "acting out" against the wishes of the group? Whether I am late for the group meeting when I arrive five minutes after the stated starting time or am "wasting the group's time" when I tell a joke depends upon the norms that have been established for the group. All relationships and small group interactions happen simultaneously on several levels. They involve what is said (the substance), the relationships and interactions between the people involved (the pattern), and the action that mediates between those two and that unites them (the process). Each group develops its own norms for appropriate group substance, pattern, and process.

Interactive Complexities

Small groups share many of the communication characteristics that make interpersonal and public communication effective, but due to the complexity of the interactions in small groups, some important differences in the communication process also need to be taken into account. Like effective interpersonal dyads, the members of small groups are mutually interdependent and, therefore, mutually responsible for the success or failure of the group's communication. Members of small groups share responsibility for speaking, listening, feedback, and empathy with dyadic communication, but in small groups those responsibilities are made more complex by the multiple sets of interactions.

Group interactions contrast with most types of public speaking. Although, in both cases, the speaker is attempting to present a message to an audience, in public speaking, the audience is not usually expected to participate, other than to listen. The preparation for and success of the presentation is placed largely on the speaker. If one member of the audience in a public speaking situation does not show up, the speech itself is probably not affected. In a small group or an interpersonal dyad, on the other hand, each member is an important part of the communication interaction. If one member does not show up or does not participate, the whole group is impacted.

Whereas public speaking can happen effectively in very large groups, a group numbering more than 15 to 20 members can no longer function effectively as a "small" group. The potential number of interactions produced by the increased number of people overwhelms the dynamics of the group process itself. Because small groups are a function of the interaction between a group of people with different points of view, they depend on the ability of the group to hear and incorporate that multiplicity of ideas. When the number of possible interactions becomes too large, that integration and merging of ideas becomes difficult or impossible.

In addition, small groups tend to have an ongoing interactive identity that may or may not be substantially altered by changes in membership. This differs from the total interdependence of a dyad and the relative independence of a public speaking forum. In a dyad, if one of the two members quits, the dyad no longer exists. In a public speaking forum, on the other hand, the speech is set ahead of time, and the make-up of the audience, while important in terms of the acceptance or rejection of the message and the speaker, plays a substantially different role. For the small group, the loss or addition of a group member may not wholly either eliminate or create the group's ability to discuss issues, function, and make progress, but it will substantially affect the group's process.

Types of Small Groups

Small groups are everywhere and are of many types. Family, work, school, and leisure activities may all involve small groups. In each context we work with others to come to common understandings and to make decisions that affect each of us to some degree. Each type of small group can be characterized by the kind of communication that takes place within it.

Our immediate family is, for most of us, a significant small group affiliation and may be referred to as a *primary* group or a basic social unit to which we belong. This type of small group tends to be the most informal, and we ordinarily remain members in it over a long period of time. *Social* and *casual* groups extend our primary-group relationships. Sports teams, discussion groups, school or church groups, leisure activities, and other special-interest or activity groups may all provide extended social primary-group relationships. Our membership in these groups may be solely for companionship, or we may use these affiliations to help us understand and deal with important issues in our lives or to develop professional, personal, or social roles and skills.

Educational or *learning* groups are concerned primarily with discovering and developing new ideas and ways of thinking. These may include educational courses, seminars, or enlightenment groups. An extension of this type of group is the *therapeutic* group, in which members come together to learn about themselves and their relationships with others. The communication in this type of group is characterized by discussion and analysis of a particular issue, but it may not be organized in such a way or vested with authority to directly solve problems. Support, therapy, and consciousness-raising groups, whose main task is the development and maintenance of group process and relationships, have been studied very little (Wyatt, 1993), but that type of group is not the main focus of this text.

Decision-making and *problem-solving* groups, on the other hand, are convened for the express purpose of making a decision, solving a problem, or dealing with specific issues. A board of directors may meet to determine company goals and policies or to deal with the latest budgetary dilemma. Committees are problem-solving groups that are assigned a task, usually by some other person or group. They may be formed either as *standing* committees that exist for an enduring period of time, or as *ad hoc* committees intended to accomplish a specific task rapidly and to be disbanded when the task is completed. Social and political organizations often have various committees ranging from personnel and membership to program and executive.

Work groups may be seen as a type of problem-solving group. Work groups have evolved in the last ten years within business organizations and occur at all organizational levels, from McDonald's crews to high-level executive retreats where organizational policy and direction are determined. The immediate office group or production team is an ongoing part of most jobs, and the effectiveness of these groups can influence both an individual's productivity level and happiness within the organization. *Quality circles* and *self-managing work* groups are two specialized examples of work groups. Their goals are to increase the quality and performance effectiveness of their groups.

In addition to problem-solving groups, *conference* groups are formed with representatives from several different groups. In many cases, their meetings provide vital information-sharing and coordinating opportunities. An extension of conference groups can be seen in *mediated communication* groups. Made possible through the use of electronic message carriers, such as computers and teleconferencing equipment, these groups permit people in disparate locations to communicate and solve problems of mutual concern. Further, the informal liaisons promulgated by the availability of electronic media for communication add another layer to these mediated communication groups. Many in the business and professional world, as well as in schools and homes, use e-mail and other Internet services regularly and are members of various on-line groups. The particular communication strategies used in small groups depends to some degree on the context of the interaction and the goals the group wants to accomplish. For example, electronic communication poses different issues for small group communication than does face-to-face communication. Different types of face-to-face situations and overall contexts also place quite different types of demands on the communication interactions.

Groups in Organizations

Groups and teams, used effectively, produce outstanding results. They can enhance creativity and expand the scope of alternative solutions. Most successful companies and large corporations have been started by brainstorming in small groups, rather than by a single individual acting alone.

Small groups are the cornerstones of many aspects of organizational behavior, operating at all levels and playing major roles in the informal and formal interactions in organizations (Harris, 2002). Organizations make use of committees, task forces, work groups, and a vast number of other types of groups and teams, ranging from electronic networks to interdisciplinary problem-solving groups.

Examples from the Automotive Industry

The Ford Motor Company provides an example of the effective use of small groups. In the early 1980s, Ford had become the butt of numerous jokes. FORD: "Found on the Road Dead," "Fix or Repair Daily." Unless you were a diehard Ford fan, you were probably shopping around for another brand. The Ford Motor Company knew it was in trouble and wanted to understand the problem and how to improve the product and its public perception, in order to increase sales. It organized focus groups to find out what people liked and disliked about Fords. The researchers asked the focus group members, "Have you driven a Ford lately?" The majority of the participants indicated that they could not even remember the last time they had ridden in a Ford (Waterman, 1987), but Ford got enough feedback to redesign the production processes and product offerings. In addition, Ford began using groups within the organization for everything from inventory control and product quality management to customer relations (Bolman & Deal, 1991; Osborn, Moran, Musselwhite, & Zenger, 1990). Now, when Ford says "Quality Is Job 1," the company is referring to the power of groups to create better automobiles, and today, Ford Taurus and Mercury Sable are considered among the best cars available. Ford now has a much different image and market share than it did in the days of the old Ford Pinto.

The General Motors Saturn plant provides another example of effective group work. This plant was considered one of the leading experiments in maximizing employee input through the use of groups and teams to produce quality automobiles in the 1990s (Woodruff, 1992). "Organized as a collection of small, self-directed business units . . . each team manages everything from its own budget and inventory control to hiring, without direct oversight from top management" (Woodruff, 1992, p. 66). By reducing the bureaucracy inherent in most large organizations, Saturn has generated some remarkable results. "Absenteeism averages just 2.5% versus 10%–14% at other GM plants" (Woodruff, 1992, p. 66). Employees have a strong commitment to their company, and "Saturn builds the highest-quality American cars, with defect rates rivaling those of Hondas and Nissans. The cars are selling so well dealers cannot keep them in stock" (Woodruff, 1992, p. 66). A J. D. Powers and Associates survey of new car owners ranked

Saturn (at $9,995–$12,895) just below Lexus and Infiniti automobiles ($35,000+) in customer satisfaction (Byrne, 1993).

Meetings

One gauge of how prevalent groups are in organizations is the role of meetings (see Figure 1.3). An estimated 11 million (Watson & Barmer, 1990) to 20 million meetings (Cole, 1989) take place in organizations in the United States every day!

A survey of chief marketing executives of the Fortune 1,000 companies revealed that they worked an average of 59 hours a week, spending 21 of those hours in meetings. That's more than one-third of their working week ("Management Meetings," 1988). In 1987, $7.1 billion was spent on corporate-wide meetings such as conferences, retreats, and strategy sessions ("What Business," 1988). In 1990 *Industry Week* estimated that organizations committed $37 billion worth of employees' time to meetings each year ("Meetings Unpopular," 1990).

Committees, conferences, and meetings have fostered many tongue-in-cheek comments such as: "A meeting brings together a group of the unfit, appointed by the unwilling, to do the unnecessary"; "A camel is a horse designed by a committee"; "A conference is a meeting of people who singly do nothing, and who collectively agree that nothing can be done"; and "A conference is a meeting to decide when the next meeting will be held." Yet, small group meetings have persisted in organizations, and as organizations move to flatten hierarchies and increase the use of self-managed work teams, the number and amount of time spent communicating in small group meetings is likely to increase. Effective small group communication has moved from an advantage to a necessity in organizational work today.

Figure 1.4 provides some guidelines for increasing your meetings' effectiveness.

Summary

As members of human society, it is almost impossible not to belong to or participate in small groups. Yet, not all such groups are equally satisfying, effective, and successful. Communication in small groups functions to allow group members to pool their individual knowledge and skills and to collectively formulate effective strategies for completing tasks (Hirokawa, 1990).

Successful small group communication depends on the willingness and ability of each member to share in the responsibility for that interaction and communication. Ultimately, the success or failure of any communication interaction depends on the individuals involved and their ability to balance the dynamic of unique interaction patterns.

Small groups may be formal or informal, ranging from family and social groups to organizational work groups or boards of directors. Small groups are dynamic systems and, as such, must be viewed as interactive communicative networks. They gain their viability through the effective interaction between the

FIGURE 1.3   Are You Lonely? Hold a Meeting!

Are You Lonely?
Work on Your Own?
Hate Making Decisions?

HOLD A MEETING

You can...

- SEE people
- DRAW flowcharts
- FEEL important
- IMPRESS your colleagues
- EAT donuts

All on
COMPANY TIME!!!

MEETINGS
...the practical alternative to work.

FIGURE 1.4   Guide to Meeting Effectiveness

Meetings are vital to the group and team process. The following suggestions summarize common problems or issues with meeting effectiveness. Specialized groups often have particular formats and expectations which might require deviations from this list.

❏ **Before the Meeting**

1. Have a clear purpose for the meeting
2. Consider using and distributing an agenda
3. Include the right people and the right number
4. Pick an appropriate meeting time
5. Choose a location easily accessible to participants
6. Avoid too many or too few meetings
7. Provide notice, often written, well before the meeting
8. Ask members to come prepared
9. Start on time

❏ **During the Meeting**

1. Limit socializing and get down to business
2. Establish an orderly process
3. If using an agenda, use it as a guide—be flexible on specifics
4. Start with the most important topics unless the meeting has a formal format

5. Keep to the agreed upon length of time
6. Make certain adequate information will be available
7. End on time
8. Summarize the meeting
9. Consider scheduling the next meeting
10. Try not to waste time
11. Make certain quiet members can contribute
12. Make certain the meeting is not dominated by a few
13. Avoid compromises that produce poor solutions

❏ **After the Meeting**

1. Record key issues, assignments, deadlines
2. Follow-up on all decisions
3. Decide if the meeting was a success or failure

---

substance (content), the pattern (relationships), and the process (action). This communicative network is what is responsible for the benefits of synergy for which small groups are uniquely suited.

Groups formed for reasons other than primary relationships—family and social companionship groups—frequently have at their core some type of problem-solving agenda (Wambach, 1992). Most formal groups have specific reasons for existing, ranging from analyzing problems to resolving issues. Groups develop their particular personalities based on the nature of the issues around which they are convened, as well as on the characteristics of the group members and the environment in which the group is formed.

Communication forms the basis for small group interactions and is a determining factor in the outcomes of the group process. Effective small group communication strategies can help assure favorable outcomes, with members feeling empowered by having participated in creative problem solving. Poor communication strategies frequently predispose a group to unfavorable outcomes and a dissatisfied membership.

Gaining competence in small group communication is a lot like engaging in a physical exercise program. In order to gain strength and body tone, we have to work out using exercises and techniques designed for the particular muscle groups we want to strengthen and tone. The better we understand the process and functions and the more regularly we exercise according to these principles, the greater the strength and body tone we are able to gain. Just working out in whatever way we feel like whenever the mood strikes does not generally produce desirable results. We need instruction in an overall exercise plan and discipline in carrying it out, in order to measure our progress and achieve our goals.

For small group communication, this analogy translates into the importance of gaining an understanding of the theories and perspectives of how small group communication works, becoming familiar with a repertoire of communication strategies shown to be effective in small groups, and knowing when those strategies can be most usefully applied. When a small group succeeds in its endeavors, a theoretical base helps us understand how that success was achieved and helps us model future interactions accordingly. When the group's communication is less successful, a theory can help us understand where and how problems occurred and how better to handle them in future small group communication interactions. In addition, regular practice using small group communication strategies helps us develop our skills and make better use of our strategies.

DISCUSSION QUESTIONS

1. What are the basic characteristics of a small group? How is a small group different from a group of friends gathering after a ball game for an evening or several members of an office getting together for lunch?

2. List three to five groups to which you have belonged in the last few years. Did you join because of:
   A. Interpersonal attraction? Was it primarily physical proximity, attitude similarity, or need complementarity?
   B. A need for affiliation?
   C. A commitment to group goals and activities?
   D. Assignment by someone else?

   Which group(s) did you enjoy best? Which group(s) did you find most gratifying in terms of accomplishing goals? Which group(s) were least satisfying? Least successful?

3. Provide an example of the (1) transactional, (2) symbolic, and (3) shared meaning aspects of small group communication. How do these examples help you understand the communication process in small groups?

4. What is meant by the statement that the whole of the group is greater than the sum of its parts? Provide an example from your own small group experiences of this phenomenon.

5. There are numerous types of small groups including primary, social, educational, therapeutic, problem-solving, work, conference, and mediated communication. Which

ones are you most familiar with? Have you participated in any such groups? Which ones? How do they differ from the ones you are least familiar with? Looking at the different types of groups, can you identify specific areas where you should concentrate your study of small groups? What are they?

6. Chapter 1 discusses several organizational small group success stories including Ford's Taurus and General Motors' Saturn automobiles. From your own work experience, can you identify some small group success stories? Do you have some examples of when small groups were not successful on the job? What are the primary differences between the two groups?

EXERCISES

1. Icebreaker: What interests other class members?; 2. The value of groups: Increasing information and insights; 3. Learning about effective groups and teams: Are you lonely? Hold a meeting!; 4. Horse trading: A test of individual versus group decision making; 5. Inventing the light bulb

1. ICEBREAKER: WHAT INTERESTS OTHER CLASS MEMBERS?

Directions

1. Put a check mark to the left of your own favorites in each category. If none of the categories apply, write in your preferred answer.
2. Then move around the room and guess what others in the group may have picked. If you can guess *on the first try* what someone else has put for a category, have him or her initial next to the category. You may not get more than two initials from the same person. Your instructor will determine how much time you will have to get the most initials.

Favorite Food
- Mexican
- American (meat and potatoes)
- Chinese
- Italian

Favorite Animal
- Dog
- Cat
- Bird
- Fish

Favorite Vacation
- Sightseeing (by car)
- Beach
- Mountains
- World travel

Favorite Time of the Day
- Early morning
- Afternoon
- Evening
- Late night

Favorite Season
- Winter
- Spring
- Summer
- Fall

Favorite Color
- Dark (brown, black, rust)
- Light (white, gray, tan)
- Pastel (yellow, pink, baby blue)
- Bright (red, orange, blue)

2. THE VALUE OF GROUPS: INCREASING INFORMATION AND INSIGHTS

Directions

First, answer the following questions individually.

A. If you had to take medication every 2 hours, how many hours will elapse before you have taken four doses of medication? _____

B. Two people are playing checkers. Each played seven games over a period of several days. Each won the same number of games, yet no game ended in a draw. How could this happen? _____

C. How far can a person run into the woods? _____

D. What does a leopard have that no other animal does? _____

E. Some months have thirty days, some have thirty-one. Which months have twenty-eight days?_____

F. A nurse takes care of a man in a hospital. The man is the nurse's brother, but the nurse is not the man's sister. How come?_____

Second, break into teams or groups and come to an agreement on the best answer. Finally, when your instructor provides the correct answers, reassemble your group and examine your decision-making process. Did you take enough time? Did you consider diverse opinions? What prevented you as individuals from seeing the correct answers?

3. LEARNING ABOUT EFFECTIVE GROUPS AND TEAMS: ARE YOU LONELY? HOLD A MEETING!

Directions

Return to the chapter and reread Figure 1.3 Are You Lonely? Hold a Meeting!

Answer the following questions. Be prepared to share your answers with other class members.

- Have you ever attended an ineffective meeting?
- What criteria are you using to judge ineffectiveness?
- Have you attended a meeting you consider very effective?
- What criteria are you using to judge the effectiveness?
- Return to the chapter and reread the "Why Join a Group" discussion. Does this provide some additional reasons for considering a meeting effective or not?
- What is the role of "accomplishing" something in how we judge a meeting?
- If you did feel a specific meeting was ineffective, did you take any actions to make the meeting more effective? If so, what actions did you take? If not, what prevented you from taking any action?

4. HORSE TRADING: A TEST OF INDIVIDUAL VERSUS GROUP DECISION MAKING

Directions

One, write your answer at the end of the following story. This is an individual activity.

As part of the class assignment, you were asked by your instructor to *waste* $50. This means that you cannot use the money for any purpose such as saving, spending on books or friends, or going out. Since this is early in the school year, you said OK. Your instructor asks you to promise to waste the money. With less than a half hour before class, you went outside the building to see if there was some quick way to waste the money.

As you look around, you see an older person with a horse carrying a For Sale sign. You are not certain if this is a set-up by the instructor, but one thing you did not need to take to class today was a horse. So you approach the individual and ask how much the horse will cost. The answer: $50! Perfect! You hand over the $50 and take the reins of this $50 horse. As the two of you walk toward the classroom building, you notice a lot of stares and you begin to wonder if you really did the right thing—too easy, perhaps. You turn around and catch up with the former owner of the horse. You explain that you have changed your mind and the former owner tells you it is OK since there were two other buyers. Being a "horse trader" yourself, you say: "Great, I'll let you have it for $60." The former owner agrees and you walk away with $60 and no horse.

Approaching the building, your instructor stops you and asks if you are carrying out your promise. You smile meekly and hastily pursue the horse and owner. Since it is a $50 horse, catching up with the two is not difficult. You explain your problem to the owner who remembers that you overcharged $10 during the last negotiation. Fortunately, the owner agrees to sell the horse—but for $70! Not wanting to break a promise, you agree and fork over the $60 plus $10 from your own pocket.

As you approach the classroom building, the janitor steps forward and explains in no uncertain terms that no horses will be entering the building. Disappointed, you turn around and catch up with the former owner again who seems to be getting tired of these transactions. You explain your new problem. The former owner, apparently taking pity on you and wanting to end this relationship, gives you $80 for the horse and makes you promise not to return.

Now the question. *Not counting the original $50,* did you make money, break even, or lose money? If you made or lost money, exactly how much did you make or lose?

Next, once you have reached individual decisions, your instructor will form groups or teams. You job is to reach consensus on the amount of money involved in terms of making, breaking even, or losing money.

Three, after you complete this activity, consider the following questions:

A. Did you have any difficulty reaching consensus?

B. What do you see as the major stumbling blocks?

C. What helped you the most in reaching consensus?

D. If you did not reach the right answer, why?

5 . INVENTING THE LIGHT BULB

Even inventions credited to a particular individual are frequently the result of group enterprise. The electric light bulb, credited to Thomas Edison (Anderson, 1992), was possible only because of the discovery of electricity and its many potential uses by a number of earlier scientists and inventors. A Dane was the intellectual source of much of electric theory. A Frenchman developed alternating current and the first spark maker. The Leyden jar and the vacuum pump were developed by Germans. The first electric-powered machine was invented by an Austrian. Professor Henry Rowland at Rensselear Polytechnic Institute invented capacitors, alternators, generators, and filters. And, of course, Ben Franklin had much earlier demonstrated the connection between electricity and light with his kite and key. So when Thomas Edison sat alone in his workshop and "invented" the light bulb, he was hardly alone. He depended upon the input of numerous individuals working on the same general problem. People acting in concert with others and working off the synergy of shared ideas can produce results far beyond those any one individual acting alone could produce. Even Einstein worked with a mathematician friend to resolve his special theory of relativity.

Choose a recent invention (such as the evolution of personal computer operating systems and software), discovery (such as some of the recent drug therapies for managing AIDS or other diseases), idea (such as workfare instead of welfare), or theory (such as a specific communication theory), about which you already know something. Do some informal research, then trace and discuss the group effort that went into making the current accomplishment possible. Next, based on the accumulation of individual contributions to the discussion, itemize and describe the effect of synergy in developing group information, knowledge, and understanding that builds on but exceeds the contribution of any one individual.

REFERENCES

Anderson, J. A., & Englehardt, E. E. (2001). *The organizational self and ethical conduct.* New York: Harcourt.

Anderson, J. V. (1992). Weirder than fiction: The reality and myths of creativity. *Academy of Management Executive, 6*(4), 40–47.

Appleby, J., & Davis, R. (2001, March 1). Teamwork used to be a money saver, now it's a lifesaver. *USA Today,* pp. 1B–2B.

Belasco, J. A. (1990). *Teaching the elephant to dance.* New York: Penguin.

Berko, R. (1996, January). Education matters. *Spectra,* p. 8.

Beyond quality at Xerox. (1992, August). *At work: Stories of tomorrow's workplaces I*(2), pp. 1, 24.

Bolman, L. G., & Deal, T. E. (1991). *Reframing organizations: Artistry, choice, and leadership.* San Francisco: Jossey-Bass.

By the numbers. (1995, August 13). *The Tuscaloosa News,* p. 1F.

Byrne, J. A. (1993, December 20). The horizontal corporation. *Business Week,* pp. 76–81.

Cohen, A. R., Fink, S. L., Gadon, H., & Willits, R. D. (2001). *Effective behavior in organizations: Cases, concepts, and student experiences* (7th ed.). Boston: McGraw-Hill.

Cole, D. (1989, May). Meetings that make sense. *Psychology Today,* pp. 12–14.

Collins, J. C., & Porras, J. I. (2002). *Built to last: Successful habits of visionary companies.* New York: Harper/Business Essentials.

Davis, S. (2001). *Old gods almost dead: The 40-year odyssey of the Rolling Stones.* New York: Broadway.

Duncan, H. D. (1962). *Communication and social order.* London: Oxford University Press.

Hackman, M. Z., & Johnson, C. E. (2000). *Leadership: A communication perspective* (2nd ed.). Prospect Heights, IL: Waveland.

Harris, T. E. (2002). *Applied organizational communication: Principles and pragmatics for future practice.* (2nd ed.). Mahway, NJ: Lawrence Erlbaum.

Hiate, J. (1999). *Learning in chaos.* Houston, TX: Gulf.

Hirokawa, R. Y. (1990). The role of communication in group decision-making efficacy. *Small Group Research, 21*(2), 190–204.

Hof, R. D. (1992). From dinosaur to gazelle. *Business Week/Reinventing America,* p. 65.

Jackson, S. E., May, K. E., & Whitney, K. (1995). Understanding the dynamics of diversity in decision-making teams. In R. A. Guzzo, E. Salas, & Associates (Eds.), *Team effectiveness and decision making in organizations* (pp. 204–261). San Francisco: Jossey-Bass.

Katzenbach, J. R., & Smith, D. K. (1993). *The wisdom of teams.* Boston: Harvard Business School Press.

Lander, M. (1994, October 10). It's not only rock 'n' roll. *Business Week,* pp. 83–84.

Management meetings mount. (1988, March 2). *USA Today,* p. B1.

McShane, S. L., & Von Glinow, M. A. (2003). *Organizational behavior: Emerging realities for the workplace revolution* (2nd ed.). Boston: McGraw-Hill.

Meetings unpopular, but still a staple. (1990, February 25). *The Tuscaloosa News,* p. 1E.

Mehta, S. N. (2000, July 10). What minority employees really want. *Fortune,* pp. 181–186.

Miller, G. R. (1990). Interpersonal communication. In G. L. Dahnke & G. W. Clatterbuck (Eds.), *Human communication theory and research* (pp. 91–122). Belmont, CA: Wadsworth.

Morris, W. (Ed.). (1981). *The American heritage dictionary of the English language.* Boston: Houghton Mifflin Company.

1995 Industry Report. (1995, October). *Training Magazine,* p. 72.

Osborn, J. D., Moran, L., Musselwhite, E., & Zenger, J. H. (1990). *Self-directed work teams: The new American challenge.* Homewood, IL: Business One Irwin.

Rolling Stones top list of 1998 concert draws. (1998, January 3–4). *Bangor Daily News,* p. D3.

Schein, E. H. (1985). *Organizational culture and leadership.* San Francisco: Jossey-Bass.

Shaw, M. E., & Gouran, D. S. (1990). Group dynamics and communication. In G. L. Dahnke & G. W. Clatterbuch (Eds.), *Human communication theory and research* (pp. 123–155).

The team as superstar. (1998). *Outlook, 01,* pp. 24–27.

Wambach, J. A. (1992). *Group problem solving through communication styles.* Dubuque, IA: Kendall/ Hunt.

Waterman, R. H., Jr. (1987). *The renewal factor: How the best get and keep their competitive edge.* New York: Bantam.

Watson, K. W., & Barmer, L. L. (1990). *Interpersonal and relational communication.* Scottsdale, AZ: Gorsuch Scarisbrick.

Watzlawick, P., Beavin, J., & Jackson, D. (1967). *Pragmatics of human communication.* New York: W. W. Norton.

What business meetings cost. (1988, September 12). *USA Today,* p. B1.

Wood, J. T. (2000). *Relational communication: Continuity and change in personal relationships* (2nd ed.). Belmont, CA: Wadsworth.

Woodruff, D. (1992). Where employees are management. *Business Week/Reinventing America,* p. 66.

Wyatt, N. (1993). Organizing and relating: Feminist critique of small group communication. In S. P. Bowen & N. Wyatt (Eds.), *Transforming visions: Feminist critiques in communication studies.* Cresskill, NJ: Hampton Press.

2

Groups as Systems of Interaction

CHAPTER OUTLINE

CHAPTER OBJECTIVES

- Understand groups as systems of interaction.
- Distinguish the four types of problem-solving groups.
- Provide a theory for small group communication.
- Explain a systems approach to small group communication.
- Comprehend the importance of system properties including wholeness, synergy, openness, transformation, interdependence, feedback, entropy, equifinality, and the environment.
- Explain complex systems, change, and learning.
- Apply the concepts of strange attractors, phase space, bifurcation points, and irreversibility.
- Introduce the five principles of small group communication.

KEY TERMS

Bifurcation points
Complex systems
Double-loop learning
Entropy
Environment
Equifinality
Feedback
First-order change
Initial conditions

Input
Interdependence
Irreversibility
Nothing never happens
Openness
Output
Phase space
Process systems orientation
Quantum change

Second-order change
Strange attractors
Synergy
Systems approach
Systems theory
Transformation
Wholeness

What color is a chameleon placed on the mirror? Stewart Brand posed that riddle to Gregory Bateson in the early 1970s. . . . Writes Brand: "Gregory asserted that the creature would settle at a middle value in its color range. I insisted that the poor beast trying to disappear in a universe of itself would endlessly cycle through a number of its disguises." The important point about the chameleon in the mirror riddle is that the lizard and glass become one system. "Lizardness" and "mirrorness" are encompassed into a larger essence—a "lizard-glass"—which acts differently than either a chameleon or a mirror. (*Out of Control*, Kelly, 1994, pp. 69–72)

Often group behaviors, processes, and decisions have properties that cannot be simply attributed to any particular group member. They may have a history and a reason, or may be a consequence of something agreed upon in the past.

Understanding Small Group Success

Small groups attempting to solve problems show four types of problem-solving abilities (see Figure 2.1). These four types can be distinguished along two dimensions. The first dimension distinguishes groups who successfully solve the problems from those who do not. The second dimension separates those groups who understand why they were either successful or unsuccessful in solving the problems from those who do not understand how they reached their particular outcomes. If those who succeeded understand why they have succeeded and if those who failed understand why they have failed, and if they each understand what strategies will help them be successful in the future, then they are more likely to succeed in their subsequent problem-solving encounters. Groups who understand the reasons behind their successes or failures are able to employ strategies that will facilitate future success and reduce the likelihood of future failure.

FIGURE 2.1   Successful and Unsuccessful Problem-Solving Groups

Unsuccessful -------------------------------------- Successful

	Unsuccessful	Successful
Understands	Group 1: Unsuccessful, but understands why. Likely to be able to: Learn from their failure, Not make the same mistake again, Apply knowledge and achieve success next time.	Group 2: Successful, and understands why. Likely to be able to: Repeat success next time, Achieve additional knowledge with each new success.
Doesn't Understand	Group 3: Unsuccessful, but does not understand why. Likely to be unsuccessful next time.	Group 4: Successful, but does not understand why. Likely to be unsuccessful next time. Lucky this time, but "clueless."

In addition, effective groups must engage in a variety of practices ranging from establishing a clear set of commonly held goals to developing norms for interpersonal communication. Six people getting together does not guarantee an effective group; nor is effectiveness guaranteed by adding one of the strategies used by effective groups, such as choosing a leader or following an agenda. Only by understanding the process through which groups develop and communicate their commonly held goals can six people transform themselves into an effective small group.

If these six people are dedicated and successful in forming a group and achieving their group purpose, they may meet again and expect to replicate their earlier success. With a theoretical base to guide them, they can analyze their success and strive to repeat those strategies that worked. Without such a theory, they must hope for the best and trust that things will work out. If the group has a long history of working together successfully, they probably have some common intuitive understanding of their communication expectations. However, even when people know each other as individuals, they frequently find the group process more challenging than they anticipated. A theoretical perspective and awareness of the complex communication network in small groups can help group members see pitfalls before they fall too deeply into them.

Although it is theoretically possible to calculate the "personality" of a group by analyzing all of the possible relationships and interactions between each and every group member, it is often not practical to do so, and a perspective that looks at a group as a whole is more practical. A transactional model of communication in which "the properties of the group are irreducible to the properties of its individual members" (Laszlo, 1996, p. 26) suggests a *systems orientation* that underscores the dynamic, complex, ongoing process nature of small groups as influenced by past, present, and future events, interactions, situations, and contexts. Treating small groups as systems of interaction with unique characteristics provides an appreciation of a group's complexity and allows us to better examine and understand small group communication.

Communication in Small Groups

From a systems perspective, there are six basic elements of human communication that underlie the study of small group communication. First, *communication is the recognition of some behavior that is meaningful to one or more participants*. Because communication is tied to meaning, we are interested in meaning-centered activities. Systems thinking helps us conceptualize the ways in which small group communication is affected by changes in any number of verbal and nonverbal activities (such as language use, tone of voice, seating arrangement, styles of dress, timeliness, and so forth).

Second, *meaning is based on a symbolic interpretation of another's communication*. Because we cannot be inside someone else's head to understand his or her intended meaning, we depend on our own interpretations of the use of symbols, such as words, gestures, or other acts that can be seen to stand for something else. When someone says, "I'm hungry," we understand the meaning. Although we don't experience her or his feelings directly, we can equate the statement with our own feelings of hunger. Because our responses to others' communication is based on our own experiences, our communication difficulties may be based on different interpretations of the same symbolic words or gestures.

Third, *communication is contextual*. Numerous parts of the system can influence how we understand and interpret the communication process. As we noted above, the same comment made in different circumstances or by a different person can be interpreted quite differently.

Fourth, *communication allows us to apply meaning to the world*. As Capra notes, in quoting Maturana and Varela, "the system 'brings forth a world' through the process of living" (Capra, 1996, p. 267). We understand and interpret our world of experiences through communication and the abstract meaning we give to various symbolic activities. The small groups in which we participate both expand and depend upon the symbolic meanings we bring to them.

Fifth, *our cognitive abilities are open systems* that learn from and respond to the different encounters we face throughout our lives. An open system, which we discuss in greater detail shortly, connects and responds to the activities occurring around it. Our earliest experiences with other people and the symbolic meanings we learn from them provide us with the initial conditions that form the basis for our subsequent learning experiences. As self-conscious beings, we reflect back on our communication, that is, we meta-communicate. This faculty allows us to think about what has occurred or is occurring. For example, we ask ourselves, "Was I successful?" "Was I right?" "Could I have said it differently?" "Am I making sense at this point in the conversation?" We take in and process information from our environments.

Sixth, *we are simultaneously senders and receivers of communication*. Although we can isolate an individual in a small group as the sender or initiator of a message for the purposes of clarity, the messenger and the message are not readily separated from the context of the group dynamics. For example, how the message is received and interpreted may be greatly divergent from the intent with which it was sent. Skillful speakers modify *how* they send a message depending on *who* will be receiving it. The message dynamics include both verbal and nonverbal elements and are continuous.

Small groups are open, complex, dynamically changing systems of communication, and learning the vocabulary of a systems perspective can help a group member see and articulate what is occurring in the group. In this chapter we examine the characteristics of open systems, the characteristics of complex systems, and the communication functions within open, complex small group systems that facilitate the processes of dynamic group interaction and change.

A Systems Approach to Small Group Communication

A system is, by definition, a collection of interrelated parts or elements that function together to make a whole that is of a magnitude and order totally different from that of any of the individual parts. It is a set of elements bound together in interdependent relationships. The integrity of the whole depends on the mutual interaction between its parts.

Systems Theory

Systems are responsive and interactive, within themselves and within their environments—which are themselves systems. They are, therefore, multitiered, with each system part of a larger one. For example, the human body is made up of organ systems, which in turn are composed of cellular systems. Human beings are also part of social systems and ecological systems. Each system affects the ones with which it interacts, taking in, transforming, and putting out energies. When they work in harmony, each survives and thrives.

Systems theory provides an overall explanation for the complexity of small groups (Harris, 2002; Tubbs, 2001), allowing us to highlight the less obvious, but important, elements of the communication interaction within small groups. Groups are made up of individuals possessing different motives, personalities, and skills. In Chapter 1, we presented the remarkable increase in interactions possible when we move from two people (two interactions) to eight people (1,016 interactions). Add roles, norms, and the myriad of other communication variables discussed throughout this text, and the group process is, indeed, complex. Accepting complexity as a fact of group life frees us from being surprised when the time of day, current personal crises, or diverse communication assumptions sidetrack

TABLE 2.1   Characteristics of Open and Complex Systems

Characteristics of Open Systems	Characteristics of Complex Systems
Wholeness	Second-order or quantum change
Synergy	Double-loop learning
Openness	Sensitivity to initial conditions
Transformation	Strange attractors
Interdependence	Phase space
Feedback	Bifurcation points
Entropy	Irreversibility
Equifinality	

even the most dedicated group. The systems perspective demands that we consider a large number of variables.

Systems theory is a way of perceiving and thinking rather than a specific "how-to-do-it" theory. As such, it has been difficult to test in a rigorous experimental way (Eisenberg & Goodall, 2001). Being provided with specific steps to make our small groups work successfully is frequently more appealing than being asked to examine the big picture, but nothing is ever as simple as it first appears, and a systems approach provides us with a broad understanding from which to develop the specifics applicable to any particular group (see Table 2.1).

Open Systems

Systems theory is essentially a way of thinking about the complexity of interactions between and within living systems. In the 1960s, scholars began reporting their views regarding living systems in an effort to create a general systems theory—one that would explain the basic characteristics of living organisms (Miller, 1978; Thomas, 1975). This exciting period opened the door to a new type of thinking about how the parts of a system interrelate to create the whole. Again, the human body provides a useful example. While we humans pride ourselves on our ability to think and self-reflect, the brain would be useless without the other organs that provide life support. Most of us have probably experienced the difficulty of thinking straight when we are distracted by the pain or disability we experience when we sprain an ankle, twist a knee, or jam a finger in a drawer. The parts of the body are intimately interconnected. In small groups, the parts are the members—their needs and backgrounds, the subject about which they are meeting, and numerous other influences and interactions—all of which are interconnected. The straightforward biological analogy that "the leg bone is connected to the thigh bone" is, however, far easier to analyze and understand than even the simplest small group interaction. The role of communication, especially as symbolic behavior between people in the form of language or nonverbal behavior, is complex (Thomas, 1975) and is the glue that holds effective small groups and teams together.

To begin applying systems thinking to the group process, we need to first understand that we are dealing with systems of behavior between participants who are interrelated and interacting. Therefore, when we look at groups, we are examining a complex set of relationships between interdependent parts (Harris, 2002). To demonstrate an application of a systems perspective to understanding small groups, we will examine the concepts of wholeness, synergy, openness, transformation, interdependence, feedback, entropy, and equifinality.

Wholeness and Synergy.   Most of us are familiar with the concept that the whole is greater than the sum of its parts. *Wholeness,* in small groups, means that the results of people working with each other are different from the results of those same people working in isolation. The result of this dynamic interaction is often referred to as *synergy.* This synergy is created through the mixing and incorporating of each other's thoughts and messages. Through this mixing the dynamic of the group interaction produces a larger, more creative solution, and it is this synergy that makes small groups so effective in solving problems. When we "brainstorm" in small groups, the outcome is usually greater than a simple adding up of the individual ideas. It leads to the creation of new ideas stimulated by the group's interaction itself. One member suggests an idea to which a second member responds. A third member combines the two ideas in a way that builds and adds onto them and stimulates the first member to have an additional thought that expands on those ideas. The process continues and produces a result that is not directly attributable to the ideas of any one of the participants, but is, rather, the result of their interaction.

Openness.   All living organisms must be open to their environment. They must take in those energies or substances they need for their survival, use them up, and get rid of what they can't use. They must self-regulate. "*Openness* refers to the energy import activities of the system, which it needs to 'stay in the same place,' that is to maintain its own dynamic steady-state" (Laszlo, 1996, p. 32). For example, as a living system, the human body must take in air, food, and water, or it will close down and eventually die. To assure effective small group process, we must maintain openness to the environment—to the context of energy and ideas in which the group operates.

In addition, while being open and receptive to their environments, small groups also need to examine the input for relevance and integrity. Just as the human body filters what it needs for its well-being from its inputs of food, water, and air and discards what is useless or harmful, so small groups must filter the input they receive to function effectively in their environments.

Transformation.   Groups represent an ongoing system of interaction, where information and energy are taken in, processed (or filtered), and expressed in new forms (*transformed*). In other words, input is transformed into output through various interactive processes. For example, if we are working on redesigning an automobile in response to poor sales of our existing cars, we would do well to listen to the consumers who are telling us what they want. However, we also need to filter what the consumers say they want against what they are actually buying—in terms of style, price, or gas mileage. After receiving and filtering the input, we then work it into our new car design. In other words, we transform it. Without that openness to the environment and processing (transforming) of the input, we could end up designing a car that either perpetuates old, failed ideas or that meets consumers' ideas of what they think they want but which is too expensive to buy and run or too unusual in appearance, and therefore is not what they actually choose to buy. Thus, openness to input—information—is required, but the information needs to be filtered and transformed.

A group meeting to decide how best to develop the new automobile designs suggested by consumers would start by looking at data (*input*)—the characteristics of the existing cars, how these characteristics differ from what consumers say they want, how much it would cost to make the changes, how much price increase consumers will absorb, and which changes are most important. With each round of discussion, new input is required. It is examined, discussed and disputed (*transformed*), and then solutions are proposed or new questions are raised (*output*). The more complex the problem, the more iterations of input-transformation-output the group goes through in its process. This process is possible because groups are open or permeable to some degree and because the synergy of the group process permits the processing and transformation of ideas.

Interdependence.   Basic to the synergy of small groups is the *interdependence* of its members. To the extent that members depend on each other and share in responsibility for the group process, the group gains the benefit of the shared ideas and interactions. When members are *in*dependent, for example, rather than *inter*dependent, the group reverts to a simple collection of individuals. In basketball, five independent players cannot win many ball games. Even a single outstanding player cannot win without the support and mutual cooperation of other team members. The star player depends on others to pass the ball, work it down the court, and set up the shots. In addition, one inspired and talented player working interdependently with teammates can inspire those less gifted to play better than they might on their own. Although many of us have felt the frustration of trying to work with team or group members who didn't carry their load, most often there is some mutual benefit to remaining involved and connected with the other members, and it can outweigh the negative aspects of depending on nonsupportive group members. When difficulties do arise, it is time to look to communication strategies to help the group or team reach their common goal. Taking advantage of interdependence requires learning how to work with the other members. For example, when the records of 23 National Basketball Association teams from 1980 to 1994 were compared, the teams with the most "shared experience"—playing time together or low turnover—had the best win-loss records (Koretz, 2002).

Feedback.   Giving and receiving *feedback* is an important consideration in small group communication. A group must pay attention both to the feedback that it

Teamwork and synergy.

receives from its larger environment in the form of its initial charge and directions, as well as to the response to its presentations. It must also recognize the processes, style, content, and effect of the feedback that it provides its members. Positive feedback encourages creativity among group members and suggests an appreciation for diversity in thinking, perspectives, and opinions. Negative feedback encourages a reduction in deviation, can fulfill a corrective function to help keep the group on task, but can also reduce creativity. If a group wants to consider new and different ideas, it needs positive feedback that encourages deviations from the expected ways of thinking and of doing things. If the goal is to maintain the status quo, negative feedback lets us know when we have strayed too far from it.

If I use *Robert's Rules of Order* (Robert, 1990) to maintain strict control over a small group discussion, I may be engaging in negative feedback. When I call the question or rule someone out of order, I have decided that he or she has violated the expected direction of the discussion or has veered off course. This kind of strict adherence to rules is likely to stifle creativity. In most organizations, pushing for changes that actually create improvement in product or performance requires positive feedback, in order to move people away from their habitual practices. After all, if the "old" ways were working, there would be no problems to address. Consideration of alternative points of view is a recognition of the role of positive feedback in helping to make the best decisions. The constructive use of feedback also helps prevent entropy.

Entropy.   Living systems tend toward *entropy*—disorganization, stagnation, and chaos. Without the energizing effect of new input, systems tend to lose focus and organization. They tend to stagnate. By increasing inputs of energy and information, groups can prevent entropy, but too much energy or information overload can cause chaos and disorganization. Openness and the filtering of inputs helps to keep the energy balance in a satisfactory realm. Groups monitor and control their internal dynamics through the use of feedback. When a group senses that it is overstimulated and is veering too far from its intended purpose, it uses negative feedback to keep itself from heading toward self-destruction. If everyone is talking at once and no one is listening, very little can be accomplished, and someone needs to insist on order. On the other hand, an overdependence on control or too many limits on new ideas through negative feedback leads to stagnation and entropy. When we as members of groups balance these competing forces, our groups can begin to move forward successfully, with an appreciation of equifinality.

Equifinality.   There is more than one way to skin a cat, suggests an old expression. *Equifinality* refers to the fact that living systems can take different routes to the same destination. This means that there does not have to be a specific formula for how every group operates to achieve success. If you are interested in maintaining your physical health, you can watch your diet, do aerobics, lift weights, play sports, or combine any of these or other activities and probably enhance your health. So too, different groups can achieve successful results by taking advantage of the unique combination of characteristics and strengths of their particular group.

Taking Account of the Larger Environment.   As we noted earlier, small groups are systems within systems. Sometimes the processes that keep individual small groups functioning work against the larger good of the system on which it depends. The federal government is a system with many smaller systems subsumed within it. Frequently, one subsystem, open and responding to the needs of its immediate environment, works in direct opposition to another, to the detriment of the whole. For example, since 1988, the Interior Department has spent $66 million subsidizing the cost of irrigating farmlands to produce corn, barley, rice, and cotton. At the same time, the Agriculture Department paid the same farmers $379 million to limit surplus crop production (Barr, 1993). Until these two departments open themselves beyond their immediate constituencies to the larger system on which they both depend, they will perpetuate waste and ineffectiveness and, ultimately, we can assume, will exhaust the financial resources on which the health and maintenance of each of the subsystems depends. Therefore, to the extent possible, small groups or teams, as systems within systems, must understand and accommodate the totality of their environments.

Because diversity is a vitally important issue, we have devoted an entire chapter to enhance our understanding. However, two examples regarding diversity provide useful insights into the systems and subsytems connection (Gardenswartz & Rowe, 1993). When people are asked the benefits of living and working in a multicultural environment, they almost always mention different and exotic foods.

At a lunch at a management meeting, the entrée is quiche lorraine made with ham. Two managers never touch their plates. Why? There could be several reasons, but a likely one would be religious prohibitions against certain foods. Kosher food laws adhered to by some Jews prohibit the eating of pork and shellfish. Devout Muslims also refuse pork and alcoholic beverages. Hindu religious beliefs prohibit the eating of meat of any kind. In addition, many individuals choose to eat a vegetarian diet. These subsystems prevail in spite of the possible clash with other subsystems because of the depth of individuals' beliefs.

Likewise, time consciousness on the part of Americans often clashes with the mañana attitude in Mexico and the *Inshallah* of the Arab world. While time is money in the United States, time is considered more elastic and relevant in terms of mañana, or sometime in the future, and of *Inshallah,* which may mean whenever it comes to pass. For some Americans, accepting that both views are legitimate perspectives has proved difficult and, ironically, time-consuming.

The massive increases in Intranet and Internet connections have expanded the small group's universe. Not only is there a great deal more information available, but opportunities to connect digitally rather than in face-to-face group meetings have increased allowing individuals from around the globe to participate in real-time decisions (Gates, 1999). At Digital Equipment computer network groups operate in 26 countries (Helm, 1988). Engineer teams exchange information and join with marketing, sales, and manufacturing people to develop new projects and products. The implications of these trends will be discussed throughout this textbook.

Complex Systems

In addition to being open systems, small groups are also complex systems. Their communication processes are often disorderly, chaotic, apparently discontinuous, and transformational. As complex systems they have additional characteristics as well. Being aware of these characteristics allows participants to more fully appreciate the communication processes that are occurring and to make effective use of them in their group's interactions. Through their communication, small groups are capable of what has been called *second-order* or *quantum change* and of *double-loop learning* (Gemmill & Wynkoop, 1991) and participate in systems that show a sensitivity to initial conditions, the presence of strange attractors, phase space, bifurcation points, and irreversibility (Fuhriman & Burlingame, 1994).

Second-Order or Quantum Change. As we have noted, openness and change are essential and are the essence of small group communication processes. Groups transform themselves simply by their acts of communicating, learning, making decisions, solving problems, and just being together. This transformation may be of two types. The first type, known as first-order change, involves a change in the content or topic of the group discussion. This type of change may involve moving from one issue to another or moving from one phase of problem solving or decision making to the next. These changes are relatively straightforward, are often explicitly undertaken, and don't require a change in the group members themselves or in the way they interact.

The second type of change, *second-order* or *quantum change*, describes a change in the group context or dynamic. It entails a change in the quality of the group interaction itself. If, for example, a group has developed a norm of polite, rational, and nonhostile discussion and at some point in that discussion a member of the group becomes angry, claims the group is ignoring the real problems by not addressing the underlying issues, and storms out of the meeting, the group is faced with responding to that outburst. The group may choose to treat it as an anomaly and ignore it, assuming, implicitly or explicitly, that the outburst is unique to that member or circumstance. They may attribute it to a personality trait, to a temporary response to a stressful life situation, or to a "power play" enacted in order to control the group discussion around a particular issue. As coping techniques, none of these responses involves a transformational change for the group. If, however, the group uses the outburst as an opportunity to reflect on their group process and to establish new patterns of interaction, then the group itself has undergone a transformation. When the transformation is positive and constructive, this second-order change may result in new levels of trust, sincerity, and openness among group members, as an extension of their expanded ways of communicating with each other. On the other hand, the resultant second-order change may disrupt the ongoing work of the group. If the outburst triggers hidden hostilities in other members, it may irreparably harm the group process, causing the group to lose cohesion. Effective groups are those that can recognize these points of choice and change, and understand the potential inherent in them for positive transformation.

Double-Loop Learning.   Single-loop learning is learning the particular procedures for doing something. *Double-loop* learning, on the other hand, is understanding the principles that underlie those procedures in ways that allow us to extrapolate, combine, and creatively invent new processes and procedures. It combines intuitive, "common sense" understanding with the more solidly grounded information-based knowledge. The following analogy distinguishes between the single-loop learning of a cook and the double-loop learning of a chef. A cook is a person who can competently follow a recipe or learned procedure for preparing a certain type of food. A good cook is one who follows a good recipe carefully and, therefore, prepares good-tasting food. A chef, however, understands the ingredients and processes described in the recipe, can read multiple recipes for the same dish and then extrapolate from the best of each recipe to create a new and unique dish through a process similar to but not exactly like any of those recipes. While a cook depends on having the precise ingredients on hand to make a specific recipe, a chef is able to make a delicious dish with what she or he has on hand. The chef does more than memorize the quantities of individual ingredients or learn the specific procedures for preparation. A chef understands a set of general principles for preparing the dish, and, based on the knowledge of these principles, can improvise and create a new dish.

Double-loop learning permits individuals and groups to apply general principles, without being tied to an exact replication of earlier successes. It depends on understanding the overriding concepts behind the procedures. Double-loop learning is important to small group communication processes, because these processes are dynamic and never happen exactly the same way twice. There is no one recipe for successful group communication. To be effective, members of small groups and teams have to learn the concepts and principles behind the processes and then, like a chef, reinvent the particulars of the process in each new group context.

Sensitivity to Initial Conditions. In complex, chaotic systems, such as small groups, tiny variations in initial or existing conditions can produce very large effects in subsequent events; and the same (or apparently same) influence can have substantially different consequences at different times in the process or in slightly different sets of circumstances. The impact of this observation on small group dynamics can be substantial, and it suggests at least two consequences. One is that first impressions are important. A second is that the same behavior may be perceived differently, depending on the context and the group's perceptions of the person doing the behaving. Although all of the consequences of first impressions may not become apparent for some time, even in "zero-history" or newly formed groups, reputations, appearance, and personal style often precede us and provide information that may influence the group process in some unexpected way. First impressions create a baseline on which subsequent interactions are built. In addition, we have all probably felt the appropriateness or inappropriateness of a particular behavior in a given situation. Whereas one person may get away with a crude comment in a meeting and even be thought funny, another may be considered rude or embarrassing. However, depending on other factors, if either of these people had chosen a different time to make the comment, their receptions might have been different. Individual characteristics and interpersonal relationships within groups, as well as timing and circumstances, determine who can say what when.

First impressions interact with group relationships and expectations to establish patterns of response. For example, if I am 15 minutes late for the first group meeting, my being even two minutes late for the second one may cause other group members to comment on my "always being late." On the other hand, if I have always been on time for meetings and am then late for two meetings in a row later in the group process, my tardiness might go unmentioned or receive a different reaction from the group. Similarly, if I have contributed substantially to the group process, my late arrival for a meeting might receive little notice; whereas if I have been perceived as a nonproductive or obstructive group member, even a small infraction of the group norm might bring a harsh censure from other members.

Strange Attractors.   Group process evolves and takes on complex patterns. These patterns of communication and behavior are more or less constructive, are often not created or caused by any one individual or other particular influence, and, while nonrepeating in an exact way, take on a recognizable form as the group is drawn into certain communication styles, topics, metaphors, turn-taking patterns, and energy levels. The complex of influences that underlie these patterns are called *strange attractors,* because, while their influence is often readily apparent, the cause of these influences frequently remains unidentified or unknown. The importance of this concept to small group communication is that it locates these attractors in the group and its processes, rather than in individual styles, personality conflicts, or other sources of individual influence. By locating the influences in the group process itself, this concept recognizes both the complexity of interaction patterns and the responsibility of the group and its participants to observe, reflect on, and take responsibility for the effectiveness of that process. We, the group members, are the system. While none of us individually, or even collectively, can control that system of communication, we do influence its patterns.

In other words, seemingly benign activities can create important influences on how the group functions and succeeds. When these attractors are assigned meaning by the group, they influence the patterns and processes (Wheatley, 1998).

Phase Space.   Systems change in time as they take in and transform information and meaning. *Phase space* describes a system's movements through time, particularly as they are affected by its sensitivity to initial conditions and strange attractors. In small groups, the communication itself changes as the group moves through different phases. Four relatively large, descriptive phases common in group development, growth, and change are the cycles of introduction (forming), conflict (storming), emergence (norming), and production (performing). The nature of these phases will be described in greater detail in a later chapter and is mentioned here only as an example of the application of the concept of phase space to small groups. Phase space conceptualizes these descriptive phases as cycles that are iterative and dynamic. They are iterative because they repeatedly stretch and fold one into another (rather than building on each other in a straightforward linear relationship). Yet, they are dynamic in their changing, spiraling, and growth. They spiral and build on each other, rather than return to their original starting places. Authentic group discussion and conflict requires that a group has formed and members have gotten to know each other. Out of the knowledge of their different perspectives, conflict often emerges and can lead to a greater understanding upon which the group can predicate their productive decision-making and problem-solving processes. Yet, within that production phase the additional greater understanding may stimulate additional conflict and even the formation of subgroup coalitions. These coalitions may themselves take different shapes as conflicts are resolved and new conflicts arise. Yet the group never truly returns to earlier phases, but builds upon them in ways that make these later phases qualitatively different in their interaction.

Bifurcation Points. All moments or points in a group's process are not the same. Nor is the process one of stable, linear, constant growth. There are thresholds, or points of decision, that are reached and crossed at times when the group is ready. *Bifurcation points* identify these decision points. At times I have sat with a group of peers listening to a discussion, made a suggestion, and found my suggestion ignored, while the group goes on discussing the issues. Fifteen or twenty minutes later, another group member will suggest essentially the same idea and the group will rally around that as *the* answer, thanking and congratulating that member on the insight. When this occurs, I sometimes feel ignored, undervalued, and perhaps inarticulate in my ability to express ideas clearly, but often the group response has little to do with any of these factors; it has to do with my timing. The group had not reached the decision threshold at the time I made the suggestion and, therefore, could not hear and act on it. At other times, I have found myself not yet ready to make a decision when the group appeared to be at that threshold. I then have to decide how important that decision is to me. If it appears less important to me than to the others, I quietly let the group continue; but if it has particular significance for me, I may ask for a fuller explanation or further discussion, so that we can all move through the decision point together as a group.

Group communication and decision making happen at bifurcation points in time. To make effective contributions to the group, I have to be sensitive to where the group is in its process and communicate at a time in that process and in a way that helps the group move through the decision threshold. If I am early, the group may not be ready, but if the group is ahead of me, I may need to ask them to help me catch up. Effective group process results when bifurcation points are negotiated and handled in ways that empower all group members to be involved in the decision making.

Irreversibility. Group communication processes often appear to be cyclical, but as we noted above in discussing phase space and bifurcation points, they happen in time. Once something is said—whether in anger, frustration, enthusiasm, or excitement—it cannot be taken back and will have some impact on the participants and later group discussion. What is said may contribute to the effectiveness or the deterioration of the group process. Our groups may be able to move beyond it, incorporating it into our process and adding to our transformational growth, but we cannot truly start over or begin again. Each new beginning will be influenced by the past communication. Group communication happens within time and is, in that sense, *irreversible.*

This discussion of complex systems might seem—well, complex. However, we all have innumerable examples of the influence of complex systems. For example, our first year of higher education with all the second-order changes (e.g., study habits, managing time); double-loop learning (making new friends, gaining skills); sensitivity of initial conditions (e.g., first week on campus); strange attractors (e.g., choosing a major); phase space (e.g., joining groups/organizations); bifurcation points (e.g., class discussion, group leadership); and irreversibility (e.g., choosing the college).

Summary

Systems thinking underscores the dynamic nature of groups. While there are limitations to systems thinking, as there are to any theoretical perspective, the basic elements of open systems (wholeness, synergy, transformation, openness, interdependence, feedback, entropy, and equifinality) and of complex systems (second-order change, double-loop learning, sensitivity to initial conditions, strange attractors, phase space, bifurcation points, and irreversibility) all explain important characteristics of the small group communication process.

Underlying the application of a systems perspective to small group communication are five principles: that communication is the study of meaningful behavior; that it is based on symbolic interpretation; that it is contextual; that it occurs in a complex open system; and that it involves multiple, embedded layers of simultaneous verbal and nonverbal elements of human communication. Small groups modify these basic communication principles with group and cultural norms and with the roles group members play.

Small groups are both open systems and complex systems. Therefore, we need to overlay our understanding of the contexts in which small groups operate with the concepts of sensitivity to initial conditions, the presence of strange attractors, phase space, bifurcation points, and irreversibility. In this way, we can appreciate the transformative roles of second-order change and double-loop learning in developing effective small group interactions.

DISCUSSION QUESTIONS

1. What are the advantages to having a small group effectiveness theory to guide you in your small group activities?

2. Groups are living systems based on interdependence and interrelationships. What happens to a small group when parts of the system do not function well? Provide two examples from your own small group experiences that show the importance of understanding interdependence and interrelationships.

3. Explain transformation. Has this happened to your small group class since the first meeting day? Explain. Apply this concept to one of your classroom group exercises or to an example from small groups outside of the classroom.

4. Explain how entropy and equifinality impact on small groups.

5. Develop an example of second-order change created in a small group in which you participated. How does it differ from first-order change? Did double-loop learning occur? Explain.

6. Everyone has been advised to dress well for a job interview. How does this relate to first impressions? Why are first impressions important to a small group? Can you find examples other than dress or your first words that show the importance of first impressions?

7. Groups can take on special characteristics. Explain strange attractors, phase space, bifurcation points, and irreversibility. Find a small group experience for each of these characteristics. Can you or your group identify a small group experience that includes all four of these characteristics? Explain.

EXERCISES

1. Systems thinking; 2. Seeing the problem; 3. Ethics and systems: Part I; 4. Ethics and systems: Part II; 5. The zoo story

1. SYSTEMS THINKING

Identify the pattern and then write the remaining letters of the alphabet on the appropriate line.

Line 1. A   E F H I K L M N

Line 2. B   D   G   J

Line 3.   C   O

2. SEEING THE PROBLEM

Directions

Individually, decide if you have enough information or data to solve the following problems. If you do, provide the answer.

Your group has decided to get together this evening to socialize. When you arrive, you spot a man in a uniform running home. The man suddenly notices another man wearing a mask and holding a dreaded object. The first man turns around and runs back to the place he had come from. Can you tell where your group members are?

_____ Insufficient information to solve the problem.

_____ Sufficient information.

Answer: _____

You have just come across a cabin in the woods. Inside there are many dead people. They are seated in rows of chairs. What happened?

_____ Insufficient information to solve the problem.

_____ Sufficient information.

Answer: _____

What do each of the following words have in common?
Picture
Door
Car

_____ Insufficient information to solve the problem.

_____ Sufficient Information.

Answer: _____

Now, form your group and reach consensus.

3. ETHICS AND SYSTEMS: PART I

Your group is to determine how your college or university should respond to a reported increase in cheating on campus. This seems to range from adapting papers from the Internet to sharing exams. There appear to be several important issues. First, what constitutes cheating? Second, what ethical rules come into play? Your group should feel free to develop additional issues. Third, think of ethics as a systems issue. What are the overriding forces that might step in between a student's ethical considerations and their actions. Be prepared to outline your group's response to cheating and how to curb it, explaining how your solution can overcome the systems issues.

4. ETHICS AND SYSTEMS: PART II

At work, cyberslacking—or doing on-line shopping, vacation planning, job hunting, or just browsing the net while at work—is on a massive rise. In response, in 2000, 74% of companies did some form of electronic monitoring of employees—up from 35% in 1997 (Nathan, 2000). As a group, decide if there is any unethical behavior occurring. If so, what is it? Who is acting unethically? Finally, can there be a definition of ethics?

5. THE ZOO STORY

Elephant handling is a dangerous occupation, and elephant keepers are more likely to be killed on the job than in any other occupation except for coal miners.

Even firefighters and police officers do not face the same levels of danger. When a keeper was accidentally stepped on by an elephant in 1991 at the San Diego Wild Animal Park, pressure began to mount for a new means of handling elephants. This tragedy coincided with years of high staff turnover, external pressure to treat elephants differently, the promise of positive reinforcement behavioral training techniques for handling elephants, and an antiquated elephant management system. Given these reasons to change, the San Diego Zoo authorized the intro- duction of an entirely different approach to training the elephants—an animal behavioral approach (Priest, 1994).

The Trainers

In the past, trainers had controlled the elephants' behavior by establishing a dom- inance over the animals that could, when it was deemed necessary, include phys- ical discipline. This approach was adapted from life in the wild. Elephant herds are led by a dominant cow, usually the oldest member of the herd, who operates as the matriarch. Deviants are dealt with quickly and severely by this single boss, so most members of the herd do what the matriarch demands. Elephant trainers adopted this form of control hundreds of years ago and have used it since with lit- tle change.

As elephants are 50 times larger than the average trainer, this method requires individuals who exhibit a great deal of self-assurance. Showing fear to the animal might be tantamount to being disobeyed. In the extreme, the elephant could even turn on the trainer. The trainers' personality profiles, therefore, make them unlikely candidates for change. If you willingly spend your working days intimidating huge animals with the latent knowledge that you might be trampled to death, you probably do not show a great deal of self-doubt about your methods or a willingness to change them.

The Behaviorists

The animal behavioral approach is based on positive reinforcement, where an ele- phant is given a reward for cooperation. This reward is often in the form of an apple, a carrot, or a verbal praise. If the elephant refuses to participate in the training, the only punishment is a loss of the reward. During the first year, the elephants caught on quickly, and only seven losses of rewards occurred for the elephants during over 1,500 training sessions. The elephants participated in the daily shows, exhibited no aggression toward the trainers, and no physical discipline was needed or adminis- tered. The zoo management then asked the remaining traditionalists to adopt the new training methods of the behavioral trainers. Since this new procedure denied over 400 years of traditional elephant training practices, and questioned the domi- nance premise upon which these trainers had always operated, the traditionalists spent most of their time trying to circumvent the new approach and to disprove its efficacy.

How would you facilitate a change in attitude and behavior among this group?

The Outcome: Making It Work

Within a short period of time, the zoo's executive director assembled all the behavioralists, trainers, curators, keepers, and any other involved individuals and dictated that the behavioral positive reinforcement approach would be the only one used at the zoo. For the next year, the group tried every type of positive reinforcement technique to get the remaining traditionalist trainers to change. Ironically, the elephants had caught on very quickly and looked forward to the goodies being provided as a reward for doing what was expected, but the traditionalists' attitudes were uniformly hostile, and most interactions among the groups of trainers and with the management were confrontational.

Finally, as one means of changing behavior, a quarterly performance review was instituted that involved the trainers and focused on specific activities needed to implement positive reinforcement training for the elephants. While these quarterly reviews were, at first, rarely positive experiences, by the third round the trainers were starting to do the right things. By the fourth reviews, the discussions were switching from arguments to positive goal setting. The group as a whole, traditionalists and behavioralists, began working well together.

Systems Principles at the Zoo

There are at least five systems principles evident in this story. Moreover, perhaps we have missed a few that you can uncover through group discussion.

First, when people work together, the interacting of the individuals, and the processes and procedures by which they work together, determine the outcome. Most individuals have their own ideas about how to deal with issues, and simply being provided information about a better alternative method does not mean they will change their minds or behaviors. They must become involved in the decision-making processes for real change to occur. The elephant trainers were being attacked, maimed, and killed. What they were doing was not working, but implementing a change was still difficult until they became involved in the process.

Second, groups do not operate in a vacuum but within larger systems, which in this case included the zoo administration, visitors, animal rights groups, and insurance companies concerned with the mortality of keepers, among others. These systems created the pressure for change within the group.

Third, theories about how something works, traditionalist or behavioralist, must be tested in practice. Individual deep-seated beliefs can be challenged in a group environment, tested, and rethought. This is one of the major assets of making decisions in groups rather than by individuals.

Fourth, change is always more complex and more difficult than we first imagine. Most problems are problems because there are no easy answers, and groups as systems within systems make arriving at solutions even more complex.

Fifth, with careful analysis and group discussions, serious problems can be solved. Being guided by theories is more useful for trying to solve problems than simply acting intuitively or out of habit and tradition. The traditionalists had trained elephants in the same manner for 400 years. They also had one of the highest mortality rates of any occupation. In the past, the response to this danger was that it was inherent in the job, but imposing a well-tested strategy—positive reinforcement—on the training of animals offered a new approach. Because the strategy could be tested, and was not based just on tradition, it had a chance of being confirmed, refined, or rejected. In this case, the strategy worked.

REFERENCES

Barr, S. (1993, January 25). $300 billion lost in waste, fraud, U.S. report claims. *The Los Angeles Times*, p. B17.

Capra, F. (1996). *The web of life*. New York: Doubleday.

Eisenberg, E. M., & Goodall, H. L., Jr. (2001). *Organizational communication: Balancing creativity and constraint*. New York: St. Martin's Press.

Fuhriman, A., & Burlingame, G. M. (1994). Measuring small group process. *Small Group Research, 25*(4), 502–519.

Gardenswartz, L., & Rowe, A. (1993). *Managing diversity: A complete desk reference and planning guide*. Chicago: Irwin.

Gates, B. (1999). *Business @ the speed of thought*. New York: Warner Books.

Gemmill, G., & Wynkoop, C. (1991). The psychodynamics of small group transformation. *Small Group Research, 22*(1), 4–23.

Harris, T. E. (2002). *Applied organizational communication: Principles and pragmatics for future success* (2nd ed.). Mahwah, NJ: Lawrence Erlbaum.

Helm, L. (1988, May 16). What next for Digital? *Business Week*, p. 96.

Kelly, K. (1994). *Out of control*. Reading, MA: Addison-Wesley.

Koretz, G. (2002, March 1). Chalk it up to teamwork. *Business Week*, p. 22.

Laszlo, E. (1996). *The systems view of the world: A holistic vision for our time*. Cresskill, NJ: Hampton.

Miller, J. G. (1978). *Living systems*. New York: McGraw-Hill.

Nathan, S. (2000, June 22). What big brother watches. *USA Today*, p. 1B.

Opportunity 2000: Creative affirmative action strategies for a changing workforce. (1988). Indianapolis: Hudson Institute.

Priest, G. (1994, October). Zoo story. *Inc.*, pp. 27–28.

Robert, H. M. (1990). *Robert's rules of order, newly revised*. Glenview, IL: Scott, Foresman.

Thomas, L. (1975). *The lives of a cell*. New York: Penguin.

Tubbs, S. L. (2001). *A systems approach to small group interaction* (7th ed.). Boston: McGraw-Hill.

Wheatley, M. J. (1998). Chaos and the strange attractor of meaning. In G. R. Hickman (Ed.), *Leading organizations: Perspectives for a new era* (pp. 158–176). Thousand Oaks, CA: Sage.

3

Norms, Roles, Cohesiveness, and Groupthink

CHAPTER OUTLINE

CHAPTER OBJECTIVES

- Describe the importance and impact of group norms.
- Clarify the different types of group norms.
- Illustrate the concept of group roles.
- Outline the different types of roles.
- Discuss the functions of norms and roles.
- Describe group cohesiveness and groupthink.

KEY TERMS

Affiliation	Formal roles	Roles
Assigned roles	Group norms	Self-centered roles
Cohesiveness	Implicit norm	Social-emotional roles
Commitment to group goals	Multiple role enactment	Task roles
Critical roles	Peripheral roles	Violating norms
Emerging roles	Role assumption	
Explicit norm	Role sharing	

I work as a nurse on the surgical recovery wing of a large hospital, and one of my patients is preparing to go home after the completion of a surgical operation in which her bladder was accidentally nicked by the operating physician. The patient has not been informed about this accident, which probably poses little danger, but about which she should take some care (such as avoid drinking alcohol) to eliminate the possibility of future health repercussions. How should I handle this situation? Should I tell the patient, call the head nurse, write up the physician, or do nothing? Whether I tell the patient, how I tell the patient, whether I report the incident to the head nurse, and whether I talk to the physician and insist that the physician tell the patient is dependent upon the hospital norms and the view of my role as a nurse within these norms. As individuals acting within groups, we are not free agents to do whatever we believe to be best; we act within the norms and roles of the group. (Marin, Sherblom, & Shipps, 1994)

Norms

Every group we join has certain assumptions about how people are expected to behave. The standards vary with each group and within each group according to the different position or role being played by each group member. The group leader and the newcomer, for example, are expected to behave differently and may be subject to different expectations. A newcomer may be expected to listen quietly and attentively rather than talk a great deal at the first meeting, for example, while a leader is expected not only to talk, but to have prepared an agenda for the meeting and to act to keep the group on task.

The Reason for Norms

Group norms define the nature of the group and the relationships among the group members by expressing the collective values of the membership and by identifying the place of group members within that value system. In every group, certain actions are approved of and others are frowned upon. Knowing the norms means you have a map, or traveler's guide, for navigating the territory of group behavior and processes.

Norms establish the accepted rules of behavior. These rules represent the shared values, procedures, and beliefs that guide group members in their communication and actions. In many cases, norms are prescribed by an organization's culture or by the prevailing understanding about how groups operate in a given situation. These are "the set of assumptions or expectations by members of a group or organization concerning what kind of behavior is right or wrong, good or bad, appropriate or inappropriate, allowed or not allowed" (Schein, 1969, p. 59). Norms define the nature of the group by telling us what we can and cannot do. The evolution of these norms is inherent in the group development process.

Group norms are not imposed, however, by some authority figure with power. They are developed and accepted by group members as the common way of operating. They may include the norms of the prevailing culture within which the group exists, as well as rules specific to the group itself. The etiquette we use when we go on a job interview is usually different from that we use to interact with our close friends. Most students address their professors more formally than they do their family members. These are norms that we recognize and accept as part of the communication expectations within a cultural context. These cultural contexts influence our small group communication patterns as well.

Norms influence our behaviors during the group process. They reduce ambiguity, help us feel part of the group, and develop our overall sense of groupness. We learn how to speak, who can participate at what time, what can be talked about, the types of language and nonverbal communication we can use, and numerous other standards of behavior. As operating procedures, norms have an important impact on how the group functions. A club, for example, might require those members arriving late for their 6:30 AM breakfast meeting to pay $1 for each minute they are late. This rule underscores the group norm of starting the meeting on time and having everyone present. The payment of the late fee is voluntarily contributed by the member to stay within the accepted group norm.

Types of Norms

Norms can be crucial or peripheral, and explicit or implicit. A crucial norm has a primary impact on how well the group performs its tasks. In some cases, this can be as simple as an expectation for regular, on-time attendance at meetings. In other cases, this can relate to how each member will contribute to accomplishing the task. A crucial norm, when violated, usually brings some type of censure. Peripheral norms outline behaviors that should be engaged in or avoided but that are rarely essential to the effective functioning of the group. Violation of a peripheral norm—such as poor social etiquette, occasional bad manners, or mildly inappropriate behavior—makes us uncomfortable.

Norms can also be explicitly stated or implicitly understood within the group. An explicit norm is outlined, in either written or oral form, as a policy or group-sanctioned procedure. An implicit norm is an unstated preference of the group but cannot usually be clearly identified by looking at the group's written guidelines or formal operating procedures.

There are two keys that identify group norms. First, activities and behaviors that occur regularly signify norms. Among other observations, group norms may be identified by communication interaction patterns in terms of who talks to whom, what they talk about, whether or not there is an order or pattern to the sequencing of who talks, whether members stay after the meeting to chat, how seating is determined, and how the meeting is brought to order and closed. Second, when a norm is violated, the group reacts. Observe, for instance, what happens when someone brings up a taboo subject or interrupts someone else. A sudden group silence or negative response to a particular action indicates a violated group norm.

Norms and Diversity

The importance of understanding norms is underscored when we examine the rapidly changing make-up of society, including dramatic changes in demographics, multicultural backgrounds, and interests (Harris, 1997). By the year 2050, "about half of all Americans will belong to what are now considered minority groups," according to the U.S. Department of Labor's 1999 report (Associated Press, 1999, p. 5B). In almost every aspect of life, we have an increasing opportunity to work with diverse groups of individuals. Whereas we devote an entire chapter to the importance of diversity later in this text, this discussion will focus on norms. As society changes, so do the group and team norms.

In organizations, the predominant pale male management culture of the past is being replaced. In fact, there is "a move away from a dominance by the European-American male toward an increasingly diverse and segmented population . . . [including] age, ethnic origins, cultures, and personal style" (Wentling & Palma-Rivas, 1998, p. 235). In addition to its being the right thing to do, "companies that pursue diversity outperform the S & P 500" (Colvin, 1999, p. 53). S & P stands for Standard & Poors, a leading institution in the investment world, which provides investment advice and is followed carefully.

We need to be aware of the impact of changing norms. Without an understanding, the "increasing diversity and team-based work structures can spark office conflict" (Pirisi, 1999, p. 18). Our age, backgrounds, ethnicity, religion, gender, education, and work experience can lead us to see difference as deviant behavior. Today's organizations are "awash with the conflicting voices and views of the most age- and value-diverse workforce this county has known since our great-great-grandparents abandoned field and farm for factory and office" (Zemke, Raines, & Filipczak, 2000, p. 10). Even if we focus only on the different generations at work, researchers have been able to draw critical distinctions between Veterans (1922–1943, 52 million people), Baby Boomers (1943–1960, 73.2 million people), Generation Xers (1960–1980, 70.1 million people), and Generation Nexters (1980–2000, 69.7 million people) that impact how we view each other, work together in groups, and value our jobs (Zemke, Raines, & Filipczak, 2000).

Violating Norms

We are likely to abide by the norms if we feel identified with the group's goals, if we plan to belong to the group for a long period of time, if we feel a high level of cohesiveness in the group, or if we decide that we are of lesser power or status than other group members. Conversely, if it is a one-time social gathering, if we don't care about the group or its goals, or if we feel we have more authority, power, or position than other group members, we might not feel compelled to abide by the norms.

When group norms are violated, the group will usually impose some type of social sanction or punishment. This may be a light punishment that then increases in intensity if the norm is violated a second or third time. A first violation may mean that I am simply avoided or ignored for a while during the group process. For example, if I am ten minutes late for a meeting, the group may not say anything the first time but also may not include me in the discussion for a while. If I am late a second time, when I arrive, group members may become more outspoken and express their irritation more directly through comments about my tardiness, or they may begin to joke about my attendance. If I am late a third time, they may express anger about my habitual lateness and remind me that it interferes with the group's ability to accomplish its task. In each case the group is asking me to conform to the norm. The sanction imposed will also be contingent upon the perception of my other contributions to the group and accomplishment of its task. If I am perceived as having contributed a great deal to the group and the achievement of its goals, my lateness to a meeting may be perceived as trivial and a sanction as unnecessary or inappropriate. If I am perceived as not having contributed my share to the group work overall, then my lateness to the meeting may become a focal point for the group's expression of anger toward my overall lack of contribution.

Few norms are carved in stone, however. They are socially constructed by the group, and as we move from group to group, the norms change. Behavior that is severely sanctioned in one group may pass apparently unnoticed in another. Norms can be modified, but it is important to remember that groups take their norms very seriously, and violating a norm can bring significant sanctions.

Group norms are not created or enforced by any one member and may change over time. Ultimately, they are maintained by the group as a whole. While individuals may represent the group on occasion in making a norm explicit, it is the force of the group's sanction that makes a rule a norm. At work, these norms are increasingly difficult to maintain without challenge or scrutiny by others. Diversity brings new insights regarding traditional norms. For example, the previously mentioned four major age groups—Veterans (born 1922–1943), Boomers (born 1943–1960), Xers (born 1960–1980), and Nexters (born 1980+)—working in most organizations. While generalizations are dangerous, studies indicate that these four generations have vastly different assumptions and expectations regarding accepted norms. Therefore violations for one group might appear entirely acceptable for another (Zemke, Raines, & Filipczak, 2000).

Roles

Norms and roles are interrelated but differ from each other. Whereas norms are expectations regarding behavior patterns for the group as a whole, the particular way we, as individuals, are expected to act in a group is our role. Hare (1994) states that a role is associated with the position and status of a member in a group and implies the rights and duties of that member toward one or more other group members. While this definition applies primarily to the formal group roles that members perform consciously, there are expectations associated with informal roles as well. These expectations may only arise during the course of interaction in a group, however, and thus may be less clear, but they are expectations just the same.

While norms direct the behavior of the group, roles apply to a particular individual's behavior. "Roles are 'packages' of norms that apply to particular group members" (Johns, 1988, p. 246). For example, we might expect someone to take notes at our meetings and distribute them to every member. The group norm of note taking suggests a specific role for one member, even if the member taking notes changes with each meeting.

Types of Roles

Historically, scholars have divided roles into two general categories—those that take into consideration the importance of the group's task and those roles necessary for the social and emotional needs of the group (Ketrow, 1991). Task roles relate to getting the job done. Social and emotional need roles relate to the group climate and working relationships. Both are essential for a group to be effective. Task role specialists help move the group toward its goal attainment and help the group to be adaptable to changes in needs and accomplishments along the way. Social-emotional role specialists assist the group with its social maintenance functions and develop ways of expressing and dealing with the emotional dimensions of discussion for its members. In addition, self-centered roles have been identified when individuals focus on their own needs, rather than contributing in positive ways to the group discussion and achievement. Table 3.1 describes these roles.

The usefulness of these descriptions is in how they underscore the many roles any one participant might play in a small group. Effective group members frequently take on a variety of roles.

Groups often present difficult situations with multiple expectations of roles for members, so that what is expected of us in groups is not always clear (Hare,

TABLE 3.1 Group Role Behavior

Group Task Roles	Group Maintenance Roles	Self-Oriented (Selfish) Behaviors; Not Positive Group Roles
Initiating: Proposing new ideas, proposing goals, plans of action, or activities; orienting; prodding the group to greater activity; defining the position of group in relation to an external structure or goal; offering suggestions and approaches.	**Encouraging:** Praising, expressing warmth, support, and appreciation; recognizing the value of others' contributions; indicating positive feeling toward group members; reinforcing group unity and cohesiveness.	**Blocking:** Preventing progress toward group goals by constantly raising objections, repeatedly bringing up the same topic or issue after the group has considered and rejected it (although it is not blocking to raise an idea or topic the group has not really considered); preventing the group from reaching consensus; refusing to go along, accept, or support a group decision.
Elaborating: Clarifying ideas, suggestions; expanding on ideas or suggestions; developing a previously expressed idea; providing examples, illustrations, and explanations.	**Supporting:** Agreeing or expressing support for another's belief or proposal; following the lead of another member; accepting another's suggestions and contributions.	
Coordinating: Integrating; putting together parts of various ideas; organizing the group's work; promoting teamwork and cooperation.	**Harmonizing:** Helping to relieve tension; mediating differences; reducing secondary tension by reconciling disagreement; suggesting a compromise or a new acceptable alternative; working to reconcile angry members.	**Being Aggressive:** Criticizing, threatening other group members, being a "noble fighter" preventing collaboration.
Summarizing: Pulling work and ideas together; orienting the group; reviewing previous statements; reminding the group of items previously mentioned or discussed.	**Gatekeeping:** Keeping communication channels open; helping "quiet" members get the floor and be heard; suggesting turn taking or a speaking order; asking someone to offer a different opinion.	**Withdrawing:** Remaining indifferent, refusing to contribute; avoiding important differences; refusing to cope with conflicts; refusing to take a stand; covering up feelings; giving no response to comments.
Recording: Keeping track of the group's work; keeping group records, preparing reports and minutes; serving as group secretary or historian.	**Process Observing:** Making comments on how the group is working, how the members are coordinating and working together.	**Dominating:** Interrupting, refusing to accept others' conclusions as being as valid as one's own, forcing a leadership role.
Evaluating: Critiquing ideas or suggestions; expressing judgments on the merits of information or ideas; proposing or applying criteria for evaluating information.		

(continued)

TABLE 3.1   Continued

Group Task Roles	Group Maintenance Roles	Self-Oriented (Selfish) Behaviors; Not Positive Group Roles
Giving or Seeking Information: Presenting data; offering facts and information, evidence, or personal experience relevant to the group's task; asking others for facts and information, evidence, or relevant personal experience; asking questions about information provided by others; requesting evaluations; asking if the group is reaching consensus.	**Setting Standards:** Helping to set goals and standards for the group; assisting in setting norms or making norms explicit; suggesting rules of behavior for members; challenging unproductive ways of behaving; giving a negative response when another violates a rule or norm.	**Status or Recognition Seeking:** Stage hogging, boasting, and calling attention to one's expertise or experience when not necessary to credibility or relevant to group's task; game playing to elicit sympathy; switching subject to area of personal expertise.
Opinion Giving: Stating beliefs, values, interpretations, judgments; drawing conclusions from facts and information.	**Tension Relieving:** Using humor, joking or otherwise relieving tension; helping new members feel at ease; reducing status differences; encouraging informality; stressing common interests and experiences within the group; developing group narratives, themes, and fantasies to build a common spirit and bond or to test a tentative value or norm.	**Special-Interest Pleader:** Demanding group time and resources for special-interest pleading; constantly advocating for one's subgroup or special interest; not allowing group influence over one's perceived self-interests.
Clarifying: Interpreting issues; making ambiguous statements more clear; asking for examples or further clarification.		
Consensus Testing: Asking if an apparent group decision is acceptable to all; suggesting that an agreement may have been reached and asking for verification of that.		
Proposing Procedure: Suggesting an agenda of issues, or a decision-making method; proposing a procedure to follow.		

1994). Sometimes roles conflict, collide, or may be confused by ambiguous or incompatible sets of expectations. You might be asked, for example, to be a group leader when, because of other obligations to the group, you do not have the time and energy needed to undertake the job. You might then experience role conflict. At another time you may not be certain what role to play or you may experience multiple and contradictory role demands from the group, leading to role ambiguity. You experience role conflict when you are expected to act in a manner different from what you perceive to be your desired role, and role ambiguity when the role you are expected to take on is unclear. An example of role conflict is being put in charge of a group when you do not want to take the responsibility. Everyone in the group says you are a natural-born leader. You want no part of this role but accept it because of the group pressure. An example of role ambiguity occurs when a group tells you they want your input and leadership but do not provide any guidelines explaining what they have in mind and, in practice, they appear to want neither your input nor your leadership. Role conflict and role ambiguity can be difficult problems for groups to deal with and may require either role analysis to determine what is expected of a particular role or role negotiation to ensure a common understanding of the role among all group members.

The Function of Roles

In addition to these issues, Bales (1950) identified four functional characteristics of roles that can create problems for groups. Certain roles can create privileged positions where there is (a) greater access to resources, (b) more direction of and control over other persons, (c) increased status—a sense of importance and prestige within the group, and (d) a greater sense of involvement in and identification with the group. Negotiating resources, direction, status, and involvement can at times be difficult for a group and can create tensions among group members.

Because a small group is a collection of individuals bound together with some common purpose, the members each have an interest in playing their respective roles to achieve that purpose. In general, group members work to foster favorable impressions of themselves; to organize their multiple relationships with other group members; to develop a common understanding shared among group members of the group's goals, ambitions, preferred style of meeting, communicating, and accomplishing tasks; and to express their feelings and thoughts while not exposing their personal vulnerabilities to too great an extent. Along these lines, Bochner (1984) developed a typology of five communication role functions that apply to communication in small groups. These functions—"(1) to foster favorable impressions; (2) to organize the relationship; (3) to construct and validate a conjoint world view; (4) to express feelings and thoughts; and (5) to protect vulnerabilities" (p. 583)—are carried out both by the individual group members in their interactions with each other within the group and by the group as a whole in its interactions with the larger external world.

The roles we assume within a group to help it accomplish these goals are the consequences of several factors. Roles can be determined, assigned, or emergent. Deterministic roles are those determined by external factors. For example, in our families, the roles of mother, father, sister, brother, daughter, son, or cousin are determined by the nature of the relationships. While each of us may act out our roles with some creativity and deviation from an established social norm, certain behaviors and expectations are fairly standard (for example, taking care of children). Formal or assigned roles exist in most small groups and include note taking, scheduling, or chairing. Emergent roles are those that are worked out among the members of the group. These roles are negotiated as the group activity proceeds and result from the interaction of the group members. For example, we might be assigned the role of chairperson only to find out that a colleague has the expertise and experience to deal with a particular issue. For a while, that person will emerge as the group leader even though we were explicitly assigned that role.

As would be predicted by systems thinking, each group will develop a differ-ent set of roles for its participants. In one group, we might be the leader, in another the devil's advocate. At other times, we might be a newcomer or decide to be a silent observer. We accept these roles through the process of role assumption. When we take on an individual role, we are going through the process of role assumption, which means trying to act in accordance with the expected behaviors anticipated by the group and with the norms associated with that role. Although the particular role may seem simple when it is described, the actual acceptance and acting out of the role can prove to be very difficult.

Cohesiveness

Cohesiveness is the "force that binds group members together" (Keyton & Springston, 1990, p. 234). *Cohesiveness* refers to the desire of members to stay in the group. While the group task and structure tend to be set, cohesiveness is a result of how well group members interact. Groups are not doomed to failure if the members do not get along, but cohesive groups fulfill important needs for the group members, increasing their willingness to contribute to the group, and cohe-sive groups have been shown to be more effective in task performance (Evans & Dion, 1991).

Cohesiveness describes a set of influences and reasons that keep members in a group and keep them motivated and willing to contribute extra time and effort to help the group complete its job (Witteman, 1991). As Zander (1982) suggested, in more cohesive groups members converse freely, are more interested in the achievements of the group, attend and actively participate in group functions, are interested in the activities of other members and willingly assist each other in achieving the group's tasks, and identify with the group through their use of lan-guage in speaking of "we" and referring to nongroup members as "they." Cohesion is frequently cited as important to a group's success (Stockton, Rohde, & Haughey, 1992).

Influences on Cohesiveness

Widmeyer and Williams (1991) identify a number of influences on the develop-ment of group cohesion. The size of the group, the background similarity of group members, the members' satisfaction with the task in which they are engaged and with the social aspects of the group, and the success of prior group performance all contribute to greater group cohesion. Larger groups, for instance, may find social and task cohesiveness more difficult as some members may find it easier to engage in "social loafing" and "going along for the ride" without investing themselves heavily or contributing fully to the group's work.

Cohesiveness develops in groups through greater communication among group members and with increased pressure for conformity to group norms. Explicitly clarifying group goals, identifying member roles, and encouraging member involvement in the decision-making process all contribute to greater cohesiveness. Other influences, such as soliciting full member involvement in the decision-making process, involving members in clarifying group goals and member roles, and recognizing members' contributions, serve to develop cohesiveness, as well. Finally, successfully accomplishing tasks, being productive, and being recognized as a successful group also strengthen and encourage group cohesion.

Consequences of Cohesiveness

Group cohesiveness brings with it many positive benefits, such as good feelings about the group and membership in it, feeling that the group activity fulfills certain personal needs or allows certain personal expressions, as well as feelings of personal success and productivity. Group cohesiveness can also enhance the decision-making process, the quality of the decisions made, and the overall productivity of the group. So, cohesion is an important factor for any group process and, in general, group cohesion and performance are positively related (Evans & Dion, 1991). However, too much cohesiveness can also impair the decision-making process and even encourage groupthink (Mullen, Anthony, Salas, & Driskell, 1994).

Teams pursue common purposes based on forces that bind them together.

Groupthink

Groupthink is defined by Janis (1982) as a strong concurrence-seeking tendency among members within a group that leads to a deterioration in the decision-making process. Group cohesion and accompanying pressures for conformity carried to the extreme can lead to groupthink. Janis developed his groupthink theory based on the catastrophic Bay of Pigs and Pearl Harbor decisions, President Kennedy's handling of the Cuban Missile Crisis, and Vietnam (see Figure 3.1). Other researchers have added breaking into the Democratic headquarters at Watergate, the arms-for-hostages deal, and the Hubble Spacecraft as examples of flawed decisions perpetuated by the groupthink process (Whyte, 1989).

These historically significant events point to the key issue in groupthink. As group members we unknowingly make unanimity or solving immediate problems our goal rather than making the best decision. In 2000, the University of Wisconsin-Madison inserted the photo of an African American male into a crowd of white football fans for its fall admissions brochure (Wyatt, 2000). The digitally altered cover was intended to convey an appearance of a diverse student body even though as of the fall 1999, fewer than 10% of the school's more than 41,000 students were nonwhite and 2.15% were black. Unable to "find an authentic picture of diversity," the university instead made a decision that created national embarrassment and required the reprinting of all 106,000 copies at a cost of $63,000 to remove the picture (Wyatt, 2000, p. 5A). In 1996, for an advertisement Ford Motor Company removed the faces of Pakistani, Indian, and black employees and superimposed white faces (Parker-Pope, 1996). The photo was printed in newspapers worldwide and the employees whose faces had been changed reacted with shock. Ford, while

FIGURE 3.1   Janis's Groupthink Framework

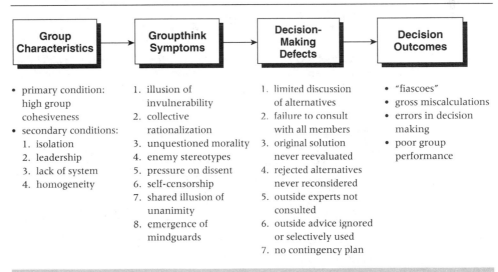

Group Characteristics	Groupthink Symptoms	Decision-Making Defects	Decision Outcomes

• primary condition: high group cohesiveness
• secondary conditions:
  1. isolation
  2. leadership
  3. lack of system
  4. homogeneity
	1. illusion of invulnerability
	2. collective rationalization
	3. unquestioned morality
	4. enemy stereotypes
	5. pressure on dissent
	6. self-censorship
	7. shared illusion of unanimity
	8. emergence of mindguards
		1. limited discussion of alternatives
		2. failure to consult with all members
		3. original solution never reevaluated
		4. rejected alternatives never reconsidered
		5. outside experts not consulted
		6. outside advice ignored or selectively used
		7. no contingency plan
			• "fiascoes"
			• gross miscalculations
			• errors in decision making
			• poor group performance

embarrassed that the changes had been made, argued that the alterations reflected the ethnic makeup of Poland, which is almost exclusively white, and that the photo was intended for that country only. The pressure to appear diverse or to conform to a particular country's culture provides current examples of the power of group-think since publishing a photo broadcasts the group's poorly conceived decision.

Ford made the news in 2000 for another tragic series of events. The Bridge-stone/Firestone ATX and Wilderness tires on the Ford Explorer were blamed for over 270 deaths and 800 serious accidents (Riley, 2002). Evidence indicated that Bridgestone/Firestone had been aware of the problem since 1996, yet continued to supply the same tires. As the story unraveled, Ford appeared to have been aware of the problem but had chosen to discount its significance—perhaps because the Explorer was the best-selling Ford vehicle and accounted for one-fourth of Ford's sales (Healey & Nathan, 2000). In response to mounting pressures, 6.5 million tires were recalled in August 2000, Ford offered replacements through any tire dealer-ship, and the inevitable lawsuits against Ford and Firestone began.

This is another example of groupthink. As early as 1996, a group of personal-injury lawyers and one of the nation's top traffic safety consultants identified a pat-tern of failures of Firestone ATX tires on Ford Explorers (Bradsher, 2001). However, they decided not to tell the National Highway Traffic Safety Administration (NHTHA) because they were "leery" of how NHTSA would handle the information. Dr. Ricardo Martinez who administered the agency from 1994 to 1999 said this behavior appalled him. He added that withholding information meant the lawyers were putting their possible benefits, winning the case and getting financial rewards, above the needs of the public which "would clearly be unethical" (Bradsher, 2001, p. 1A).

Groupthink Characteristics

Groupthink is evidenced when the following characteristics emerge during small group interactions:

1. Group members rush to a conclusion without considering all the alternatives.
2. Decisions are not carefully reexamined, even when there are indications of possible dangers.
3. Little time is spent discussing the reasons alternative courses of action were rejected.
4. The group limits itself to a small range of possible alternative courses of action.
5. Members create rationalizations to avoid dealing directly with warnings.
6. Group pressure is put on any individual who expresses doubts or questions the group's arguments or proposals.
7. Group members censure their own doubts.
8. Members believe everyone is in unanimous agreement without any testing of the premise.

Examine for a moment the University of Wisconsin and Ford/Firestone examples and see how many of the groupthink characteristics you can identify. Effective decision making depends upon full consideration of a variety of dissenting points of view. Group consensus is best arrived at after a full and critical discussion of alternative views. When discussion is cut off and consensus is arrived at too early, the quality of the group decision can suffer.

Kroon, Kreveld, and Rabbie (1992) suggest that more diverse, heterogeneously composed groups are less susceptible to groupthink. The need for the group to critically evaluate ideas and arguments from diverse perspectives can make it more vigilant and less likely to have groupthink tendencies.

Summary

Norms, roles, cohesiveness, and the potential of groupthink all present challenges for effective small group discussion, decision making, and problem solving. A small group can improve their chances of being effective by including three things in their discussion. First, the group should be conscious of the way they develop group norms and should explicitly review and discuss them, asking how effective they are for achieving group social-emotional and task needs. Second, they should discuss the roles that need to be undertaken by group members. Before assigning roles, however, they should clarify the role expectations and when and how they need to be accomplished. Then, through group discussion and negotiation, they should match group members to appropriate, desirable, and compatible roles. Third, they should discuss group cohesion. How can the group maintain the social-emotional cohesiveness to work effectively together, while still maintaining the critical differences in perspective necessary to withstand the threat of groupthink. Maintaining this balance can be difficult but is imperative for a group to maintain their long-term happiness, productivity, and effectiveness.

DISCUSSION QUESTIONS

1. Are there group norms at your educational institution? What are they? In the group of individuals you spend time with, are there group norms? What are they? In both cases, how did you identify these norms? How did you adapt to these norms?

2. What are the functions of norms in groups?

3. At this point in your small group and team communication course, what roles have you accepted and performed? Explain. Have you experienced any role conflict(s)? Explain.

4. What is an emerging role?

EXERCISES

1. Norms; 2. Assuming norms; 3. Norms and roles by generation; 4. Ethics—Photo substitutions; 5. Role conflict and role ambiguity; 6. Your roles; 7. The new truck

1. NORMS

Think about your current class. How diverse is the class? What norms seem to operate as you progress through this course? Are people on time? Is everyone prepared for class each time? Do most people participate? How? Are differences of opinion and perspective encouraged, tolerated, or restricted? Are there acceptable deviancies that are tolerated or sanctioned by the teacher and/or the class? Are some of these norms "carryovers" from other class experiences?

Directions

Answer these questions considering the earlier discussion of norms in your text. Compare your answers with other class members. Develop some generalizations concerning the class norms *and* the implications of these norms for the course.

2. ASSUMING NORMS

1. Based on your own experiences and understanding, write down as many words as possible to explain what norms mean to you in terms of your expectations for small groups and teams. Work by yourself and *do not* share the list with anyone else. Strive for at least ten words.

2. Check the words you associate with norms with the members of your group. Give yourself a point for each word that every group member had on his or her worksheet. Words must be "almost" identical. Give the group one point for every word that appears on all the worksheets. Compare your scores with other groups.

3. How many points did your group have? What does this tell us about the real meaning of norms? Is it important to not assume norms? How should we discuss norms in our group or team? What are the key issues and potential problems? How can we prevent misunderstandings?

4. Did you respond that "we need to check for understanding and common definitions"? If so, how would you proceed to accomplish that goal? Are expectations regarding the group or team process important to consider before launching into examining issues or solving problems?

3. NORMS AND ROLES BY GENERATION

1. Veterans, Boomers, Xers, and Nexters. In your experience, what differences have you noted between these four groups in terms of accepted norms and roles? List three differences that you feel exist between each of these groups.

2. In your small group, try to develop a "master list" of the differences. Has the group experienced problems and issues because of these differences?

3. What process could be followed to create norms given these diverse backgrounds?

4. ETHICS—PHOTO SUBSTITUTIONS

Ethics is a difficult issue. Anderson and Englehardt (2001) conclude that "ethics concerns the rights and responsibilities, privileges and obligations of our conduct within and between . . . relationships" (p. 6). They add: "A primary goal of ethics, then, is to establish appropriate constraints on ourselves . . . These constraints are necessary because we have conflicting interests and selfish desires that can inflict harm on ourselves and others" (p. 7).

As a group, decide: (1) Do you agree with this definition of ethics? If not, what other definitions would you offer? (2) Did the University of Wisconsin and/or Ford and/or Bridgestone/Firestone engage in unethical behavior? Be prepared to explain why or why not.

5. ROLE CONFLICT AND ROLE AMBIGUITY

Background

Your new job includes assignment to the OIG (Organizational Improvement Group) and you are excited with the opportunity to work on such a high-priority project. Anissa, the leader, opens the first meeting by explaining that OIG needs to: (1) understand where the organization stands in terms of areas for improvement; (2) examine the current trends in the industry as a whole; (3) develop some interviewing processes; and (4) establish some roles for each member to play. No one speaks up to question these choices, so she asks for volunteers to take responsibility for the OIG items: areas for improvement, current trends, and developing interviewing processes. You and Judy volunteer for areas for improvement; Electra and Jack volunteer for studying the current trends; and your leader appoints Mike and Marsha to develop some interviewing processes, since no one volunteered. Being team players, Mike and Marsha agree although somewhat hesitantly. Everyone agrees to meet at the same time in a week to review progress.

At the second meeting, you and partner, Judy, explain that you are new to the company and are finding it difficult to interview effectively; Electra and Jack haven't seen a library in years and neither one enjoys surfing the net; and Mike and Marsha simply do not want to work on interviewing.

Assignment

Step 1: Knowing what you do about role conflict and role ambiguity, how would you act as the OIG leader? (1) Review the task, maintenance, and self-oriented roles and see if some important questions were missed. (2) Why is role clarification an important step in working with a task-oriented team? (3) How can the OIG process be "saved"?

Step 2: In your group, share your responses and develop a common strategy for reducing role conflicts and role ambiguity. This can apply to a team designed for the entire course or for a particular problem-solving team. Be prepared to share your responses with the rest of the class.

6 . Y O U R R O L E S

Return to the three role categories—task, maintenance, and self-oriented—discussed in the chapter. Place a check mark next to each of the behaviors you feel you currently engage in while working in small groups. Place an "X" next to those behaviors you feel are important but that you do not currently pursue. Compare your self-assessment with the assessment of someone in the class who has had the opportunity to observe your small group behaviors. Is the dyad in agreement regarding the other's self-assessment? How can you work to diminish those behaviors that are less than productive and increase the productive behaviors?

7 . T H E N E W T R U C K

The following group role-play exercise is based on a modified version of Maier and Hoffman's "New Truck Exercise" (Maier & Hoffman, 1963). It provides a good discussion starter of group process, norms, values, and roles.

A telephone company's repair team consists of five telephone line repair persons: Pat, Lee, Chris, Jo, and BJ. They all do essentially the same job—fix phone lines that are out of order. This requires knowledge and diagnostic skills, as well as muscular ability. Each person ordinarily works alone and drives a small truck around to do several jobs in one day.

Every so often the crew gets a new truck to replace an old one. The last time this happened the supervisor assigned the new truck and heard so much grumbling and so many complaints that this time the supervisor has called a team meeting to make the decision. The supervisor is willing to allocate the new truck according to team consensus and will not intervene in the decision-making process but must be convinced that a team consensus has been reached.

Pat: You have worked for the phone company for seventeen years and drive a two-year-old Ford truck, which you maintain and keep running well. You think that you should get the new Chevrolet truck because you have the most seniority and because you don't like your present truck. Your personal car is a Chevrolet, and you prefer a Chevy truck such as you drove before you got the Ford.

Lee: You have worked for the phone company for eleven years and drive a five-year-old Dodge truck, which you have taken excellent care of. You feel that you deserve the new truck. Your present truck is old, and since the more senior repair person has a fairly new truck, you should get this next one. You have taken excellent care of your present Dodge and have kept it looking and running like new. A person deserves to be rewarded for taking good care of a truck.

Chris: You have worked for the company for ten years and drive a four-year-old Ford truck. You have more driving to do than most of the others because you work primarily in the suburbs. You have a fairly old truck, and you feel you should get the new one because you do so much driving.

Jo: You have worked for the company for five years and drive a three-year-old Ford truck. The heater in your present truck doesn't work well and is inadequate to heat the truck. Ever since BJ backed into the side door of your truck, it has never closed right and lets in a cold draft. You attribute your frequent colds and sick time to your cold truck and want a warm one, since you have a good deal of driving to do in the suburbs. As long as your truck has good tires and brakes and is warm and comfortable, you'll be happy.

BJ: You have worked for the company for three years and drive a five-year-old Chevrolet truck. You have the poorest truck in the crew. Not only is it five years old, but before you got it, it had been in a bad wreck. It has never been totally reliable, and you have put up with it for three years. It's about time you got a good truck to drive, and it seems only fair that the next one should be yours. You have a good accident record. The only accident you had was when you sprung the door on Jo's truck when he opened it as you backed out of the garage. You had hoped that the new truck would be a Ford, since you prefer to drive a Ford.

Several groups of five participants each can simultaneously role-play this group discussion. Allow approximately 20 minutes for the groups to reach consensus. Additional non–role-playing observers of the group interaction can use the observation form (see Table 3.2 on page 64) to take notes identifying the communication roles each participant performs, providing examples of those roles, and identifying the consequences. Ask groups who arrive at a consensus early to reflect on their decision-making process while the other groups arrive at consensus. They can review the turn taking, persuasive strategies, use of interruptions, phases of group process, developing norms, assumed roles, and expressed values that occurred in the group.

Follow-up Questions
1. Who gets the new truck? (Did each group give the new truck to a different person?)
2. What was the conversational process by which the decision was made? (Participant and Observer comments are helpful here.)
3. Were there identifiable stages or phases in the discussion and decision-making process?
4. What were the rules of discussion developed and the implicit norms used in making the decision?
5. What were the values and assumptions underlying the decision to give the new truck to a particular person? Were other arrangements made for other participants and what were the values underlying those decisions?

TABLE 3.2   Observer Form for the New Truck Exercise

Communication Role Performed	Person Who Performed Role					Example of Role	Consequence
	Pat	Lee	Chris	Jo	BJ		
Initiate							
Question							
Interpret							
Suggest							
Facilitate							
Evaluate							
Provide feedback							
Clarify							
Summarize							
Terminate							
Actively listen							
Confront							
Model							
Reflect on feelings							
Provide support							
Empathize							

REFERENCES

Anderson, J. A., & Englehardt, E. E. (2001). *The organizational self and ethical conduct.* Orlando, FL: Harcourt College Publishers.

Associated Press. (1999, September 3). Demographics will challenge employers and government. *The Tuscaloosa News*, p. 5B.

Bales, R. G. (1950). *Interaction process analysis: A method for the study of small groups.* Reading, MA: Addison-Wesley.

Bochner, A. (1984). The functions of human communication in interpersonal bonding. In C. Arnold & J. Bowers (Eds.), *Handbook of rhetorical and communication theory* (pp. 544–621). Boston: Allyn & Bacon.

Bradsher, K. (2001, June 24). Defects in SUV tires discovered, kept quiet by lawyers. *The Tuscaloosa News*, pp. 1A, 8A.

Colvin, G. (1999, July 19). The 50 best companies for Asians, Blacks, and Hispanics. *Fortune*, pp. 53ff.

Evans, C. R., & Dion, K. L. (1991). Group cohesion and performance: A meta-analysis. *Small Group Research, 22*(2), 175–186.

Hare, A. P. (1994). Types of roles in small groups. *Small Group Research, 25*(3), 433–448.

Harris, T. E. (1997). Diversity: Importance, ironies, and pathways. In C. D. Brown, C. Snedeker, & B. Sykes (Eds.). *Conflict and diversity* (pp. 17–34). Cresskill, NJ: Hampton Press.

Healey, J. R., & Nathan, S. (2000, September 21). Further scrutiny puts Ford in the hot seat. *USA Today*, p. 1B.

Janis, I., (1982). *Groupthink* (2nd ed.). Boston: Houghton Mifflin.

Johns, G. (1988). *Organizational behavior: Understanding life at work* (2nd ed.). Glenview, IL: Scott, Foresman.

Ketrow, S. M., (1991). Communication role specializations and perceptions of leadership. *Small Group Research, 22*(4), 492–514.

Keyton, J., & Springston, J. (1990). Redefining cohesiveness in groups. *Small Group Research, 21*(2), 234–254.

Kiley, D. (2002, May 20). Part of tire settlement used to warn of under inflation risks. *USA Today,* p. 8B.

Kroon, M. B. R., Kreveld, D. van, & Rabbie, J. M. (1992). Group versus individual decision making: Effects of accountability and gender on groupthink. *Small Group Research, 23*(4), 427–458.

Maier, N. R. F., & Hoffman, L. R. (1963). Seniority in work groups: A right or an honor? *Journal of Applied Psychology, 47,* 173–176.

Marin, M. J., Sherblom, J. C., & Shipps, T. B. (1994). Contextual influences on nurses' conflict management strategies. *Western Journal of Communication, 58,* 201–228.

Mullen, B., Anthony, T., Salas, E., & Driskell, J. E. (1994). Group cohesiveness and quality of decision making. *Small Group Research, 25*(2), 189–204.

Parker-Pope, T. (1996, February 2). Ford puts blacks in whiteface, turns red. *The Wall Street Journal,* p. B8.

Pirisi, A. (1999, November/December). Teamwork: The downside of diversity. *Psychology Today,* p. 18.

Schein, E. H. (1969). *Process consultation: Its role in organizational development.* Reading, MA: Addison-Wesley.

Stockton, R., Rohde, R. I., & Haughey, J. (1992). The effects of structured group exercises on cohesion, engagement, avoidance, and conflict. *Small Group Research, 23*(2), 155–168.

Wentling, R. M., & Palma-Rivas, N. (1998). Current status and future trends of diversity initiatives in the workplace: Diversity experts' perspective. *Human Resource Development Quarterly, 9*(3), 235–253.

Whyte, G. (1989). Groupthink reconsidered. *Academy of Management Review, 14,* 40–56.

Widmeyer, W. N., & Williams, J. M. (1991). Predicting cohesion in a coacting sport. *Small Group Research, 22*(4), 548–570.

Witteman, H. (1991). Group member satisfaction. *Small Group Research, 22*(1), 24–58.

Wyatt, S. (2000, September 23). Doctored photo highlights need to diversify. *The Tuscaloosa News,* p. 5A.

Zander, A. (1982). *Making groups effective.* San Francisco: Jossey-Bass.

Zemke, R., Raines, C., & Filipczak, B. (2000). *Generations at work: Managing the clash of veterans, boomers, xers, and nexters in your workplace.* New York: AMACOM.

4

Four Phases of Group Development: Forming, Storming, Norming, and Performing

CHAPTER OUTLINE

CHAPTER OBJECTIVES

- Understand the four phases of group process.
- Explain the importance of the forming stage and its communication characteristics.
- Outline the factors occurring in the storming phase.
- Illustrate how the norming phase occurs.

- Discuss the performing phase.
- See how the termination phase operates.
- Understand modifications to the phase model.
- Specify the kinds of communication occurring during each phase.
- Introduce the role of organizational teams.

KEY TERMS

Cohesiveness	Making decisions and solving problems	Secondary tension
Conflict		Self-disclosure
Emergence	Norming	Social dynamics
Formal group	Organizational teams	Storming
Forming	Orientation	Task dynamics
Group identity	Performing	Termination
Inclusion	Phase model	
Informal group	Primary tension	

They were a consulting team brought together for this project of investigating business opportunities in Argentina, Brazil, and Chile. Each had an individual expertise to contribute to the team effort. Two were fluent in Spanish, and one of them knew South American business culture. Another was an industry expert. A fourth knew marketing, and the fifth member was a communication and negotiation expert. They met for the first time as a team in January, and I sat in as they began to talk about the project. First, over coffee, they shared their backgrounds, expertise, got to know each other, and shared what each of them knew about the project. It was a fun session that started quietly but soon became marked by laughter, good-natured fun, verbal repartee, and jocular conversation. This was a good beginning, but as we met more times and had more serious discussions of the project, disagreements that occurred over travel plans and the structuring of the project's priorities became heated arguments. Fortunately, group members stepped in to facilitate the discussion and find ways around apparent impasses. Gradually the parameters and pressures of the project became clear, and the group developed discussion standards and performance expectations. Even during the constant travel and tight living conditions that followed during the next four months, group members became close friends and performed together as a team to generate an outstanding and useful report. When they parted, it was with a sense of sadness as well as one of accomplishment.

Newly formed groups frequently go through a set of identifiable stages or phases that have come to be known by the informal identifiers of forming, storming, norming, and performing as indicated in Figure 4.1. Forming describes the initial orientation phase of getting to know other group members. Storming describes the conflict phase that often occurs once group members have gotten to know each other well enough and become comfortable enough with each other to state their opinions openly and honestly. Norming describes the emergent process through which common group understanding, rules for discussion, focus on issues, and an orientation to task become established within the group. Performing describes the phase of task accomplishment, social reinforcement, and goal achievement. For many task-oriented groups, these phases are followed by a termination phase, once the task is accomplished.

Early group researchers, led by Tuckman (1965, 1977) and Fisher (1970), identified these group phases. While not all groups follow them, or follow them in order, the phases describe common group experiences (Verdi & Wheelan, 1992; Wheelan & McKeage, 1993). Recognizing the phases can be important to facilitating group process because the communication of the group usually changes with the phase they are in, and the way the group deals with these changes can affect how they deal with challenges and make decisions.

Therefore, while it would be misleading to suggest that the group process will always be orderly and move through these phases in a linear sequence, a discussion of these phases provides a descriptive picture of what to expect, in a general way, of a group engaged in decision making and problem solving. If a group skips

FIGURE 4.1   The four phase model can be plotted on an "S" curve. This curve indicates that groups work through the phases, although not necessarily in the orderly pattern shown on this curve. At some point, the group will terminate or disband because their tasks have been completed. For teams, a point is reached where some reforming is necessary to replace unnecessary steps, change ineffective procedures, or develop new goals.

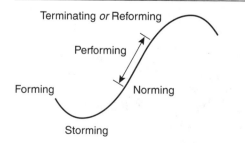

one of these phases, there is the possibility that the group decision-making process will be incomplete or that the phase will be revisited at a later point in time.

Forming: Hello, Orientation, and Inclusion

The first stage for any group is *forming*. During this period, we are deciding who we are as a group, what our purpose is, whether or not we want to be a member of the group, who the other group members are, and what our place or role will be in the group. This phase in group development focuses on issues of inclusion and attempts to identify the parameters of acceptable behavior within the group (Wheelan & McKeage, 1993). During this phase of a group's development, members are uncertain about the other members and how the actual group process will unfold and are often hesitant to contribute much (Wellings, Byham, & Wilson, 1991).

As a new group member, I observe you and you observe me. I would like to appear attractive, competent, pleasant, and bright. I am likely to smile, act pleasant, and make small talk. I am not likely to be overtly disagreeable, become argumentative, be confrontational, or be overly revealing about my personal life. I would like to know if you are friendly, intelligent, and nice, or arrogant, mean, and hostile. So, I will probably be quiet, observant, and somewhat inquisitive.

These initial periods hold some uneasiness and awkwardness that are normal and to be expected, as we do not know each other well and have not as yet established group operating procedures, norms, or roles. This initial uneasiness and uncertainty is called primary tension and is evidenced in the small talk, awkward silences, and search for friendly faces that often surround the initial conversations. When members introduce themselves and identify their reasons for being in the group, people gradually begin to relax. Humor can be used to release some of these tensions and feelings as well.

Once the primary tension is released, the group begins to devote itself to the task at hand, trying to define the group's purpose, establish some type of agenda, develop some working rules, and begin the group process. Important characteristics in this first phase are that most of the communication is tentative as the group devotes itself to becoming oriented to its goals; conflict is avoided, played down, or ignored; and group members usually ask more questions than making statements regarding their beliefs.

The forming phase should include some important communication characteristics as summarized in Figure 4.2:

1. This phase contains a number of questions that can help group members develop a clear understanding of the task at hand.

2. The goals of the group become generally understood, although they may not be explicitly articulated.

3. Some uncertainty regarding the group's task may be expressed. Articulating this uncertainty and the task at hand is important, otherwise, there may be only apparent or pseudo agreement, as members simply "go along to get along." A lack

FIGURE 4.2   **Forming—Key Elements to Facilitate Good Communication**

✓ Group Norms—Accepted Standards (see Chapter 3)   ✓ Group Goals
✓ Rules—Guidelines for Proceeding   Realistic
✓ Roles—What members are expected   Clear
    to do (see Chapter 3)   Attainable
✓ Structure—How to organize

of a clear understanding and consensus on this task can create the basis for conflict later in the group process.

4. While tentative, there may be some role assignments. In particular, a leader is likely to emerge or be explicitly selected. Depending on the group, this may be seen as an important status symbol that can create difficulties during the storming phase, or it may be perceived as a simple formality or as necessary to the functioning of the group.

The key elements to facilitate good communication in this phase are the establishment of group norms, rules, roles, and structure. Group goals need to be established that are realistic, clear, and attainable within the time available.

In general, this phase is marked for members by an initial uncertainty and often a hesitation to disclose personal information, creating a primary tension. Supportive group behaviors can help members build an interpersonal trust and get better acquainted. Precautions should be taken to provide an open, safe environment for the giving and receiving of information and expression of feelings. Any issues of confidentiality must be understood so that group members can build interpersonal trust. It is important for members to explicitly assess their commitment to the group and the task, recognizing any ambivalence and coming to terms with any approach–avoidance feelings toward other group members, the task itself, and the time and energy commitments that will be required of them. The purpose of the group must be clearly and openly discussed so that members can match their individual expectations against the group's aim. Misconceptions concerning the purpose of the group and role confusion can create negative emotions that distort group functioning, leading to silent withdrawal by group members or expressive acting out of self-oriented roles by some members. These feelings may also affect attendance at meetings, timeliness in accomplishing tasks, and drop-out rates of group members during the later phases of task accomplishment. Since this is the first step in group formation, productivity or group accomplishments tend to be low since members are still exploring this new collective (Montebello, 1994, p. 35).

The group can maintain some flexibility in topic areas to be discussed to meet the needs of individuals in the group, but all topics should be put forward at this time. Once we get to know the members of a group, we may still experience anxiety concerning the group's overall purpose, process, and goals; or about the other group members, their perspectives, and their intentions. These types of concerns, based upon our understanding of the group and other group members, bring us to the second phase of group process—storming.

Storming: Conflict in Groups

The storming phase is the most complex phase in a group's process. Conflict frequently erupts over issues of power, authority, and competition within the group (Wheelan & McKeage, 1993). We have gotten to know each other well enough to work through our initial polite or "niceness" phase with each other. Now we can be more honest and forthright in our opinions and positions. As this happens, we discover our areas of disagreement. Conflicts may occur over task issues as we begin presenting our ideas. Different views are expressed. Some are accepted; others are rejected. Members vie for control of the discussion. People take sides and break into different factions and coalitions. This is an important phase for the group, and rather than avoiding or glossing over conflict in this phase it should be seen as a way for a group to begin to define and deal with the difficult issues inherent in the task at hand.

Conflict occurs, in part, because group members are now comfortable enough with each other to present their real views and opinions. For example, do you argue more often with your friends or with strangers? With strangers we tend to be more polite and "on our best behavior." With friends—the people we feel the most comfortable with, care about the most, spend the most time with, and who know us the best—we are likely to be more honest, forthright, and more willing to state and argue our beliefs. Similarly, in small groups, as we get to know each other and each other's positions better, we are likely to become more honest and less tentative in stating our positions. This more open communication brings us into honest disagreements and conflict.

A number of theorists have suggested that this initial phase of group conflict is important to fostering subsequent group feelings of cohesion and cooperation, as well as leading to a more effective decision-making process (Verdi & Wheelan, 1992; Wheelan & McKeage, 1993). Yet, some groups become so concerned with these inevitable conflicts that they attempt to avoid them, and in avoiding them, they avoid or suppress important aspects of the group's issues. Through this avoidance, a secondary tension may be created that stifles the development of long-term group cohesion and of effective group decision making and problem solving.

As the group continues to meet and the primary tension subsides, an interdependence based on sharing and association develops, resulting in a group identity and sense of cohesion. Cartwright (1968) describes the factors that influence the development of this sense of cohesion. These include the developing of clear goals, activities that are within the members' capabilities, similarity among group members, cooperation and interdependence among members, interaction among members with a democratic leader, and a group a climate that results in feelings of being valued and accepted.

There are also factors that threaten cohesion. These are an unstable membership, goal uncertainty, group deviants who do not conform to group norms, cliques that are more committed to the needs of a particular subgroup than the group as a whole, and a lack of leadership in developing cohesiveness (Arrow & McGrath, 1993).

Several important communication concerns affect group cohesion during the conflict phase, including disruptive behavior, interpersonal conflict, and lack of interpersonal skills in listening, providing feedback, and developing supportiveness (see Figure 4.3). Members do not always know how to give and receive feedback that is both supportive of other members and constructive in developing the group cohesion and task. Sometimes people think giving advice or solving another's problems for them is support. These techniques are not often advantageous in a group setting and can create disruptive patterns of talk and behavior within the group. In addition, it is difficult for some people to talk openly about their opinions and feelings, or to openly disagree with another member. An atmosphere of trust and acceptance must be felt within the group for this to occur. To create this supportive climate, group members must practice empathetic listening and be able to communicate nonjudgmental acceptance and disagreement.

Despite group selection practices, a group may have a member who is not well suited to the particular group, and who is causing disruption. It is important to decide whether the disruptive behavior is an expression of either primary or secondary tension that may subside as the group progresses or is indicative of a more long-lasting problem. The group must decide because it cannot function well if the disruptive behavior continues. Either the leader or the group as a whole must speak with the member in a sensitive way to explain the effect the disruptions are having on the group, and offer a constructive way of contributing to the group discussion.

Occasionally, some members may experience periods of dissatisfaction with the group or with some of its members. They may perceive someone in the group as having a pessimistic attitude, or they may be uncomfortable with someone's communication style. These issues and concerns need to be dealt with openly in the group.

In addition, members take risks and feel vulnerable when they open up to the group. So, members may not easily express themselves, may feel inhibited, or

FIGURE 4.3   Storming—Communication Concerns

Disruptive behavior

Interpersonal conflict

Lack of interpersonal skills in listening

Providing feedback

Developing supportiveness

may lack the necessary social skills, resulting either in silence or in acting out against others.

Members need to feel that they are being heard. No one member should dominate the discussion. One technique to facilitate this is the "group round." At the beginning of each meeting, members are asked how much time they will need during the meeting to share their ideas and information. Time is set aside for each member and carefully monitored. Members are notified when their time is up. If more time is needed, the member may ask for more and another member may volunteer some of his or her time to allow the person to continue speaking. Another way to approach the time issue is to create a round in which everyone has a designated amount of time to speak. When time is up for one, the speaker is notified and attention shifts to the next person. Rules can be established for whether or not cross talk will be allowed. Sometimes feedback is left to the end of a full round. The norms developed by the group for the sessions reflect the group members' priorities. Early meetings may be guided by a leader who is responsible for promoting discussion and interaction among members and creating an atmosphere of open communication and nonjudgmental, empathic listening. The leader may also provide information and assist members in understanding how they can integrate the information and members' contributions.

Also, some members may feel threatened by others, and it may take time for them to develop a basic trust. There is a normal resistance to self-disclosure that can make a leader's task more difficult in these early sessions. As the group becomes more cohesive, members can share more leadership responsibility and have more input into the content of the sessions. In a supportive group, vulnerability is sensed by the other members and efforts are made to help the individual feel accepted. It is important for the group to feel comfortable and know how to respond supportively to disclosure and emotional expression. Members may need to be encouraged to take the time they need to contribute to the group discussion.

Besides performing managerial functions, setting limits, and monitoring rules and procedures, a facilitative group member must demonstrate kindness, warmth, openness, and sincerity, taking an active role in encouraging other members to express feelings and model ways to share concerns in the group (Lieberman, 1991).

The secret to effective group process is to try to air, hear, and accept as many conflicts as possible during this phase in order for the group to recognize multiple perspectives and develop a better understanding of the full complexity of the issues to be faced. Interpersonal and group conflicts are inevitable and an important part of the group process. Working through these conflicts depends on several factors, including the group members' amount of understanding and agreement, the group members' apparent satisfaction, and the willingness of group members to trust each other's good will, and to communicate empathy for diverse perspectives.

These attitudes help group members resolve conflict in this phase. If the conflicts are not fully resolved, however, this phase may be revisited, perhaps even repeatedly, as the group moves to phase three. If we do not understand, feel satisfied, or trust, we have difficulty becoming a cohesive emergent group capable of making a decision or solving a problem.

Norming: Emergence as a Group

At this point in a group's evolution, differences have been expressed and the storm of conflict is subsiding. Member relationships are becoming more open and trusting, and the group begins to feel more cohesive. Open negotiation of goals, roles, expectations, group structure, and the division of labor is undertaken. Even though members have developed their positions and come to some understanding of the positions of other members of the group, there is a tendency for groups to move back and forth between conflict and emerging cohesiveness. Disagreements are rarely fully and permanently resolved. The major issues may have been resolved, but there are countless issues to be worked through, as the group begins working toward defining problems and solutions. While the interaction remains tentative, cooperation is on the rise. During this phase, there are both primary and secondary tensions as new issues occur, raising primary tensions, and proposed solutions bring secondary tensions.

Ideally, groups should proceed through phase two (storming) before tackling phase three (norming), but two human characteristics tend to muddy the process. First, we like to solve problems, even before we have fully defined them. So, during phase two it is very tempting to propose our own personal solution before the group completes a thorough examination of different viewpoints and issues. Second, as the group proceeds through the emergence phase, group members may feel the need to revisit issues that were in conflict during phase two because some aspect of the analysis appears incomplete. In this case, individuals may feel that they have not represented their position adequately and wish to restate it in order to become more comfortable with the outcome. If the conflict experienced in phase two has not been well managed or fully resolved, the group will, sooner or later, return to phase-two issues.

A group is likely, from time to time, to hit periods of silence. This silence may be marked by tension, as one tries to think of what to say next, or a member may withdraw from the group if he or she feels pressured to speak up when not ready to do so. Silence can also be a time for introspection, looking inside oneself for answers or reflecting on what has just been shared. A group facilitator must judge what type of silence is occurring in order to help the group progress.

Norming describes the groups' willingness to settle upon specific rules for how discussions will take place and decisions will be made. It is an important phase in the group process and sets the stage for the group's performance.

Performing: Making Decisions and Solving Problems

Performing identifies the real work phase of the group. It is characterized by an increase in task orientation and by open exchange and feedback. The group's social tension usually decreases as a sense of relief occurs and the group begins moving toward some type of solution, examines that solution, and begins to assess the impact it will have on the problem.

A problem-solving process consisting of four or five distinct steps can help the group function more effectively during this phase. Each of these steps is distinct and calls for different communication behavior from the leader and group members working through the problem-solving process. Table 4.1 shows some of the "do's" and "don'ts" for group members in this problem-solving process.

TABLE 4.1   Group Members' Responsibilities for Facilitating Problem Solving in the Performing Phase

Step 1: Defining the Problem

DO'S:

- Do provide the pertinent data that you possess.
- Do provide the background context for the problem.
- Do explain how this problem relates to others.
- Do ask other group members for whatever facts and data they possess.
- Do make sure that everyone understands all the facts and data.
- Do restate the definition of the problem to ensure that all members are aware of what you have and what you want.

DON'TS:

- Don't discuss solutions.
- Don't blame or assess fault regarding the problem.
- Don't move on in the process until everyone is clear about the definition of the problem.
- Don't supply a lot of irrelevant information.
- Don't act as though you have already decided on a solution and are involving other members of the team as merely a formality.

Step 2: Generating Possible Solutions

DO'S:

- Do encourage "off the wall" comments.
- Do challenge the group to push for as many possible solutions as they can think of.
- Do "prime the pump" with your own ideas, especially if the group is stuck.
- Do set a time limit.
- Do invite everyone to participate, even if you have to ask them explicitly.
- Do ask open-ended questions to spark the team's thinking.
- Do write down all ideas generated.
- Do assure the team that all ideas are welcome, and that no idea is silly.
- Do piggyback off each other's ideas.

DON'TS:

- Don't allow editing, evaluating, or criticizing of ideas.
- Don't settle on the first "good" idea that surfaces.
- Don't punish other members who criticize ideas—just remind them of the ground rules.
- Don't spend much time advocating your ideas.
- Don't spend much time on any one person or one good idea.
- Don't go beyond the time limit set unless the team explicitly wants to.
- Don't quit until the time limit is up.

(*continued*)

TABLE 4.1   Continued

Step 3: Evaluating Solutions

DO'S:
- Do review all the items on the list of possible solutions and eliminate those with no support.
- Do keep any item on the list that anyone is willing to discuss.
- Do focus on looking at the positive and negative aspects of each solution.
- Do anticipate the consequences of each solution.
- Do make sure that each member has ample opportunity to provide their input.
- Do invite members to combine solutions.
- Do ensure consensus by getting everyone's input.
- Do frequently restate what you hear to clarify the meaning.

DON'TS:
- Don't allow the team to judge each other as they judge the ideas.
- Don't get bogged down discussing the pros and cons; assess value quickly.
- Don't quit until you have clear consensus.

Step 4: Creating an Action Plan

DO'S:
- Do generate alternative how-tos for implementation before choosing an action plan.
- Do make sure that specific tasks are assigned.
- Do make sure that time frames are set.
- Do empower the members with the authority to complete their tasks.
- Do arrange a method of following up to ensure completion of the tasks.
- Do include yourself as a person responsible for a task.
- Do restate each member's role to clarify and ensure commitment.

DON'TS:
- Don't state roles and tasks in general, unmeasurable terms.
- Don't assume that brilliant solutions produce brilliant action plans; be creative in your planning.
- Don't forget to follow up.

Terminating

"Groups that have a distinct ending point experience a fifth phase" (Verdi & Wheelan, 1992, p. 357). This final phase in a group's process is termination. In the original forming, storming, norming, and performing model, this phase was called adjourning (Tuckman & Jensen, 1977). Even ongoing groups may reach a termination point through membership attrition or changing group needs. Loss of individual group members can also create small points of termination within the group. Finally, many task groups experience a time of completing their task and terminating their meetings.

If the group has really become interdependent in their working together— enjoy talking with each other, the regularity of meetings, and the forum for expression of themselves, are cohesive in their relationships, enjoying the interactions with each other as well as the tasks—then the termination phase can be an awkward and stressful phase for group members (Keyton, 1993). Impending termination may cause disruption to the group's processes and conflict among the group members (Verdi & Wheelan, 1992). Many people find it difficult to terminate relationships and would simply rather avoid saying good-bye. There may also be an unwillingness to deal with the emotions tied to ending the group. Keyton (1993) observes that the termination phase may be characterized by anxiety about separation and conclusion, a degree of sadness, and some self-reflective evaluation, as well as positive feelings toward the group and its project.

A group's termination may form a pivotal point in an individual's life and activities, and members of groups can benefit by reflecting on, coming to terms with, and talking about the termination of the group. People say good-bye in different ways, but a special event that marks the end of the group may help members experience a sense of closure.

Keyton (1993) suggests that not acknowledging the termination of a group may mean, for many people, not having to admit the end of a good group experience or the presence of bad ones. Yet, she argues, this is an important phase in the group process. How we terminate our group activities affects how we will interpret, in retrospect, what we have accomplished and experienced as a group and what we expect of future groups. Good-byes, and their sense of closure, feelings of task accomplishment, and positive relational expression, are an important aspect of small group process.

Usefulness of the Phase Model

This phase-model approach to understanding group process suggests the importance of waiting to solve a problem until all the issues surrounding it have been discussed. People in Western societies, and Americans in particular, tend to be "can do" individuals (Quick, 1985). When we are faced with a problem, we prefer making a decision and acting on it, rather than going through the time and energy-consuming steps of analysis. In acting quickly, however, we tend to miss some critical issues in the process. The phase approach outlines what should be done and operates as a functional checklist for a group.

Modifications

Not all groups follow this phase model in a strictly linear process. Poole and Roth (1989) studied groups and found that they frequently go through periods of disorganization. This disorganization creates cycles in their process, meaning the group can repeat some of the phases several times. A group might, for example, simultaneously operate with one foot in phase two and one foot in phase three in an effort to move forward. This is OK and may even be effective for the group. Group process can be messy.

The types of communication that occur in a group also shift and change from one phase to the next. Seven categories of statements have been described by Verdi and Wheelan (1992). In the forming phase "dependency" statements are common. These seek direction, show an inclination to conform to the dominant mood of the group, and express a desire to follow the general direction of the suggestions made. In the storming phase "counterdependency" statements that assert independence and reject other members' attempts at leadership and authority become more prominent. "Fight" statements that imply participation in struggle through argumentativeness, criticism, and aggression also become more common. These are followed in the norming phase with "flight" statements indicative of avoidance of confrontation and perhaps of task. The "counterpairing" statements of this phase, expressing an avoidance of intimacy and of cohesion and a desire to keep the discussion distant and intellectual, gradually give way to an emergence of "pairing" statements that express a warmth of friendship, support, greater intimacy, and a general positive regard for other group members. Finally, in the performing phase, "work" statements representing the purposeful accomplishment of goal-directed, task-oriented activities become more prevalent (Verdi & Wheelan, 1992).

This phase interaction theory suggests that effective groups are attentive to the group process and to assessing: (a) the nature of the task; (b) the standards for evaluating various decision options; (c) positive qualities of the various possible choices; and (d) negative qualities of various options (Hirokawa & Rost, 1992). In other words, effective groups pay attention to the decision-making process itself and, even when they modify or deviate from the phase model, they make certain that the task is clearly analyzed before deciding on a solution.

Organizational Teams

This phase model also identifies the major points in organizational team development and of the leadership roles necessary in those teams. In stage one, primary organizational team issues are those of inclusion and acceptance. At this point, the team gets to know each other and gathers information regarding the job at hand. One major difference between a decision-making group outside an organization and an organizational team is the assignment of a leader. In an organization, a leader is normally assigned and the leader's job is to provide structure and direction for the organizational team members. In other decision-making groups, a leader is more likely to emerge during the group process, and the group members will have more influence on determining the role of the leader.

In stage two, issues of control and influence arise. Team members discover who has the power and decide which individuals to listen to. This stage is similar to the storming and norming phases, and the leader's role is to offer support and guidance without directing or controlling the group.

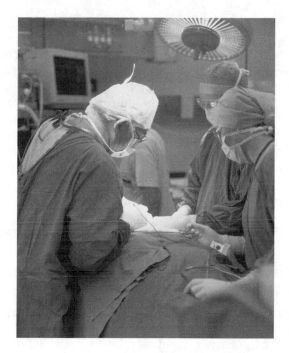

Surgery teams require outstanding teamwork and common goals.

Stage three deals with commitment and cohesion. The team performs the actual task, and the leader focuses on facilitating their performance, providing the team the freedom and resources to act.

Overriding Influences

Three major influences affect a small group's process of working through these phases. These influences are: whether the group is a formal or informal body; the task and social dynamics; and how the primary and secondary tensions affect the group dynamics.

Formal or Informal Group

A group is a formal one when it has been sanctioned or mandated by some organization. In other words, the system (that is, an organization, social body, university, club) decides it needs to establish an additional subsystem with some specific duties. A committee is formed, a team is chosen, or a task force is named that is governed by a particular set of rules or procedures. In formal groups, the social structure is relatively well established, norms and roles are explicit, and group members are aware of the relationships within the group. When you are assigned to a task force, the purpose, goals, and membership are determined by the larger organization (your university or employer), and the group is formal.

An informal group emerges and forms itself because of the interests of the members. While a formal group has specific rules and operating procedures, informal groups develop their own rules and procedures as the need arises. Their interacting process is frequently based on implicit or larger social rules. Informal groups often fulfill social needs, while formal groups are more oriented toward accomplishing a specific task or goal. Finally, an informal group can disband spontaneously, while formal groups have a more permanent status or defined period of existence.

Both formal and informal groups can be highly effective. For example, at the world renowned Mayo Clinic, groups and teams are an integral part of the patient care process. "Specialists don't just visit a patient; they swarm the patient with an integrated team, diagnosing a complex problem, proposing treatment—and often slotting the patient for surgery within 24 hours of diagnosis" (Roberts, 1999, p. 150). Starting as an informal arrangement, teamwork is now "built into the treatment of patients, and it's integrated into the clinic's fabric of governance" (Roberts, 1999, p. 150).

Task and Social Dynamics

Task and social dynamics are interdependent issues that continually interact in the group system. A task orientation deals with a group's purpose, structure, rules, procedures, and individual task-oriented assignments. The goals and objectives of the group, or getting the job done, can be viewed as the overriding group purpose. Using the systems analogy, our major concern with task dynamics is the group's output, accomplishments, or productivity.

Appropriate Task Questions

1. Why are we here?
2. What is to be accomplished?
3. What information and background is needed?
4. Do the group members have the ability, knowledge, and skills to do the assigned job?
5. What are the components of the problem?
6. What purpose(s) and goal(s) are driving this group?
7. What rules, procedures, and operating methods should be used?
8. How predictable is the outcome and is it clear?
9. By what criteria will we be judged?
10. Can it be done?

Social dynamics describes the ability of individuals to work together as a group. The synergy created by bringing together individuals who possess different backgrounds also means that there are significant issues regarding membership composition, group processes, norms, roles, status, and leadership. In order to be an effectively functioning system, the parts of the system must develop an ability to work well together. If group members do not have a desire to understand and deal with the task, the group will founder and probably fail, or a few dedicated individuals will have to do all of the work. If group members do not have some compatibility or enjoy each other's company, the group's cohesiveness will also suffer, but incompatibility among group members can be overcome. Open, involving communication motivates members to invest themselves in the process and builds a group's cohesion.

Social Loafing—A Threat to Group and Team Success

We've all been there. A group is formed and it soon becomes obvious that some members do not plan to contribute a great deal. They seem to be along for a free ride. This phenomena is called *social loafing* which is the tendency to exert less effort when working in a group than when working alone (Cohen & Fink, 2001). Some members might just be lazy or have other pressing commitments. Perhaps they do not care about the issues being discussed or feel they have little to contribute. Finally, the U.S. is one of the most individualistic nations in the world (Sweeney & McFarlin, 2002). This might explain our tendency to look out for number one or to avoid group commitment over the needs of the group.

There are consequences however. We can resent the free riders and the group is denied potentially useful input, the productivity (e.g., grades, income) might be lessened, and there can be an erosion of group cohesiveness.

What can be done to overcome social loafing? First, we can obtain a commitment from each group member to the purposes of the group. Second, we can make certain the rewards for participating are greater than not participating. Finally, we can actively involve reticent members through verbal and nonverbal communication and active listening.

Primary and Secondary Tensions

When the expected, initial period of uneasiness, awkwardness, and uncertainty within the group that is indicative of primary group tension lasts too long it can negatively impact the normal development of a group's dynamics and process. The group's pattern of communication and interaction; its development of norms, roles, and operating procedures; and its members' concerns for inclusion, acceptance, interpersonal trust, and support may all be adversely affected. When a period of extended primary tension occurs, a group may find it difficult to arrive at a consensus in defining its purpose, establishing an agenda, developing working rules, and beginning its work. Likewise, an avoidance of secondary tension through the suppression of conflict may stifle the development of group cohesion and of effective group decision making and problem solving. Group cohesion depends on the consensual development of clear group goals, member cooperation and interdependence, and individuals' feeling valued and accepted. Achieving these feelings of cooperation, interdependence, and acceptance requires that conflicts be dealt with thoughtfully and respectfully, but openly and honestly. Avoidance of conflict will, in the long term, impede the progress of the group. To be successful, groups must openly confront both primary and secondary tensions as issues to be worked through rather than as problems to be avoided.

Summary

Groups proceed through specific phases during their development. The orientation or forming phase is how the group sets itself up. This "first impressions make lasting impressions" phase is significant. During conflict or storming, we see the importance of diverse positions and work through issues. After sufficient discussion, we move to phase three, emergence or norming. After this consensus phase, we begin the performing phase during which we make a commitment to the outcome.

Small groups tend to have messy processes. The phase model helps us describe the essential issues raised by group processes. During these four phases, norms will be established and reinforced. Knowing what is expected from the group helps us succeed.

DISCUSSION QUESTIONS

1. What are the advantages of a phase model of group development? Are there any weaknesses? Can any of the phases be skipped? Can they be rearranged?

2. What important communication characteristics occur in the forming stage? Why are these important?

3. Does conflict have a role in developing group cohesion? What is it?

4. During the forming stage, what actions and behaviors should be encouraged to create an effective group?

5. From your own group experience, identify some examples of the norming phase in a group.

6. How would you define cohesion in a small group or team? Why is it important?

EXERCISES

1. Forming: Last night—Learning about other group members; 2. Bluffing and disclosing—Forming stage; 3. Blizzard; 4. Expectation and trepidation; 5. Problem-

solving group exercise: Cheating; 6. Performing stage—Basic questions; 7. The consulting firm

1. FORMING: LAST NIGHT—LEARNING ABOUT OTHER GROUP MEMBERS

Instructions

1. Write on a piece of paper something that you did last night. Do not write something you have already told other class members. Turn the piece of paper in to the instructor.
2. Your instructor will read each piece of information aloud and the order in which they are read will be the number assigned to that set of information: First read is #1, second read is #2, and so forth.
3. Write down the number and then write the name of the person who you think is the author next to the appropriate number.
4. Your instructor will reread each piece of information and you will be asked to call out the name of the person you think is the author.
5. Your instructor will then ask the real author to "please stand up."
6. Give yourself one point for every correct connection that you made between the author and what he or she did last night.

Debriefing

What does this demonstrate about the forming phase? Why were some activities easier to guess than others? How important is it to allow some self-disclosure before the group gets "down to business?" Do we need to take a proactive role in the forming stage by expressing our expectations and fears regarding the group process? What precautions should we take regarding forming impressions without actually knowing the individual?

2. BLUFFING AND DISCLOSING—FORMING STAGE

Directions

(1) Each team member should write four statements about herself or himself. Three of the statements must be true and one must be false. (2) Each team member should read the four statements and the other team members should try and determine which statement is false. (3) Depending on the team's progress toward investigating a specific issue or topic, an alternative would be to write four statements about what you have done to further the team's progress or found out about the issue—three true and one false. (4) Once you have shared, are you surprised with the diversity of experiences? How will this impact the ability of this team to work together? What steps can be taken to increase our understanding of other group members?

3. BLIZZARD

The Situation

Your group has gone on a hiking trip in the northern U.S. backcountry—a wilderness area. Since it was a nice-looking day, everyone dressed in comfortable clothes with some wearing hiking shoes, others sneakers, and one a pair of sport sandals. But, expecting a nice day, no one dressed for a potential problem. On the way into the hills, the weather was fine and everyone was enjoying the day. Slowly, it began to rain but the group wanted to travel just a little farther since it was still early. After about an hour, the blizzard hit. In what seemed minutes, an inch of snow had covered the ground. Gusts of wind brought an increasing amount of snow and it was soon up to your knees. Getting back to your car seems impossible. Would you know how to survive?

Step 1: Answer the following questions individually without consulting the other members of the group.

1. You're thoroughly lost so you should sit down and wait for someone to find you. True or false? Explain _____

2. What's more important in a survival situation: food or water? _____

3. How much water should you drink every day in this situation? _____

4. If you're stranded without food, eating anything is better than eating nothing. True or false?

5. You're out of water. What should you do to prevent dehydration?
   a. Drink sea water
   b. Drink alcohol, especially in winter because it'll keep you warm.
   c. Drink your own urine.
   d. None of these.

6. Check the three items you should always carry with you in the backcountry.

   ____ Map   ____ Knife
   ____ Chocolate bar   ____ Vitamins
   ____ Loaded pistol   ____ Change of socks
   ____ Garbage bag   ____ Sun glasses
   ____ Compass   ____ Cigarette lighter

7. Psychologists say there are four traits common to survivors. Pick the four from the following list.

   ____ Stubborn   ____ Having a will to survive
   ____ Humorous   ____ Optimistic
   ____ Stoic   ____ Flexible
   ____ Compassionate   ____ Fiery
   ____ Introverted   ____ Able to tolerate bizarre experiences

8. Rank (1, 2, 3) the following in terms of survival importance.

   a. Common sense _____
   b. Proper equipment _____
   c. Physical toughness _____

9. What is the most common cause of death in the backcountry?

Step 2: Assemble your small group and compare answers. Reach consensus regarding the best answers.

Step 3: Your instructor will provide the correct answers according to survival experts. For each correct answer (a) give yourself 2 points and (b) give the group 2 points. Add up the points and compare your individual chances for survival with the group's chances.

Step 4: Did the group progress through the four phases? Specifically, was there rigorous discussion (storming) before any decisions were made? Was the first "logical" answer accepted rather than a careful examination of all opinions? Did the loudest voice or the voice that claimed expertise win out even when some group members were not certain? Did any of the group members have important insights that they chose not to share? Why? If the group had the wrong answers, would a more careful discussion of the possible responses been helpful?

4. EXPECTATION AND TREPIDATION

The group process has promise and possible limitation. To clarify your own feelings when you enter a group, respond to the following two issues:

1. What are your expectations about working in groups and teams? What positive benefits do you foresee? Rank these in terms of how important they are to you individually. 1 = of primary importance, 2 = moderately important, 3 = somewhat important, 4 = nice to have, 5 = will probably occur but not too important.

Expectations	**Ranking**
1. _____	_____
2. _____	_____
3. _____	_____
4. _____	_____
5. _____	_____

2. What are your concerns about working in groups and teams? What limitations do you foresee? Rank these in terms of how important they are to you personally. 1 = of primary importance, 2 = moderately important, 3 = somewhat important, 4 = nice to have, 5 = will probably occur but not too important.

Trepidations   **Ranking**

1. _____   _____

2. _____   _____

3. _____   _____

4. _____   _____

5. _____   _____

Analysis

In your small group, compile a list of expectations and trepidations for small group and team work. What are the similarities? What are the differences? How can the positives be maximized and the concerns minimized?

5. PROBLEM-SOLVING GROUP EXERCISE: CHEATING

Step 1. In your group, examine with the following situation.

Cheating, plagiarizing, and other similar activities are on the rise throughout college and university campuses. Your group has been asked to develop an appropriate and effective response to this problem by deciding: (1) if there is an issue on your campus, (2) what are the manifestations, and (3) what solutions can be used. Be as specific as possible.

Step 2. Present your solution to the rest of the class. Solicit additional insights for use in step 3.

Step 3. Examine your group decision-making process. Did you go through the four stages? If you skipped one, did it impact on the quality of your decision? Did you "miss" anything important? Did you rush to finding the solution without allowing for storming and norming to have an impact?

Alternative topics

If cheating is not of interest to the group or providing different topics for each group would prove more interesting, consider one of the following.

How to deal with increased crime on your campus.
Deciding the theme for an upcoming campus party or dance.
The role of sports in higher education.
Reducing the digital divide.

Effectively dealing with discrimination.
Raising the drinking age to 25.
Requiring people to vote.

6. PERFORMING STAGE—BASIC QUESTIONS

Moving from good intentions to actions can be complicated. As a group, pick a problem that seems to have a relatively straightforward solution. To better guarantee performance, apply the following format.

Step 1: What must be done?
Step 2: Why must it be done?
Step 3: Where should it be done?
Step 4: When should it be done?
Step 5: Who should do it?
Step 6: How should it be done?

7. THE CONSULTING FIRM

Your group is a small, independent communication consulting firm that has formed to provide services to area businesses. In a 20 to 30 minute discussion, develop some initial ideas and reasons for a company name, logo (symbol), and slogan (catchy phrase). The goal is to clearly identify the character of your firm and the types of communication services you can provide to businesses to help them improve their employee communication and relations, their community relations, and their public relations. Your group's name, logo, and slogan should all be integrated and work together to create a clear, coherent impression of your firm, its identity, and its purpose.

Although this discussion may be too short to show a complete group development, you should be able to see (1) some evidence of the group phases at work in an initial hesitancy of group members to suggest ideas or to take on specific roles in the discussion; (2) more open disagreements and frank discussions of the appropriateness of potential names, logos, and slogans; (3) the development of some implicit or explicit criteria to judge and decide on appropriate items; and (4) a coalescing around some ideas and working together to modify those items. If these didn't happen in this order, did they happen in a different order or did different phases emerge? How would you best describe the group process?

The company name, logo, and slogan evaluation form can be used by the group, the entire class, or the instructor to evaluate and provide feedback on the products of this exercise (see Table 4.2). Often, the small working teams presenting their work to the entire group or class and receiving appropriate feedback (specific, positive, and with suggestions for improvements) on their ideas can enhance the overall team experience and productivity.

TABLE 4.2   Company Name, Logo, and Slogan Evaluation Form

Company Name						
Expressive and informative	5	4	3	2	1	Dull, uninformative
Logo						
Expressive and informative	5	4	3	2	1	Dull, not expressive
Slogan						
Expressive and informative	5	4	3	2	1	Dull, uninspired
Overall Integration of All Three						
Expressive and informative	5	4	3	2	1	Loose, not adequately integrated

The BEST part of the presentation?

Suggestions for improvements:

REFERENCES

Arrow, H., & McGrath, J. E. (1993). Membership matters. *Small Group Research, 24*(3), 334–361.

Cartwright, D. (1968). The nature of group cohesiveness. In D. Cartwright & A. Zander (Eds.), *Group dynamics: Research and theory* (3rd ed. pp. 91–109). New York: Harper & Row.

Cohen, A. R., & Fink, S. L. (2001). *Effective behavior in organizations: Cases, concepts, and student experiences.* Boston: McGraw-Hill Irwin.

Evans, C. R., & Dion, K. L. (1991). Group cohesion and performance: A meta-analysis. *Small Group Research, 22*(2), 175–186.

Fisher, B. A. (1970). Decision emergence: Phases in group decision-making. *Speech Monographs, 37,* 53–66.

Hirokawa, R., & Rost, K. (1992). Effective group decision making in organizations. *Management Communication Quarterly, 5,* 267–288.

Keyton, J. (1993). Group termination: Completing the study of group development. *Small Group Research, 24*(1), 84–100.

Lieberman, D. A. (1991). Ethnocognitivism and problem-solving. In L. A. Samovar & R. E. Porter (Eds.), *Intercultural communication: A reader* (pp. 229–234). Belmont, CA: Wadsworth.

Montebello, A. R. (1994). *Work teams that work.* Minneapolis: Best Sellers.

Poole, M. S., & Roth, J. (1989). Decision development in small groups V: Test of a contingency model. *Human Communication Research, 15,* 549–589.

Quick, T. L. (1985). *The manager's motivation desk book.* New York: Wiley.

Roberts, P. (1999, April). Total teamwork: The Mayo clinic. *Fast Company,* pp. 149–162.

Sweeney, P. D., & McFarlin, D. B. (2002). *Organizational behavior: Solutions for management.* Boston: McGraw-Hill Irwin.

Tuckman, B. W. (1965). Developmental sequences in small groups. *Psychological Bulletin, 63,* 384–399.

Tuckman, B. W. (1977). Stages in small group development revisited. *Group and Organizational Studies, 2,* 419–427.

Verdi, A. F., & Wheelan, S. A. (1992). Developmental patterns in same-sex and mixed-sex groups. *Small Group Research, 23*(3), 356–378.

Wellings, R. S., Byham, W. C., & Wilson, J. M. (1991). *Empowered teams: Creating self-directed work groups that improve quality, productivity, and participation.* San Francisco: Jossey-Bass.

Wheelan, S. A., & McKeage, R. L. (1993). Developmental patterns in small and large groups. *Small Group Research, 24*(1), 60–83.

Widmeyer, W. N., & Williams, J. M. (1991). Predicting cohesion in a coacting sport. *Small Group Research, 22*(4), 548–570.

5

Diversity in Groups: The Strength of Different Perspectives

CHAPTER OBJECTIVES

- Define diversity and its role in small groups.
- Understand the impact of stereotypes.
- Discuss the concept of communication contexts.
- Explain the role of language use on diversity.
- Elucidate the impact of nonverbal communication on diversity.
- Outline the impact of diversity on group commitment and consensus.
- Present the strength obtained through diversity.
- Suggest ways to make diverse groups work.

KEY TERMS

Assumptions
Commitment and consensus
Communication contexts
Conflict management
Diversity
Hierarchies of power

High-context environment
Insider/outsider
  allegiances
Language use
Low-context environment
Myths

Nonverbal communication
  and diversity
Power
Pressures for conformity
Stereotyping
Synergistic impact of diversity

No one can play a game alone. One cannot be human by oneself. There is no selfhood where there is no community. We do not relate to others as the persons we are; we are in relating to others. (*Finite and Infinite Games,* Carse, 1986, p. 45)

We can regard strangers with fear and treat those who are different with hostility, or we can treat strangers as potential friends. Those who are different may prove to be interesting and to have something valuable to contribute to our group discussion and to our experience of community (Barnlund, 1989).

Defining Diversity and Its Place in Small Groups

Diversity describes the reality of a national and world community made up of people from cultures with languages and social customs very different from our own. In addition, people in the United States may speak the same language (although even that is not always true) and share the same overall cultural value system, while having a relationship to that value system that is quite unlike what we might expect. Diversity is a fact of life in the United States today and has an impact upon small group communication. If a small group consists of members from diverse backgrounds, that diversity influences the group discussion. If the group itself is not diverse in its membership, the diversity of the larger community of which it is a part means that it may have difficulty representing and adequately responding to the multiple needs of that community. Either way, increased diversity must be considered and can have a positive effect on the decisions that are made in small groups.

When we try to define the term *diversity,* we come up against our discomfort with acknowledging differences that we may have branded as inferior (Witherspoon & Wohlert, 1996). However, in order to capitalize on the contributions of all members of our social, political, organizational, and group environments, we must first come to understand diversity as precisely what the term means—difference.

TABLE 5.1   Diversity and Differences—Some Categories

Gender	Race	Age	Religion
Ethnic Heritage		Geographic Location	
Social and Economic Class		Access to Education	Physical Ability
Sexual Orientation		Different Communication Contexts	
Family Status	Physical Attractiveness		First Language

This concept of difference implies not a hierarchy of value, but, rather, a conception of different perspectives on given issues based on different life experiences as outlined in Table 5.1.

As a concept, diversity often refers to the "other"—people who look, speak, or behave differently from what we expect and accept in those with whom we are familiar (Madrid, 1991). In an organizational context, diversity often refers to people who are other than white males of Western European descent—which implies different socialization experiences, different access to the dominant economic structure, and possibly a first language other than English. Beyond gender, race, and ethnic heritage, diversity also relates to differences in social and economic class, access to education, physical attractiveness and ability, and sexual orientation. Thus, diversity means that we may not share a common set of experiences or assumptions in certain important ways with those with whom we work and communicate. Communication in terms of shared meaning, therefore, cannot be taken for granted but must be actively pursued (Beamer & Varner, 2001).

Diversity does not necessarily make life easier for us. It is often simpler when we share cultural values, common experiences, and basic assumptions with those with whom we interact. A common culture provides us with a measure of predictability in our interactions with the people around us, defining the ground rules for our behavior and communication (Neher, 1997; Barnlund, 1989). When we put people with very different life experiences and sets of assumptions together in a group or team and ask them to work together toward a common goal, difficulties often arise. In response to these difficulties, organizations have had to institute diversity training programs for their employees. A college in Massachusetts has even had to institute civility rules for its faculty to ensure that unpopular points of view are allowed to be voiced. Although deeper cultural values and beliefs may not change, changes in behaviors can effectively be made, indeed must be made, in order for us to live and work together and to maintain a civil society (Neher, 1997).

Assumptions and Stereotyping

In order to understand how we have come to have such different life experiences, we need to understand a little about the internal matrix—the pattern—that culture creates in our lives. As human beings, our relationships within social groups begin at birth. We depend on each other for our physical and psychological well-being, as well as for our survival throughout our lives. We learn our automatic and perceptual responses to our surroundings from those who nurture and care for us. We learn how to behave and what cues to look for in any number of complex interactions that will lead to our survival, as well as to our acceptance and continued nurture. Thus, our values and systems of defining and understanding the external world are inculcated in us from the very beginning of our lives, when we begin to develop our basic assumptions, stereotypes, and prejudices.

The late Maine Senator Edmund Muskie was fond of telling a joke about a Maine farmer who met a Texas rancher. The Maine farmer was bragging about how large a potato farm he owned when the Texan responded, "You only have 150 acres! Why, in Texas I could get into my truck and drive a day and a half and still not reach the end of my land." To this the Maine farmer responded dryly, "Yes, I once had a truck like that myself." Aside from the humor, this joke illustrates how our basic assumptions about, and perspectives on, even physical realities such as size and distance are culturally defined.

Each cultural group learns and perpetuates the truths and myths that have helped prior generations of that group survive and adapt to their surroundings. Part of that cultural adaptation includes stereotyping. Stereotyping as a form of categorization is part of the human condition. Because of the myriad of stimuli constantly coming into our awareness, we need to learn to categorize those stimuli that indicate danger to our survival and then develop appropriate responses to them. Stereotypes help us make immediate and potentially critical decisions, saving us from having to sort through each individual circumstance and from overloading our mental circuits (Neher, 1997).

In the United States, many different cultural traditions coexist. Within the changing context of our country and communities, even stereotypes that may have been relevant to prior generations (and many were not relevant then) no longer serve the purposes of our larger social matrix (Calloway-Thomas, Cooper, & Blake, 1999; Zemke, Raines, & Filipczak, 2000). Because stereotypes are slower to change than the context in which they are applied, they frequently result in harmful, if sometimes unintended, consequences.

When we know few, if any, people from a different, identifiable group, each individual member of that group with whom we come into contact becomes a "token," representing all the members of the group (Powell, 1988). To the extent that this person confirms our stereotype, the stereotype, rather than the individual, is likely to become the focus of our response. If the person behaves in a way noticeably different from our stereotype, we may attribute that to the person's being an exception, rather than to the stereotype's being inaccurate or inappropriate for gauging our responses to members of that group. Research has shown that when we get to know members of groups other than our own, we tend to see them as individuals, rather than as members of the groups to which they are assigned by our stereotyping (Powell, 1988).

Thus, stereotypes can be damaging to all of us. They tend to perpetuate myths about groups of people and to disallow for the valuable differences and positive contributions we all receive from each unique individual. None of us perfectly fits a stereotype in its unidimensionality. However, we may each find ourselves at times bound up in living within the confines of the stereotypes imposed upon the groups of which we are members, interfering with our personal development as whole human beings. Learning to relate to each other in more appropriate ways is critical not only to working in diverse groups, but to our growth as individuals, as well.

Stereotyping can deny us the benefits of a multifaceted perspective. For example, when U.S. workers were asked who is most likely to be treated unfairly at work, 21% responded African Americans, 18% responded Arab Americans, 13% responded Hispanics, 12% responded Muslims, and 8% responded women (Haralson & Lewis, 2002). Part of the impetus for some of this mistreatment stems from a backlash after September 11, 2001 against Arab, Middle Eastern, South Asian, and other groups who are seen as different from others (Armour, 2002). Regardless of the reasons, we can conclude that diversity is a complex, multitiered phenomenon and requires active thought and communication.

Communication Contexts

Different subcultures within the United States develop different "rules" of communication. Communication is more than language use and nonverbal behavior. Communication takes place within a context. Because our ways of thinking and our orientations to our environments are enculturated, we each learn diverse, culturally based sets of perceptual screens for viewing and compartmentalizing experience, as well as for communicating that experience (Lieberman, 1991; Samovar & Porter, 1991).

In addition, as individuals, we operate quite separately from one another. We think, feel, and respond within the confines of our own skin and minds. We can never really know what another person is thinking or would like to communicate (Neher, 1997). In order to cross the barrier between our individual selves, therefore, we each encode and send our messages according to the rules of communication we have learned and incorporated from our cultural environment. In turn, we each decode and interpret each others' messages according to these same learned and adapted rules of communication. In the process of encoding and decoding the messages between one another, a great deal of interpretation and hence misunderstanding can, and frequently does, occur (Cason, 1997). This happens even between people who share cultural norms and assumptions. When people have different sets of cultural assumptions, the misunderstandings are likely to be greater.

The more that can be taken for granted in the communicative interaction, the "higher" the communication context is said to be. Communication in a high-context environment means that less of the meaning needs to be explicitly stated. Much is simply understood by virtue of the situation itself (Victor, 1992). On the other hand, a group from diverse backgrounds, cultures, and understandings must be assumed to be low in common context, and therefore, meanings need to be explicitly communicated.

A clash of communication cultures happened in the skies over New Jersey in 1997, when a passenger airplane preparing to land at an airport was inadvertently flying in what had just been designated as an off-limits military training airspace. Apparently unknown to the civilian pilot, two military jets approached the civilian aircraft in a reconnaissance maneuver to ascertain the identity of the aircraft. The civilian plane, with an onboard computer programmed to avoid mid-air collisions, automatically took sudden evasive action, with some injury to passengers. Each air traffic system—civilian and military—was operating on its own set of assumptions and responded to the situation based on those assumptions. Neither was aware of or heeded the other's intentions. If this can happen between different flying subcultures operating within carefully constructed air traffic control guidelines and rules—a relatively high-context environment—it can happen between individuals from diverse subcultures attempting communication in a small group. For this reason, we need to establish explicit, mutually agreed upon sets of communicative codes, rules, and patterns for our group interactions (Neher, 1997).

Language Use

One of the most obvious communication codes is that of language. Language is the principal way we cross the barrier between our own interior world and that of others (Neuliep, 2000). Our culture provides us with certain assumptions about the appropriate use of language. Different cultures often make quite different assumptions about not only particular words and grammar (the language per se), but the ideas and purposes for which those words can and should be used.

For example, in the Japanese culture, words are assumed to be used for social purposes to ensure harmony between group members, rather than for argument or settling differences in points of view (Beamer & Varner, 2001). Other social systems based on direct experience or pictographic representation of oral speech may have less language for abstract problem solving than those social systems based on more indirect relationships with their environments (Becker, 1991; Hoijer, 1991; Shuter, 1991). In many African cultures, the *word* is preeminent. Imaginative and vivid language is important, as is a call-and-response mode of communicating, indicating a link between the speaker and the listener. Interruption of the speaker, therefore, is expected and appreciated, and those who speak well in this type of exchange are likely to become leaders (Weber, 1991).

Moreover, beyond overt differences in language, most cultures treat men and women differently and teach them different ways to use language and to communicate nonverbally (Stewart, Cooper, Stewart, & Friedley, 2003). Even within a common language, particular inflections, vocabularies, and grammatical usage become enmeshed with the associative meanings we assign based on their presumed use by a particular identifiable group. Aside from regional identification, this attribution frequently occurs along a hierarchical continuum, reflecting the values of the social context in which we are operating. In this way, language use can convey cultural differences that may lead others to judge a person based on assumptions about racial, ethnic, educational, or class background (Victor, 1992). Language use can also act as a code that promotes insider–outsider allegiances within and between groups of people. In order to really hear each other, therefore, we need to be willing to forgo listening for educational, racial, or class privileging codes of language use and to listen consciously for the content and the intent of the message being communicated.

Nonverbal Communication

Nonverbal communication complements the use of language and is made up of deeply ingrained response patterns. It is often subtle and multidimensional (Remland, 2000) and may take the form of body or facial gestures, tone of voice, turn taking, use of time, or habits of dress or hairstyle. It is important to understand that different cultures attach different standards of appropriateness to nonverbal expressions, particularly those that are more easily controlled (Gardenswartz & Rowe, 1993). Although facial expressions, for example, may express the same emotions across cultures, the appropriateness of expressing those emotions may vary depending on culture and the context of the communication event (Victor, 1992). Even something as commonplace as a smile has different meanings in different cultures and contexts (Barna, 1991).

In addition, different subcultures in the United States communicate their understanding of what is being said differently. Some research indicates that African Americans may give more subtle conversational feedback in certain contexts than their white American counterparts, causing some white American speakers to assume their African American listeners have not understood what was said (Victor, 1992). Verbal and nonverbal communication is discussed at length in another chapter, but it is important to understand that we each communicate and interpret others' communication differently.

Interestingly, however, research undertaken to look for universally agreed upon traits for effective group leaders found that particular personality traits, such as "a sense of humor, flexibility, patience, resourcefulness, and consideration for others" (Neher, 1997, p. 218), were commonly held to be important across most cultures. Therefore, it would appear that beneath the surface of quite different communication styles runs an undercurrent of a common human orientation toward social interaction.

Diversity in Small Groups and Teams

Group Commitment and Consensus

Within our small groups, we depend on each other for the success and productivity of those endeavors we share. To the extent that we each hold a stake in the outcomes of the decisions we make in the groups in which we participate, we benefit from everyone's involvement. People are more committed and work harder in a group if they feel their input and contributions are valued (Neher, 1997). If some members feel excluded or disenfranchised from those groups, we not only lose the benefit of their unique contributions and their support (Schreiber, 1996), but we may even invite their sabotage of our efforts.

Our diverse backgrounds and relationships lead to different experiences and expectations within groups and organizations, as well as within the culture at large. People of different genders, racial characteristics, and sexual orientation experience life, the workplace, and groups differently and are sensitive to different issues and concerns (Schreiber, 1996; Gemmill & Schaible, 1991). Their varied personal experiences produce multiple and diverse opinions that can enhance the decision-making process and can lead to higher-quality decisions (Jackson, May, & Whitney, 1995). In organizations, homogenous teams gel more quickly than do diverse teams, which makes sense since the members share a common background. However, given time, diverse teams outperform homogenous teams in decision making and in gaining the members' commitment to the team's goals (Hickman & Creighton-Zollar, 1998).

Being insensitive to these diverse perspectives can lead to bad feelings. Indeed, the result of such insensitivity has led to an increasing number of charges of sexism and racism, as well as complaints of sexual harassment and "gay bashing" since 1990 (Neher, 1997). What some of us may take as a joke or a humorous remark in a small group or team can make others feel uncomfortable, unwelcome, discounted, or insulted—even if that was not our intent.

In addition, when we solicit and pay attention only to those contributions we expect from a participant based on her or his membership in a recognizable stereotyped group, we miss out on the true value of that person's perspectives. For example, if we expect a woman to act only as the group nurturer or "social specialist" within the group, rather than as a contributor to the task-oriented goal at hand, we overlook her valuable experience and expertise (Powell, 1988). If we look to a man only for solutions to the task problems, and do not engage him in relationship issues and assumptions, we are not getting the maximum from his potential contribution. Likewise, if we dismiss the contributions of someone who has difficulty articulating a train of thought, who is quiet and slow to contribute, who seems to us to ramble on incessantly without ever making a point, or who we assume is a member of the group only for political reasons, we have diminished the potential contributions of that person to the group. Alternately, if we assume that certain people have power, authority, knowledge, or the right answers, we may feel intimidated and find it difficult to challenge their points of view. This internal censuring and shutting ourselves down also reduces the quality of the group discussion and potential for creative decisions. Group potential is maximized when all participants feel comfortable in making contributions during every step of the process. Furthermore, we cannot arrive at a true group consensus in our decisions if we have not heard equally from all of the perspectives and considered all points of view.

People are created equal. Cars are not.

Mercedes-Benz U.S. International. MBUSI, the first U.S. enterprise by Daimler-Benz, AG (predecessor to DaimlerChrysler), makes the popular M-Class Sport Utility Vehicle. Everyone is a team member and MBUSI has a firmly stated policy of valuing diversity. They are committed to promoting and supporting an inclusive environment free from discrimination against any person on the grounds of race, color, religion, national origin, disability, sex, marital status, sexual orientation, or citizenship. Their success as a diversity centered, team organization can be seen in their production of 80,000 M-Class vehicles a year, a current workforce of over 2,000 team members, and a doubling in size by 2005.

Strength in Diversity

We have noted that the diversity of a small group is part of what makes it effective for solving difficult or complex problems. The strength of diversity is in the creative problem solving that comes from including different perspectives—perspectives not formed by the same background and context. A homogeneous group with a shared set of assumptions is less likely to come up with an innovative solution to a difficult problem. A diverse group has the advantage of bringing a variety of points of view.

Organizations, for example, have found that diversity initiatives significantly improve their bottom line. A survey by the Society for Human Resource Management and *Fortune* magazine found that "91% of respondents say their diversity initiative helps their organization keep a competitive edge" (Survey says, 2001, p. 8). General Electric Power Systems reported a 13% gain in productivity from cross-functional and multicultural teams versus homogeneous teams (Robinson & Dechant, 1997).

Groups are dynamic interactive systems, depending upon the experience and abilities of their participants. The synergistic effect of group process is achieved through a combination of the contributions and influences of the members. The more diverse the members of the group, the more potential for varieties of interaction and, therefore, the more potential for arriving at new and creative solutions.

In order for small, diverse groups to achieve these optimal results, however, they need to begin with open-minded participants and the concept of equifinality—that is, that there are many different ways to solve a problem or achieve the overall goals. When we start with an assumption that there is more than one right way to solve a problem and more than one right answer, we open ourselves to hearing and understanding important differences in perspective among group members, rather than silencing those differences and members, intentionally or unintentionally. If everyone agreed on the best course of action, there would be no purpose in meeting. Likewise, if we already had the best answer to the problem, why convene the group? Diverse groups provide the opportunity to explore different perspectives on a problem and make possible innovative solutions that result from combining those perspectives. When group members bring different viewpoints and backgrounds to the decision-making process, "they achieve a competitive advantage against organizations that are either culturally homogenous or fail to successfully utilize their diversity" (Gardenswartz & Rowe, 1998, p. 52).

To the extent that our groups and the organizations within which they exist are themselves part of the larger environment of social and economic realities, optimum solutions are relative to that total environment. Appropriate answers "emerge" from the context of the larger environment in which the problem is located, from an open exchange of ideas among the group members, and from the interaction between the group and its larger environment. For that reason, obtaining the contributions and commitment of as many diverse and representative members as practical offers the best hope for an optimal solution to a problem at any particular time and place.

Making Diverse Groups Work

Research has shown that the more individual group members participate and understand each other, the more creative solutions they are likely to develop (Kirchmeyer, 1993). However, in order for the group process to work the way it is intended and for each member to feel involved and appreciated, ground rules need to be established and maintained. Different groups come up with different ways of approaching this issue, and, obviously, the more diverse the group in terms of attitudes and communication assumptions, the more difficult and time-consuming this transactional aspect of group process becomes. However, the more important the task, the more important it is that all members be heard and understood, and therefore, the more important it may be to spend the time needed to focus on the communication process itself (Witherspoon & Wohlert, 1996).

Conflict Management

Among the most important communication rules and expectations to be established in small groups are those surrounding conflict. Within the U.S. cultural model, conflict is an inevitable part of group creativity and communication. Differences between members and open confrontation of those differences are frequently seen as positive indicators of the creative process in action (Neher, 1997). On the other hand, research has shown that Asian cultures make different assumptions about the appropriateness of confrontation than the U.S. culture does. Whereas in the United States and many Western cultures, truth resides in logic and debate, in Asian cultures, it is to be found in the totality of the person, and maintaining harmony is the goal of communication (Becker, 1991). Within the United States, Native American children raised in a tradition that emphasizes harmony with nature and the importance of the group over the individual learn better in a noncompetitive and cooperative environment. Children from a Mexican background are taught to believe in cooperation and feel that sharing answers or homework is a sign of solidarity and generosity (Calloway-Thomas, Cooper, & Blake, 1999). For many North American students, individual success is valued and sharing is seen as cheating. These diverse backgrounds, so critical to the successful analysis and resolution of issues, can create barriers if they are not recognized and accepted.

Regardless of the cultural orientation to conflict, however, working with it is almost never easy. Whether or not conflict has a positive effect depends in large measure on how it is handled. If it leads to simmering animosities and an individual's withdrawal from participation in the group process, it may lead to negative impacts on the group and on the task at hand. When conflict is taken as a necessary and inevitable part of the creative process apart from personalities, however, it can be constructive (Neher, 1997) and lead to more balanced involvement by minority as well as nonminority members (Kirchmeyer, 1993). Conflict management is dealt with at length in another chapter, but it is important to consider it explicitly within the context of managing the communication process in groups of diverse people.

Hierarchies of Power

Power is another of the sometimes subtle but pervasive issues with which we must deal within the context of diversity. Each of us makes assumptions regarding where and with whom power lies in any context. There are hierarchies of power throughout our socialization processes that we have come to take for granted, sometimes without being aware of the way in which we situate ourselves along the continuum. Clearly, the overriding assumption of social, economic, and political power in this country has long resided with upper-class and upper-middle-class white European males of wealth and privilege. Other members of society have implicitly been located along multiple hierarchies of power in relation to this group. It is important to note, however, that embedded within this larger social context are subcultural hierarchies with different assumptions of what constitutes power. As Nathan McCall (1994) notes in his book, *Makes Me Wanna Holler*, the apex of power in the inner city neighborhood in which he came of age rests with those young men who most flout the rules of the larger white society.

In the workplace, however, and in many of the public groups in which most college graduates participate, the power paradigm of the predominantly white social and economic system continues to prevail. Within the United States, organizational behavior and expectation has been defined within the context of that privileged upper-middle-class, middle-aged, able-bodied, white male experience (Fine, 1993; Gentile, 1996). Within that paradigm, the experiences and voices of women, people of color, the elderly, those with other than attractive able bodies, the poor, and the undereducated have often been subordinated to that privilege. This being the case, it is not surprising that research indicates that these "diverse" people have very different employment experiences, particularly in the areas of "hiring and promotion, job satisfaction, sexual harassment, and affirmative action" (Fine, 1993, p. 149). As we enter the twenty-first century, this often remains the case in spite of legal attempts to level the playing field by means of affirmative action (Mehta, 2000). The social norms that underlie the economic realities of our culture have proved highly resistant to long-term change (Powell, 1988).

Moving beyond the mistrust of people in positions of power in a group is hard work for those accustomed to being marginalized. It is incumbent, therefore, on those who have been implicitly empowered by the culture to do all they can to hear what people with different experiences have to say and to offer. A necessary first step may be for the empowered people to place themselves consciously at the margins of the group process, permitting members they may consider to have less expertise to take the reins of power in the group and to be heard. Difficult as that may be, it can allow us all an opportunity to listen and gain valuable insights into our colleagues' frames of reference, thereby expanding our own understanding of the issues we share as a group (Fine, 1993).

Power is a shared responsibility. We each participate in its use and abuse. Although theoretically we cannot be overpowered unless we acquiesce at some level, it is certainly the case that the means to economic and social security can be effectively blocked by those who wield more power. It is, therefore, the responsibility of each of us as members of groups, and society in general, to play our part in assuring that all voices, including our own, are heard and fully considered (Wyatt, 1993).

Pressures for Conformity

In spite of our best intentions, there is frequently a pull toward conformity in groups in order to get the job done and to move on. Group process is hard work, and it is particularly difficult when members come from widely different sets of assumptions, not only about the task but about the process itself. Even between individuals who share the same cultural norms and expectations, different experiences may cause one or another to approach a given task from a different perspective than that of the apparent majority of group members. There is frequently discomfort or outright hostility toward those members who consistently raise seemingly irrelevant issues or who refuse to go along with what appears to be a majority opinion. On the other hand, it is often "the deviant" who brings up issues that may otherwise go unnoticed or unacknowledged, thereby moving the group toward creative thinking and problem solving.

Although there is much agreement about the need for diverse perspectives in the development of creative solutions, the actual application of this notion in groups of diverse people is frequently fraught with difficulty. The social stigmas we attach subconsciously to those we deem less experienced or less able in some perceivable way interfere with our seriously taking account of their contributions and may interfere with their comfort in offering their points of view (Schreiber, 1996). Conflicting opinions and diverse perspectives are more easily expressed and entertained in groups of social "equals" than they are in groups of people from diverse ethnic or class backgrounds. Moving beyond our stereotypes, therefore, remains the challenge in making real diversity work in our small groups and organizations. Equality does not imply that people are the same; it recognizes their differences and values them equally (Weber, 1991). In fact, the value of differences is that they represent different experiences and different points of view, and bring them to bear on the decision or problem at hand. Therefore, setting explicit guidelines for overcoming pressures for conformity is essential to effective work in diverse groups and teams.

Summary

Changes in the U.S. workforce are moving everyone into an examination of diversity and group norms (Harris, 1997; Hudson Institute, 2000). Changes in workforce demographics include: increases in the average age of employees, a smaller pool of young workers, more ethnic and racial minority members entering the workforce, increasing numbers of women, and more immigrants ("The New America," 2000). By the year 2000, Caucasians of Western European ancestry will be outnumbered by Americans from Asian, African, Hispanic, Middle Eastern, and Eastern European ancestry (Henry, 1990). Legal and moral issues have been added to the basic issue of employee availability, including the importance of organizations accommodating varying types of ablebodiedness and diverse family patterns (Harris, 2002).

Many companies, as well as universities and other nonprofit groups, are implementing diversity initiatives to make members aware of the importance of recognizing, accepting, and effectively utilizing differences occurring as a result of ethnicity, cultural heritage, gender, age, physical challenge, and other circumstances (Wynter, 1994). Ethnic and cultural diversity is an issue that must be addressed as groups and organizations enter the new millennium (Loden & Rosener, 1991). With the turn of the century, most new entrants into the workforce will be women and people from cultural minorities. This is a dramatically different composition of new recruits than has been faced by organizations in the past (Gardenswartz & Rowe, 1993).

Overcoming our complex and deeply ingrained biases and prejudices against people different from ourselves, however, can prove a difficult stumbling block in the path of our ability to make the best use of the diverse perspectives offered in many of our small group and organizational settings. Our first instinct is to assume that what we know and expect is right (Barna, 1991). Because we all experience the need to reduce the uncertainty of interaction with strangers, we form ideas of what to expect from them based on certain categories or stereotypes that our socialization process has deemed important. Based on this categorical information, we then "know" how to behave with those strangers. Although this is "natural," the categories are often inadequate. We need to expand our points of view to take into account what is natural for those with whom we interact, as well as for ourselves, and see each other as unique individuals with diverse experiences and abilities.

Research has shown that incorporating diverse perspectives helps groups make better and more creative decisions most of the time. Difficult as it may be, therefore, when interactions within a small group are consciously monitored and directed toward the inclusion of all members, the resultant synergistic effect of the group process is superior to any that could be achieved by a homogeneous group of people who share the same biases and perspectives. Therefore, as we participate in groups with people different from ourselves, we need to examine and take into account our own perceptual biases and filters and allow others to be heard from their own points of view.

Taking different points of view and different ground rules for communication is time-consuming and often difficult, but is worth the effort, if the result is a superior decision or an improved working or living environment. As Madrid (1991, p. 118) says, "what keeps our society together is tolerance for cultural, religious, social, political, and even linguistic difference; what makes us a unique, dynamic and extraordinary nation are the power and creativity of our diversity." Beyond tolerance, it is the willingness to seek out, listen to, and appreciate difference that will be our greatest asset as we participate in diverse small groups.

DISCUSSION QUESTIONS

1. Define diversity. Does your definition take into account the members of your small group class? Is it inclusive of your educational setting? Is it too broad to be immediately useful?

2. Does valuing diversity come easily? Why or why not? Can you make some suggestions to enhance your group's ability to value diversity?

3. Are you a member of a group that has been stereotyped? Does your experience reflect the concepts identified in this chapter? How? Are there differences? What are they?

4. What is a communication context? What role does communication context play in our understanding of others?

5. Language use and nonverbal communication can convey cultural differences. From your own background, provide examples of both of these.

6. How is small group effectiveness diminished by not valuing diversity or by believing in stereotypes? Provide at least three conclusions.

7. Explain the concept "white men of privilege." Do you agree with the concept? Why or why not?

8. How does the pressure for conformity work against the valuing of diversity?

EXERCISES

1. Diversity and living together; 2. Words and gender; 3. Stereotypes; 4. Try reversing the bigotry of language; 5. What have you experienced?

1. DIVERSITY AND LIVING TOGETHER

The following exercise, although addressing simple issues, makes an interesting discussion starter to address questions of diversity in values and perspectives, what influences those differences, and how we can resolve them through listening, discussion, arriving at consensus, and the development of group norms.

Each person in the group should respond to the following questions individually and in writing. Then answers can be compared and discussed in small groups of four to six participants and finally in the larger group of the whole. Can we come to a common group understanding or at least hear the different values and reasoning behind the different perspectives?

There are no right or wrong answers to the following questions, so please be honest and respond by choosing the most appropriate answer according to your personal habits, customs, desires, and most common behaviors over the last six months.

1. Frequency of Washing the Dishes
    A. Dishes must be washed immediately after every meal or snack, and never left in the sink.
    B. Dishes should be washed after every meal or placed in the dishwasher.
    C. Dishes should be washed at least once a day and not left overnight.
    D. Dishes should be washed once a week.
    E. Dishes should be washed once a month.
    F. Dishes should be washed when the sink and counter are full.
    G. Dishes should be washed when we are out of clean dishes, just like laundry.
    H. Whatever, I have no schedule. I wash dishes whenever I think of them.
2. Someone gives you an unexpected and very nice gift. How do you say "thank you"?
    A. Saying "thank you" in person at the time of receipt is appropriate and adequate.
    B. Saying "thank you" over the phone is appropriate and adequate.
    C. Saying "thank you" via electronic mail (e-mail) note is appropriate and adequate.
    D. Saying "thank you" with a formal, handwritten, follow-up note is appropriate and adequate.

3. The standard U.S. home toilet consists of a base unit in which there is a basin of flushable water. On top of this base is a ring called a toilet seat, and on top of this seat is a cover referred to as a toilet seat cover. Both the seat and the cover are generally designed to be raised to a vertical position or lowered to a horizontal position. After use, what position should the toilet seat *cover* be left in?
   A. the down, horizontal position
   B. the up, vertical position
   C. It doesn't matter; either position is fine and appropriate.
   After use what position should the toilet seat *ring* be left in?
   A. the down, horizontal position
   B. the up, vertical position
   C. It doesn't matter, either position is fine and appropriate.

After responding individually and in writing, discuss your responses in the group. What are the different perspectives expressed by group members? How diverse are these perspectives? What informs the diversity of these perspectives (functional use, habits, values such as convenience or appearance, other types of influences)? Apply the problem-solving sequence described in Table 4.1 to resolving any issues raised by these questions.

2. WORDS AND GENDER

Directions

1. Certain words tend to be perceived as female or male. Assume that the following words refer either to a male or female. Circle F if you think the word is more likely to refer to a female, M if a male. While the words could refer to either category, if you had to choose male or female, which would it be?

F	M	Wealthy	F	M	Tries
F	M	Aggressive	F	M	Marries
F	M	Vulnerable	F	M	Hires
F	M	Outspoken	F	M	Supportive
F	M	Cares	F	M	Selfish
F	M	Confident	F	M	Works
F	M	Nurturing	F	M	Independent
F	M	People-oriented	F	M	Individualist

2. In your group, compare your choices (F, M) with the other group members. Are there similarities? Differences?
3. Which characteristics does the group consider most desirable for group membership? What does it take to be a productive group member?
4. As a group, add five to ten additional words that seem to connote a gender-specific trait. Are there specific occupations that are associated with a specific gender? Is the stereotype accurate?

5. How does stereotyping impact on the group? What limitations do stereotyping place on potential contributions by male or female members?

3. STEREOTYPES

Directions

Step 1. We hear numerous statements about other groups and cultures. Upon examination, we can discover that these statements are weakly supported or unfounded. Try the following exercise. For each statement, place a check mark if you have heard the statement about other groups. Then, write in the group (if any) that comes to mind. Finally, write in an example that disproves the generalization.

	GROUP	DISPROVES
_____ 1. Are bigoted, prejudiced, and biased.	_____	_____
_____ 2. Are smart and work hard.	_____	_____
_____ 3. Are aggressive and pushy.	_____	_____
_____ 4. Are associated with organized crime.	_____	_____
_____ 5. Are lazy and unreliable.	_____	_____
_____ 6. Laugh and smile a lot.	_____	_____
_____ 7. Are very good at sports.	_____	_____
_____ 8. Are nurturing and supportive.	_____	_____
_____ 9. Are conceited.	_____	_____
_____10. Drink and party too much.	_____	_____

Step 2. As a group or class, share your responses. Are there similarities or differences? How confident can we be in any stereotypes? Why do we use stereotypes? Are there other examples on your campus of stereotypes? Try to list five more.

4. TRY REVERSING THE BIGOTRY OF LANGUAGE

The prejudice against the color black and for the color white permeates our language. A few examples:

black-hearted	White Christmas
black thoughts	Snow White
Black death (plague)	white magic

1. As a test of the strength of this phenomenon, try to think of words or phrases that use (1) the color black in a *positive* way or (2) the color white in a *negative* way. We'll get you started with "in the black" and "white as a ghost." Make two columns on a blank sheet of paper. Label the first column POSITIVE BLACK and the second column POSITIVE WHITE. Try to list 25 words or phrases in each column.

2. For small groups, combine lists, brainstorm additional examples, and try to list 50 words or phrases in each column.

3. Debriefing: Was this exercise difficult? What does it tell us about the ability of words to limit our perception. Did some of the examples provided by your instructor surprise you? Why did you not remember them?

5. WHAT HAVE YOU EXPERIENCED?

1. Many of us have traveled to different parts of the United States or abroad. Consider some of the regional or international differences you have encountered or you know about.

Concept	Examples of differences
1. Language	_____
2. Distance	_____
3. Assertiveness	_____
4. Clothing	_____
5. Touch	_____
6. Manners and/or eating habits	_____
7. Relationships with family	_____
8. Time consciousness	_____

2. In your small group, share your examples. Work to develop additional examples based on the group discussion. What are some of the differences in your group?

3. Considering your campus or your possible work environment, how does the group feel these differences will impact on a group or team's effectiveness?

4. Devise a strategy to overcome these differences and be prepared to present it to the class.

REFERENCES

Andersen, P. (1991). Explaining intercultural differences in nonverbal communication. In L. A. Samovar & R. E. Porter (Eds.), *Intercultural communication: A reader* (pp. 286–296). Belmont, CA: Wadsworth.

Armour, S. (2002, May 10). Reports of workplace bias still on rise since Sept. 11. *USA Today*, p. 1B.

Barna, L. M. (1991). Stumbling blocks in intercultural communication. In L. A. Samovar & R. E. Porter

(Eds.), *Intercultural communication: A reader* (pp. 345–353). Belmont, CA: Wadsworth.

Beamer, L., & Varner, I. (2001). *Intercultural communication in the global workplace* (2nd ed.). Boston: McGraw-Hill Irwin.

Becker, C. B. (1991). Reasons for the lack of argumentation and debate in the Far East. In L. A. Samovar & R. E. Porter (Eds.), *Intercultural communication: A reader* (pp. 234–243). Belmont, CA: Wadsworth.

Calloway-Thomas, Cooper, P. J., & Blake, C. (1999). *Intercultural communication: Roots and routes.* Boston: Allyn & Bacon.

Carse, J. P. (1986). *Finite and infinite games.* New York: Ballantine Books.

Cason, R. E. (1997). *Writing for the business world.* Upper Saddle River, NJ: Prentice Hall.

Fine, M. G. (1993). New voices in organizational communication: A feminist commentary and critique. In S. P. Bowen & N. Wyatt (Eds.), *Transforming visions: Feminist critiques in communication studies* (pp. 125–166). Cresskill, NJ: Hampton.

Gardenswartz, L., & Rowe, A. (1993). *Managing diversity: The complete desk reference.* San Diego: Pheiffer.

Gardenswartz, L., & Rowe, A. (1998, July). Why diversity matters. *HR Focus,* pp. 51–53.

Gemmill, G., & Schaible, L. Z. (1991). The psychodynamics of female/male role differentiation within small groups. *Small Group Research, 22*(2), 220–239.

Gentile, M. (1996). *Managerial excellence through diversity.* Prospect Heights: Waveland.

Haralson, D., & Lewis, A. (2002, April 10). Unfair treatment in the workplace. *USA Today,* p. 1B.

Harris, T. E. (1997). Diversity: Importance, ironics, and pathways. In C. D. Brown, C. Snedeker, & B. Sykes (Eds.), *Diversity and conflict* (pp. 17–34). Cresskill, NJ: Hampton.

Harris, T. E. (2002). *Applied organizational communication: Principles and pragmatics for future practice* (2nd ed.). Mahwah, NJ: Lawrence Erlbaum.

Henry, W. A. (1990, April 9). Beyond the melting pot. *Time,* pp. 29–35.

Hickman, G. R., & Creighton-Zollar, S. (1998). Diverse self-directed work teams: Developing strategic initiatives for 21st century organizations. *Business Source Elite, 27,* 44–47.

Hoijer, H. (1991). The Sapir-Whorf hypothesis. In L. A. Samovar & R. E. Porter (Eds.), *Intercultural communication: A reader* (pp. 244–251). Belmont, CA: Wadsworth.

Hudson Institute. (2000). *Halfway out the door.* Indianapolis, IN: Walker Information.

Jackson, S. E., May, K. E., & Whitney, K. (1995). Understanding the dynamics of diversity in decision-making teams. In R. A. Guzzo, E. Salas, & Associates (Eds.), *Team effectiveness and decision making in organizations* (pp. 204–261). San Francisco: Jossey-Bass.

Johnston, W. B., & Packer, A. E. (1987). *Workforce 2000: Work and workers for the 21st century.* Indianapolis, IN: Hudson Institute.

Kirchmeyer, C. (1993). Multicultural task groups: An account of the low contribution level of minorities. *Small Group Research, 24*(1), 127–148.

Lieberman, D. A. (1991). Ethnocognitivism and problem-solving. In L. A. Samovar & R. E. Porter (Eds.), *Intercultural communication: A reader* (pp. 229–234). Belmont, CA: Wadsworth.

Loden, M., & Rosener, J. B. (1991). *Workforce America! Managing employee diversity as a vital resource.* Burr Ridge, IL: Irwin.

Madrid, A. (1991). Diversity and its discontents. In L. A. Samovar & R. E. Porter (Eds.), *Intercultural communication: A reader* (pp. 115–119). Belmont, CA: Wadsworth.

McCall, N. (1994). *Makes me wanna holler.* New York: Vintage Books.

Mehta, S. N. (2000, July 11). What minority employees really want. *Fortune,* pp. 181–186.

Neher, W. W. (1997). *Organizational communication: Challenges of change, diversity, and continuity.* Boston: Allyn & Bacon.

Neuliep, J. W. (2000). *Intercultural communication: A contextual approach.* Boston: Houghton Mifflin.

Powell, G. N. (1988). *Women & men in management.* Newbury Park, CA: Sage.

Remland, M. S. (2000). *Nonverbal communication in everyday life.* Boston: Houghton Mifflin.

Robinson, G., & Dechant, K. (1997, August). Building a business case for diversity. *Academy of Management Executive,* pp. 21–27.

Samovar, L. A., & Porter, R. E. (Eds.). (1991). *Intercultural communication: A reader.* Belmont, CA: Wadsworth.

Schreiber, E. J. (1996). Muddles and huddles: Facilitating a multicultural workforce through team management theory. *The Journal of Business Communication, 33*(4), 459–473.

Shuter, R. (1991). The Hmong of Laos: Orality, communication, and acculturation. In L. A. Samovar & R. E. Porter (Eds.), *Intercultural communication: A reader* (pp. 270–276). Belmont, CA: Wadsworth.

Stewart, L. P., Cooper, P. J., Stewart, A. D., & Friedley, S. A. (2003). *Communication and gender* (4th ed.). Boston: Allyn & Bacon.

Survey says diversity improves bottom lines and competition. (2001, July). *HR Focus,* p. 8.

The new America. (2000, September 18), *Newsweek,* p. 48.

Victor, D. A. (1992). *International business communication.* New York: HarperCollins.

Weber, S. N. (1991). The need to be: The socio-cultural significance of black language. In L. A. Samovar & R. E. Porter (Eds.), *Intercultural communication: A reader* (pp. 277–282). Belmont, CA: Wadsworth.

Witherspoon, P. D., & Wohlert, K. L. (1996). An approach to developing communication strategies for enhancing organizational diver-

sity. *The Journal of Business Communication, 33*(4), 375–399.

Wyatt, N. (1993). Organizing and relating: Feminist critique of small group communication. In S. P. Bowen & N. Wyatt (Eds.), *Transforming visions: Feminist critiques in communication studies* (pp. 51–86). Cresskill, NJ: Hampton.

Wynter, L. E. (1994, July 20). The price of diversity varies by consultant. *The Wall Street Journal,* p. B1.

Zemke, R., Raines, C., & Filipczak, B. (2000). *Generations at work: Managing the clash of veterans, boomers, xers, and nexters in your workplace.* New York: AMACOM.

6

Verbal and Nonverbal Communication

CHAPTER OUTLINE

CHAPTER OBJECTIVES

- Discuss the functions of verbal communication.
- Explain group fantasies, metaphors, and narratives.
- Identify the structures of meaning in verbal communication.
- Outline the types and functions of group talk.
- Explain the principles of nonverbal communication.
- Illustrate the types of nonverbal communication.

KEY TERMS

Body language
Chronemics
Connotative meaning
Consciousness-raising talk
Denotative meaning
Encounter talk
Ethnocentrism
Eye contact
Facial display
Fantasy
Functions of verbal
   communication

Group fantasies
Group talk
Humor
Inferences
Judgments
Kinesics
Metaphors
Narrative
Nonverbal communication
Observations
Paralanguage
Process orientation

Problem-solving talk
Productivity
Proxemics
Role-assumption talk
Semantics
Sex-role stereotyping
Silence
Symbolic
Synchrony
Task ordering
Verbal communication

There is a joke about a man who visited a retirement home and who was being shown around by the manager. They came out onto a large porch, overlooking the lawns and gardens, upon which a number of the current residents were sitting. As they stood there, one of the residents suddenly called out "34," and the rest of the group broke into laughter. After a few minutes of silence, another resident said "27," and again they all laughed. At this point, the man turned to the manager and said, "What is going on? Why are they laughing? What is so funny?" The manager replied that these residents had been there together as a group for so long that they had learned each other's jokes and had decided to number the jokes so that whenever someone wanted to tell one, they could just call out the number and the rest of them would remember the joke and laugh. The man asked if he could try. The manager said "Sure" and the man called out "32"! The residents looked puzzled, but remained silent. When the man asked the manager why no one had laughed, the manager simply replied, "Well, some people just don't know how to tell jokes."

Small group communication is a combination of verbal and nonverbal communication, and small groups build expectations about what these verbal and nonverbal communication characteristics will be like. Jokes, like other forms of communication, are told both verbally and nonverbally within this context of group expectations. What makes jokes funny is a combination of the verbal and nonverbal components.

Nothing never happens within the context of small group communication. Nonverbal communication is always occurring, whether or not anyone is speaking. As we have said, we simply cannot not communicate, for the act of not speaking is itself communicating something to those around us. When a person finds meaning in an action or a statement, whether accurate or misinterpreted, communication has taken place. In this chapter, we discuss the various aspects of verbal and nonverbal communication, the role of denotative (dictionary) meaning and connotative (associative) meaning in verbal communication, and the symbolic meanings assigned to both verbal and nonverbal communication. We begin with verbal communication and conclude with nonverbal communication. Although we consider them separately in this chapter, they occur simultaneously and work together, complementing or contradicting each other.

Functions of Verbal Communication

In discussing the role of verbal communication in groups, we will first examine three *functions* of verbal communication—task ordering, process orientation, and narrative.

Task Ordering

Task ordering involves cognitive meaning that focuses on either/or choices and which creates an understanding about the group's purposes and processes. Specifically, language draws attention to particular items and provides the *backbone* of the group interaction.

Small groups are usually formed to achieve some goals. To achieve those goals they must order their activities into some sequence that can be attended to and followed. For example, if we are asked to serve on a task force, one of the first questions we might ask is, "What are we trying to accomplish?" We are also interested in the time constraints, the resources available, and other pertinent data. One of our goals is *productivity*—that we accomplish the purpose for which we were convened.

If our group has an agenda, keeps notes, or takes minutes, verbal communication is being used to order the task. In the end, it is *task ordering* that permits us to judge whether or not the group has been a success or a failure. However, as important as the *destination* of verbal communication is the *journey* itself. The importance of this function can been seen when we form a small group in one of our classes. The tendency of the group is to move directly to performing tasks rather than allowing the phases we discussed (Chapter 4). Because time has not been put into establishing the group's purposes or processes, the results frequently are substandard. We are dealing with the issue without determining how to order tasks.

Process Orientation

Process orientation, or *how* we say something, is frequently as important as *what* we say (task ordering). The norms, roles, and process all influence how well the group functions. For example, in a small group, interrupting another member before she or he is finished may be considered rude. Alternately, a participant who is unable to contribute to the discussion may resent the meeting and its outcome. Many excellent meeting plans have been derailed because the *how* was not adequately attended to. Process orientation allows us to gently and diplomatically address issues that can create great difficulties if left to a no-holds-barred task orientation.

Because small groups involve the use of interpersonal influence, verbal strategies that heighten that influence while achieving the desired goal serve both the individual and the group. In studying interpersonal influence strategies, Newton and Burgoon (1990) found that those who used positive, supportive verbal communication felt most satisfied with the results of their interaction.

When you design your resume in order to obtain employment, you should spend some time determining which items to include or exclude. Interestingly, the most studied aspect of resumes by researchers is the content (Plung & Montgomery, 2004). However, once you have made your choices, you still need to design the resume which involves trying to determine how the potential employer will react to how the the resume looks. This is a process question.

One of the best ways to differentiate between task and process orientations is to examine the concept of leadership. At the task level, someone is a successful leader if the goal is accomplished. At the process level, we look at how the leader accomplishes the goal, and whether she or he was successful as a facilitator, coach, persuader, and participant (Kotter, 1990). At this level, we are concerned about *how the person leads,* not if he or she always wins. In making the determination as to the success or failure of a group's verbal communication, the data we use are called narrative.

Narratives and Group Fantasies

How we talk *about* our group may determine the way we feel and act toward the group. This narrative combines both myth and reality. When a team leader tells the members that they were picked because they are the "best and the brightest," there may be some wishful thinking, along with, perhaps, some partial truth; but to five people facing a difficult task, this can also be an excellent motivational statement.

A leader may refer to the group as a "well-oiled machine." This metaphor can then take on significance as a defining concept for the group. The use of a metaphor "makes us conscious of some likeness, often a strikingly novel and surprising likeness, between two fundamentally different things or processes" (Clancy, 1989, p. 24). Implicit in the comparison is a vision of how the group operates. However, using metaphors to compress complicated concepts into more readily understandable ones needs to be done with some caution. Imagine the different interpretations we would have for our group based on the following metaphors from column A or B. For most of us, column A provides more attractive descriptions of groups.

Descriptions of Groups	
A	**B**
One big happy family	Insane asylum
Athletic team	Snake pit
First class	Zoo
Explorers	Quicksand
Warriors	Boiling cauldron
Stage	Swamp

Groups may also develop fantasies and stories that perpetuate the group image and serve either to motivate or derail the group's process toward its goal. Being considered "the best and the brightest" may be a fantasy, but it can provide a strong group incentive toward achieving excellence and living up to its perceived reputation.

Fantasy is "the creative and imaginative shared interpretation of events that fulfills a group's psychological or rhetorical need to make sense of their experience and to anticipate their future" (Bormann & Bormann, 1992, p. 110). Fantasies indicate the willingness of the group members to see events in a new or unique manner that has developed through the group's interactions. These fantasies can be either positive and enhancing or negative and destructive. When stories and fantasies are shared by the group, they help develop a group's identity. Delta Air Lines, for example, has used the slogans "The Delta family feeling" and "We love to fly and it shows." If the majority of Delta team members accept these slogans as fantasy themes, they operate on the same level and carry out the same principles—they are willing to use them as guidelines—they will pursue the same goals and carry out the same principles. Often, the creation of a story, a dramatized narrative, provides a clear illustration that increases interaction and identification among group members (Witherspoon, 1997). For example, sharing with other group members examples of your own successful and unsuccessful group experiences can offer guidelines for your current undertaking.

The narrative process also provides *sense-making and values* for group members. When we say the customer is always right, we are telling people who work for our organization that the customer is valued over other issues. If our school claims to be the best in a particular aspect of higher education because it fosters creativity, the people who attend or work for the school know that creativity is a value. On the other hand, groups seen as dysfunctional or serving no worthwhile purpose will likely live down to that expectation.

Structures of Meaning
in Verbal Communication

The functions of verbal communication could not be achieved if it were not for the meaning we associate with words. In discussing meaning in verbal communication, we will examine denotative and connotative meaning, semantic and symbolic meaning, group talk, and the use of humor.

Denotative and Connotative Meaning

Denotative meaning is what the word literally means or represents. It is the dictionary meaning of the word. When we ask someone what he or she means, we are requesting a denotative description. However, this is often easier said than done. Of the 500 most used words in the English language, there are over 14,000 dictionary definitions. To understand what is being said, therefore, we depend not only on the denotative meaning, but also on the *connotative* meaning—the context and associations we hold for the word(s) being used.

Connotative meaning depends upon the multiple subjective realities carried by group members. Words have fuller meanings than those provided by a dictionary. When we respond that an idea is a "winner," the word in that context may have little denotative meaning, but it does have a clear connotative meaning suggesting that the idea is excellent, full of potential, exciting, and promising. In verbal communication, the group, as well as the larger social context, determines the meanings we assign to words.

Frequently, we accept connotative meanings as if they represented facts rather than an interpretation of the facts. If we call someone "differently abled" instead of "handicapped" or "disabled," we may change the way we view the individual, rather than simply how we refer to them. Labeling someone a "yuppie" is more likely to lead to a negative image than saying "a young professional." Renaming group managers as team leaders, facilitators, and coaches can make a difference by redefining their roles, functions, and acceptance by the group. Would you rather be an employee or a team player? Do you want a manager to tell you what to do, or a leader to help you develop your abilities? Language use is powerful and more than "mere semantics." Our language defines the world we see, live in, and respond to. It brings certain observable facts to our attention, while muting or ignoring others. An interesting example of this is Ervin-Tripp's (1968) interviews with Japanese-American war brides living in the United States after World War II. These interviews showed that the women had substantially different outlooks on life when they spoke in Japanese than when they spoke in English. When they spoke in English, they were more self-assertive and expressed more independence, especially when talking about a woman's ability to work outside the home, than when they spoke in Japanese. Li—a speaker of Chinese who is fluent also in both English and Japanese—suggests that the language and syntax of Japanese itself shapes a female's speech to be more tentative and less assertive, while English allows more assertive expression and the more assertive conceptualizations associated with it (1996, personal communication). "Language is a guide to social reality" (Orbe & Harris, 2001, p. 52).

Semantics

The study of meaning construction in language is called *semantics*. Three principles underlie the role of semantics, and they help us understand how verbal communication functions. First, *meanings are in people, not in words*. A word means something because those who developed and who continue to use the word have agreed, and continue to agree, that it should mean that. Richard Lederer's interesting examples from his column in *The Patriot Ledger* (1996, July 27–28, p. 36) illustrate how the circumstance of meanings in people rather than in words can generate some unintentionally ambiguous and possibly humorous messages, such as those that have appeared in actual newspaper headlines.

Ambiguous Meanings

"Prince Charles backs bicycles over cars as he opens world talks."
"Iowa man's soon-to-be-amputated hand could hold key to murder."
"Beaches all washed up."
"Shop sells soup to nuts."
"One-legged escapee still on run."
"Fire officials grilled over kerosene heaters."
"Legislators tax brains to cut deficit."
"Man minus ear waives hearing."
"Bar trying to help alcoholic lawyers."

Second, *language is symbolic*—that is, it is something that *represents* something else. Language is not itself that something. For example, a school's grading scale *represents* something. If we say we have a 2.5 grade average, that does not indicate what we actually learned, earned, or achieved, but it does function as a symbol of that learning for some people in some contexts. Likewise, language is symbolic and represents, but is not the same as, experiences, observations, and feelings.

Third, language conveys meanings about *observations, inferences, and judgments*. Observations are based on *factual* occurrences, can be verified, and deal with the past or present. Inferences are *deductions* based on facts or indicators. Judgments are *opinions, beliefs, or thoughts* based on interpretations of a given set of facts or indicators.

During the O. J. Simpson trial, for example, there were *observations* made that Simpson had a temper. His wife had called 911 and started to file a complaint, claiming that he was violent and threatening her. From that information, some individuals *have inferred* that he *might* have killed her. Finally, in deciding that he was not guilty beyond a reasonable doubt, the jury offered a *judgment* based on their interpretation of the facts as presented to them. Individuals and groups must take care in identifying their level of abstraction along the scale from objectively verifiable observations, to inferential opinions, to judgmental conclusions. Note that the first level, observation, allows for true or false, correct or incorrect conclusions. The second level, inference, is less certain since we are taking information provided us and interpreting it. The third level, judgment, involves assumptions about the truth based on subjective responses to our interpretations.

Group Talk

Effective groups first define their goals and objectives using task-oriented language. However, as noted above, problem solving is rarely accomplished by task orientation alone. Because it occurs in the context of a group made up of individual members, each with different experiences, strengths, weaknesses, and styles of interaction, process must be attended to. While a group works toward solving problems, in the process of using language that addresses the perceived issues each member also plays a role in offering meanings above and beyond the task-oriented problem-solving talk. For example, we may talk about something in a manner that indicates we perceive our role differently than the simple language we are using. If I speak with authority and particular knowledge on a given subject, I may be placing myself in the role of an expert. If I respond "Really?" or "I wouldn't have thought that to be true," to your comment, my use of different tones and facial expressions may change the expressed meaning of my words and may place me in the role of an adversary. Table 6.1 shows examples of some challenging statements that tend to reduce group discussion.

Often, when a task is overwhelming, or a great deal of time is being spent going in circles, groups try to reestablish their primary motivations. It would not be unusual for an individual to move away from role talk to consciousness-raising talk, which is primarily motivational, in an effort to refocus the group or keep them on target. In addition, in any group, there is the social-emotional discussion, which allows the members to become more familiar with each other. When group members stop talking about the task and decide to discuss their own interpersonal needs and orientations, they engage in encounter talk. Group talk is, therefore, multifaceted and multifunctional. At any given time, group members may use verbal communication to convey any of the four types of messages: problem-solving talk, role-assumption talk, consciousness-raising talk, or encounter talk.

Humor

Finally, an important area of communication that is frequently overlooked is that of humor. Humor is based on our ability to take advantage of inconsistencies and incongruencies (Duncan & Feisal, 1989). Humor uses the power of verbal communication to share messages, relieve stress, support group fantasies, integrate ideas, support common values, convey messages and meaning to people, and help

TABLE 6.1   Examples of Challenging Statements

1. We tried that before.	24. I don't like the idea.
2. Our problem is different.	25. You're right, BUT . . .
3. It costs too much.	26. You're two years ahead of your time.
4. That's beyond our responsibility.	27. We're not ready for that.
5. That's not my job.	28. Has anyone else ever tried it?
6. We're all too busy to do that.	29. It isn't in the budget.
7. It's too radical a change.	30. Can't teach an old dog new tricks.
8. We don't have the time.	31. Good thought, but impractical.
9. We don't have enough help.	32. It's too much trouble to change.
10. What you are really saying is . . .	33. Let's give it more thought.
11. We've always done it this way.	34. It won't work here.
12. Our group is too small for that.	35. Put it in writing for us to consider.
13. That's not practical for us.	36. We'll be the laughingstock.
14. I don't see the connection.	37. Not that idea again.
15. Bring it up in six months.	38. Let's all sleep on it.
16. We've never done it before.	39. Where'd you dig that one up?
17. We should look into it further before we act.	40. We did all right without it.
18. It will run up our overhead.	41. It's impossible.
19. We don't have the authority.	42. It's never been tried before.
20. That's too ivory tower.	43. Lets shelve it for the time being.
21. Let's get back to reality.	44. Let's form a committee.
22. That's not our problem.	45. It can't be done.
23. Why change it? it's still working OK.	

listener acceptance (Bolman & Deal, 1991). Studies of effective groups support the importance of humor (Kiechel, 1986).

The effectiveness of groups, such as committees, however, has been the brunt of many jokes. Arthur Goldberg, an associate justice of the U.S. Supreme Court, observed: "If Columbus had an advisory committee, he probably would still be at the dock." Milton Berle, the comedian, described a committee as "a group who keep minutes and waste hours." Although this is not a call for a house comedian or a "class clown," humor is a useful tool for keeping the group cohesive and on task.

Nonverbal Communication

While verbal communication directs the task and process aspects of the group discussion, nonverbal communication forms the context in which we discuss them. Our lives are filled with highly symbolic nonverbal communication activities. For example, most college students go through the formal graduation ceremony, replete with caps and gowns, speeches, hugs, and handshakes, even when there is no requirement that they attend or participate in graduation. They could, instead, be mailed their diploma. Why do they take part? The nonverbal behavior is meaningful to them and to those individuals who supported their undergraduate careers. The public ceremony holds significance as a symbol of their achievement.

By definition, all behaviors that are not consciously verbal and that are assigned meaning by one or both of the parties in a communication interaction are nonverbal communication. It has been estimated that between 65% (Birdwhistell, 1970) and 93% (Mehrabian, 1981) of a message's meaning is nonverbal. We judge the strength and validity of messages dealing with affiliation, positive regard, power, interest, dominance, credibility, status, attitudes, and competence primarily through nonverbal communication (Andersen, 1999). In a group discussion, whether an idea is accepted, valued, and added into the mix and to what degree frequently has as much to do with the presenter and the manner of presentation as with the literal meaning of the words used to express it.

Principles of Nonverbal Communication

For purposes of our discussion of nonverbal communication, we will assume the presence of eight guiding principles in small groups and in communication generally which are summarized in Table 6.2.

The first is that *the quality of the relationships between group members is established and perpetuated through nonverbal behavior.* We provide a great deal of communication nonverbally to others that indicates how we feel about them. Sitting next to someone at a meeting usually indicates some liking or attraction. Getting up and moving when someone sits next to us provides a message that may be interpreted negatively. In addition, our nonverbal behavior gives off information that allows other group members to interpret our words, as well as our actions.

Second, *when what we do and what we say are inconsistent, nonverbal communication is more likely to be believed* (Harris, 2002). A popular saying expresses this in the words: "You can't talk your way out of something you behaved your way into." If what we do contradicts what we say, people usually believe what we do. It is not

---

TABLE 6.2   Nonverbal Communication—Principles and Impact

1. Impacts the quality of relationships
2. More likely to be believed
3. One or both parties can assign meaning
4. Behaviors are guided by context and power relationships
5. Norms and expectations of culture guide the group
6. Things we notice lead to meaning
7. Women are more sensitive to nonverbal cues
8. Concentrate on improving our own actions

enough to say a group is important to us; we must participate in the group's activities to demonstrate that importance.

Third, *nonverbal communication becomes meaningful when one or more parties assign meaning to it.* The importance of this is demonstrated when someone in our group assigns meaning to our actions, even when we did not intend to communicate that meaning. Thus, nonverbal communication can be assigned meaning if only one of the parties decides to pay attention to it.

Fourth, *our interpretations of participants' behaviors are guided by context and power relationships.* Organizational background, setting (e.g., family versus sports team), occupational and group affiliations, size of the group, the role of the individual in the group, and numerous other issues operate as intervening variables in the interpretation process. For example, two men weighing over 250 pounds each can happily slap each other on their rear ends if they are playing professional football but are not likely to engage in the same behavior in a business meeting. Doing the right thing at the right time in the right place summarizes this fourth principle. Table 6.3 shows some likely interpretations of behaviors based on the context and power relationships of the people engaging in them.

Fifth, *groups operate within the norms and expectations of the culture of which they are a part.* The way we respond to time, age, gender, race, class, ethnicity, or any number of other variables varies with the sociocultural context. The dominant culture of the United States dictates many of the norms and mores of smaller groups within that culture. For example, while a person in the United States, whose social and economic order is clock-time based, may notice someone's promptness or tardiness, a Latin American may be much less likely to see this as an important issue.

Sixth, *the things we notice, or our perceptions of nonverbal cues, lead to meaning.* Under this principle, relaxed posture, forward leans, decreased distance, increased touching, and enhanced attention all provide positive messages in U.S. cultures (Hackman & Johnson, 1991).

TABLE 6.3   Relational Statements

People we like:	People we do not like:
Are assertive	Are pushy
Are good on detail	Are picky
Work well under pressure	Can't stand the heat
Are confident	Are conceited
Are task oriented	Are impossible to work with, real hard-nosed
Are enthusiastic	Are emotional
Follow through	Don't know when to quit
Stand firm	Are bullheaded
Have sound judgment	Have strong prejudices
Are open, speak their minds	Are mouthy
Are quiet, shy	Are secretive

Seventh, women and men may differ in their sensitivity to nonverbal cues and in their accuracy in decoding them. Some researchers have suggested that *women, in general, are often more sensitive to nonverbal cues and more accurate in sending nonverbal messages* (Anderson, 1999).

In line with this seventh principle, the eighth suggests that, although we can learn to be better at interpreting other people's nonverbal cues, *we will have greater success in using the principles of nonverbal communication if we concentrate on improving our own actions* (Hackman & Johnson, 1991).

While these eight principles help us frame our understanding of the role of nonverbal communication, it is important to note that nonverbal communication can be ambiguous and misleading. Because it is framed within personal and social contexts, it is always important to try to understand the larger personal context of the communicator and to look for patterns of nonverbal communication, as well as for verbal corroboration.

Types of Nonverbal Communication

Others interpret our involvement through our nonverbal communication, which is closely linked to our involvement in a conversation or group. Coker and Burgoon (1987, p. 463) found that "the behaviors that most strongly discriminated high from low involvement were general kinesic/proxemic attentiveness, forward lean, relaxed laughter, coordinated speech, fewer silences and latencies, and fewer object manipulations. Behaviors most predictive of magnitude of involvement change were facial animation, vocal warmth/interest, deeper pitch, less random movement, and more vocal attentiveness." In the present discussion, we will focus on five issues in particular: facial display, paralanguage, body language, proxemics, and chronemics.

Facial Display.   We judge a person's willingness to interact by how he or she uses facial expression (Remland, 2000). Restricting our facial communication suggests a lack of involvement and interest. Smiling, for example, is considered a positive communication behavior that indicates to others that we are honest, intelligent, and worth joining in some venture (Grazian, 1987).

Eye contact is also critical to and indicative of effective small group and interpersonal communication but is full of complex meanings and context-based assumptions. While other cultures make different assumptions, in the United States, we generally interpret direct eye contact as an indication of credibility, honesty, and power (Andersen, 1999). In addition, we tend to look at people with greater power more often than at people we consider to have less power. On the other hand, showing deference to power is accomplished through diminished eye contact by subordinates. A speaker is perceived as more confident if she or he maintains eye contact (Andersen, 1999).

In small group communication, eye contact can be used to increase or decrease the amount of interaction in the group. Those group members who are looked at most frequently tend to feel more empowered and involved. They may be more likely to contribute to the group than those who are not looked at. On the other hand, if we ourselves refuse to look at the other group members, we will be left out of the conversation.

When we have to convey bad news, we tend to decrease our eye contact. On the other hand, in a leaderless performance group, such as a band or a dance company, eye contact may be the principal means of communication between members to assure that everyone works together (Rose, 1994). To be an effective group member, therefore, we need to be aware of and use effective eye contact and other facial expressions. This means we need to be aware of different cultural, personal, and role-related expectations and interpretations surrounding eye contact.

Paralanguage.   Paralanguage is the meaning that is perceived along with the actual words used to deliver a message. It is *how* we say something. This is a broad category that includes dialects, accents, pitch, rate, vocal qualities, pauses, and silences. A pleasing voice, for example, will make people more likely to listen to us and a modulated voice is seen as more attractive and as indicating a better education and higher socioeconomic position than is a dynamic voice (Andersen, 1999). Particular accents and dialects carry associations that enhance or undermine our power and credibility in a group. Responses to certain vocal cues vary according to communicator and context (Buller & Burgoon, 1986; Buller & Aune, 1988). On another level, however, our emotions are clarified through our pitch, tone, rate, and other vocal behaviors that add to the words.

Paralanguage can be used to regulate the small group discussion. Our tone of voice can let the other group members know if we are approving, uncertain, or disagreeing with their contributions, and often in a group, "it's not what you said that bothered me, but how you said it."

Silence also has a number of uses. It can be used to create interpersonal distance or as an emotional response to a situation. It can indicate agreement or dissension, or be used as a way of opting out of conflict. Silence may be used in response to respect for authority or as a means of defying that same authority. Thus, silence itself sends a message (Burgoon, Buller, & Woodall, 1996).

Body Language.   *Kinesics,* the study of body language, consists of the messages we deliver through our physical appearance and by our movements and gestures. Before we move, our physical appearance sends a message, either positive or negative, depending on the context and the individuals receiving the stimulus. We all have built-in biases based on past experience and acculturation. For example, in the United States, studies have shown that tall, slim men are perceived as more qualified than short, stout men (Andersen, 1999; Remland, 2000).

Body movement and gesture provide a number of cues to the success or failure of group interactions. When successful communication between equals is taking place, there is frequently a *synchrony* in the body movements between individuals. "Rhythm seems to be the fundamental glue by which cohesive discourse is maintained" (Erickson, 1987). Being in sync with other members of your group means you all "march to the same basic tune." On the other hand, Hickson and Stacks (1985) found "that mirroring the behaviors of others is a sign of conceding or according status or power to them" (p. 202), and Burgoon and Saine (1978) noted that numerous studies indicate that higher-status individuals have greater movement and more relaxed posture. As with most nonverbal communication, it is difficult to generalize to all situations. However, in general, the cues we get from body movements give us the sense of whether or not someone else is "on the same wavelength," thereby encouraging us to be, or discouraging us from being, open, forthcoming, and developing a group spirit. When individuals do not open up, other group members tend to view those members as judgmental, uncooperative, and nonresponsive (Remland, 2000).

How we clothe ourselves and our general appearance also have an impact. This is made explicit when we are told to dress for the occasion or to "look the part." The underlying issue is what is significant. If other group members do not think we appear to fit the group norms, they will not assign us credibility. Without credibility, we will have little, if any, influence. Sooner or later, we will lose interest in the group and will become ineffective. Table 6.4 summarizes the critical nonverbal actions.

The way we move also has an impact. If we sit squarely facing the group, we will most likely be perceived as open and forthcoming and as interested in the group functions. If we sit with our arms crossed, looking away from the group, or laid back in our chair, the message we are giving is one of disinterest. Other group members interpret our actions as indications that either we do or do not want to be a part of the group.

We are judged by our behavior, not our words. If what we do does not fit with what we say, group members tend to believe what we do. Therefore, positive nonverbal actions, as outlined in Table 6.5, are vital to our success in a group.

Proxemics.   "How we structure, use and are affected by space in our interactions with others" (Harper, Wiens, & Matarazzo, 1978, p. xii) constitutes *proxemics*. Hall (1963) identified the study of the structuring of personal space—the invisible boundary individuals draw around themselves as proxemics. This boundary is greater or lesser depending on the circumstances and the relationships with the other people in an interaction. More powerful people have freer use of the space around them than do less powerful individuals.

TABLE 6.4   Critical Nonverbal Actions

Facial Display	**Body Language** (Kinesics)
Facial expression	Movements
Eye contact	Gestures
Paralanguage (How we say something)	**Clothing and General Appearance**
Silence	

TABLE 6.5   Positive Nonverbal Behaviors

1. Time	Don't keep people waiting.
	Give adequate time.
2. Setting	Avoid furniture as a barrier.
	Create pleasant surroundings.
3. Physical Proximity	Closeness reduces status differences.
	Closeness promotes warmth.
4. Gestures	Make frequent use of open-palm gestures.
5. Head Movements	Use head nods.
	Tilted head indicates suspicion.
6. Facial Expression	Smile frequently.
7. Eyes	Make frequent, direct eye contact.
8. Voice	Communicate warmth.
	Avoid sounding bored or disinterested.

There are significant issues surrounding physical setting and seating arrangements in the communication patterns experienced in the small group communication as well. Sommer (1969) identified several types of seating patterns. These seating arrangements are shown in Figure 6.1. Individuals sitting across a table from each other maximize their interpersonal distance, increase their potential for sending and receiving both verbal and nonverbal messages and thus perhaps conflicting messages, and increase the likelihood of becoming competitive. Sitting with a corner of the table between participants reduces interpersonal distance, focuses attention on the project and materials rather than on the individuals' nonverbals, and may help enhance the cooperativeness of the participants. Sitting side by side reduces the interpersonal distance still further and, unless that interpersonal distance is too intimate to feel comfortable, may also be a cooperative seating arrangement. In meetings, different seating positions have been described as power spots (Kordia, 1986). Dominant positions are at the ends of a rectangular table (Cooper, 1979) and on the corners (Kordia, 1986). The middle of the table sides are considered less powerful places to sit, but may be good places from which to observe the group interaction without getting drawn into the discussion. Also sitting on a side next to a powerful individual may represent a powerful coalition within the group setting. While it is easy to make too much of seating patterns and lose sight of discussion patterns in groups, a creative group who are experiencing discussion difficulties may find that rearranging the seating influences that discussion.

Chronemics.   Chronemics is the study of the use of time. Western cultures are particularly oriented toward clock-based time as an organizing principle in the work world (Calloway-Thomas, Cooper, & Blake, 1999). In our culture, time is money. Small groups organized in this context must be sensitive to the time-based

FIGURE 6.1   Seating Arrangements

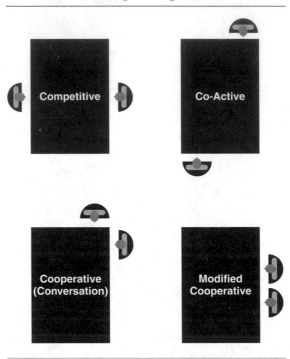

expectations of many of their members and of the organizations within which they operate. Promptness is important but is also negotiable (Burgoon & Saine, 1978). The manipulation of time is an important dynamic in small group interactions. An individual who takes too much of a group's time may be poorly perceived and his or her contributions discounted. On the other hand, a person in an influential position may be granted more leeway in bending the expectations for the use of time. As in all the areas of nonverbal communication, in order to be effective, small group members must be sensitive to the time orientation of the group.

Powerless Stereotypes

Because we judge others based, in part, on their nonverbal actions, we can also be guilty of drawing invalid conclusions regarding others. Because we have certain culturally based expectations, we are prone to misjudge others, thereby reducing our group's effectiveness.

Sex-role stereotyping continues in many groups and organizations fostering expectations that men will act like leaders and women will act like subordinates (Remland, 2000). Consider how this stereotyping adversely impacts our group effectiveness. Two critical assets needed by a group—communication effectiveness

TABLE 6.6 **Functions of Nonverbal Communication**

Function	Explanation
Repetition	Reinforcing verbal messages with nonverbal behaviors. Examples: A supervisor moving his or her arms while giving instructions. Telling and showing someone how to do a job. Giving an OK signal, or a pat on the back, along with verbal praise. The verbal and nonverbal are the same and work together to carry the message.
Complement	Using nonverbal messages to supplement, expand, modify, or provide details to a verbal message. Examples: Looking confident while conducting a briefing enhances the quality of the presentation. Speaking softly while discussing delicate information. The nonverbal adds to and facilitates the verbal message.
Accentuation	Using nonverbal communication to provide emphasis. Examples: The loudness of a person's voice often conveys the true strength of the message. A secret can be forecast by a whisper. A wink or a furrowed brow can add to the impact of the verbal message. Distance can indicate seriousness. The nonverbal accentuates and increases the power or effectiveness of the verbal message.
Substitution	Using a nonverbal behavior in place of a verbal one. Examples: A head nod to indicate yes, a "pat on the back," a "knowing glance," or a "thumbs up" for success. When the action is symbolic, it is called an emblem.
Contradiction	Making the nonverbal and verbal messages incongruent. Examples: A colleague's facial expression, or vocal inflection, gives a message opposite to the verbal one. Sarcasm is one of the best examples, since the tone of voice provides a meaning that is quite different from the stated one. Making someone wait and then saying that he or she is important can be an example. Someone's asking you what is wrong because of your appearance and your saying, defensively, "nothing," is another example.
Regulation	Using nonverbal behaviors to initiate, continue, interrupt, or terminate interactions. Examples: Eye contact, gestures, nods, head motions, and numerous other behaviors indicate how the interaction should progress.

and leadership—might be denied because of stereotyping. First, "numerous studies have shown that women throughout the world are more accurate, sensitive receivers of nonverbal communication than men" (Andersen, 1999, p. 122). Second, this stereotyping reduces the possible success of a group. Numerous recent studies indicate that women are more effective as managers and leaders in the areas of motivating others, fostering communication, producing high-quality work, and listening to others than are men (Sharpe, 2000). According to the same studies, male managers tie female managers in the areas of strategic planning and analyzing issues. "But, women often find themselves penalized no matter what they do" (Remland, 2000, p. 320).

Ethnocentrism can also diminish a group's success. The assumption that the traditional nonverbal actions seen as important to successful group work should be expected in our multicultural society can lead to incorrect judgments and loss of important input. For example, the nonverbal rules of an Arab's native communication behaviors support speaking loudly and standing close, which might be interpreted as pushy. A Middle Easterner has been schooled to take the time to chitchat before getting down to business, which a group might see as inefficient and obtrusive (Gardenswartz & Rowe, 1993). Needless to say, these examples can be expanded to include different parts of the United States, as well as our neighbors to the North and South and throughout the world. We must make certain that we do not interpret the nonverbal actions of others as indications of powerlessness, lack of interest, or incompetence. *Homophily*, which is our tendency to want to be in groups with people who are similar to us, can deny us important viewpoints from our multicultural world. Instead, we need to create group situations conducive to being inclusive—both because it is the right thing to do and because it will enhance the group process.

Summary

Once we gather a group of interested individuals to work on an issue, the most significant area in determining our success or failure will be the quality of the communication—both verbal and nonverbal. It is through that interaction that group and personal meanings are established.

Verbal communication allows group members to order the tasks, understand the process, and develop symbolic meaning through a group narrative. Traditionally, misunderstandings have been blamed on the way language was used to establish the group's "job." While the task is important, the power of language comes from its semantic and symbolic capacities. In addition, when groups use humor and engage in specific types of group talk, they often increase their chances for success.

Nonverbal communication includes all behaviors, other than verbal communication, that are assigned meaning by one or more of the participating parties. Among other things, it includes facial display, paralanguage, body language, proxemics, and chronemics. Effective group members understand the importance of both verbal and nonverbal communication.

DISCUSSION QUESTIONS

1. Distinguish between the task-ordering, process-orientation, and narrative functions of verbal communication. Why are these important to the small group and team communication process?

2. "We're Number One!" is a popular characterization for a group, school, or organization. Identify three similar phrases used with groups you have been associated with. Were these metaphors or fantasies or both? Explain.

3. Identify five words you are certain will carry the same meaning—denote the same thing—for three other people. Reexamine the list and see if you can provide some connotative meanings for the words. Share your list with several other people and see if your denotative words have the same meaning for the other group members.

4. Distinguish between problem-solving, role assumption, consciousness-raising, and encounter talk. From your own experiences, provide an example of each one.

5. Think of a joke about your college or university—or, perhaps, your college or university's chief rival. How does the telling of the joke, or humor, function in a group?

6. Return to the eight principles of nonverbal communication. Pick two principles and provide new examples of how they operate in a group or team.

7. How can you use eye contact to increase your small group or team effectiveness?

8. What is synchrony? How does it function in small groups or teams?

9. Explain proxemics and chronemics. Are there universal rules for all cultures regarding these concepts? Explain.

EXERCISES

1. Find a metaphor; 2. A slogan or name for your group; 3. Humor—Tell a joke; 4. Nonverbal observation; 5. Overcoming discrimination; 6. Silent films, videos, or TV shows; 7. To catch a spy

1. FIND A METAPHOR

1. A metaphor, as explained in the chapter, is an unrelated concept that offers insights regarding something you are examining. Your goal is to use one idea to make sense of another.
2. For this exercise, concentrate on a past group or team experience. To get you started, did the experience have any similarities to conducting an orchestra, playing a sport, refereeing a contest, constructing something, going on a diet, putting out a fire, or any other activity?
3. Does the metaphor allow you additional insights into the group process? How does it shape your understanding?
4. If you are in a group or team for the entire course, what metaphors would you use to describe the experience? Share your metaphors with the rest of your group or team and see if you can agree on several specific metaphors.

2. A SLOGAN OR NAME FOR YOUR GROUP

1. Perception is guided and sometimes controlled by the names we use for activities. In the '70s, small truck frames with passenger bodies were called SUVs and an entire industry was created. Customer service consultants argue that a customer complaint is really an opportunity for improvement turned upside down. A door can become a passageway, a problem can be a challenge, and so on.

2. What name can you create for your group or team that captures the essence of group work without simply calling it a group? Share your answer with your group and adopt a slogan or name that reflects the group or team's understanding and aspirations.

3. HUMOR—TELL A JOKE

1. Some jokes are generic. For example, sport-related jokes can be told by any college or university about any rival—just substitute the school name. How do you get a(n) _____ graduate off of your front porch? How many _____ freshmen does it take to change a light bulb? What are the longest three years of a _____ (*name sport*) player's life? Answers. Pay for the pizza; none, that's a sophomore course; first year. Corny, but they usually bring a smile.

2. To be effective, humor should not be directed at other groups since the joke is at someone else's expense. So avoid racist, sexist, age-related, disability-related, or other forms of negative humor. While the sports-related jokes might seem group directed, they are much too shallow to create any harm.

3. What humorous incident has happened in your small group class this semester? Why it is funny? Share your example with a small group.

4. In your group, examine the use of humor and fun as a means for creating a better working relationship. Remember, we do not have to be funny, but we do need to have a sense of humor.

4. NONVERBAL OBSERVATION

1. Spend an hour at your student union, local eatery, library, or other public place observing nonverbal communication activities. Be prepared to report your findings.

2. What types of nonverbal communication were most prevalent? What surprised you regarding nonverbal communication? What types of nonverbal communication would you suggest using more? What types seem to be ineffective or should be avoided?

3. Notice the nonverbal communication between superiors and subordinates. How does it differ from the nonverbal communication between apparent equals?

4. As we discussed in the chapter, research reports differences in how men and women use nonverbal communication. Do you observe differences in how touch, space, eye contact, attention, and dominance are occurring? What are they?

Alternate Procedure

Observe a group of people holding a meeting. Observe the nonverbal characteristics: Where do people sit? Do they lean forward or lean back, look tense or relaxed, look interested or bored? Are their motions synchronous, that is, when one person leans forward does another person lean forward or back in response? Do people look at the speaker, take notes, or eat during the discussion? What is your impression of the overall tone, energy level, collaborativeness, and participation of the group members? Observe the verbal characteristics of a group discussion. Who speaks first, who talks and how much, who gets interrupted and by whom? Is there a pattern or sequencing to the talking? Do people take turns in an orderly fashion, and do some people generally speak after the same other people in a repeating sequence? Do members of the group engage in private conversations aside from the general group discussion?

5 . OVERCOMING DISCRIMINATION

Overview

More than half the U.S. population is now considered overweight and nearly 18% obese, or about 30 pounds or more overweight. As early as nursery school, children prefer drawings of peers in wheelchairs or with facial disfigurations over those of fat children. A National Education Association position paper says that "for fat students, the school experience is one of ongoing prejudice, unnoticed discrimination, and almost constant harassment" (Goldberg, 2000, p. 11A). This discrimination based on persons' weight impacts their college and job experience. In college, students indicated they would rather marry an embezzler or blind person than an obese person. One study found that highly obese women earn 24% less, while the moderately obese earn about 6% less, than their nonobese colleagues. Ironically, white men who are a little heavy receive a 7% higher salary than slimmer men. As with other marginalized groups, obese individuals want inclusion, encouragement and opportunity.

Adapted from: Asher, D. (2000, May/June). Discrimination: A weighty matter. *Psychology Today*, p. 14; Goldberg, C. (2000, November 11). Study: Obesity prejudice appears early and in most spheres of life. *The Tuscaloosa News*, pp. 1A, 11A; Mehta, S. N. (2000, July 10). What minority employees really want. *Fortune*, pp. 181–186.

1. What are your personal feelings, insights, or observations regarding the paragraph about excess weight? How do you react to an obese individual? Are your reactions based on informed information justifying your interpre-

tation of someone else's nonverbal presence? What judgments have you made that might be open to question?

2. As a group, determine if you agree that obese individuals are subject to discrimination. List the kinds of stereotypes applied to this particular group. Decide what information your group has to support these stereotypes. In terms of verbal communication, at what level of abstraction are these stereotypes? How valid are the generalizations?

3. Is it ethical to discriminate based on body shape? What do we lose by marginalizing a specific group of individuals based on their nonverbal actions?

4. Devise a plan of action to reduce overweight-based language and nonverbal perceptions. Is this difficult? What does this tell us about the power of verbal and nonverbal communication to shape our perceptions, attitudes, and actions?

6. SILENT FILMS, VIDEOS, OR TV SHOWS

1. Watch a video, film, or TV show without any sound.

2. Individually, decide: What nonverbal activities are occurring? Which ones would you not have noticed if there had been sound? Which ones make little sense without sound? Which ones "speak" to you even though there is no sound? Does this support the notion that actions speak louder than words?

3. As an alternative, watch the video, film, or TV show with others and then compare notes. Which nonverbal actions did all the group members notice? Which seemingly important nonverbal cues did some take note of and others miss? What possible explanations can you develop for this disparity?

7. TO CATCH A SPY

1. The Spies and Citizens Exercise: This small group exercise divides a group into two subgroups of spies and citizens. The spies make up approximately one-quarter to one-fifth of the total group. The citizens make up the other three-quarters or four-fifths. Both citizens and spies know how many spies there are, but only the spies know who they are. The object of the exercise is for the citizens to figure out who the spies are and eliminate them from their community. Spies go to jail when they are found out, but wrongly accused citizens also leave the community. For citizens, the experience of being accused is so traumatic that they move away to start their lives over in a new community.

Procedure

Everyone gets a sheet of paper identifying him or her as either a spy or a citizen. Then all players close their eyes with their heads facing down and only the spies are allowed to look around and identify each other. Next, everyone meets as one big group and discusses the problem with having spies in the community and how many spies there are known to be there. Once they have discussed this problem for a short while, members accuse two people of being spies. These two people each get to make statements arguing and providing evidence of their good citizenship. Then the entire group gets to vote on which one they think is a spy, and that person is eliminated from the community and from further group discussion. That person then reveals whether he or she is in reality a spy or a citizen, and the exercise proceeds with further discussion, accusations, voting, and elimination of members from the community. Once members are eliminated from the group discussion, they become observers of what are effective verbal and nonverbal strategies for being believed by the group that they are good citizens. What are effective verbal and nonverbal strategies? What are ineffective ones? How are group decisions influenced by the use of these effective and less effective strategies?

2. Alternately, observe a group of people holding a meeting. Observe the nonverbal characteristics: Where do people sit, do they lean forward or lean back, look tense or relaxed, look interested or bored? Are their motions synchronous, that is, when one person leans forward does another person lean forward or back in response? Do people look at the speaker, take notes, or eat during the discussion? What is your impression of the overall tone, energy level, collaborativeness, and participation of the group members? Observe the verbal characteristics of a group discussion. Who speaks first, who talks and how much, who is interrupted and by whom? Is there a pattern or sequencing to the talking? Do people take turns in an orderly fashion, and do some people generally speak after the same other people in a repeating sequence? Do members of the group engage in private conversations aside from the general group discussion?

REFERENCES

Andersen, P. A. (1999). *Nonverbal communication: Forms and functions.* Mountain View, CA: Mayfield.

Birdwhistell, R. L. (1970). *Kinesics and context: Essays on body motion communication.* Philadelphia: University of Pennsylvania Press.

Bolman, L. G., & Deal, T. E. (1991). *Reframing organizations: Artistry, choice, and leadership.* San Francisco: Jossey-Bass.

Bormann, E. G., & Bormann, N. C. (1992). *Effective small group communication* (5th ed.). Edina, MN: Burgess.

Buller, D. B., & Aune, R. K. (1988). The effects of vocalics and nonverbal sensitivity on compliance: A speech accommodation theory explanation. *Human Communication Research, 14,* 3, 301–332.

Buller, D. B., & Burgoon, J. K. (1986). The effects of vocalics and nonverbal sensitivity on compliance: A replication and extension. *Human Communication Research, 13,* 1, 126–144.

Burgoon, J. K., Buller, D. B., & Woodall, W. G. (1996). *Nonverbal communication: The unspoken dialogue.* New York: McGraw-Hill.

Burgoon, J. K., & Saine, T. (1978). *The unspoken dialogue.* Dallas: Houghton Mifflin.

Clancy, J. J. (1989). *The invisible powers: The language of business.* Lexington, MA: Lexington Books.

Coker, D. A., & Burgoon, J. K. (1987). The nature of conversational involvement and nonverbal encoding patterns. *Human Communication Research, 13*(4), 463–494.

Cooper, K. (1979). *Nonverbal communication for business success.* New York: AMACOM.

Duncan, W. J., & Feisal, J. P. (1989). No laughing matter: Patterns of humor in the workplace. *Organizational Dynamics, 17,* 4, 18–30.

Erickson, F. (1987). The beat goes on. *Psychology Today, 21,* 38.

Ervin-Tripp, S. M. (1968). An analysis of the interaction of language, topic, and listener. In J. A.

Fishman (Ed.), *Reading in the sociology of language*. The Hague: Mouton.

Gardenswartz, L., & Rowe, A. (1993). *Managing diversity: A complete desk reference and planning guide*. Chicago: Irwin.

Grazian, F. (1987, September). Smiling equals trust. *Communication Briefings, 6*, p. 6.

Hackman, M. Z., & Johnson, C. E. (1991). *Leadership: A communication perspective*. Prospect Heights, IL: Waveland.

Hall, E. T. (1959). *The silent language*. Garden City, NY: Doubleday.

Hall, E. T. (1963). A system for the notation of proxemic behavior. *American Anthropologist, 65*, 1003–1026.

Harper, R. G., Wiens, A. N., & Matarazzo, J. D. (1978). *Nonverbal communication: The state of the art*. New York: Wiley.

Harris, T. E. (2002). *Applied organizational communication: Principles and pragmatics for future success*. Mahwah, NJ: Lawrence Erlbaum.

Hobbs, C. R. (1987). *Time power*. New York: Harper & Row.

Kiechel, W., III. (1986). Executives ought to be funnier. In P. J. Frost, V. F. Mitchell, & W. R. Nord (Eds.), *Organizational reality* (3rd ed., pp. 363–366). Glenview, IL: Scott, Foresman.

Kordia, M. (1986). Symbols of power. In P. J. Frost, W. F. Mitchell, & W. R. Nord (Eds.), *Organizational reality: Reports from the firing line* (3rd ed., pp. 145–156). Glenview, IL: Scott, Foresman.

Kotter, J. P. (1990). *A force for change: How leadership differs from management*. New York: Free Press.

Lederer, R. (1996, July 27–28). Some headlines say far more than they mean to. *The Patriot Ledger*, p. 36.

Mehrabian, A. (1981). *Silent messages: Implicit communication of emotions and attitudes* (2nd ed.). Belmont, CA: Wadsworth.

Newton, D. A., & Burgoon, J. K. (1990). The use and consequences of verbal influence strategies during interpersonal disagreements. *Human Communication Research, 16*, 4, 477–518.

Orber, M. P., & Harris, T. M. (2001). *Interracial communication: Theory into practice*. Belmont, CA: Wadsworth Thomson Learning.

Plung, D. L., & Montgomery, T. T. (2004). *Professional communication: The corporate insider's approach*. U.S.: Thomson South-Western.

Remland, M. S. (2000). *Nonverbal communication in everyday life*. Boston: Houghton Mifflin.

Rose, J. (1994). Communication challenges and role functions of performing groups. *Small Group Research, 25*, 3, 411–432.

Sharpe, R. (2000, November 20). As leaders, women rule. *Business Week*, pp. 75–84.

Smith, D. R., & Williamson, L. K. (1985). *Interpersonal communication: Roles, rules, strategies, and games* (3rd ed.). Dubuque, IA: Brown.

Sommer, R. (1969). *Personal space: The behavioral basis of design*. Englewood Cliffs, NJ: Prentice-Hall.

Witherspoon, P. D. (1997). *Communicating leadership: An organizational perspective*. Needham Heights, MA: Allyn & Bacon.

7

Listening and Feedback: The Other Half of Communication

CHAPTER OUTLINE

Motivation

The Four Components of Listening
Sensing (Hearing the Message)
Interpreting the Message
Evaluating the Message Content
Memory: Retaining and Responding
to the Message

Active Listening
Barriers to Active Listening
Active Listening Response Methods

Feedback: Responding to the Message
Providing Constructive Feedback
Receiving Feedback

Summary

Discussion Questions

Exercises

References

CHAPTER OBJECTIVES

- Explain the importance of listening.
- Identify the role played by motivation in effective listening.
- Outline the four components of listening.
- Identify the barriers to effective listening.
- Define active listening.
- Clarify the barriers to active listening.
- Elucidate the four response methods of active listeners.
- Discuss the eight guidelines for feedback.
- Describe constructive feedback techniques.

KEY TERMS

Active listening
Arrogance
Constructive feedback
Disrespect
Distracting delivery
Evaluating
Expressing understanding
External noise
Feedback

Internal noise
Interpreting
Lack of interest
Long-term memory
Memory
Noise
Paraphrasing
Pre-programmed emotional
    responses

Receiving feedback
Questions
Selective attention
Sensing
Short-term memory
Thought speed
What's in it for me

Who's on First?

ABBOTT: They give ball players nowadays very peculiar names.

COSTELLO: Funny names?

ABBOTT: Nicknames. Pet names. Now, on the St. Louis team we have Who's on first, What's on second, I Don't Know is on third.

COSTELLO: That's what I want to find out. I want you to tell me the names of the fellows on the St. Louis team.

ABBOTT: I'm telling you: Who's on first, What's on second, I Don't Know is on third.

COSTELLO: You know the fellows' names?

ABBOTT: Yes.

COSTELLO: Well, then, who's playin' first?

ABBOTT: Yes.

COSTELLO: I mean the fellow's name on first base.

ABBOTT: Who.

COSTELLO: The fellow playin' first base for St. Louis.

ABBOTT: Who.

COSTELLO: The guy on first base.

ABBOTT: Who is on first.

COSTELLO: Well, what are you askin' me for?

(from *The Naughty Nineties* as quoted in: Furmanek & Palumbo, 1991)

In any human communication process, effective listening is equally as important as clear, articulate speaking. Sensitive, articulate expression of ideas is one half of communication; careful, effective listening is the other. Receiving the message being sent by the other person and accurately assigning meanings to that message are required for understanding and for any real communication to take place. Abbott and Costello's "Who's on First?" misunderstanding can bring a smile to your face, but small group misunderstandings are not usually as funny.

Small groups are effective because of the group synergy that develops through a common group understanding. This common understanding and synergy are made possible by effective listening, then incorporating the individual ideas in new ways and into new forms. In order to take advantage of everyone's input, we must be good listeners. Without careful listening, the group is simply made up of individuals with independent and often competing or conflicting ideas. The goal of small group communication is to create and develop ideas together (Stewart & Thomas, 1990). Listening plays a key role in achieving that goal, and if no one is listening, the group fails to achieve the larger unity for which it was convened. In organizations, the high-performance and successful teams have "an open communication structure that allows all members to participate. Individuals are listened to regardless of their age, title, sex, race, ethnicity, profession or other status characteristics" (Wheelan, 1999, p. 42).

Research indicates, however, that while about half of our communication time is spent listening (Johnson, 1996), most of us are not very good listeners (Alessandra & Hunsaker, 1993). Many physicians, for example, do not listen carefully enough to their patients' stories to make accurate diagnoses (Nyquist, 1996). It has been argued that the average college student listens effectively to only about 50% of what is said and remembers only 25% of that content after two days (Wolvin & Coakley, 1985). Indeed, most individuals listen at about a 25% effectiveness level. In addition, the 50% I hear may not be the 50% you thought was the most important, and the 25% I remember is unlikely to be the 25% you intended as your main message.

Why are we such poor listeners? Some scholars have suggested that, while we have all been encouraged to talk, few of us have been taught how to listen. As Johnson (1996, p. 91) puts it, "No parent waits eagerly for a child to learn to listen. Rather, the emphasis is on learning to talk." We tend to believe that talking is the same thing as communicating. Yet, as the expression goes, "God gave you two ears and one mouth."

We incorrectly identify talking with leading and following with listening. Often, listening is the more important skill (Ray, 1999). A transcript from an actual radio conversation of a U.S. Navy ship with Canadian authorities off the coast of Newfoundland in October 1995—released by the Chief of Naval Operations on October 10, 1995—makes the point.

CANADIANS: Please divert your course 15 degrees to the South to avoid a collision.

AMERICANS: Recommend you divert your course 15 degrees to the North to avoid a collision.

CANADIANS: Negative. You will have to divert your course 15 degrees to the South to avoid a collision.

> **AMERICANS:** This is the Captain of a U.S. Navy ship. I say again, divert YOUR course.
>
> **CANADIANS:** No, I say again, divert YOUR course.
>
> **AMERICANS:** This is the aircraft carrier USS *Lincoln*. The second largest ship in the United States 92 Fleet. We are accompanied by three destroyers, three cruisers, and numerous support vessels. I demand that you change YOUR course 15 degrees north. I say again, that is one five degrees north, or countermeasures will be taken to ensure the safety of this ship.
>
> **CANADIANS:** This is a lighthouse. Your call.

Listening can be a critical leadership skill.

Mediators, negotiators, and other individuals who are trained to work through problems must first learn to listen effectively. In negotiator training seminars, for example, the negotiator trainees are reminded that they never learned anything while they were talking and that they cannot succeed in a negotiating session until they fully understand the other side (Asherman & Asherman, 1990). When they are talking, they are sending messages but are not developing much insight into how other people think or feel.

In *The Seven Habits of Highly Effective People*, Covey (1989) identifies one of the seven habits as: "Seek first to understand, and only then to be understood." Ineffective people, he explains, are eager to be heard but often do not take the time to understand the other person's perspective before speaking. Highly effective people place understanding the other person first, and that understanding comes only through listening.

Motivation

No one becomes a better listener without the motivation to do so. Essentially, we all ask, "What's in it for me?" In small groups the payoff is clear. Effective listening, with the consequent synergy of shared ideas, allows for successful solutions to problems, the achievement of goals, and the personal satisfaction of a job well done.

Listening has been shown to be a vital skill for successful managers, supervisors, and professional employees, taking over 60% of their average day on the job (Peters, 1987; Wolvin & Coakley, 1985). However, "only about one-third of employees say that their managers listen to them" (Sweeney & McFarlin, 2002, p. 294).

The rewards of effective listening include many life-enhancing experiences, such as learning, building relationships, being entertained, making intelligent decisions, saving time, enjoying conversations, settling disagreements, getting the best value, preventing accidents and mistakes, asking intelligent questions, and making accurate evaluations (Bone, 1988). Finally, good listeners get a great deal more out of small group membership and are more appreciated by their fellow members.

Good listening is, however, a very complex process. As with any complex process, there are numerous ways to parse it into its component parts. In this chapter, we present several ways of looking at the listening process. First, we examine the four components of listening: hearing, interpreting, evaluating, and responding. Then we examine active versus passive listening and group climate.

The Four Components of Listening

Listening involves four sequential components experienced in rapid succession. We must sense or hear the message, interpret or provide meaning to the message, evaluate the content of the message, and retain and respond to the message in the context of an ongoing communication event. Each of these components is in itself a complex process. For this reason, a more detailed examination of each follows.

Sensing (Hearing the Message)

Hearing the sounds, and even being able to repeat the words, is not the same thing as sensing, or hearing, the message. Hearing is the involuntary "physiological process of receiving aural stimuli" (Johnson, 1996, p. 91). Thus, the act of hearing the sounds is nonselective. Sensing or hearing the message, on the other hand, is a voluntary act whereby we choose certain sounds and noises to pay attention to, while avoiding others. This is an important part of listening and happens as a result of our decision to attune to certain messages. Hearing and listening to the message are influenced by selective attention and the amounts of external and internal noise.

Selective Attention. Choosing one message over another is called *selective attention*. The messages we attune to are the ones that have some "pre-programmed" importance for us. If I am an avid football fan, for example, I will be drawn toward football-related messages. If I'm interested in social or environmental issues, I will tune in to those. If I am a quilter, I will selectively attend to messages related to quilting. If I am committed to social justice, I am more likely to pay attention when civil rights issues are discussed. On the other hand, if I don't follow the soap operas on TV, I am not likely to pay attention to someone discussing the latest gossip about one of the stars.

There are several reasons we engage in this practice of selective attention as indicated in Table 7.1. To start, some things are simply more important to us. For example, when someone calls our name, we are more likely to respond. With the barrage of stimulation that assaults us from all directions in our daily lives, we must learn to discriminate those stimuli that are necessary either to our survival or to our well-being from those that make little difference to us in our ongoing lives. Because we cannot possibly process all the stimulation that surrounds us, we have learned to pay attention to those stimuli that are familiar to us and that have particular significance for us. These can range from issues of crucial importance to

TABLE 7.1   Selective Attention—Reasons

1. Some things are more important
2. More likely to listen when the content supports our point of view
3. Messages contradicting what we believe are likely to be rejected
4. Expertise or understanding can decrease interest in other viewpoints
5. Difficult material may be ignored

those that appear trivial. They can include basic survival, our jobs, our relationships, popular cultural icons, or any number of other stimuli in our environments.

Because small groups are convened for any number of purposes, we may be called upon to listen to discussion ranging from subjects in which we have little or no interest, to those in which we have strong feelings or feel particularly expert, to those which excite great controversy. In each of these cases, we are presented with particular challenges to our ability to listen carefully and to contribute meaningfully to the group discussion.

In addition, small groups are frequently made up of individuals from a variety of backgrounds, experiences, and points of view. If we have been asked to join a group convened to come up with solutions to a given problem in our community, we are more likely to pay attention to, and to side with, individuals, arguments, or examples that support our point of view on the issue than to those that oppose it, particularly if the topic is a controversial one. In a sense, we put "emotional cotton" in our ears when certain topics are broached. Even when we are ready to listen, anger, frustration, or hostility may interfere and make us defensive rather than good listeners.

When messages contradict or challenge our way of thinking, we may tend to reject them. Prejudices, stereotypes, and preconceived ideas can prevent us from fully hearing issues and alternative viewpoints on topics. If, for example, we hold preconceived ideas about the place of women in our society, assume that older people have little to contribute to the economic base of our society, make assumptions about the general characteristics of people based on their racial or ethnic backgrounds, hold stereotypes about gay people, or believe adamantly in one side of an issue, such as the right to die or the right to choice, then it becomes difficult for us to hear other people's views on these topics when they oppose or even question our own.

In addition, we make conscious decisions to pay attention to some messages and ignore others. As we become more expert in a particular subject, we may tend to dismiss what we consider unsophisticated viewpoints. This can become a problem in small groups, when ideas are weighted toward the opinions of the "experts" and miss the potentially broader and sometimes innovative views of those on the "outside" of the issue.

Finally, difficult material may discourage us from listening carefully. If we feel we don't understand the issue in question, we may simply drop out of the discussion, assuming we have nothing to offer to it anyway. This robs the group of our potential input from a fresh perspective, while robbing ourselves of an opportunity to learn something new and perhaps beneficial in some way. In a small group, members with particular expertise need to take responsibility for clarifying the issues and helping all members overcome the barriers to understanding, but they must also be open to listening to new and innovative approaches to the issue under discussion.

Noise. Noise is a useful term for the interference that occurs between the spoken message and hearing. There are two types of noise: external and internal. External noise includes distractions that make it difficult to hear the other person. For a small group, these can include extraneous sounds, a telephone ringing, bad acoustics, poor visibility between the speaker and the listener, an uncomfortable physical environment, other people talking, coughing, or moving around, or any number of other physical distractions. Comedian George Carlin's quip: "Aren't you glad the phone wasn't invented by Alexander Graham Siren?" alludes to the distraction and irritation caused by certain sounds. Remember the last beautiful spring day when you were sitting in a hot, stuffy classroom and you could hear music and people having fun outside? That is the essence of external noise.

Internal noise includes a preoccupation with personal issues, charged-up emotional states, stereotyping and prejudice toward the sender or toward his or her message, or distractions from other aspects of our lives. All of these interfere with our hearing. We are not blank slates that unconditionally accept all incoming verbal and nonverbal messages. If we do not make a conscious effort or are not trained in active listening, we frequently allow noise to interfere with our hearing.

Interpreting the Message

Assigning meaning to someone's message is a complex task. In hearing the message and choosing to pay attention, we accept the message into our memory system. Interpreting the message is the next step. Our goal in this should be to understand the other person's meaning. We are all limited in our perspective and understanding, however, by our perceptions of others' verbal and nonverbal communication. As I listen to someone else, I filter my interpretation of their message through my own attitudes, assumptions, needs, values, past and present experiences, knowledge, expectations, fears, goals, educational background, and emotional involvement. Thus, we each bring our own particular limitations to hearing and accurately interpreting someone else's message.

A much cited story provides an example of the preconceptions we frequently bring to our interpretations. A little boy is involved in a serious automobile accident in which his father, who was driving the car, is killed instantly. The boy is rushed to the hospital in critical condition. The emergency room doctor takes one look at the boy and shouts: "Oh my God, it's my son!" How is this possible? For some of us, the answer is not immediately apparent. Our implicit assumption that doctors are ordinarily men can make the interpretation process difficult. In this case, the doctor is the boy's mother. Recognizing our assumptions and interpretations can be tricky business.

During a job interview, the interviewer tells the interviewee that "only the top 10% get jobs with this company." Is the interviewer boasting, trying to show the exclusiveness of the company, explaining how selective the process can be, letting the interviewee know there is little chance of being hired, or making the chance to be hired seem like an honor? There are many possible interpretations of this type of statement. As the interviewee, we will likely adopt the one that reflects our own prior experiences and sets of assumptions. This interpretation will, in turn, likely influence our interview performance. This is true in small group discussions, as well.

Although we all use pre-programmed assumptions to interpret and understand communication events, we can retrain those assumptive bases (Sashkin & Kiser, 1993). For example, customer service personnel in some companies are trained to see a complaint or problem as just an opportunity turned upside down (Zemke & Schaaf, 1989). The staff are trained to accept criticism of their organization as valued input, rather than to react defensively. Thus, our interpretation of others' messages can be consciously affected by our attention to our own assumptive bases. The more we learn to move beyond our unexamined assumptions and the more we allow ourselves to understand others' perspectives, the more accurate or mutually beneficial our interpretations of their messages can become.

Evaluating the Message Content

This stage involves forming an opinion or making a judgment regarding the messages. We are asking ourselves if the "facts" support the points being made or justify the positions being taken. It is a quality-control step, which poor listeners frequently overlook in their rush to judgment. Too often we don't stop to make certain that all the information is carefully gathered and weighed.

When we are asked to serve on a jury, we are admonished by the judge to refrain from making any final decision until all the evidence has been heard. This is a reminder of the importance of the evaluation stage of listening. Evaluation is the process of taking in various inputs, filtering out those that we consider unimportant, interpreting those that are important in our schema, and then making decisions about how to deal with them. In the decision-making process, it is important not to evaluate before collecting enough information.

Memory: Retaining and Responding to the Message

Everyone in good mental health has both short-term memory and long-term memory. Short-term memory is our working memory. It lasts from 1 to 60 seconds and decides which incoming messages should be preserved. If we do not recognize the messages as important, they are dismissed. Through our selective attention, we may concentrate on certain types of messages. If we are distracted by external or internal noise, however, there is a good chance we will temporarily lose a portion of the message, and unless there is some compelling reason to retain the input, the

Successful group decision making requires outstanding teamwork and common goals.

message may be easily overridden by competing stimuli. In the first meeting of a small group, for example, we may be so intent both on making sure others perceive us well and on monitoring our own external performance that we don't concentrate on introductory information given during the meeting. In so doing, we may effectively undermine the good impression we had wanted to make.

If we are stimulated to process and store particular bits of information, those bits gain access to our *long-term memory*. Although this part of our memory is relatively unlimited in its capacity, the message must first gain entry. Often, we must hear something several times before it gains access to our long-term memory. The first component of listening is that of acting on which messages to admit to our short- and long-term memory bases. Selective attention, external and internal noise, and our memory system all play important roles in our ability to hear the message.

Each of the four components of listening plays a vital part in how well we participate in small groups. As we have shown, each component can be either a building block or a barrier in our listening process, and active, effective listening is key to the success of small groups.

Active Listening

Active, effective listening is hard work. When we engage in active listening, we respond verbally and nonverbally to the other group members, letting them know we are paying attention. We become part of the transaction and take responsibility for understanding their meanings. These active listening behaviors and skills are not intuitive and do have barriers to their effective achievement. We present nine of those barriers (Golen, 1990).

Barriers to Active Listening

Lack of Interest.   The first barrier has to do with lack of interest in the subject matter, either because we find it inherently uninteresting or because we have determined it is too difficult for us to understand. This can lead to boredom, impatience with the speaker, daydreaming, or becoming preoccupied with something else instead of listening. To work with this barrier and contribute meaningfully to the group process, we need to find areas of interest. We may even tell ourselves that, since we are there at that moment, we might as well pay attention to the content of the discussion.

Distracting Delivery.   A second barrier to good listening is our tendency to judge the speaker's personal characteristics. If someone fidgets, refuses to be efficient in his or her comments, seems disorganized, speaks in an accent or cadence different from our own, dresses in an unusual way, or behaves in any number of other ways distracting to us, we may become impatient and inattentive, or begin concentrating on the speaker's mannerisms or delivery, rather than on the message (Pearson & Davilla, 1993). We need to remember, however, that it may be the least likely person who offers the greatest insight on a particular issue. All too often, we miss that when we allow ourselves to be distracted by superficial aspects of a person's presentation style. We need to remind ourselves to judge content, not delivery, and we need to exercise patience, allowing the other person to develop her or his ideas before rejecting them based on irrelevant criteria.

External and Internal Noise.   In line with distracting delivery is the third barrier—external and internal noise. As we discussed earlier under "Noise," this can prevent us from hearing the messages conveyed during a small group session. During any conversation, a phone ringing, a lawn mower running, or someone hammering nearby is a distraction. Whether the noise is external or internal, it is up to each of us to make an effort to hear past it—to concentrate on the message. We might remind ourselves that the information we miss by being distracted will have to be regained sometime in the future. Essentially, not listening at this moment is an opportunity lost that will require our time and energy later, and in a group, it may be difficult to recreate the messages that are missed, since the dynamics of the group process are difficult to recreate.

Arrogance and Disrespect.   The fourth barrier relates to our emotional responses to behaviors that show arrogance or disrespect. People with know-it-all attitudes or who use generalizations such as "you always," or "you never" may create hostility in us. If we are attacked personally or treated with disrespect, we are less likely to listen carefully to what is being said. This may be difficult for individual group members to deal with effectively, but a strong group leader should be able to moderate that kind of behavior in the interest of the group as a whole. In the case of behaviors that are simply annoying, each of us as group members must try to overlook them and to see through the behaviors to the contributions the individual is making to the group process.

Pre-Programmed Emotional Responses.   A fifth barrier to effective listening comes when a group member touches on an issue to which we have a strong emotional reaction. Groups may refuse to maintain a relaxing and agreeable environment for the speaker or refuse to relate to and benefit from the speaker's ideas, may disagree or argue outwardly or inwardly with the speaker or become emotional and excited when the speaker's views differ from their own, and the discussion can quickly degenerate into an argument of already established biases, rather than airing different points of view. Frequently, the more important the topic, the more likely group members are to respond from a pre-programmed point of view than from a rational response to the issue at hand. When this happens, we are best advised to sit back, relax, and hear the other person out. If we have really listened carefully, we may find there are points on which we can agree. If not, we have still heard the speaker and can make a relevant reply based on what was really said, rather than on our pre-programmed emotional reaction.

Ambushing.   This sixth barrier often comes hand-in-hand with the fifth barrier. We disagree with the individual and simply wait for a chance to interrupt or debate. We rehearse our own rebuttal while the individual is speaking and wait for the chance to ambush. Some listeners listen intently for points on which they can disagree and then just wait for their chance to attack the individual.

Listening for Facts.   A seventh barrier to effective listening is getting past our training in school, which was to listen only for the facts in order to recall them for a test. In a small group discussion, delivering a series of facts is not the sole purpose of communication. Rather, the purpose is to achieve some degree of mutual understanding. Deliberative listening, or listening only for facts, can actually blind us to the overall point being made by the sender. Understanding comes from sensing the other person's point, not just from developing a catalog of the facts presented. Thus, effective listening looks for the overall themes that encompass the facts and the reasoning behind them.

Faking Attention—Pseudolistening.   The eighth barrier to effective listening— faking attention—may also have its genesis in our school training. Usually some time around second or third grade, we are singled out by a teacher who admonishes us to "Pay attention!" After that, we become quite adept at faking attention, and before long we fake more than we listen. The only solution to this problem is to recognize it and work at really listening.

Thought Speed.   Thought speed is the ninth barrier to careful listening. Because we can think three to four times faster than anyone can talk, our temptation is to make use of the "free" time by allowing ourselves to wander around mentally. We may formulate our responses to what we think is being said; we may be triggered into thoughts on totally unrelated subjects; or we may simply feel bored and stop listening altogether. We can, however, train ourselves to use our thought energy to concentrate more fully on what is being said and intended—listening carefully to the phrasing of the message, observing the manner of presentation, looking for any other clues that may be apparent in the delivery of the message. This concentration is a clear competitive advantage effective listeners can use.

Other Barriers.   Other barriers to active listening are: laziness or tiredness (avoiding a subject because it is complex or difficult or because it takes too much time); and insincerity (avoiding eye contact while listening and paying attention only to the speaker's words, rather than to the speaker's meaning).

Active Listening Response Methods

Active listeners take advantage of the opportunity to listen carefully and understand each person during a group discussion. This enables them to participate more effectively and offer constructive feedback during the process. Four response methods that active listeners use are paraphrasing, expressing understanding, asking questions, and using nonverbal communication.

Paraphrasing.   Considered one of the secrets of effective listeners, paraphrasing is stating in our own words what we think the speaker intended to say. The description should be objective. Essentially, we are responding to the verbal and nonverbal signals given by the speaker.

Among other things, paraphrasing is an excellent way to fight daydreaming. If we are concentrating on developing an internal summary of another individual's thoughts and ideas, we do not have time to daydream (Wolvin & Coakley, 1985). We can paraphrase verbally to the speaker or simply paraphrase internally by mentally summarizing the other person's points.

In addition, in group meetings, there is a tendency for the discussion to go off on tangents. Thus, a second value of paraphrasing lies in its ability to bring the discussion back to the points being made at that time and to put group members back on the same track. A simple comment such as: "So I understand that what you are concerned about is . . ." allows a clear response by the speaker. Whether she or he says yes or no, everyone is back talking about the same issue. Used in this context, paraphrasing is a no-lose technique, and it helps the group stay focused.

Finally, paraphrasing can move emotional issues from the personal back to the objective. If one of the group members has been complaining that, "You never listen to my comments about . . . !" a careful restatement, such as: "OK, what I hear you saying is . . ." can allow the other group members to focus on the crux of the problem. The complaining member is treated with respect, and the discussion is turned toward something that involves content, not emotion.

Expressing Understanding.   At times, it may seem more appropriate to focus on the feelings of the speaker, rather than to restate the content of the message. This type of statement of understanding allows the group to assess more accurately how well the speaker's feelings have been perceived and understood, and this may permit the speaker to view her or his own feelings more accurately, as well. "You sound hopeful about . . ." allows the speaker to clarify or modify his or her meaning and the group to better understand the totality of the message. In order to enhance clarity, we should note the nonverbal communication of the speaker, as well as the actual statements she or he made. This is more than saying, "I know how you feel."

Asking Questions.   Part of paraphrasing and expressing understanding is the effective use of questions. This is a skill rarely taught and frequently used in ways that discourage, rather than enhance, discussion. Questions can be seen as challenges to our honesty or position on an issue, or they can be seen as manipulative. A question such as: "You don't really believe those people, do you?" does not invite an open discussion of the respondent's point of view. In a small group, the goal of questioning should be to clarify the other person's perspective, open up the discussion, or follow up on a previous idea. It should not be used as a thinly veiled attempt at putting the respondent on the spot. Combined with paraphrasing and expressed understanding, questions allow the listener to both indicate an interest and clarify the message. A simple, "Do you mean . . . ?" may clear up any possible misunderstandings.

Using Nonverbal Communication.   Since more than 50% of all meaning is communicated nonverbally, effective listeners make use of nonverbal gestures. Making eye contact, nodding our heads, and sitting in an attentive manner all indicate that we are interested and listening, and they encourage the speaker to continue talking. Fidgeting, frowning, looking at our watches, reading our own notes, or behaving in other distracting ways gives the opposite message.

Feedback: Responding to the Message

Listening is an active process. Feedback is a vital part of the process. Since we cannot not communicate, no response is nonetheless a response. After carefully listening to the message as openly and completely as we can, we are in a position to respond to what was communicated. We should respond nonverbally during the message with good eye contact and some head nods. Feedback plays an important role in the effective listening process, but it is intricately tied to the first three components: hearing the message, interpreting it, and evaluating its content. The most effective feedback indicates to the sender that we are listening to the content of the message, interpreting it accurately, and understand it.

   Feedback is vital to any group process committed to improving itself, for it is the only way to know what needs to be improved. Giving and receiving feedback should be more than just a part of a team member's behavior; it should be part of the whole group's culture. It has two purposes. One is to reinforce verbally and nonverbally the other group members. The other is to focus on the content of their messages, rather than on their attitudes or attributes. To be effective, feedback should be used to further the quality of the discussion.

Providing Constructive Feedback

When offering feedback, use descriptive statements without judgment, exaggeration, labeling, or attribution of motives. State the facts as specifically as possible. Tell how the behavior affects you. Say why you are affected that way and describe the connection between the facts you observed and your feelings. Let the other person respond. Describe the change you want the other person to consider. Describe why you think the change will alleviate the problem. Listen to the other person's response. Be prepared to discuss options and to compromise to arrive at a solution, rather than argue specific points. For example: "When you are late for meetings, I get angry because I am a busy person and dislike wasting time sitting and waiting for you to arrive. Is there another time that we could schedule our meetings so that you could get here on time?" will probably be more effective than: "You are always late for meetings. I'm tired of you being so irresponsible and wasting my time like that. When will you ever grow up, learn to take your commitments seriously, and take some responsibility for being places on time?"

Talk first about yourself, not the other person. Use "I" not "you" as the subject of your feedback statement. Speak for yourself. Be careful about statements such as "The group feels," or "The group doesn't like." Encourage others to state their own complaints.

Phrase the issue as a statement, not a question. Questions appear controlling and manipulative and can cause people to become defensive and angry. Consider the difference between: "Can you stop that so we can get down to business?" and "I would like to get on with our meeting and business."

Restrict your feedback to things you know for certain. Don't present opinions as facts. Speak only of what you saw and heard and what you feel and want.

Provide positive feedback as well as negative. Many people take good work for granted and give feedback only when there are problems. People are more likely to pay attention to your complaints if they have also received your compliments. It is important to remember to tell people when they have done something well. Help people hear and accept your compliments when giving positive feedback. People sometimes feel awkward when told good things about themselves and will fend off the compliment or change the subject. Reinforce the positive feedback and help the person hear, acknowledge, and accept it.

Scholtes (1988) suggests some additional positive ways of providing effective feedback. These include acknowledging the need for feedback, giving both positive and negative feedback, and understanding the context in which feedback is given. To provide constructive feedback, don't use labels, don't exaggerate, don't be judgmental, and speak only for yourself. Think ahead of time about what you want to say and plan out carefully how you will phrase it sensitively.

Understand the context. An important characteristic of feedback is that it is always in a context. You never simply walk up to a person, deliver a feedback statement, and then leave. Before you give feedback, review the actions and decisions that led to that moment. Determine if the moment is right. You must consider more than your own need to give feedback. Constructive feedback can happen only within a context of listening to and caring about the person. Do not give feedback when you don't know much about the circumstances of the behavior or will not be around long enough to follow up on your feedback. "Hit and run" feedback is not fair.

Don't use labels. Describe the behavior. Be clear, specific and unambiguous. Calling someone a "Fascist"; a "Male Chauvinist Pig!"; or an "Unthinking Politically Correct Clone" are labels that are likely to be taken as insults rather than as legitimate feedback.

Be careful not to exaggerate. Be exact. An exaggeration will invite an argument from the feedback receiver rather than dealing with the real issue. Saying "You're always late for meetings" invites a defensive response of "Well, not always," or "I'm not usually very late," rather than a thoughtful one.

Don't be judgmental. Evaluative words like "good," "bad," and "should" make implicit judgments that make the content of the feedback difficult to hear.

Guidelines for Providing Effective Group Feedback

1. Effective feedback should describe our interpretation of the other person's message. The focus should be on what we think we heard, rather than on our perception of the quality of their statements. "That's stupid" is clearly a poorly phrased feedback statement. Feedback should be descriptive, not evaluative.
2. Effective feedback should be designed to clarify the process. The feedback should be understood by both parties and, if possible, the rest of the group.
3. Effective feedback should take into account the needs of the group, not just our own feelings. Is providing feedback useful to the group purpose?
4. Effective feedback should be directed toward helping to move the group process along. Simply making judgments rarely helps the group. The feedback should be constructive for everyone, not a show of one-upmanship.
5. Effective feedback should be well timed. We should distinguish what is better left unsaid, or said later in private, from what is relevant and timely now but will be irrelevant or unproductive if said later. Group work is a process and "when it's over, it's over." Timing is important, and some issues cannot or should not be revisited.
6. Effective feedback should not be stored up so it can be "dumped" later. Sandbagging, or waiting until we can score, will subvert the group process.
7. Effective feedback should be tentative. Regardless of how astute we are as listeners, we cannot know for certain what others really mean or why they act as they do. We can practice introducing our responses with tentative phrases like, "It seems to me . . ."
8. Effective feedback should be honest. Manipulative or political actions in a group label us as the problem, not the person toward whom we have directed our attack.

Receiving Feedback

When you are receiving feedback, the first thing to do is to breathe. Receiving feedback is stressful, and our bodies react by getting tense. Taking slow, full, deep breaths helps our body relax and allows our brain to maintain greater alertness. Listen carefully. Don't interrupt. Don't discourage the feedback-giver. Ask questions for clarity or for specific examples. Acknowledge the feedback. Paraphrase the message in your own words to let the person know you heard and understood what was said. Acknowledge the valid points and agree with what is true. Acknowledge the other person's point of view and try to understand his or her reaction. Then take time to sort out what you have heard.

There may be a time when you receive feedback from someone who does not know feedback guidelines. In these cases, help your critic refashion the criticism so that it conforms to the rules for constructive feedback.

Summary

Listening and feedback are vital group communication skills. We are not naturally proficient at either of these. Hearing and listening are not the same thing. To learn to listen, we must understand the process.

There are four components to listening: sensing, which involves understanding the roles of selective attention, external and internal noise, and short- and long-term memory; interpreting, which means assigning specific meaning to what we paid attention to; evaluating, which involves placing importance on certain issues; and responding, which involves providing feedback.

Active listening involves becoming part of the communication transaction and taking responsibility for understanding the speakers' intentions. It means learning to overcome the barriers to effective listening to which many of us are subject and responding appropriately to what is being said. Small groups are most effective and produce the best results when members listen and respond with care to each other's input.

DISCUSSION QUESTIONS

1. In what ways is listening important to effective group and team communication?

2. What's in it for you or your group and team members to be good listeners? Can you add some additional items beyond the ones discussed in your text?

3. Explain selective attention. Why do we engage in selective attention?

4. In your small group and team communication class, what are some examples of internal and external noise?

5. Think of a recent situation in which you found listening difficult. Which one (or more) of the four phases presented the most difficulty for you? Why? How could this have been overcome?

6. How can paraphrasing be used for effective listening? Provide three specific examples.

7. How can expressing understanding, asking questions, and nonverbal communication be used for effective listening? Provide an example for each concept.

8. What are the guidelines for giving feedback?

9. How can you give positive feedback?

10. When you receive feedback, what are the important concepts to remember?

EXERCISES

1. Listening riddles; 2. Listening and understanding; 3. Group and team members feedback form; 4. The nondebate

1. LISTENING RIDDLES

Answer the following questions. If you do not know the answer, take your best guess.

1. Is there any federal law against a man marrying his widow's sister?
2. Do they have a Fourth of July in England?
3. If you had only one match and entered a cold room that had a kerosene lamp, an oil heater, and a wood stove, which would you light first for maximum heat?
4. How many animals of each species did Moses take aboard the Ark with him during the great flood?
5. The Yankees and the Tigers play five baseball games. They each win three games. No ties or disputed games are involved. How is this possible?
6. How many birthdays does the average person have?
7. According to International Law, if an airplane should crash on the exact border between two countries, would unidentified survivors be buried in the country they were traveling to, or the country they were traveling from?
8. An archeologist claims to have dug up a coin that is clearly dated 46 BC. Why is the archeologist a liar?
9. You build an ordinary house with four sides, except that each side has a southern exposure. A bear walks by the house. What color is the bear?

Compare your answer with those of someone else or in a small group.*

While you read these statements, what do they tell us about the difficulties in listening? Return to the discussion in this chapter of "Barriers to Active Listening." Why did you miss the answer? What lessons about listening can you develop from this exercise? Are you tempted to dismiss it as a "gimmick"? If others were able to answer the questions correctly, what strategies did they employ? What does this tell us about empathetic listening?

Your instructor will provide the correct answers.

2. LISTENING AND UNDERSTANDING

1. Spell out two words from these letters: OODRWWTS.
2. Identify the letter of the alphabet that logically follows this sequence of seven letters: OTTFFSS
3. Print the word "Xerox" in the blank spaces. ___ ___ ___ ___ ___
4. How do you spell silk? Say it out loud. S－－－－. What do cows drink? _____

Procedure
     Once you have answers to these four questions, compare them with those of another class member or a group. Your instructor will provide the correct answers after you have discussed them.
Processing the Exercise
     Why did you have difficulty with answering these questions? Return to the text's discussion of listening and apply the appropriate concepts. What can you do to prevent these types of listening errors?

3. GROUP AND TEAM MEMBERS FEEDBACK FORM

Directions
     Learning to give and receive feedback is an essential skill as we work to become more effective group and team members. Feedback from the other members allows us to recognize our contributions and work on areas in need of improvement. Your own and your group's success depend on the success of the other team members. Address one sheet to each member of your group or team.

Message from: **To:**

     It would be more comfortable and beneficial for me if you would...
     It would also be beneficial to me for you to follow up with me if my comments need clarification. That way, I can continue to learn how to provide useful feedback.

BE SPECIFIC AND FOCUS ON BEHAVIORS THAT CAN BE CHANGED, NOT ATTITUDES.

1. Continue acting in the following ways and doing the following things:

2. Do the following things more:

3. Reduce or discontinue acting in the following ways or doing the following things:

4. Start doing these things:

Feedback Form for the Feedback Recipient

Respond to the following questions.

1. Was the feedback from the other group/team members consistent with your own views regarding your performance and actions?

2. What changes can you make to respond to these comments? Check the materials you have already read in the text concerning roles and communication.

3. Was it difficult for you to provide feedback to others? Why? How can this process be made easier?

4. Did others disagree with your assessments? How did you respond?

5. Since groups are living systems, does the importance of communicating with other group members regarding their actions seem like a useful tool? Why, or why not?

4. THE NONDEBATE

Pick a controversial topic about which members of a group disagree. A debate around the pros and cons of "the death penalty" works well for this exercise. The "right to life"/"right to choose" issue is also a good (although potentially volatile) discussion starter. Other issues can also be used. Have group members initially state their personal opinions in writing and then divide the group by their opinions on the topic. If the division is too uneven, ask some members to take the opposite point of view. Each side has approximately ten minutes to develop their main points, arguments, and supports. At the end of that time, one side presents its case. The other side must listen carefully, take notes, and at the end must paraphrase that argument to the satisfaction of the first group and any independent observers. The first group listens quietly and carefully to this paraphrasing of their position, then at the end provides feedback on completeness of the verbal content, and on the nonverbal tone, as well as facial and body language, with which it was presented. Then the process is repeated, with the second group presenting their position and the first group paraphrasing it and receiving feedback.

REFERENCES

Alessandra, T., & Hunsaker, P. (1993). *Communicating at work.* New York: Simon & Schuster.

Asherman, I., & Asherman, S. (1990). *The negotiation sourcebook.* Amherst, MA: Human Resource Development Press.

Bone, D. (1988). *The business of listening.* Los Altos, CA: Crisp.

Covey, S. R. (1989). *The seven habits of highly effective people.* New York: Simon & Schuster.

Furmanek, B., & Palumbo, R. (1991). *Abbott and Costello in Hollywood.* New York: Putnam.

Golen, S. (1990). A factor analysis of barriers to effective listening. *The journal of business communication, 27,* 25–36.

Johnson, D. (1996). Helpful listening and responding. In K. M. Galvin & P. J. Cooper (Eds.), *Making connections: Readings in relational communication.* Roxbury, MA: Roxbury Publishing Company.

McIntyre, R. M., & Salas, E. (1995). Measuring and managing for team performance: Emerging principles from complex environments. In R. A. Gauzzo, E. Salas, & Associates (Eds.), *Team effectiveness and decision making in organizations.* San Francisco: Jossey-Bass.

Nyquist, M. (1996). Learning to listen. In K. M. Galvin & P. J. Cooper (Eds.), *Making connections: Readings in relational communication.* Roxbury, MA: Roxbury Publishing Company.

Pearson, J. C., & Davilla, R. A. (1993). The gender construct. In L. P. Aaliss & D. J. Borisoff (Eds.), *Women & men communicating: Challenges and changes.* Orlando, FL: Harcourt Brace Jovanovich.

Peters, T. (1987). *Thriving on chaos.* New York: Knopf.

Ray, R. G. (1999). *The facilitative leader.* Upper Saddle River, NJ: Prentice-Hall.

Sashkin, M. & Kiser, K. J. (1993). *Putting total quality management to work.* San Francisco: Berrett-Koehler.

Scholtes, P. R. (1988). *The team handbook.* Madison, WI: Joiner Associates.

Stewart, J., & Thomas, M. (1990). Dialogic listening: Sculpting mutual meanings. In J. Stewart (Ed.), *Bridges not walls* (5th ed., pp. 192–210). New York: McGraw-Hill.

Sweeney, P. D., & McFarlin, D. B. (2002). *Organizational behavior: Solutions for management.* Boston: McGraw-Hill Irwin.

Wheelan, S. A. (1999). *Creating effective teams.* Thousand Oaks, CA: Sage.

Wolvin, A. D., & Coakley, C. G. (1985). *Listening* (2nd ed.). Dubuque, IA: Brown.

Zemke, R., & Schaaf, D. (1989). *The service edge.* New York: New American Library.

8

Group Evolution: Teams

CHAPTER OUTLINE

The Scope of Employee Involvement Programs

Teams
    Quality Circles
    Self-Managing Work Teams

Summary
Discussion Questions
Exercises
References

CHAPTER OBJECTIVES

- Explain employee involvement as a part of team development.
- Understand the scope of employee involvement.
- Define teams.
- Discuss the importance of teams.
- Distinguish the characteristics of parallel structures.
- Identify the structure and role of quality circles.
- Explain the three limitations to quality circles.
- Outline the characteristics of self-managing work teams.
- Discuss the benefits and costs of self-managing work teams.

KEY TERMS

Cross-disciplinary teams
Employee involvement
Group evolution
Individual rewards
Leading
Managing

Not invented here
Organizational development
Parallel structures
Power
Problem-solving groups
Quality circles

Segmentalism
Self-directed teams
Self-managing teams
Semiautonomous work units
Team facilitator role
Teams

Every so often a Celtic game would heat up so that it became more than a physical or even mental game and would be magical. The feeling is difficult to describe, and I certainly never talked about it when I was playing. When it happened I could feel my play rise to a new level . . . It would surround not only me and the other Celtics but also the players on the other team, and even the referees. . . . The game would be in the white heat of competition, and yet I wouldn't feel competitive . . . The game would move so fast that every fake, cut, and pass would be surprising, and yet nothing could surprise me. It was almost as if we were playing in slow motion. During those spells, I could almost sense how the next play would develop and where the next shot would be taken. (Bill Russell, as quoted in *The Fifth Discipline*, Senge, 1990, p. 235)

Senge, Kleiner, Roberts, Ross, and Smith (1994) trace the origin of the word *team* back to the Indo-European word *deuk,* which means "to pull." They argue, therefore, that the essence of the word team means "to pull together" and that the modern sense of the team emerged in the sixteenth century, meaning a group of people pulling and acting together. From these origins they define a team to be "any group of people who need each other to accomplish a result" (Senge, Kleiner, Roberts, Ross, & Smith, 1994, p. 354).

When the interests and expectations of the individuals in a small group come into alignment so that there is a consensus on purpose, task, and how to get things done, a feeling and experience of synergy develop that go beyond the efforts of the individual members, or even the group as a whole, to a new level of creativity and task accomplishment. While sports might provide an obvious example of teamwork, "in high pressure workplaces, such as nuclear plants, aircraft cockpits, or the military, teamwork is essential to survive" (Appleby & Davis, 2001, p. B2). An equally stressful environment, health care organizations, "increasingly rely on interdisciplinary teams for comprehensive diagnosis and treatment of patients" (Ellingson, 2003, p. 93). Fast paced sports or stressful environments offer dramatic examples of the importance of teamwork. However, as we observed earlier in this book, the majority of U.S. corporations use teams which have provided significant gains in productivity, effectiveness, and employee satisfaction with their jobs (Shockley-Zalabak, 2002).

Small groups increase involvement and commitment on the part of active participants. Groups can make better decisions than individuals and provide a forum for creative solutions. However, traditional group discussion approaches and meetings do not take full advantage of the power of small groups (Peters, 1992). This chapter will explain the move by organizations toward the use of self-managing work teams and the emergence of groups as teams. Successful organizations now rely on teams to achieve improved quality, greater creativity, and increased employee involvement (Deetz, Tracy, & Simpson, 2000; Dumaine, 1993). The principles of involvement through teamwork have also been applied to voluntary organizations, ranging from school committees to community groups, as well as to traditional corporations and small businesses (Morrison, 1994). Throughout our professional careers, we take part in large numbers of committees and teams. Increasing our involvement in an effort to solve problems is a fundamental purpose of these activities. While we will concentrate on examples and information derived from organizations, the importance of involvement, teams, and self-management applies to all types of groups.

The Scope of Employee Involvement Programs

Employee involvement programs, which frequently involve small group activity, are efforts that include employees in the information-gathering, decision-making, and implementation stages of problem solving (Moorehead & Griffin, 1998). Actively involving employees in an organization is a vital component in any developmental effort (Murrell & Meredith, 2000). Employee involvement programs enlist various degrees of participation in the management process, ranging from making suggestions to semiautonomous work units. In the view of many analysts, employee involvement is the way to manage in the new century (Boyett & Boyett, 1998). Because they influence efficiency, quality, and morale, employee involvement programs provide an important method for making companies more competitive (Murrell & Meredith, 2000; Truell, 1991). Innovation is tied directly to the use of effective communication through these programs (Kouzes & Posner, 1990; McShane & Von Glinow, 2000). Employee involvement in the initiation of ideas creates understanding, shared vision, buy-in to group and team goals, and a collaboratively developed strategy (Lewis, 1998).

Employee involvement programs already exist in the majority of organizations (Greenwald, 1992). The Center for Effective Organizations at the University of Southern California found that 68% of the Fortune 1,000 companies used self-managed or high-performance teams, which represent the highest form of employee involvement (Dumaine, 1993).

The General Accounting Office (1989) categorized employee involvement programs ranging from suggestion systems, which have the lowest amount of active employee participation, to self-autonomous work units. There are dramatic examples of successful teamwork in organizations (for example, Corning, Motorola, Xerox, GE, A. O. Smith, Boeing, Kodak, Cummings, Polaroid, Ford, Federal Express, and Procter & Gamble). Table 8.1 shows the transition from group involvement to teams to self-directed units. Over 70% of all U.S. firms have teams and their popularity is rising ("Teams," 1995; "Trying," 1994). The Texas Center for Productivity and Quality of Work Life's study of teams "shows the clear financial effect of the team approach in dozens of organizations" (Manz & Sims, 1993, p. 189). We need to remember that with teams, one size does not fit all. For example, Texas Instruments (TI) uses teams extensively, but only 5% of its employees are in self-directed teams. The remaining 95% are included, as needed, on

TABLE 8.1   From Involvement to Self-Direction

Traditional Group Involvement

Group/team leader/manager
Sets agenda
Directs problem solution
Establishes limits and uses rules
Controls disruptive behaviors
Task focus over member focus

To Teams

Leader facilitates meetings
All members contribute to success
Members take responsibility
Everyone helps with agenda
Member's needs recognized
Members control disruptive behaviors

To Self-Directed

Everyone shares leadership
Members set guidelines for success
Working procedures decided by team
Meetings owned by members
Members are accountable

project teams that can last as little as two weeks. Their strategy has "improved annual revenue per employee from $142,000 to $227,000 in two years" (Neuborne, 1997, p. 2B).

Teams

Teams are ongoing, coordinated groups of individuals working together, even when they are not in constant contact. These groups can include special task forces, intact work groups, new work units, or people from various parts of an organization who must work together to achieve a common goal (McShane & Von Glinow, 2000). Teams differ substantially from many small groups, because the teams themselves, rather than the leader, control the group process. Although many group communication textbooks recognize the value of sharing the leadership role among group members in many situations, the means for reducing the power and influence inherent in the role of an individual manager are not always as clear.

The importance of teams and teamwork is obvious to anyone working with organizations (McShane & Von Glinow, 2000). Examples of the power of teamwork to assist in transforming organizations are provided in practically any discussion of organizational renewal and change (Boyett & Boyett, 2000; Wellins, Byham, & Wilson, 1991). When team members are actively involved in the initiation of ideas and procedures, there is a marked increase in understanding, shared vision, collaborative team strategy, and buy-in to the final plan (Lewis, 1998). Team building represents the most widely used form of organizational development, because it offers a systematic method for improving the interpersonal and task aspects of regular work groups (Sweeney & McFarlin, 2002). Table 8.2 shows the evolution of teams.

For our purposes, teams are divided into groups seeking solutions to particular problems (e.g., task forces, specialized work groups, quality circles), and the semiautonomous, self-directed, or self-managing work teams. Although both approaches represent important attempts to involve employees in the problem identification and solution processes, the self-managing work team encompasses participative management. As such, self-managing work teams are becoming an even more potent means for organizational development, transformation, and renewal. We will cover the following approaches to teams: (1) quality circles, and how they represent the successes and limitations of parallel problem-solving groups, and (2) self-managing teams, with discussions of participative management and the barriers to building such programs.

TABLE 8.2   The Evolution toward Self-Directed Teams

Underdeveloped Group	*To*	*Traditional Teamwork*	*To*	*Self-Directed Team*
Stage 1	**Stage 2**	**Stage 3**		**Stage 4**
Unempowered	Somewhat unempowered	Somewhat empowered		Empowered
Members do as told	Team/group somewhat parallel	Team parallel		Team independent
Members execute leader's directions	Members react, request make suggestions	Members participate in directing		Members take responsibility for process
High leader control, plan, direct	Less leader control, coach, counsel, open communication	More participant control, critical thinking, involve team members		Control planning, leader teaches other to lead themselves
Traditional Groups	*To*	*Enlightened Leadership*	*To*	*Super Leadership*

The Human Resources team at American Cast Iron Pipe Company (ACIPCO). ACIPCO has been selected for Fortune Magazine's "100 Best Companies to Work for" for the last seven years.

Photo Courtesy of American Cast Iron Pipe Company

Quality Circles

Quality circles are one of the best-known parallel approaches. Although there are a variety of definitions for quality circles, "in essence, such circles are voluntary groups of employees who work on similar tasks or share some area of responsibility, and who agree to meet on a regular basis to discuss—and perhaps solve—key problems related to their work" (Baron, 1983, p. 558). These small teams of employees usually meet once a week to analyze work-related problems and to propose solutions to them. Typically, a quality circle has little or no authority to spend organizational resources and has no direct control over the acceptance or implementation of the quality circle's solution. Most quality circles are limited to making an analysis and providing recommendations for improvement to management.

Pushed by the Japanese success in the early 1980s, American businesses rushed to adopt quality circle approaches, with 80% of the Fortune 500 companies having some type of quality circle and 44 percent of all companies with more than 500 employees using quality circles (Lawler & Mohrman, 1985). There are numerous documented examples of quality circle successes (Johns, 1988), especially with specific quality issues and for employee morale building (Baron, 1983). A sample of the Fortune 1,000 companies indicated that 68% of the companies had some form of quality circle (Marks, 1986). These companies reported a 69% success in productivity improvement and a 72% success in quality improvement (*Employee Involvement in America*, 1989).

However, "in more than 60% of the American organizations in which they have been tried" (Marks, 1986, p. 38), quality circles failed. Many organizations abandoned their quality circle program within a year (DuBrin, Ireland, & Williams, 1989). Some experts argue that the problem is not in the patient, but in the prescription. Too often, quality circles were used as an attempt at quick fixes for serious problems. The natural tendency to resist change, the lack of incentive for managers to actually listen to employees, and inadequate training of both managers and employees led to these failures (Karp, 1983; Marks, 1986).

Inherent Limitations to Quality Circles.   There are numerous reasons for the failure of quality circles and other team-building programs. At various times, union objections, time away from the job by employees, unrealistic expectations, threat of change, and inadequate training have led to their failure (Gutknecht & Miller, 1986).

Three very specific problems confronted in most quality circle efforts are the tendency of providing individual rewards, inappropriate management styles, and segmentalism (Kanter, 1983). Because these barriers can be overcome by self-managing work teams, they warrant further analysis.

Individual Rewards.   First, the reliance on individual rewards is counterproductive to team building ("Work Incentives," 1994). One of the vital components in effective organizational change is teamwork (Anderson & Anderson, 2001). The tendency of American organizations to reward individual performance is a major stumbling block in team building efforts (French, Bell, & Zawacki, 2000). The outcome of this can be conflict within a team over perceived scarce resources. In education, we have the well known competition for grades which provides a clear example of individual rewards. The measurements used by organizations to gauge individual success provide one of the major reasons for choosing personal recognition and glory over positive team-building behavior. For American corporations, success often is based on short-term criteria such as a department's bottom-line profit. In our school systems, we have the same tendency to respond to one semester's work rather than the total learning accomplished. Thus, there is little incentive to build a group into a team for a course that ends in four months. In fact, our background and training rarely teaches us how to work for team goals. If you have had extensive team training in athletics or interscholastic events (such as debate), you might feel that this has prepared you for teamwork in an organization. There are differences, however, between an athletic team where the goals are fairly clear (win) and an organization attempting to solve a significant problem (Bolman & Deal, 1991). In addition, the rules are clearer in competition (such as time available, referees), roles are assigned (such as quarterback, second affirmative speaker), and the time span (season) is laid out.

In addition, because effective team building requires a relatively long time frame, there is a natural inclination to circumvent the group process in order to achieve the short-term rewards. Organizations reinforce this perspective by focusing on market leadership, strong profits, and high stock prices rather than developing team concepts based on strong cultural affiliation. Many corporate bureaucracies have established counterproductive norms of good management behavior (defined as behavior leading to advancement and job security), which include ignoring the long term, avoiding responsibility, concentrating on appearances rather than reality, hypocrisy, and slavish acceptance of current dogma (Gabriel, Fineman, & Sims, 2000).

Inappropriate Management Styles.   Second, many managers and supervisors are ill equipped to encourage team building. This is true for two reasons. They fear a loss of power, and they are more comfortable managing from their position than leading a team.

Loss of Power. Often, managers and supervisors view employee involvement in the decision-making process as a threat to their own power and authority (McShane & Von Glinow, 2000). This perceived loss of power has led first-line supervisors to resist quality circle and team efforts.

Managing versus Leading. Underscoring the difference between managing and leading has become a very popular means for focusing on productive and counterproductive behaviors (Harris, 2002). Managing is required to plan, budget, organize, and control. Someone, for example, must schedule the group meetings, set the agenda, and perform other such mundane duties. Overreliance on these managerial tools, however, tends to sabotage employee involvement and quality circle programs. A well-intentioned manager might design an agenda that excludes important information, topics, or input. Too little time might be allocated for a full discussion of the issues. As we discovered earlier, both agendas and time allocation are important issues, but they can be imposed to limit the group's synergy or success.

Leading involves developing strong subordinates and group members (Kotter, 1990). Although the leader bears the responsibility for implementing effective team building concepts, overreliance on the leader for heroic attempts at motivating and developing individuals is counterproductive (McShane & Von Glinow, 2000). Leaders need to empower teams by strengthening the teams' control throughout the decision-making process (Conger, 1989).

Autocratic management and heroic leadership can be significant impediments in the team process. If team-building efforts are successful, supervisors and managers will assume entirely different roles from their traditional ones. Instead of being the boss, reward dispenser, and coordinator, managers and supervisors become liaisons, linking pins, and facilitators. Power has thus shifted through the empowerment process, and leading—rather than managing—becomes the expected behavior. Without proper training, managers and supervisors will conduct business as usual, rather than deal with the uncertainties inherent in employee involvement through teams.

The most important behaviors for managers and supervisors as team facilitators are to encourage the following: open communication; team problem solving; two-way interaction team decision making; self-management; cross-training and performance monitoring; listening, sharing information, giving verbal and written feedback, and attending to nonverbal clues; working through conflicts and developing a climate of teamwork; and continuously learning, while tolerating ambiguity and uncertainty (Burress & McElhenie, 1992). Two conclusions are clear from this list. First, few individuals can accomplish all of these behaviors, so shared leadership within the group is important. Second, some training in group process is critical for successful group leadership. Unfortunately, too few managers and supervisors have learned the basics of effective facilitation.

Segmentalism.   Segmentalism is the tendency of separate units within the same organization to be indifferent to the success of other units—or actually to be competing with those other units. As an organization works toward change, segmentalism prevents effective team building. According to Egan (1988, p. 146), "Isolationism and empire building instead of system enhancing integration of the subunits of a corporation or institution constitute one of the main forms of corporate irrationality." Universities provide an excellent example with their "untouchable departmental system" (Egan, 1989, p. 273). Groups isolate and tend to take on problems that are particular to their own areas of interest. Therefore, they are limited in their abilities to respond to problems that are not "theirs." So prevalent is this issue that it is labeled the NIH factor (not invented here). NIH prevents collaboration in at least two ways. First, inherent in NIH is that the idea cannot be very good because it was created somewhere else. Apple Computer became so ingrained in the NIH syndrome that, during the 1990 corporate reorganization process, Chief Operating Officer Spindler decreed that NIH would no longer be tolerated (Buell, Levine, & Gross, 1990). His reasoning was simple—Apple's arrogance was decreasing productivity and marketing effectiveness. Second, the groups who were asked to produce or sell the product did not understand or identify with it. In the extreme, the process of developing a product in engineering and handing it over to production is called the "over the wall" syndrome where one department of an organization completes a part the job and then just hands over that part to someone else. So, it goes "over the wall" with no collaboration or coordination. Needless to say, the unit receiving the partially completed work is unlikely to fully understand why the job looks like it does. In the past, building small empires in individual departments or units, guarding turf against any intrusions, and maintaining control have proven to be powerful deterrents to effective team building (Kanter, 1983; Sweeney & McFarlin, 2002).

Self-Managing Work Teams

These inherent limitations to many parallel problem-solving and team efforts underscore the differences between parallel problem-solving groups, as exemplified by quality circles, and self-managing work teams. In almost all cases, team development efforts such as quality circles do provide a useful initial step in the self-managing work team process (McShane & Von Glinow, 2000).

The Differences That Characterize a Self-Managing Work Team.   What differentiates the parallel structure approach to problem-solving teams and the self-managing approach are the powers vested in the two types of problem-solving groups. Parallel problem-solving groups maintain the traditional reporting structure and do not provide for control of resources. Contrast that to self-managing teams where there is team management of the problems involved in completing the work. Recall that parallel groups are limited in their chances for success because of individual rewards, a restrictive management style and perception of employees' abilities, and segmentalism.

So, what is so different about self-managing teams? First, self-managing teams are self-regulating. This independence from outside authority represents a significant movement from small problem-solving groups to a more participative management system (Torres & Spiegel, 1990). After sufficient training and experience, self-managing work team members operate together as one to complete a total job. As teams develop, they increase the group's knowledge and understanding and gradually take shared responsibility for planning, organizing, decision making, controlling, scheduling, and goal setting. The group leads itself. Self-managing work teams work toward regulated, continuous improvement in the performance of their work units. When they are introduced carefully into subunits of organizations, self-managing work teams have a remarkable record of achievement in a variety of organizational settings.

This record can be measured in the six performance areas of increased productivity, improved quality, reduced turnover, reduced absenteeism, increased innovation, and cost savings from 30 percent to 70% (Boyett & Boyett, 1998). Kodak high-performance teams, for example, "improved productivity so much at one plant that the work of three shifts could be completed in one" (Boyett & Boyett, 1998, p. 139). At Motorola, teams improved quality by 50 percent and reduced late deliveries by 70 percent. Federal Express was able to reduce the number of lost packages and billing errors by 13 percent in one year. Diamond Packaging Services Division, a family-owned business, used teams to win the 1998 RIT/USA TODAY quality cup for small business. Teams were able to reduce customer complaints by 25 percent, increase profits by 350 percent from 1996–1997, and substantially increase employee earnings (Choquette, 1998).

The power of shared responsibility is impressive. Allowing group members to become part of the solution by assuming a variety of roles leads to better solutions to problems and a stronger commitment to implementing those solutions.

Remember, self-managing work teams represent a structural and procedural change in traditional organizational operations (Torres & Spiegel, 1990). Rather than operate as a parallel structure, the problem-solving group becomes a fundamental work unit. The group becomes a team of individuals, working together as one to complete a total job. With experience and training yielding knowledge and understanding, these individuals gradually take shared responsibility for planning, organizing, decision making, controlling, scheduling, goal setting, and in general, regulating continuous improvement in the performance of their work unit. In the past, for example, a typical employee response to a production problem in a traditional organization would be to sit down and wait for a foreperson or manager to solve the problem. In self-managing work teams, employees take on the responsibility of solving problems themselves. They do so because their knowledge, involvement, power, and responsibilities are expanded. In sum, a team is more than just a group. Although problem-solving groups are important, a team shares common boundaries, interdependent tasks, articulated purpose, and well-understood, personally owned goals. Perhaps most important self-managing work teams seem to overcome the three barriers faced by many problem-solving groups.

Overcoming the Barriers to Self-Managing Team Building.   First, self-managing work teams help overcome the impact of *individualized rewards* because self-managing work teams are designed to create member interaction and interdependence. In the examples cited earlier regarding the effectiveness of self-managing work teams, employees are also better paid, because they are rewarded on a team success basis (Boyett & Boyett, 1998; Choquette, 1998). Rather than viewing colleagues as competitors, individuals have powerful incentives for working together to maximize success. In addition, self-managing work teams provide for a group identification and increased job satisfaction (Dalziel & Schoonover, 1988). Task excellence is achieved because employees identify with the issues and the solutions. Being part of the solution, individuals feel a greater incentive and obligation to guarantee successful implementation.

Second, the *role of managers and supervisors is dramatically different* in the self-managing work team. In traditional organizations, leadership is based on the manager's having the decision-making power, the information, the responsibility for distributing rewards, and in many cases, the expertise. The result is that the manager tells people what to do and becomes an administrator, rather than a leader. Shared responsibility and control take the place of the traditional manager's carrying the responsibilities and burdens of managing performance alone. The primary roles for the manager are those of facilitator and coach. The self-managing work team leader constantly asks: "How can each problem be solved in a way that further develops the team's commitment and capabilities?" These team leaders learn to empower others, move decisions to the proper levels, provide a vision and communicate it, and build trust and openness.

Third, self-managing work teams *overcome segmentalism*. Subordinates' and managers' perspectives are broadened beyond a narrow concern for a specialized area. Instead, team members identify with the problems associated with the overriding issues of productivity and quality. In addition, learning to solve problems as they develop makes each team member increasingly better qualified to solve future problems.

After reviewing various studies, Boyett and Boyett (1998) and Olsavsky (1990) drew several conclusions about the benefits and costs of self-managed work teams. Although self-managing work teams are touted as solutions to a wide variety of organizational issues, seven specific benefits consistently occur. The benefits of self-managing work teams are (a) improvement in work methods and procedures; (b) gains in attraction and retention of employees; (c) increases in staffing flexibility; (d) increases in service and product quality; (e) improvements in output; (f) enhanced quality of decision making; and (g) reductions in supervision and staff support.

These factors lead to better productivity. Teams set the production goals, which tend to be higher. Feedback is employed effectively to improve performance. Cross-training enhances the ability of team members to help out and replace each other. The cost of labor is reduced 20% to 40%, in many cases. There are, however, drawbacks to these team approaches. If self-managing work team programs are to be implemented successfully, costs and pitfalls must be considered carefully. There are at least five costs occurring in many self-managed work team programs: (a) increased training costs, including the use of staff or outside consultants to facilitate the implementation; (b) unmet expectations for organizational change; (c) conflicts between participants and nonparticipants, occurring if only a few teams are formed; (d) time lost in team meetings and a slower decision-making process; and (e) resistance to the change by some staff-support groups.

In addition, there are seven possible pitfalls, which include: (a) insufficient training or training that is too late for the teams; (b) management that is too impatient for results; (c) failure to acknowledge that people will test the system; (d) trying to implement when the technology for a particular change is insufficiently known; (e) inadequate time allowed for the experience to gel before it is evaluated; (f) inappropriate boundaries chosen for team membership or responsibilities; and (g) a corporate culture that is radically counter to the self-managing team philosophy.

Thus, self-managing work teams require a substantial investment in time, forethought, and commitment to be successful. Implementation can be difficult, but the successes of self-managing work teams make this approach to organizational transformation exciting and important.

Under the very best of circumstances, change is difficult. In the attempt to redefine employment relations, identifying and pursuing common interests seems to be a vital component. The learning process, which requires management and employees alike to reconsider many underlying—and often incorrect—assumptions, might be the most important outcome of any self-managing work team process.

Summary

We have discussed three issues. First, the importance of considering means for increasing employee involvement through the use of groups. Second, the role of problem-solving groups as parallel organizational structures, such as quality circles, was presented, and the successes and the three inherent limitations to the use of these groups offer insights into the use of such teams. Third, given these limitations, we examined groups and teams that utilized shared power and responsibility. Our summary of the successes of self-managing work teams points to one viable alternative to traditional group structure. Because self-managing work teams are a significant structural and psychological change, the basic concepts behind the self-managing work team were outlined.

Too often, organizations have rewarded values such as, "If it ain't broke, don't fix it." By passing managerial power to self-managing work teams, new values can be encouraged, such as "Do your job well and find ways to constantly improve it!" Constant innovation and quality improvement are ends sought by most organizations.

The goal is to create group and work environments where power, knowledge, information, and rewards are shared. By assuming more responsibility, group members become self-managing through their work teams. Although implementation is difficult, the rewards can be remarkable for the organization and its members.

DISCUSSION QUESTIONS

1. What is an example of an employee involvement program? Why would employee involvement be beneficial to an organization?

2. What is the difference between groups and teams?

3. Define a parallel team structure. Will these types of teams be limited in their effectiveness in organizations? Why or why not?

4. What are the inherent limitations for quality circles?

5. Define a self-managing work team. How do self-managing teams overcome the limitations inherent in quality circles?

6. What are some of the pitfalls for self-managing teams? Why should these be considered before adopting this process?

EXERCISES

1. Teams—Developing feedback to work toward self-direction; 2. The research team; 3. Who's in charge?; 4. Differentiating past team experiences and organizational teams

1. TEAMS—DEVELOPING FEEDBACK TO WORK TOWARD SELF-DIRECTION

Underpinning the concept of self-direction is the ability to help other team members through feedback. Answer the following questions about your team. Share your responses with the other team members and discuss any improvements that can be made.

1. What's going well on this team?
2. What are the areas of concern?

3. What skills would make the team more effective?
4. What type of support needs to be provided to the team members from other team members?
5. What are my positive team behaviors?
6. What will the other team members say are my positive team behaviors?

2. THE RESEARCH TEAM

1. Teams are characterized by members who engage in complementary and interdependent roles. These roles can be taken on or assigned. One way to form groups is to ask individuals to rank-order the roles according to their individual preferences or abilities, then form groups with the best combination of roles available. Five identifiable useful roles for members of groups are:

   A. Researcher: An individual with the ability, experience, and desire to work individually and coordinate the efforts of other group members in library research, interview with expert sources, and survey as necessary for the group projects. The ability to accomplish tasks, pay attention to details, and coordinate the efforts of others is important for this role.

   B. Materials Organizer: An organized responsible person, able to collect, collate, and compile documents. Some facility with a word processor is helpful. Organizing, summarizing, and acting as a repository for collected group documents and products are important skills.

   C. Technical Support Person: A person having some facility with or willingness to learn about the use of technical equipment—such as overhead projectors, camcorders, VCRs, film projectors, and/or computer multimedia, desktop publishing, and presentational graphics equipment useful in putting together exciting and informative group presentations. A willingness to locate and develop skills using some type of equipment to enhance the group's project is also important.

   D. Process Recorder: A person observant and sensitive to group process and task. The ability to hear and record the group's sentiments, positions, discussions, decisions, and agreed-upon responsibilities. An interpersonal sensitivity in reflecting and evaluating the group's process and progress is an essential skill. Note taking and word processing skills are also helpful to this role.

   E. Facilitator: A discussion organizer and idea stimulator. A person with an involving, democratic style, good listening skills, and an ability to summarize group decisions. Primary responsibility is to develop meeting agendas, suggest topics to be discussed next, and organize meeting times. Must be a good listener, able to summarize members' main points, and able to stay calm and mediate the group's discussions.

2. A second way is to ask all participants to rank-order a set of skills or competencies that they possess and then form groups having the most comprehensive combination of skills or competencies for the task. The form provides a means of obtaining a rank-ordering of 12 useful skills to research teams.

Skills Selection Form

Select one of the following skills (rank a skill as 1 to indicate your BEST skill).

Rank-order the rest of the skills (2 = next best, 12 = least skillful).

_____ (A) Speaking in public

_____ (B) Facilitating small group meetings, developing agendas

_____ (C) Researching a subject in the library

_____ (D) Conducting surveys or informational interviews

_____ (E) Typing or word processing

_____ (F) Writing clear technical reports

_____ (G) Experience with video equipment

_____ (H) Experience with computer graphics and desktop publishing

_____ (I) Artistic drawing, sketching, painting, creative abilities

_____ (J) Poster board or sign lettering and layout

_____ (K) Using computer presentation software experience

_____ (L) Researching information on the World Wide Web

Claiming a skill does NOT mean you will be solely responsible for it in the group. Groups will divide up tasks once formed.

3. Exercise for the research team: Choose a significant and important topic to research. This topic may be a current local, national, or international social issue (such as local housing conditions, national homelessness, or world famine). Form a group with members taking on specific roles. Divide the tasks of researching the topic by these roles and then make a group presentation of the results of that research. Is the researching task made easier by dividing it along specialized roles? How much specialization of task is appropriate to a team? Does it help to have some overlap in group member roles or does individual responsibility work best? Can a group become a team if their individual roles are highly specialized? What happens if some of the roles are not filled for a particular group or if a role is particularly well done?

3. WHO'S IN CHARGE?

One of the most significant differences between a traditional group discussion and a developing team is the role of leader. At one time, a group leader planned, scheduled, and organized the group meetings and often did the majority of the work. Teams require a better distribution of roles, including the leadership functions. In self-directed teams, all the members share the vast majority of functions. Examine the following list of functions and the traditional roles played in groups and teams. *Speculate* on what would change if you were moving toward a self-directed team. What would be the differences between traditional team and group behaviors and roles and those in a self-directed unit?

Function	Traditional	Speculation—Self-Directed
Leadership	Leader performs special duties. Plans, directs, has oversight. Leader gets special recognition.	
Decision making	Rewards for being finished first, contributions by a few.	
Meeting facilitator	Assigned to the leader.	
Planning	Leader responsible for scheduling, etc.	
Research	Individual assignments.	
Member evaluation	Leader or outside authority.	
Length of membership	Until project completed.	
Other:		
Other:		
Other:		

Discussion

Share with the other teams/groups the speculations your team developed. What are the similarities and differences? What possible hurdles does your team foresee in becoming a self-directed work unit? Would you be willing to undertake these responsibilities?

4. DIFFERENTIATING PAST TEAM EXPERIENCES AND ORGANIZATIONAL TEAMS

Sports provide a large number of examples on how to succeed. Numerous team development experts point to important differences between organized sports and the types of team we are most likely to be a part of in an organization. In your group, develop a list of *differences* between organized sports teams and organizational teams. These differences fall into the specific categories provided. Your group might find additional categories.

Organized Sports Teams	Your Organizational Team
Coach's role	
Team player compensation	
Choosing team players	
Player qualifications	
Rules of play	
Seasons	
Practice/training	
Officials	
Measuring of success	
Opponents	
Other	
Other	

Debriefing

While organized sports offer many important opportunities, we must be very aware that the type of team we will join in an organization is fundamentally different in many important aspects. As a team, develop a set of strategies to compensate for these differences.

REFERENCES

Anderson, L. A., & Anderson, D. (2001). *The change leaders's roadmap: How to navigate your organization's transformation.* San Francisco: Jossey-Bass/Phiffer.

Appleby, J., & Davis, R. (2001, March 1). Teamwork used to be a money saver, now it's a life saver. *USA Today,* pp. 1B–2B.

Baron, R. A. (1983). *Behavior in organizations: Understanding and managing the human side of work.* Boston: Allyn & Bacon.

Boyett, J., & Boyett, J. (1998). *The guru guide.* New York: John Wiley.

Buell, B., Levine, J. B., & Gross, N. (1990, October 15). Apple: New team, new strategy. *Business Week,* p. 88.

Burress, A., & McElhenie, M. (1992, June). Facilitator behaviors. *Self-Managed Work Teams Newsletter, 2,* 4.

Byrne, J. A. (1993, December 20). The horizontal corporation. *Business Week,* pp. 76–81.

Choquette, K. K. (1998, May 1). Team approach wins points with workers. *USA Today,* p. 5B.

Conger, J. A. (1989). Leadership: The art of empowering others. *The Academy of Management Executive, 3,* 17–24.

Dalziel, M. M., & Schoonover, S. C. (1988). *Changing ways: A practical tool for implementing change within organizations.* New York: AMACOM.

Deetz, S. A., Tracy, S. J., & Simpson, J. L. (2000). *Leading organizations through transition.* Thousand Oaks, CA: Sage.

DuBrin, A. J., Ireland, R. D., & Williams, J. C. (1989). *Management & organization.* Cincinnati: South-Western.

Dumaine, B. (1993, December 13). Payoff from the new management. *Fortune,* pp. 103–104, 108, 110.

Egan, G. (1988). *Change agents skills: Assessing & designing excellence.* San Diego: University Associates.

Egan, G. (1989). Model: A design, assessment, and facilitation template in the pursuit of excellence. In J. W. Pfeiffer (Ed.), The 1989 annual: Developing human resources (pp. 267–275). San Diego: University Associates.

Ellingson, L. L. (2003, May). Interdisciplinary health care teamwork in the clinic backstage. *Journal of Applied Communication Research, 31,* 93–117.

Employee involvement in America. (1989). Washington, DC: General Accounting Office.

French, W. L., Bell, C. H., Jr., & Zawacki, R. A. (2000). *Organization development and transformation: Managing effective change*. Boston: Irwin McGraw-Hill.

Gabriel, Y., Fineman, S., & Sims, D. (2000). *Organizations and organizing* (2nd ed.). London: Sage.

General Accounting Office. (1989, June). Miles to go . . . Or unity at last. *Journal of Quality and Participation*, 60–67.

Greenwald, J. (1992, January 27). Is Mr. nice guy back? *Time*, pp. 42–44.

Harris, T. E. (2002). *Applied organizational communication: Perspectives and pragmatics for future success*. Mahwah, NJ: Lawrence Erlbaum.

Kanter, R. M. (1983). *Change masters: Innovation for productivity in the American corporation*. New York: Simon & Schuster.

Karp, H. B. (1983). A look at quality circles. In L. D. Goodstein & J. W. Pfeiffer (Eds.), *The 1983 annual for facilitators, trainers, and consultants* (pp. 157–163). San Diego: University Associates.

Lawler, E. E., III, & Mohrman, S. S. (1985). Quality circles after the fad. *Harvard Business Review, 63*, 65–71.

Lewis, J. P. (1998). *Team-based project management*. New York: AMACOM.

Manz, C., & Sims, H. P. (1993). *Business without bosses*. New York: Wiley.

Marks, M. L. (1986, March). The question of quality circles. *Psychology Today*, pp. 36–44.

McShane, S. L., & Von Glinow, M. A. (2000). *Organizational behavior*. Boston: McGraw-Hill.

Moorehead, G., & Griffin, R. W. (1998). *Organizational behavior: Managing people and organizations*. Boston: Houghton Mifflin.

Morrison, E. K. (1994). *Leadership skills: Developing volunteers for organizational success*. Tucson, AZ: Fisher.

Murrell, K. L., & Meredith, M. (2000). *Empowering employees*. New York: McGraw-Hill.

Neuborne, E. (1997, February 25). Companies save, but workers pay. *USA Today*, pp. 1B–2B.

Olsavsky, M. A. (Ed.). (1990). *The new work systems network: A compendium of selected work innovations cases* (BLMR Report No. 136). Washington, DC: U.S. Government Printing Office.

Peters, T. (1992). *Liberation management*. New York: Alfred A. Knopf.

Schaef, A. W., & Fassel, D. (1988). *The addictive organization*. San Francisco: Harper & Row.

Senge, P. (1990). *The fifth discipline: The art and practice of the learning organization*. New York: Doubleday.

Senge, P. M., Kleiner, A., Roberts, C., Ross, R. B., & Smith, B. J. (1994). *The fifth discipline fieldbook: Strategies and tools for building a learning organization*. New York: Doubleday.

Shockley-Zalabak, P. (2002, April). Protean places: Teams across time and space. *Journal of Applied Communication Research, 30*, 231–250.

Sweeney, P. D., & McFarlin, D. B. (2002). *Organizational behavior: Solutions for management*. Boston: McGraw-Hill.

Teams. (1995, Oct.). *Training*, p. 72.

Torres, C., & Spiegel, J. (1990). *Self-directed work teams: A primer*. San Diego: University Associates.

Truell, G. F. (1991). *Employee involvement: A guidebook for managers*. Buffalo, NY: PAT.

Trying to increase worker productivity, more employers alter management style. (1994, Feb. 13). *The Wall Street Journal*, p. B1.

Waterman, R. H., Jr. (1987). *The renewal factor: How the best get and keep the competitive edge*. New York: Bantam.

Wellins, R. S., Byham, W. C., & Wilson, J. M. (1991). *Empowered teams. Creating self-directed groups that improve quality, productivity, and participation*. San Francisco: Jossey-Bass.

Work incentives: Bonus busting. (1994, January/February). *Psychology Today*, pp. 20–21.

Zenger, J., Musselwhite, E., Hurson, K., & Perrin, C. (1994). *Leading teams*. Homewood, IL: Business One Irwin.

9

Decision Making and Problem Solving

CHAPTER OBJECTIVES

- Explain the importance of defining the problem.
- Understand internal and external constraints.
- Identify the process of developing alternatives.
- Determine what issues must be considered in making the choice or decision.
- Outline the implementation stage process.
- Elucidate the decision evaluation step.
- Define the factors important to the group process.
- Apply systems thinking to the group process.
- Discuss the decision-making process.

KEY TERMS

Alternatives
Concurrence-seeking
Criteria
Evaluating the decision
External constraints
Five Ws and the H

Goals
Group process
Implementing the decision
Intended consequences
Internal constraints
Refining goals

Symptom
T chart
Underlying causes
Unintended consequences

I grind the last of my French vanilla coffee beans and perk myself a large cup of coffee. I set the cup on the desk next to my computer. I turn on my computer, get it all set up, and reach over for my first sip of coffee. Savoring the aroma as I bring the cup to my mouth, I notice a small fly squirming on the surface of the coffee. I think flies are dirty little creatures who walk in all kinds of disgusting things, and who knows where this one has been? They carry germs and possibly even diseases. What should I do? I could pick the fly out and drink the coffee. I could throw the coffee away and go without, today. I could perk and drink another kind of coffee. Or I could go to the store, buy more French vanilla coffee beans, and make another cup. I have to make a decision.

This is a decision-making incident, because I have a goal—to enjoy my favorite coffee, while I work on my computer. And I must make a choice among competing options—to drink this coffee, drink another kind, or forgo the pleasure—within a given set of constraints—risk getting a disease or spend time, money, and energy going to the store. It is a personal decision, rather than a group decision, and it (most likely) has minimal foreseeable consequences and only for me. Many other decisions in my life are more complex in nature, are made by groups of people, and may have consequences for larger numbers of people. Whether made by an individual or a group, a decision holds an underlying assumption of a conscious, considered judgment, and it takes place within the constraints of a complex environment.

Decision Making and Problem Solving

Both decision making and problem solving involve making choices. A *problem means there is a gap between the current situation and a desired solution.* Problem solving involves the generation of alternatives aimed at movement from an existing state to a preferred state. *Decision making is making a choice among two or more alternatives to solve the problem.* Both processes end in an *act of choice* even if the choice is not to make a choice. While decision making can be a complex process, it can be described in six discreet, but interrelated, stages, as outlined in Table 9.1.

TABLE 9.1   Decision-Making Process

Simplified

1. Identify a goal and a problem preventing goal achievement
2. Examine constraints
3. Develop and analyze alternative ways of responding
4. Make a choice
5. Plan of action and implement the decision
6. Evaluate the results or consequences

First, we have to identify a goal to achieve and a problem or set of problems that stand in the way of reaching that goal. (My goal is to enhance my experience of working through the enjoyment of my French vanilla coffee, but that dirty little fly presents a problem for me, standing in the way of obtaining my goal of enjoying that coffee.)

Second, we come up against constraints on our choices of action regarding our response to this problem. (French vanilla coffee is my favorite coffee; other coffees aren't as enjoyable for me. I don't have any more French vanilla coffee beans. Going to the store to buy more coffee beans will take time, energy, and money, and will disrupt my work schedule and the flow of my ideas. If I drink this cup of coffee I could get sick from the diseases the fly might be carrying. These are constraints I consider in making my decision.)

Third, we develop and analyze alternative ways of responding to the problem and its constraints. (I could perk and drink another kind of coffee. I could go without coffee today. I could go to the store and buy more French vanilla beans to grind and perk. I could pick the fly out of my coffee and drink it.)

Fourth, after consideration of the possible alternatives, we finally have to make a choice. (I decide to drink the coffee.)

Fifth, we develop a plan of action and implement the decision we have made. (I reach in with my spoon, pick the fly out, and drink the coffee.)

Sixth, we evaluate the results, or consequences, of our decision and of the process itself, completing a "feedback loop," which informs our decision making the next time. (If the coffee tasted good, I didn't get sick, I had an enjoyable experience drinking it, and I got a lot of work done that morning, I'd probably make the same decision next time. If, however, I got violently ill or I simply couldn't enjoy the coffee because I kept thinking about the fly, I might reconsider my decision next time.)

Each of the stages has a connection to every other stage, forming a negotiated interaction among them. The problem exists only within a given context and a set of desired goals. (If drinking the coffee wasn't important to me, or if I didn't think about the fly, I wouldn't have had a problem or have had to make a decision. My actions would have been automatic. I would either drink the coffee or not.)

The context and goals relate to the implementation of the solution, and may relate to the constraints on which we have chosen to focus. The alternatives we develop and consider depend on our definition of the problem, the goals we hope to achieve, and the constraints we have established, as well as on the context in which we expect to implement the solution. Behind the surface level of the decisions being made lies a substratum of a complex pattern of assumptions and expectations that give substance to the meaning of that decision.

The Stages of Decision Making and Problem Solving

Defining the Problem

Most problems are problems because they are not easily understood or solved. As H. L. Mencken, a famous American editor and political commentator, said: "There is always an easy solution to every human problem—neat, plausible and *wrong*." To reach a desirable and effective solution, we need to clearly understand what it is we want to achieve. Without a clear goal in mind, we are like Alice in Wonderland when she came upon the Cheshire Cat.

> "Would you tell me, please, which way I ought to go from here?"
> "That depends a good deal on where you want to get to," said the Cat.
> "I don't much care where—" said Alice.
> "Then it doesn't matter which way you go," said the Cat.
> "—so long as I get *somewhere*," Alice added as an explanation.
> "Oh, you're sure to do that," said the Cat, "if you only walk long enough."
>   (Guiliano, 1982, pp. 39–40).

If we don't know where we want to go, and if we don't know what to expect when we get there, it doesn't really matter how much effort we put into making our decision. We have no parameters for it. Therefore, our first step in understanding a problem is to clearly define our goals and the criteria we will use to recognize and evaluate our achievement of those goals. The six steps covered are outlined in Table 9.2.

TABLE 9.2   Decision-Making and Problem-Solving Stages

In-Depth

1. Defining the problem
2. Constraints in the context of goals
3. Searching out alternatives
4. Making the decision
5. Implementing the decision
6. Evaluating the decision

Once we have established our goals, we then need to understand what it is that stands between us and them. However, getting to the root of what it is that is keeping us from our desired outcome is not always easy or obvious. What may initially appear to be the obstacle may simply be a symptom of a deeper underlying issue that, without resolution, may continue to create the undesirable effects we had hoped to overcome. For example, I may see myself as overweight and out of shape. I know how to lose weight: Stop eating. I know how to get in shape: Work out five times a week for at least an hour at a time. These solutions appear straightforward, but they may not address the underlying problem. Why have I gotten myself into habits that make me overweight and out of shape? Do I perpetuate life situations and attitudes that lead to my using food as a coping mechanism or to exhaustion as an excuse to avoid exercise? Are there other underlying problems that need to be addressed before I can effectively address my health or fitness problem? *What at first appears to be the problem may simply be a symptom.* Attempting to solve that issue merely glosses over the deeper problem, which will manifest continuously until we address its root cause. Individuals and groups have a tendency to *follow the path of least resistance* when trying to make a decision. A quick fix diet or a membership in the local gym might seem to solve the overweight and out of shape problem. But, I was not working out before so why would this actually work? Easy solution, yes. Correct solution, perhaps. Expediency in resolving a problem can often lead to hasty decisions where we pick the most obvious decision rather than the best (Beach, 1997).

To really solve problems, it is our challenge as individuals and as small groups to first come to understand the deeper levels of the real problem to be solved. We may or may not be aware of the hidden agendas we carry around with us that keep us from seeing and addressing these underlying issues. In addition, it may appear inefficient or even threatening for us as a group to spend valuable time and energy looking beneath the surface when we have immediate goals to reach or needs to attend to. Real and effective solutions depend on appropriately defining the underlying issues.

When the United States launched the *Challenger* spacecraft on January 28, 1986, there was strong evidence available to the decision makers that it might explode (Kruglanski, 1986). That information was ignored, discredited, and downplayed (Gouran, Hirokawa, & Martz, 1986). At each successive level of the decision-making process, decisions were made to either discount or not pass along the relevant information. "In short, it appears that the decision makers responsible for the *Challenger* launch, while still concerned about safety, were also influenced by the objective of maintaining their launch schedule" (Hirokawa, 2003, p. 130).

In response to the 1986 disaster, NASA created a safety office. However, on February 1, 2003, the *Columbia* shuttle broke apart while trying to return to earth killing the seven astronauts aboard. The subsequent inquiry revealed that many of the same decision making issues that caused the *Challenger* disaster still remained (Eisler, Watson, & Levin, 2003; Levin, 2003). In a safety meeting prior to the *Columbia* launch, a fateful decision was made to go ahead despite the revelation that a large chunk of foam came off on a mission in late 2002 (Watson, 2003). The investigating group's final report of the incident concluded that "NASA's overconfident management and inattention doomed *Columbia* every bit as much as the chunk of foam that struck the shuttle with deadly force" (Dunn, 2003, p. A3).

As we noted earlier, *what at first appears to be a problem might actually be a symptom.* With NASA, the lack of a safety office was not the problem. Instead, the problem was the culture and attitudes of the agency itself since the newly created safety office (1986) was quickly underfunded and ignored (Eisler, Watson, & Levin, 2003; Watson, 2003).

In a less tragic example of poor decision making, the Coca-Cola corporation introduced "New Coke," apparently expecting it to become an overnight taste sensation. Coca-Cola was forced to reverse its decision quickly, however, and reintroduce "Coke Classic" when sales dropped off and consumers protested (Whyte, 1991). In these situations, highly skilled individuals and groups made decisions with negative impacts on their long-term goals and with consequences for large numbers of people. They made these decisions because they failed to adequately address the larger contexts and dynamic interactions surrounding their decisions—the weather at the time of the *Challenger* launch, which exacerbated the problem with the faulty O-rings, the inherent tendency of foam to dislodge during shuttle launch which was underplayed with *Columbia*, and the taste desires of the consumers of Coca-Cola. In hindsight, we can see that misreading the information on the initial problem allowed NASA and Coca-Cola to ignore critical information.

If the decision-making processes had been working effectively, the larger issues surrounding the goals and immediate problems would have been openly discussed, with the problem definition expanded, the constraints acknowledged, and possible alternative solutions sought. More fully conscious decisions could have been made, incorporating an understanding of the possible or likely consequences of the decisions taken and assuring a better outcome.

Constraints in the Context of Goals

Constraints are a nearly inevitable element of any decision-making process and may be of two types: external or internal. External constraints are those imposed on the decision-making process, such as the time, money, resources, energy, knowledge base, or other resources that the group or individual has to use for the process. Internal constraints are those integral to the problem. They may have instigated the initial problem, or they may have to do with limitations on the implementation, such as government regulations, the physical location, technical or design difficulties, or any number of other constraining factors and circumstances.

For example, a community that has disposed of its solid waste at a local dump may be told by the state that it must close and seal its dump and find more environmentally sound ways of disposing of its solid waste. A committee may be formed to come up with alternative solutions and may be faced with external constraints, such as having little expertise in solid waste management, little meeting time, and a short time frame in which to develop its recommendations. Internal constraints may include funding limitations imposed by the community, as well as technical and regulatory constraints on the disposal of solid waste. When we examine the underlying causes of our difficulty with weight loss and physical fitness, we may come up against external constraints imposed by our current life situation, our lack of knowledge of the depth of the problem, or lack of access to the range of possible alternative solutions. Our internal constraints may relate to the effect on our health of rapid weight loss or the impact of a sudden intensive fitness program.

NASA and Coca-Cola were each operating under clearly defined goals, with initial sets of external and internal constraints that apparently closed their minds to negotiating those constraints. Consequently, they were unable to expand the scopes of their goals, to identify the problems to be addressed, or to explore alternative solutions. Goals and constraints are an aspect of decision making, but they should not be allowed to dictate the solutions. They need to be acknowledged and weighed, but not to the exclusion of understanding their interactions with other important criteria. To the extent that we are conscious of our decision processes—taking our goals and constraints into account but not letting them overshadow our search for a fuller understanding of the problem and additional constraints or our creative search for solutions—we allow ourselves to make the best possible decision at a particular moment in time.

Searching Out Alternatives

In the simple example of the fly in my coffee, my constraints and alternatives were straightforward. They involved one person, and the expected consequences of a wrong decision were relatively minor. In the case of the *Challenger* and *Columbia* disasters, however, the consequences of the wrong decision were enormous. While the search for alternatives may be constrained by time, resources, knowledge, or energy, if the decision is consequential, it is worth a commensurate effort to negotiate those constraints, in order to pursue optimum solutions. Finally, we must remember that one clear choice is to decide not to make a choice. Sometimes we invest so many resources in examining a problem that we feel we must make a change. But, what if the real problem with my weight is my own unrealistic expectation about my ideal size? Perhaps, after examining all the alternatives, I would be better off just staying as I am.

Developing alternatives is frequently the most creative and exciting part of the process. Since it involves gathering as much information from as many sources as possible, digesting and synthesizing that information, and forming it into a workable shape that responds to the problem at hand it can be the most difficult and frustrating. An essential part of this exploration of possible courses of action is bringing into focus the unintended consequences, along with the scope of a proposed solution and its long- or short-term goals and expected results. *Unintended consequences* are those results that occur because of the decision but were not expected or planned. For example, in July 2003, an 86-year-old retiree drove his car through an open-air market in Santa Monica, California, killing 10 people and injuring dozens more. Almost immediately, "California Highway Patrol Commissioner Dwight O. "Spike" Helmick called for reconsideration of legislation to require road testing for drivers age 75 and older" (Barnhill, 2003, p. 10). On the surface, tougher testing for older drivers would seem to make sense and 20 states and the District of Columbia do have some type of special relicensing requirements. However, what if a large number of the 18.9 million drivers age 70-plus ceased to drive? An unintended consequence would be that someone would have to drive them requiring families, communities, and others to adjust their lives. This does not mean the relicensing approach is incorrect, but it does demonstrate what happens when we make changes. Along the same vein, the federal government's decision to create the interstate highway system had the unintended consequence of isolating many smaller towns.

If possible, every alternative should be considered. Frequently, a solution derived from a far-out idea may be key to solving a difficult problem. For example, suggesting the U.S. abandon the space program, while not necessarily a popular idea, could help a decision-making group grapple with the underlying reasons for the disasters—the flights themselves. Developing additional alternatives increases the statistical chances that the group will locate the best solutions or isolate the most significant issues (Herek, Janis, & Huth, 1987; Katzenback & Smith, 1993).

In 1982, Johnson & Johnson was faced with a major disaster—seven deaths in two days from the ingestion of cyanide-laced, Extra-Strength Tylenol (Trujillo & Roth, 1987). Four years later, in February of 1986, a 23-year-old New York woman died after ingesting two Extra-Strength Tylenol capsules, and cyanide was found in the body of a Nashville man and in his bottle of Tylenol capsules (Benson, 1988). Johnson & Johnson took an almost unthinkable set of actions— ones far from normal for a profit-making organization. In spite of the costs and logistical hurdles, they discontinued production of over-the-counter capsules and replaced 15 million capsule products already on the market. The company's CEO, James Burke, appeared on television on the Phil Donahue Show, spoke at the National Press Club, and held press conferences to confront negative news coverage. He wanted to calm public fears, distinguish the contaminated Tylenol capsules from caplets and other Tylenol products, and assert that the capsules had been contaminated after they left the manufacturing and distribution facilities. As a result of their efforts, Johnson & Johnson and Tylenol emerged from this crisis with an effective response that saved their reputation and maintained their market share (39% of the market share 12 weeks after the second crisis, close to their 42% all-time market high), dramatically demonstrating how well groups can solve problems when they engage in an open decision-making process (Benson, 1988).

In a community group dealing with new ways of disposing of solid waste, different members, having different backgrounds and expertise, can offer diverse perspectives. Some may have connections with people in other communities who have had experience with the same issues; some may have expertise in a particular aspect of waste disposal technology; and others may have a political sense of what will or will not be acceptable to the community they are serving. The more different sets of experiences and knowledge bases that we as a group can bring to bear on developing alternative solutions to a problem, the more likely it is that a satisfactory solution will be found.

Once a variety of alternative solutions have been placed in discussion, the focus shifts to the possible consequences—intended and unintended—of each of the alternatives. This is sometimes more difficult than we at first think. There may be hidden effects in areas we may not be taking into account. If, for example, as an unforeseen consequence of my deciding to drink my coffee, I get sick and am unable to work for a month, I may not be able to pay my rent and may be kicked out of my apartment. I may get fired from my job and may now be homeless and penniless. Even small decisions can have large unintended consequences. While this consequence appears highly unlikely, so did the *Challenger* and *Columbia* disasters to the NASA team (before they happened), and it must be considered a possible outcome. Being aware of this possibility and then weighing its likelihood and its seriousness, should it occur, against the more likely possibility—that the distraction of having to make new coffee or of going to the store to buy more French vanilla coffee beans might cause me to lose my concentration on the job at hand and leave undone the work I wanted to accomplish—is an important part of the decision-making process. As individuals and as groups, we may not always make the right decisions, but when we consider all of the possible outcomes before making those decisions, we are more likely to make better ones.

Making the Decision

After defining the goals and the underlying problem to be addressed, coming to an understanding of the constraints on solving the problem and examining alternative solutions and their likely consequences, we are ready to decide which of the available alternatives best meets the goals we have set out to achieve. Our choice needs to take into account the costs and consequences of our best long-term solution and compare them with the less ideal, but perhaps more affordable or more easily implemented and maintained, solutions. Restating the original objective is one way to make certain the group does not travel too far from its original purpose (Schultz, Ketrow, & Urban, 1995).

If I want to lose weight and develop a healthy exercise regimen but find that my underlying problem relates to my current work situation, it may be that the ideal solution is to quit my job and go to a high-cost therapeutic retreat. For obvious reasons, this may not serve the other interests of my life and may not be possible. Rather than ignoring the consequences of a life-changing solution or opting for either no solution or the ideal one only, I might do better to plan a staged, long-term solution that incorporates the full complexity of my life. I can then implement a strategy that will take me where I want to go in discreet and achievable increments. On the other hand, I may be able to renegotiate some of my external constraints. If, for instance, I have a spouse or partner who can take over the responsibility of earning some of the family income, freeing me to pursue a more satisfying, if less well-paying job and life situation, I might be able to consider my choices in a different light. Changing the focus of the problem and the constraints on the alternative solutions makes our choices and the possibilities for their implementation quite different. In most decision-making and problem-solving situations, there are a number of interrelated and negotiable possibilities. It is important to keep this in mind when trying to solve what appear to be insurmountable problems. Groups have to look for ways to evaluate choices in realistic scenarios, without giving up or accepting an all-or-nothing solution.

In addition, we need to keep in mind that our choices are ultimately constrained by the small choices we have made at each step along the way, including the sets of priorities we have chosen to follow. The choice we make incorporates all of the previous choices we have made both consciously and unconsciously. We can probably never make perfect choices all of the time, but we improve our odds of making good choices based on the available information and through the effective use of the decision-making process.

Implementing the Decision

The implementation stage frequently is ignored or given inadequate attention in the decision-making process. Assume for a moment that relicensing was required for all older drivers. How would it be done? Who would pay for the additional personnel? What provisions would be made to guarantee fairness between states and to rectify unfair decisions? These, and many more questions, would face the implementation process. Elaborate reports generated for government agencies or private corporations that have taken months of time and great financial investment to produce are often shelved, because those charged with the implementation are not vested in the project or because implementation is too costly or requires infrastructure that is not in place. Everyone feels cheated, and the process itself takes on an expectation of failure.

As an example, when an outside consulting firm was hired by the U.S. government to evaluate the economic development potential of one Native American Indian reservation, none of the Native American residents were asked to serve on the decision-making/problem-solving team. Although information and ideas were sought from those impacted by the proposed development, none of those people were involved in actually developing the goals, assessing the problems and constraints, brainstorming alternatives, choosing the proposed solutions, or developing the implementation strategy. Those it was intended to serve were not involved in making the decision. Consequently, a very fine report was written and submitted to the government but never acted upon.

Our community solid waste group may have decided that the best solution to the waste disposal problem is to recycle as much as possible of the wastestream and truck the remainder to the nearest waste-to-energy plant. When the plan is put in place, it may turn out that there is no market for much of the recycled waste, forcing the community to send that to the waste-to-energy plant, as well. This may change the terms of the contract for the tonnage of hauled waste and greatly increase the cost of the waste disposal, as well as cause confusion among the residents who had just begun to sort their household trash for recycling. If the committee had anticipated this result and had negotiated their original contract for their waste disposal accordingly, or if they had joined with other communities to give themselves more access to the recycling market, they might have saved money and valuable implementation time, as well as the good will of the community. To the extent that the committee anticipates the impacts of implementing its decision and the constraints imposed on it, it may be able to offset some of the unintended negative political, technical, and economic consequences.

Evaluating the Decision

The decision-making/problem-solving process is not finished until we have seen whether or not it has accomplished its goals or whether it has better or worse consequences than we expected. After the fact, NASA was forced to examine its decisions on the *Challenger* and *Columbia* launches and examine its decision-making process, as well. Had this evaluation occurred as part of the initial decision-making process, the disasters might have been averted. Large decisions are the result of many small ones made throughout the entire decision-making process. Each phase of the process opens certain sets of possibilities, while closing others. In order to learn from our decision-making process, we need to examine the outcomes in terms of both those we expected and those we did not expect, and we need to understand how we predicted accurately, as well as where we went wrong in not predicting actual consequences and limitations.

The decision-making process is most effective when we take the evaluation stage into account in the beginning, as we are defining the problem. Part of an effective evaluation is to set up a procedure for measuring the success of our outcome as it relates to the definition of the original problem. We should be able to say at the beginning of the process that a given desired outcome will be apparent if it meets certain specific criteria. These criteria become the basis for the evaluation.

In addition, in order to be able to replicate and understand the process itself, we should document it at each step along the way so we can rethink our solution if it is flawed. The composition and working relationships of the group or team, the goals we identify, the ways we define the problem, the reasons for narrowing or expanding its scope, the constraints we choose to consider and why, our information-gathering tools and strategies, the alternatives we develop and pursue or decline to pursue and why, our choice of a solution and the reasons for it, the implementation process we develop and propose, the implementation process that actually takes place, the results of the implementation, and, finally, the effects of the process itself on the outcome all need to be examined. Evaluating our decisions and the processes we used to make them helps us avoid repeating disastrous decisions, while giving us the tools to replicate positive ones.

Patterns of Decision-Making and Problem-Solving Groups

While the stages of the decision-making process form the structure that shapes it, the interaction between those stages gives the decision-making process its energy. Making decisions in groups and teams helps us address the underlying interrelationships of the problems and issues to be resolved by making it possible to examine a problem from multiple and often discrepant perspectives. This examination helps develop solutions that take into account the complex environment of the problem and its solution. When NASA sent the Hubble spacecraft into orbit, the telescope did not work. The NASA corporate culture has been blamed, in large part, for this setback, as that culture encouraged individuals to make autonomous decisions without seeking or paying attention to dissenting opinions of an expert group (Capers & Lipton, 1993; Stein & Kanter, 1993). As with the *Challenger* and *Columbia* disasters, extremely bright and dedicated NASA scientists and engineers made a poor decision. That decision might have been avoided, if they had made use of the wider range of expertise and perspectives available to them.

Many have suggested that NASA succumbed to *groupthink*. As originally conceived, groupthink signaled a highly cohesive group's stress on *concurrence-seeking* (Janis, 1983). Cohesive groups can develop a similarity in thinking or purpose that blinds them to considering important alternative ideas or actions (Street, 1997). The University of Wisconsin-Madison apparently became a victim of groupthink when it tried to develop an image of a diverse student body. After the search for an authentic picture of diversity to put on its fall 2000 admissions brochure became difficult, they inserted the photo of an African-American male into a crowd of white football fans (Wyatt, 2000). At the time, fewer than 10% of the school's more than 41,000 students were non-white and 2.15% were black. Once exposed, the University subjected to national embarrassment and reprinted 106,00 copies at a cost of $63,000 (Wyatt, 2000). Time or other external constraints may predispose a group to limit its discussion of possible alternatives, and once the decision is made, it may spend little or no time reexamining its decisions, even when there are indications of possible dangers. Engaging in groupthink can be a way of avoiding conflict, despite the fact that healthy conflict is frequently required to reach the most constructive and innovative decisions.

Group Composition

Deciding the makeup of a decision-making or problem-solving group or team itself is a significant part of the group process. The membership composition should reflect the larger social and organizational environment in which it takes part, as well as the nature of the problem and the context in which it occurs. The Native American Indian reservation economic development group clearly should have included those expected to implement the solution, as well as those expected to be impacted by it. The community group charged with developing solid waste disposal options would do well to include at least one or two members with some knowledge of the technical, market, and cost aspects of the problem, as well as members with an understanding of the social and political characteristics of the community to be served. Informed human resources managers recognized some time ago how ironic it was for managers to try and make decisions regarding what motivates employees (Harris, 2002). Since these groups have different jobs, skills, and working conditions, the best decision-making group would consist of representatives from both.

Group Process

Once the group membership has been determined, there are at least three steps, as shown in Table 9.3, that the group must take before it can effectively begin the task at hand. First, it needs to address the external constraints on the group process itself. These include the time frame for completing the task, the time and commitment each of the members has to give the group, the knowledge and understanding individual members bring to the problem at hand, the availability of outside sources for technical expertise, and any other relevant concerns. Each group has its own strengths and weaknesses, and it is wise to understand and take these into account, in order to make the best use of everyone's time, particular abilities, and interests.

Second, the group needs to decide how it will run itself. Will it elect a chair and someone to keep the minutes of the proceedings, or will there be no formal group leadership? Who will be in charge of setting the agenda for meetings? Who will call the meetings, and how frequently does the group need to meet? If the group is within an organizational context, these decisions may be made by those who have established the group and charged it with a given responsibility. If the group is not already structured, however, it may fall to the members themselves to decide how best to meet their goals. Group dynamics may evolve over time with shared decision-making and problem-solving successes and failures. Leadership may shift and change according to topics under consideration, or leadership may be stable. It may be based on personality or expertise. Ways of dealing with disruptive members may be formally addressed or informally handled as situations arise, or the issue may be left unaddressed. Whatever the decisions made about group leadership, structure, and process, those decisions can become critical to the overall success or failure of the group effort.

TABLE 9.3   Three Preliminary Steps

1. External constraints on the process—What are the limitations?
2. Procedural issues—How to run the group?
3. Voting or consensus—How will decisions be made?

TABLE 9.4

Consensus Includes	Consensus Does Not Include
1. Seek everyone's ideas—Prevent group-think and take advantage of all ideas.	1. Voting—It creates a win/lose outcome since the minority is told it does not matter.
2. Listen—Work toward understanding of other group/team members.	2. Majority rule—People not included in the outcome have little motivation to help carry out the decision.
3. Discuss ideas. Encourage and explore differences.	3. Bargaining—Consensus seeks the best outcome not a compromise.
4. Not getting all you want—A group/team should work toward integrating everyone.	4. Minority rule—If you disagree with the proposal, offer a viable alternative or let the process continue.
5. Agreement to the point that everyone can live with it—Avoid win/lose perspectives.	

Third, the group must decide how the outcome of the problem-solving process itself will be determined—whether by a majority vote or by overall consensus (Wood, 1992). These two methods are quite different and may make a great deal of difference in the acceptance and effectiveness of the implementation of the decision. Voting yes or no on a particular issue indicates how the group members feel, but obtaining consensus among the group members enhances their commitment to the decision (Ellis & Fisher, 1994). The nature of the problem to be addressed may dictate whether consensus is possible, desirable, or necessary, whether a vote by a two-thirds majority or by 51% of the members will suffice, or whether the leader of a subgroup should make a particular decision. Once these aspects of the process have been adequately addressed, the group is ready to move on to the issues at hand. Table 9.4 outlines the concensus process.

The Decision-Making and Problem-Solving Process

Problem Identification and Information Gathering

If we embark on our journey in the wrong direction, all of our efforts could be lost. The following discussion provides an extensive roadmap to help make certain you reach the desired location. Asking questions is at the heart of group decision making. It is essential to identifying the problem to be solved and to gathering the relevant information to solve it. Six types of questions are important to ask. They are sometimes known as the five Ws and the H. These questions should be asked for any problem.

Who, What, Why, When, Where, and How

It is important to ask:

> For whom is it a problem?
> What is the problem?
> Why is it a problem?
> When is it a problem?
> Where is it a problem?
> How is it a problem?

Specific questions include:

How does the problem relate to our stated goals?

Will resolving it assure that our goals are met?

When, how, and by whom was this problem brought to our attention?

What difficulties are being created by it?

What harm or lack of benefit important enough to justify investigation does it create?

What, if any, aspects of the problem or the solution are potentially catastrophic? (Earthquakes, tidal waves, botulism, and nuclear war are all events that rarely occur, but they can be devastating when they do. If some aspect of the problem has this type of potential and occurs even once, is that too often?)

What are the other harms that must be considered?

What are the benefits that are being denied?

What has been violated by a deviation from standard procedures?

When does the problem occur? When doesn't it occur?

What locations, people, and situations are most likely to have the problem?

What other problems consistently (always or almost always) occur with this problem? Can these be related somehow? Do we have the correct cause and effect?

Once the group has asked and answered all the questions it can on its own, it then must analyze what else it needs to know in order to more fully understand and define the issue and develop meaningful alternative solutions.

What are we trying to evaluate, understand, and comprehend?

What data will help? (Samples, surveys, books, articles, research, interviews, site visits?)

How will the data be recorded, shared, synthesized?

What special skills are needed to gather the information?

What obstacles exist to gathering the information? Time, expertise, availability?

Who else can be included in the discussion?

How did we get our information? Is it first- or secondhand? Is it rumor or verifiable?

How current, representative, respected are our sources?

How complete is the picture? Are there obvious gaps?

Refining Goals

Once the information has been gathered and discussed, the group reexamines its original goals and evaluation criteria in light of the expanded understanding of the problems and constraints. It then decides what expectations or criteria are relevant or possible to apply to the final decision and to its evaluation. The group might start with visualizing the ideal solution. What would be included in this outcome and what could be excluded? Next, because the ideal may not be workable or practical, the group must decide what must be present at a minimum to make it acceptable. One way of arriving at these solutions is to brainstorm all the criteria that the group thinks essential or important to the final resolution. For example:

A solution must not exceed a particular cost ceiling.

A solution must be cost effective.

A solution must be acceptable to particular groups.

A solution must be acceptable to particular individuals in positions of power.

A solution must be capable of quick implementation.

A solution must be easy to maintain and administer.

A solution must be a useful base for future planning.

A solution must be easily justified to a given audience.

A solution must meet certain regulatory standards.

A solution must provide recreational opportunities for particular groups.

A solution must be accessible or usable by handicapped people.

A solution must. . . .

Once a list has been generated, the group can go back and:

1. Assign an *A to the top one-third* of the items that are absolutely essential for the decision to be acceptable.

2. Assign a *C to the bottom one-third* of the items that really are not critical. In any problem-solving situation, there are numerous nonessential or cosmetic items that do not need to be considered at that moment.
3. The *middle one-third automatically receive a B.*
4. Go back to the Bs and force them into the A column or the C column.
5. Forget the Cs and eliminate them from discussion.
6. Prioritize the As, and you have developed a good starting point for developing the essential criteria.

Using the A list, the group can now refine its goals and evaluation criteria, writing them down to clarify them and to assure that all members understand and agree with the decision on them. This is an essential part of the process, and it is important to document it. This will form the basis for making the choice from alternatives and for evaluating the implementation of that choice.

Refining Alternatives

Once the goals have been refined in light of the information and data that have been gathered and analyzed, the group is now able to search for alternative solutions. Members should be encouraged to be as creative as possible, drawing from each other's ideas and insights. The group can use any number of techniques (see Chapter 11) in developing this list of alternative solutions. When the list is developed, the group must then go back and examine each of the alternatives it is considering for any possible consequences of their implementation—intended or unintended. The group should keep a careful record of this discussion of the alternatives. Some piece of an alternative discarded along the way may prove useful when combined with another.

Making the Choice

When the list of alternatives and their foreseeable consequences has been developed, it is time to choose which one best fits the goals and solves the problems the group has outlined. Each alternative should be discussed in relation to how well it fits within the parameters established for the decision. Some questions the group might ask themselves include:

How well does the alternative meet the goals we have established?
    Does it meet the most important ones?

How well does it solve the problem?
    Which parts of the problem will be solved?
    Which will be left unsolved?
    Is that acceptable?

Do the advantages of this solution outweigh any possible disadvantages?

Are there reasons why this solution will not be implemented?

If it is implemented, will it be easy or difficult to maintain?

Are there concomitant problems that should be addressed?

    For example, is this solution going to drain away important resources (money, personnel, time) from other problems?

    Will this solution impact individuals or groups not considered in this discussion or have other unintended consequences?

    Are there ways in which this alternative ignores important research data or other information obtained by this group?

    Is this alternative justifiable to those who will be asked to pay for it or who will be impacted by it?

The group can use a T chart, in which the advantages of each alternative are listed on one side and the disadvantages are listed on the other side (see Figure 9.1). This gives the group a way to answer the simple question: Do the advantages outweigh the disadvantages? When each alternative has been weighed and the decision made, the group must develop a strategy for the implementation of that decision.

Implementing the Decision

Although the original decision-making group may not be responsible for the actual implementation of the decision, it is its responsibility to design a strategy that helps assure that it is implemented, because a *solution that is not implemented is not a solution; it is just a good idea.* As we have noted earlier, the implementation stage is frequently where the decision-making process breaks down. Although the difficulties in this stage should have been anticipated earlier in the process, there may be various reasons why they may not have been adequately addressed. The group can begin by asking itself a few questions:

FIGURE 9.1   A T Chart for an Alternative Solution

Advantages	Disadvantages

Are there adversarial groups or individuals that will try to block the implementation of this decision? Can we alter the solution to gain their allegiance? If not, can we safely ignore or go around them?

Have each of the implementation steps been considered carefully, including who does what, when, where, and how (person, activity, time, place, and method)?

Table 9.5 outlines the stages of decision making and problem solving. Once the decision has been implemented, we must follow up with our evaluation of the

---

TABLE 9.5   The Stages of Decision Making and Problem Solving

Define the Issue or Problem.

Identify the problem and specify the symptoms of the problem.
Gather information on the size and scope of the problem.
Research the seriousness, urgency, and implications of the problem.
Look for causes and underlying conditions of the problem.

Consider the Goals to be Achieved and the Contextual Constraints on the Goals.

Identify the criteria that would indicate successful achievement of the goals.
Rank-order the criteria in importance and specify criteria that must be met.
Identify which criteria must be met and which are less essential.
Refine the goals, based on criteria, to be satisfactory, realistic, achievable.

Search Out Alternative Solutions.

Suggest as many alternative solutions as possible.
Refine and combine alternative solutions.

Make the Decision.

Evaluate the alternative decisions or solutions using the goal criteria.
Rank-order the solutions based on how well they meet the criteria.
Does any one solution or solution combination meet all criteria that must be met?
If not, reevaluate solutions and goals. Are goals achievable? Other solutions?
If yes, does solution meet goals that should and can be met?
If not, is there another solution or set that can meet these criteria as well?
Does the solution create additional problems? How can they be resolved?

Implement the Decision or Solution.

Develop a procedure for implementing the solution that best meets criteria.
Evaluate the implementation: Is it achievable, too expensive, take too long?
Evaluate the decision or solution.
Identify criteria and method to evaluate the decision once it is implemented.
Does the decision or solution accomplish its goals?
Implement an ongoing evaluation plan that occurs at regular intervals.

solution and of the process. Even if the decision is not implemented, the evaluation stage is critical for understanding the reasons for that result and how we might have avoided it.

Summary

Two assumptions underlie our discussion: that the group is formed with a particular problem or issue to resolve and that there are particular results or goals that it hopes or expects to achieve. Research shows that groups are more successful at achieving their goals when they approach a problem systematically and rationally (Hirokawa, 1983). Understanding the decision-making stages can help groups structure their process. Although the individual stages of the decision-making process can be described separately, they are, as we have noted, interrelated. In defining the problem, understanding the constraints, searching for alternatives, deciding on a solution, and understanding the consequences of the implementation of that solution, a group moves back and forth between stages, balancing each stage against the others, while keeping the goals in mind.

We may find that what initially presented as the problem is, in fact, only a symptom of the underlying problem. By carefully articulating the expected outcome or goals we hope to achieve, we can reexamine the original issue or problem with which we are presented. Throughout the process, these goals can provide structure and order to the discussion and keep the decision-making process on track. They can act as directional signs and allow us to measure our progress as a group. They can also give us a sense of closure when we are finished. The first step, therefore, in solving the problem for which a group has been convened is to understand clearly the goals to be achieved.

In discussing the goals, the group must understand the internal constraints under which it is operating—whether those be financial, technical, political, environmental, or other constraints. Within that context, the group will want to decide which goals are the most important, which are necessary, which would be desirable, and which might be excessive, for the given purpose and set of circumstances. For example, if our initial stated goal is to close, cover, and secure our town dump, as required by state environmental regulations, we might be tempted to expand that goal to create a park or recreational area on top of the old dump site. This has been done in some other communities, but is it practical for ours? Will our citizens value it enough to pay for the extra cost of bringing the site to that standard and then maintaining it as a park in the future? On the other hand, as the costs of waste disposal escalate, we might be tempted to scale back our dump closure plans to simply closing the gates and hoping that the environmental regulators don't bother us about it. In that case, we might find in a few years that the runoff from the site pollutes neighboring wells and water supplies, leading to lawsuits and a requirement that the town supply clean water to the affected residents. In considering our goals, therefore, we need to think through the potential impacts of their implementation. The scope of the goals will dictate the scope of the problem to be resolved.

DISCUSSION QUESTIONS

   1. Why is defining the problem important to effective decision making?

   2. Distinguish between internal and external constraints. Provide an example of each one from your own experience.

   3. Why should you be careful about accepting the first answer to a difficult problem? What decision-making principle does this highlight?

   4. What constraints do we face when we make a final choice?

   5. When implementing a decision, what actions should be considered?

   6. What elements are important for an effective evaluation stage?

   7. What is meant by concurrence-seeking? Why would a group be prone to trying to achieve concurrence-seeking?

   8. Do you agree with the conclusion that groups are more successful when they approach a problem systematically and rationally? Why or why not?

   9. Briefly outline the systematic problem-solving approach provided in this chapter.

EXERCISES

1. Survival strategies: Effective problem solving; 2. Critical and creative steps in decision making; 3. Evaluating the decision-making and problem-solving team process; 4. Evaluating the group contribution process

1. SURVIVAL STRATEGIES: EFFECTIVE PROBLEM SOLVING

Problem solving and decision making require careful analysis to develop successful solutions. This exercise will allow your team to practice these techniques.

Step 1. Individually answer the following survival questions. What would you do if you were confronted with the potentially dangerous situations? Consider the situation and develop a strategy for survival.

   1.1 Runaway Car. You have lost control of the car and cannot stop it.
   1.2 Sinking Car. You are trapped in a car that has gone into a lake or river.
   1.3 Earthquake
   Indoors
   Outside
   In a car
   1.4 Adrift at sea. You have no means of propelling the boat.

Step 2. *Balanced input strategy.* Form teams of eight or fewer members. Before beginning, develop a strategy for obtaining the greatest amount of input and ideas for each situation. Do not allow anyone to dominate the discussion. Reach consensus on the best answer. Do not accept "I don't know" since these are life-threatening situations.

Step 3. Compare your responses to the experts' suggested solutions provided by your instructor. Your team might have developed additional strategies based on specific training or knowledge and, if no, the suggested strategies will provide a basis for comparison.

Step 4. Analyze the effectiveness of your team. These types of crisis situations can highlight issues in the team's problem-solving habits. Consider the following questions: 1. Did emotions overshadow the discussion? 2. Did people push for a solution even though this was a hypothetical planning opportunity for a future survival situation? In other words, did the group allow a few responses to determine the solution? 3. Did some members chose to not participate since it has not really happened? 4. Did the team operate as a self-managed unit or was there a strong desire to have some authority figure intervene? 5. Was there balanced input or were there a few strong voices? 6. How could you redesign the discussion to create an equal-voice approach without assigning roles? 7. Did you find the team rushing to solve the problem without careful analysis? 8. What does this tell you about the difficulty of developing effective teams? 9. Did the group attempt to solve the problem quickly without a systematic approach? 10. Return to the chapter and determine which steps were not carefully considered. 11. Review your answers and determine how closely they match the experts' answers provided at the end of the exercise section of this chapter. What decisions did the group make that were correct? What was missed? How can this be avoided in future group decision-making situations? 12. What other observations can you make about the team process?

2. CRITICAL AND CREATIVE STEPS IN DECISION MAKING

As a discussion group, pick a significant problem or social issue (for example, a current community or school issue such as parking, landlord relations, or tuition and fee increases) and pay particular attention to working through a problem-solution sequence for it. Use a flip chart or board to write the definitions and lists generated in each step. In this procedure it is important to do each step individually and sequentially and not jump ahead or combine the steps. It is especially important to engage in serious critical thinking in the critical thinking steps and not to be critical in the creative thinking steps. This may prove more difficult than it first appears.

Step 1. Define the problem. Generate a clear, concise, delimiting definition of the problem. This definition should identify precisely what the problem is and its major underlying causes. This phase requires critical thinking.

Step 2. Brainstorm all of the relevant aspects, influences, consequences, and tangential pieces of the problem. This is a noncritical, creative, fun, and synergistic step during which no idea is too wild, outlandish, or silly. All ideas should be entertained and listed. No critical responses are allowed; only requests for clarification or elaboration, supportive statements, or comments building upon an idea can be made. This phase requires creative thinking.

Step 3. Identify and rank-order the aspects of the problem that are the most important to be resolved. These aspects identify the criteria that a solution must address. This step requires critical thinking.

Step 4. Brainstorm as many solutions as possible. Again, this is a noncritical, creative, fun, and synergistic step during which no idea is too out-of-bounds. All ideas should be entertained and listed. No critical responses are allowed, only requests for clarification or elaboration, supportive statements, or comments building upon an idea can be made. This phase requires creative thinking.

Step 5. Identify and rank-order the possible solutions for their potential to resolve the problem. Critically assess the solutions for how many of the criteria they address and how well they satisfy those criteria. This step requires critical thinking.

Step 6. Identify the best solution, which may be a combination of solutions, then discuss how that solution addresses each of the criteria and how the solution can be implemented. This step requires critical thinking.

Step 7. Identify how to evaluate the effectiveness of the solution once it is implemented. This step requires both creative and critical thinking.

3. EVALUATING THE DECISION-MAKING AND PROBLEM-SOLVING TEAM PROCESS

Consider the team you are currently working with and respond, individually, to these issues:

1. How well has the group defined the problem? Has there been a systematic approach to decision making and problem analysis?
2. What are the team goals? Are they clearly identified?
3. Has the team searched out enough alternatives?
4. What steps have been taken to carefully make the decision?
5. Are the appropriate actions in place to implement the decision?
6. How will the team evaluate the decision?

Compare your responses with the rest of the team. Do you need to return to a specific step or phase? If there are different assessments, work to resolve these differences.

4. EVALUATING THE GROUP CONTRIBUTION PROCESS

Step 1. It is important to have some gauge of how the group is functioning. This is one of the best ways to utilize problem solving. Your group is the ideal model for actually identifying and dealing with process issues.

Directions

(1) Rate each of the following questions and (2) add some relevant example or comment. 4 = Very; 3 = Quite a Bit; 2 = Somewhat; 1 = Not Very

_____ 1. How clear are the group member's roles and responsibilities?

Comment:

_____ 2. How well are group members' talents used?

Comment:

_____ 3. How willing are group members to be fully involved in the group process?

Comment:

_____ 4. How good is the group members' active participation during meetings?

Comment:

_____ 5. How well do group members keep commitments?

Comment:

_____ 6. How good is attendance at group meetings?

Comment:

_____ 7. How obvious are the benefits to contributing to the group process?

Comment:

Step 2. Group members should share their scores for the seven items to produce a group total. The group should congratulate itself for the highest-ranking items. The group should then turn to the lowest-ranking items and determine what the problems seem to be that are creating the lower rankings. Consider using the different problem-solving techniques already provided.

Step 3. Develop an action plan to assist the group in being successful.

REFERENCES

Barnhill, W. (2003, September). New focus on older drivers. *AARP Bulletin,* pp. 10–11.

Beach, L. R. (1997). *The psychology of decision making: People in organizations.* Thousand Oaks, CA: Sage.

Benson, J. A. (1988). Crisis revisited: An analysis of strategies used by Tylenol in the second tampering episode. *Central States Speech Journal, 39*(1), 49–66.

Capers, R. S., & Lipton, E. (1993). Hubble error: Time, money and millionths of an inch. *Academy of Management Executive, 7*(4), 41–62.

Dunn, M. (2003, August 27). Investigators issue scathing report of NASA's management. *The Tuscaloosa News,* p. A3.

Eisler, P., Watson, T., & Levin, A. (2003, August 27). Report flays NASA culture. *USA Today,* p. 1A.

Ellis, D. G., & Fisher, B. A. (1994). *Small group decision making: Communication and the group process* (4th ed.). New York: McGraw-Hill.

French, J. R. P., & Raven, B. (1968). The bases of social power. In D. Cartwright & A. Zander (Eds.), *Group Dynamics.* New York: Harper & Row.

Gibb, J. (1961). Defensive communication. *Journal of Communication, 11*, 141–148.

Gouran, D. S., Hirokawa, R. Y., & Martz, A. E. (1986). A critical analysis of factors related to decisional processes involved in the *Challenger* disaster. *Central States Speech Journal, 37,* 119–135.

Guiliano, E. (1982). *The complete illustrated works of Lewis Carroll.* New York: Avenel Books.

Harris, T. E. (2002). *Applied organizational communication: Principles and pragmatics for future practice* (2nd ed.). Mahwah, NJ: Lawrence Erlbaum.

Herek, G., Janis, I. L., & Huth, P. (1987). Decision-making during international crisis: Is quality of process related to outcome? *Journal of Conflict Resolution, 31,* pp. 203–226.

Hirokawa, R. Y. (1983). Group communication and problem solving effectiveness: An investigation of group phases. *Human Communication Research, 9,* 291–305.

Hirokawa, R. Y. (2003). Communication and group decision-making efficacy. In R. Y. Hirokawa, R. S. Cathcart, L. A. Samovar, & L. D. Henman (Eds.), *Small group communication: Theory & practice: An anthology* (3rd ed., pp. 125–133). Los Angeles: Roxbury.

Jablonski, J. R. (1992). *Implementing TQM* (2nd ed.). San Diego, CA: Pfeiffer.

Janis, I. L. (1983). *Groupthink: Psychological studies of policy decisions and fiascoes* (2nd ed.). Boston: Houghton Mifflin.

Katzenbach, J. R., & Smith, D. K. (1993). *The wisdom of teams: Create a high-performance organization.* Boston: Harvard Business School Press.

Kruglanski, A. W. (1986, August). Freezethink and the *Challenger. Psychology Today,* pp. 48–49.

Levin, A. (2003, August 27). Board found agency full of flaws. *USA Today,* p. 5A.

Schultz, B., Ketrow, S. M., & Urban, D. M. (1995). Improving decision quality in the small group:

The role of the reminder. *Small Group Research, 26,* pp. 521–541.

Seibold, D. R., & Krikorian, D. H. (1997). Planning and facilitating group meetings. In L. R. Frey & J. K. Barge (Eds.), *Managing group life: Communication in decision-making groups* (pp. 270–305). Boston: Houghton Mifflin.

Stein, B. A., & Kanter, R. M. (1993). Why good people do bad things: A retrospective on the Hubble fiasco. *Academy of Management Executive, 7*(4), 58–62.

Street, M. D. (1997). Groupthink: An examination of theoretical issues, implications, and future research. *Small Group Research, 28,* pp. 72–93.

Trujillo, N., & Roth, E. L. (1987). Organizational perspectives for public relations research and practice. *Management Communication Quarterly, 1,* 218–224.

Watson, T. (2003, May 15). Probe slams NASA safety. *USA Today,* p. 1A.

Watson, T. (2003, June 24). Records show NASA safety office cuts. *USA Today,* p. 3A

Weick, K. E. (1979). *The social psychology of organizing.* (2nd ed.). Reading, MA: Addison-Wesley.

Whyte, G. (1991). Decision failures: Why they occur and how to prevent them. *Academy of Management Executive, 5*(2), 23–31.

Wood, J. T. (1992). Alternative methods of group decision making. In R. S. Cathcart & L. A. Samovar (Eds.), *Small group communication: A reader* (6th ed., pp. 158–164). Dubuque, IA: Wm. C. Brown.

Wyatt, S. (2000, Sept. 23). Doctored photo highlights need to diversity. *The Tuscaloosa News,* p. 5A.

Yalom, I. (1985). *The theory and practice of group psychotherapy.* New York: Basic Books.

10

Creativity in the Small Group Process

CHAPTER OUTLINE

What Is Creativity?

Creativity Means a New Way of Looking

Barriers to Creativity
Perceptual Barriers
Cultural Barriers
Emotional Barriers

Techniques for Encouraging Creativity
Idea Needlers
Manipulative Verbs
Association and Metaphors
Analogy

Solving Problems Creatively

A Creative Group Climate
Openness
Sharing
Gibb's Communication Climate
Comparisons

Summary

Discussion Questions

Exercises

References

CHAPTER OBJECTIVES

- Understand creativity.
- Explain creativity as a new way of looking.
- Outline the perceptual, cultural, and emotional barriers to creativity.
- Demonstrate the use of idea needlers and manipulative verbs.
- Examine the importance of association, metaphors, analogy, and fantasy for creativity.
- Discuss ways of solving problems creatively.
- Provide the elements of a creative group climate.
- Review and explain Gibb's group climate factors.

KEY TERMS

Algorithms
Analogy
Association
Certainty versus
  provisionalism
Control versus problem
  orientation
Creativity
Cultural barriers

Emotional barriers
Equifinality
Evaluation versus description
Group climate
Heuristics
Idea needlers
Imagination
Manipulative verbs
Metaphors

Neutrality versus empathy
Openness
Paradigmatic thinking
Paradigms
Perceptual barriers
Reciprocity
Sharing
Strategy versus spontaneity
Superiority versus equality

Lewis Thomas tells an intriguing story about the wasp called *Sphex*. At egg-laying time, she flies looking for caterpillars. When she finds one, she swoops down, paralyses it, and carries if off to the entrance of the burrow to her nest. The caterpillar is placed right at the "front door," and the wasp goes inside to check that everything is in order. She then returns to pull the caterpillar in. If, however, the caterpillar is moved just a short distance while she is inside, we begin to see the limits of her well-managed behavior. She will search for the caterpillar, deposit it at the front door, and engage in the nest-checking procedure all over again. If the caterpillar is removed a second time, the dragging back and checking procedure will be repeated in exactly the same way. If you wish, by moving the caterpillar every time the wasp enters the nest, you can lock the creature into an endless cycle of mindless behavior. (*Imaginization*, Morgan, 1993, p. 264)

Groups must do more than simply reproduce the existing system. They must create something new. This creative process is facilitated by a creative group interaction. This chapter focuses on the concepts behind group creativity. It defines creativity and examines some of the myths surrounding it, exposes some of the barriers to creativity, provides techniques for increasing creativity and steps for solving problems creatively, and outlines the requirements for a creative climate.

What Is Creativity?

When what you do is new, different, and helpful, it is creative (Goman, 2000). "Creativity is . . . going beyond the current boundaries of technology, knowledge, social norms or beliefs . . . [or] seeing and acting on new relationships, thereby bringing them to life" (Anderson, 1992, p. 41). "Creativity in this sense involves the power to originate, to break away from the existing ways of looking at things, to move freely in the realm of the imagination, to create . . . new ideas and strong feelings" (Sacks, 1995, pp. 241–242).

Trying something new, invoking new perceptions, or providing a new response are creative approaches to problem solving. If you drive a new route to work to avoid a traffic jam, you are using creativity. Adding a new spice or other nonstandard ingredient to the chili recipe is a creative act. Such ideas enhance and expand the possibilities of a product, a way of doing something, or a way of seeing things. After all, what is an Egg McMuffin but egg, cheese, ham, and a muffin (with lots of cholesterol)? Sometimes "boldly going where no one has gone before" is a group's goal, but more often the desired outcome is finding a better solution to a mundane problem.

Albert Einstein is credited with having said: "Imagination is more important than knowledge"; "Our thinking creates problems that the same type of thinking will not solve"; "Everything should be made as simple as possible, but not simpler"; and "To raise new questions, new possibilities, to regard old problems from a new angle, requires creative imagination and marks real advance" (Morgan, 1993). Imagination, insightful understanding, and creativity are at the core of these statements.

In our thinking and behaving, we sometimes find ourselves locked in boxes of closed perspectives with actions that prevent us from discovering insights or developing solutions. As a simple example, it took years before someone asked the obvious question: Why do freezers have to lie on their sides and not stand up like refrigerators? The first freezer was prone, so subsequent freezers were also made prone, but now we have upright freezers. Bose asked a similar question about the size of the traditional speaker: Why so huge? Now we have very good small speakers.

What makes creativity possible is the concept of an underlying system, or ground, beneath the surface of our perceptions of apparently disparate and unrelated phenomena. Because of this unifying ground, there are innumerable ways of getting to the same place (equifinality). Einstein's famous statement, "God does not play dice with the universe," suggests his assumption of such a system. Problems do not occur randomly or in isolation. A systematic and open-minded approach to small group problem solving should yield answers to the underlying causes and consequences of a problem, directing us toward a simple, but not simplistic, solution. Often, this means unlocking ourselves from our habitual ways of thinking.

In popular myth and fiction, creativity is often associated with people who are considered weird or strange. We tend to imagine that creativity is linked to an impoverished antisocial individual locked away in a top-floor garret, finally emerging after years of experimentation, with a grand invention. At the very least, we see a McGuiver-like character creating simple and innovative solutions to complex problems, using only the minimal materials at hand. In the real world of everyday life, creativity is much less dramatic and much more common.

Creativity Means a New Way of Looking

Creativity is the result of looking at things in a new way, synthesizing two or more previously unrelated phenomena or modifying something that already exists. One way to understand creativity is to draw the distinction between *heuristics* and *algorithms*. A task is heuristic if it involves learning by doing, perhaps through trial and error. It is algorithmic if it imposes a straightforward, tried-and-true solution. Most tasks, even mundane ones, such as driving to work, completing a research paper, or arranging a room, do not have single, precise formats or answers. They partake of equifinality and are, therefore, open to creative solutions. We all engage in creative problem solving on a daily basis. If you change your study habits and the result is a better grade, you have been creative. When you rearrange your room or apartment so there is better access to certain areas, you have been a creative problem solver.

Creative individuals generate ideas *and* make something happen as a result. For example, a plain iron bar is worth $5. When someone took that iron bar and forged horseshoes from it, the value increased to $11. At some point, it was also used to make needles and the price rose to $3,285. Someone else decided to make watch springs from it and its value went to $250,000. The ability to see the same iron bar and realize its many uses is creativity. In this case, the difference between $5 and $250,000 (de Janasz, Dowd, & Schneider, 2002).

Some guidelines for creative problem solving include: keeping an open mind; withholding premature judgments; looking at problems in new ways and as opportunities, rather than as obstacles; accepting different opinions; avoiding too heavy reliance on logic; allowing for ambiguity; being willing to break the rules and "draw outside the lines"; and asking why and what if.

Reviews of business success stories reveal several attributes of creative people. Among other characteristics, innovative individuals tend to see combinations not obvious to everyone else. For example, "it was Craig McCaw's gift . . . to look across the traffic jams and see a nation of people talking on car phones. In September of 1994, Mr. McCaw made himself $800 million by selling McCaw Cellular Communications Corp., Kirkland, Wash., to New York–based AT&T Corp. for a total of $11.5 billion" (Bowers & Gupta, 1994, p. A1). Other innovative people simply spot the obvious and look at it in a new way. Quicken, the successful and profitable personal-finance software, is based on the simple principle that most people hate to balance their checkbooks. Scott Cook, a former brand manager at Procter & Gamble, observed this and came up with a solution. "People don't buy technology," Mr. Cook suggested. "They don't say, 'Fill 'er up. I'll take 10 gallons of technology.' They buy what technology does for them" (Bowers & Gupta, 1994, p. A13). Entrepreneurs who strike it rich are the ones who take existing concepts and find new ways of utilizing them. Organizations must be creative in order to survive in the twenty-first century (Robinson & Stern, 1997; Senge, Keliner, Roberts, & Smith, 1999).

Creative thinking is available to all of us, but too often, we stifle it in ourselves. One advantage of working in a group is being able to take advantage of the creative processes of a number of people working simultaneously. People think, make decisions, and solve problems in different ways. A group can explore and take advantage of those alternative approaches to a problem or a decision and thereby develop creative new insights, decisions, and solutions.

Barriers to Creativity

In general, we limit our creativity because we lack self-confidence, fear taking risks, feel a need to conform, do not feel we are in an environment that encourages creativity, or find ourselves locked into our habitual ways of looking at the world—our paradigms. These blocks to our creativity can often be traced to our social training, beginning at a very young age.

The vast majority of our education and acculturation has been based on learning the right way to do something. Rarely are we rewarded or provided positive recognition for being wrong or marching to the tune of "a different drummer." Being different can mean we will be ostracized. Perception, culture, and emotion stand as barriers to the free use of our creative imaginations.

Perceptual Barriers

Perceptual barriers are those characteristics that blind us to the hidden dimensions of an issue. Perceptual barriers include: difficulty in isolating the problem; narrowing the problem so much that we see only the immediate issue and not the larger context; overlooking "trivia" that may be at the base of the problem; overlooking the obvious or failing to investigate it fully; accepting superficial similarities with our prior experiences as indicative of sameness; inadequately defining terms or isolating attributes; and failing to distinguish between cause and effect (Adams, 1986).

Many of these perceptual barriers result from paradigmatic thinking. As Marshall McLuhan stated, we shape our tools and then our tools shape us. Our tendency is to define issues in terms of the ways we have already defined them. The following exercise illustrates this concept. Put nine dots on a piece of paper (as shown Figure 10.1). Connect all nine dots using four straight lines without lifting your pen or pencil from the paper. The solutions are revealed later in this section. (The secret is to try thinking outside the box.)

A paradigm is the preformed model we use for our thinking. It is the container within which acceptable discourse about an issue is defined. Thomas Kuhn (1962) outlined the impact of paradigms on how we think. Although Kuhn was focusing on scientists when he explained how their paradigms, or views of the world, limit their scopes of inquiry, the paradigmatic box that encloses our thinking applies to all of us. We each use paradigms to understand and respond to the problems, people, and ideas we encounter on a daily basis.

A paradigm will blind us, however, to certain facts, ideas, and problems, because we have come to accept it without question. In our search for understanding, we want certainty, but being certain means we have not left room for doubt in our world. In order to be creative, we must be willing to challenge the current paradigms, in order to see outside our boxes, or views, of the world and to open ourselves up to other options.

FIGURE 10.1   The Nine-Dot Puzzle

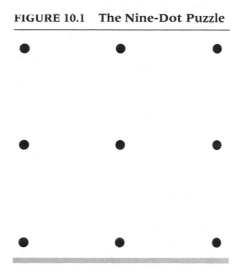

The letters Q W E R T Y U I O P form an all too familiar pattern for anyone using a computer keyboard. These are the top row of letters and they have appeared on typewriters since the 1870s (Oech, 1992). The original manual typewriters could not respond as quickly as an operator could type, so the keys would jam. Sholes & Co., a leading typewriter manufacturer, decided to slow down the operators by making the keyboard more difficult to use. This inefficiency was created by including the "O" and "I", the third and sixth most frequently used letters, in the top row, thereby slowing down the operator. Because this pattern worked to resolve the original manual typewriter problem, it has remained in spite of its built-in inefficiency.

As you can see by looking at Figure 10.2, the answer to the nine-dot exercise is not all that difficult, if you go outside the apparent box established paradigmatically by the nine dots. Alternately, all nine dots can be connected with one line—just use a very broad, felt marker roller and cover all nine dots in one sweep. Other creative solutions include bending the paper in a circular form so that you can move your pen or pencil around the paper and connect all nine dots, or folding the paper so that all nine dots are on top of each other and pushing the pencil through the page, so that the pencil pierces all nine dots. One line and all nine dots are then connected.

The following is another creativity exercise (Mattimore, 1994). Which of the following numbers is most different from the others?

1) Three
2) Thirteen
3) Thirty-one

Most people have difficulty with this exercise. The number that is really different is "2" since it is an even number, while the other five are odd, but we tend

FIGURE 10.2   The Nine-Dot Solution

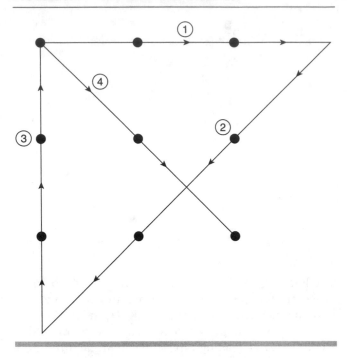

not to see the "2" since it is bracketed ")" off from the other numbers. We tend to define the problem in a standard, paradigmatic manner. By assuming the 1), 2), and 3) are simply organizing symbols, we miss the obvious—three additional numbers.

Paradigmatic thinking creates blocks to our thinking, leading us to assume we are inherently not creative people. When we are in trouble, however, we all find we have the ability to be creative.

Common Blocks and Creative Responses

Blocks	Creative Responses
That's impossible.	See the ways in which it is possible.
It's not exactly right.	Assume no solution is perfect.
I might appear foolish.	So did Albert Einstein.
Let's get serious.	Then, when do we get to have fun?
That's not logical.	Neither is the theory of light as both wave and particle.
That's not practical.	Who says?

Cultural Barriers

Behind perceptual barriers are those formed by cultural expectations. Our basic social and emotional needs are met through our membership and acceptance in a cultural network. The barriers presented by our cultural system are based on the expectation of conformity with rules and standard norms of thinking, behavior, and interaction. Cultural barriers include: a requirement for conformity; an expectation of practicality and efficiency; particular arenas for competition or cooperation; an expectation of politeness and following rules for social order; a reliance on statistical proofs; a dependence on generalizations; a trust in the power of reason and logic; a belief in an either/or perspective on issues; and a reliance on expert knowledge.

We learn early that playing by the rules will assure us a place in the game. We were also taught in our early schooling to stay in line, not to cheat, and not to talk out of turn (raise your hand). But, when we become too orderly, we lose the ability to see things from a different perspective. The nine dots and the "2)" examples make that point.

Our experiences in school and in the work world also teach us that life, after all, is serious business. However, in order to move beyond "business as usual," we need to relax and play with things, words, ideas, and concepts. Sometimes we need to be bold and "just do it." Although society places a great deal of emphasis on seeing things as they are, creativity involves seeing things slightly differently. For instance, write down all the uses you can think of for a Styrofoam cup. Can you name one hundred? It's not hard, if you realize the cup can be used to mold (as a cookie cutter or to make sand castles), for packing (break it up), and to store things (nails, pennies). Some groups have used the cup for pets (to hold fish), telephones, and for numerous other nonstandard uses. Just because the cup was designed for coffee does not limit its potential for other creative uses.

Like individuals, organizations can develop working habits that restrict creativity. Different divisions or departments focus on their expertise and areas of responsibility which can lead to perceptual barriers. *Creative abrasion* is being used by some organizations to overcome this limitation (Leonard-Barton & Sensiper, 1998). This involves bringing people together with different skills, ideas, and values to generate new ideas, problem-solving approaches, and products. "This process breaks traditional frames of thinking by having diverse perspectives rub creatively against each other to develop innovative solutions" (Cummings & Worley, 2001, p. 527). In addition, organizations often turn to outside consultants who offer different perspectives regarding issues or problems (Davenport, Prusak, & Wilson, 2003). Both approaches allow individuals access to different ways of viewing a problem.

Some of our most creative moments occur when we are willing to play, question, challenge, and enjoy solving problems (Mattimore, 1994; Thompson, 1992). Being naive or a little disrespectful of the "way things have always been done" can pay off when we confront serious issues.

Emotional Barriers

In addition to and closely associated with perceptual and emotional barriers to creativity are the personal, emotional barriers we place in the way of our creative abilities. There are risks and hard work associated with "going out on a limb" and trying something new. We may have to take more time than we would like; we may make a mistake; we may risk the censure of our peers by looking foolish or being judged incompetent.

Creativity can appear to be a chancy pursuit, so we tend to be very tentative in our attempts. We often seek the approval of others for our ideas, rather than risk being wrong. Most significant inventions throughout history have been initially rejected by the majority of people. Although our schooling and upbringing have emphasized being careful to find the right answers before we raise our hands, creative answers require a willingness to take a chance, to think out loud, and risk being wrong. If we miss the target on the first try, we can practice, and eventually, we will be on target and find appropriate answers. Fear of making a mistake often causes us to limit our creativity. In a sense, we have lost our right to be wrong.

Because our society rewards being "right" and having particular knowledge, we are sometimes caught in the net of our own expertise. If we know too much about a subject, we may lose our ability to see new and different approaches and concepts. All too often, we assume that the current standard of knowledge and ways of doing things are the best. There are numerous examples of highly placed people being overly certain. To name only one, in 1899, the director of the U.S. Patent Office said that "everything that can be invented has been invented" and requested that the Patent Office be dismantled and that he be transferred to a new position in government. Today, however, the average American automobile contains as much information-processing computing power as was on board the *Apollo* moonlanding craft in 1969, and more than a 1970s mainframe computer (Davis & Davidson, 1991).

We also frequently assume that only large research organizations or experts with particular qualifications can come up with innovative and relevant ideas. When we think of grand inventions, we imagine the Apple Computers, Sonys, or Whirlpools of the world, but "two-thirds of all inventions are created by individuals on their own time or by small organizations" (Thompson, 1992, p. 190). We are all familiar with the concept "nothing ventured, nothing gained." Creativity requires that we risk something in order to find a better solution. As Picasso said, "Every act of creation is first of all an act of destruction." We must be willing to destroy some of our preconceptions. Picasso's experiments with new ways of seeing, challenging the traditional western view of what constituted a suitable viewpoint for paintings, gave us Cubism and other innovative ways of viewing reality. We need to be willing to challenge existing paradigms, in order to open the door to creativity.

Techniques for Encouraging Creativity

Although we are all naturally creative, we tend to squelch our abilities in our efforts to conform to social expectations. Four specific techniques can help us find ways of opening ourselves up to our creativity. These are idea needlers, manipulative verbs, association and metaphors, and analogy.

Idea Needlers

In a vein similar to the Styrofoam cup exercise, imagine how many uses there are for baking soda. A few years ago, we might have limited its use to a cooking ingredient. Now it is used to keep refrigerators odor free, to clean carpets, and to brush teeth. There are probably many other uses for baking soda that you can think of. "Tea bags" are now used for instant coffee, premeasured doses of medicine, and numerous other applications. What if you wanted to question the design of the typical college classroom or the arrangement of the chairs in the classroom? The idea needlers in Table 10.1 are designed to help us raise the questions that enhance our ability to discover ideas.

TABLE 10.1   Idea Needlers

How much of this is the result of custom, tradition, or opinions?	Will it be better standing still?
Why does it have this shape?	What other layout might be better?
How would I design it, if I had to build it in my home workshop?	Can cause and effect be reversed? Is one possibly also the other?
What if this were turned inside out? reversed? upside down?	Should it be put on the other end or in the middle?
What if this were larger? higher? longer? wider? thicker? lower?	Should it slide instead of rotate?
What else can it be made to do?	Demonstrate or describe it by what it isn't.
What other power would work better?	Has a search been made of the patent literature? trade journals?
Where else can this be done?	Could a vendor supply this for less?
What if the order were changed?	How could this be made easier to use?
Suppose this were left out?	Can it be made safer?
How can it appeal to the senses?	How could this be changed for quicker assembly?
How about extra value?	What other materials would do this job?
Can this be multiplied?	What is similar to this, but costs less? Why?
What if this were blown up?	What if it were made faster?
What if this were carried to extremes?	What motion or power is wasted?
How can this be made more compact?	Could the package be used for something afterwards?
Would this be better symmetrical or asymmetrical?	If all specifications could be forgotten, how else could the basic function be accomplished?
In what form could this be? Liquid, powder, paste, or solid? Rod, tube, triangle, cube, or sphere?	Could these be made to meet specifications?
Can motion be added to it?	How do noncompetitors solve problems similar to this?

These idea needlers offer us the opportunity to use a different perspective, or lens, to view the problem.

Manipulative Verbs

When we decide to alter, multiply, eliminate, divide, or transpose, we are using manipulative verbs to change the way we view a particular process. Changing a verb can completely alter the sense of a statement and can have a dramatic effect on preconceived meanings. "For instance, a baseball or softball manager can shuffle the team's batting order 362,880 times by merely rearranging his or her starting players" (Osborne, 1963, p. 273). Table 10.2 shows some manipulative verbs that can be used to rephrase questions in ways that can transform our thinking about a problem or issue. Whatever the problem area, changing key words can open up possibilities for ways of seeing an issue that might never have occurred before.

Association and Metaphors

Robert Frost once said, "an idea is a feat of association." When we use concepts such as "most like" or "least like," we are using association. Metaphors associate unlike phenomena and help us visualize concepts. When Shakespeare called the world a "stage," he made clear his idea of life and of society. There are numerous ways to include metaphors in creative thinking. Metaphors such as "a breath of fresh air," "the new kid on the block," "an interesting window on the world," or "back to square one" all provide expanded insights into meaning beyond the literal definitions of the words. Additionally, "metaphors play a critical role in the communication process. They are the best devices to use when describing abstract concepts and expressing emotions" (Johnson & Hackman, 1995, p. 100).

In addition, particular terms carry connotations we associate with prior experiences and previously heard uses. When we talk about "eradicating poverty," we associate the term with other things we have "eradicated," such as tuberculosis, hunger, other diseases. Perhaps we find "eradicate" is too strong a word for

TABLE 10.2 Manipulative Verbs

magnify	complement	minify	submerge	modify	add
alter	soften	adapt	fluff up	combine	lighten
substitute	by-pass	reverse	subtract	divide	stretch
multiply	repeat	eliminate	thicken	separate	protect
subdue	extrude	invert	repel	distort	symbolize
transpose	segregate	unify	integrate	squeeze	
rotate	abstract	flatten	rearrange	freeze	

what we consider possible, given our associations with that word. Can we "alleviate" poverty? What are other problems we have alleviated? The associations may or may not involve the same subject or class of subjects. We may associate herds of elephants or horses, packs of dogs, or flocks of chickens with a particular group of people or with the clouds in the sky. Try looking at the descriptions in Table 10.3 and see if they free up your conception of groups.

Analogy

The use of analogy is similar to that of association and metaphor, but it is understood here to refer to the ways in which we broaden our senses of what is actually possible. Tunnel vision limits our perspective to a small set of ideas and frequently hampers our quest for creativity. The use of analogies, a comparison between things that are similar in some respects but quite different in others, helps to open up our perceptions to other useful concepts. For example, when Procter & Gamble tried to solve the problem of how to package delicate potato chips they found themselves limited to the traditional "bag full of air" answer. Then they considered other fragile and brittle items. The most obvious analogy was dried leaves. A new way of packaging potato chips came about when the group asked themselves, "Is there a time when leaves are *not* fragile?" A walk through the woods showed that leaves, when they are wet, are not fragile and they conform to the mold they land on (a branch, rock, or pile). So, the answer was to package potato chips when they are wet, conform them to a preset form, and then dry them. The ultimate product was Pringles potato crisps.

   Dr. Rene Lanennec, the inventor of the stethoscope, got his inspiration from observing children sending signals to each other by tapping on the end of a log. Henry Ford visited a slaughterhouse and was inspired to produce a better way to mass-produce cars. Carrier was watching water condensing on the side of a glass and got the idea for an air conditioner. Eli Whitney found a means for inventing the cotton "gin" (short for en*gin*e) when he saw a cat reaching through a fence trying to grab a chicken (Mattimore, 1994). Thus, idea needlers, manipulative verbs, association, and analogy are four techniques that tap into our creative potential.

TABLE 10.3   Concepts of Groups

A shrewdness of apes	A down of hares	A leap of leopards
A murder of crows	A drift of hogs	A nest of vipers
An unkindness of ravens	An exaltation of larks	A parliament of owls
A crash of rhinos	A gam of whales	A pitying of turtle doves
A charm of finches	A grist of bees	A rafter of turkeys
A covey of quail	A kindle of kittens	A smack of jellyfish

Organizations train group creativity by presenting building materials and asking the participants to design an "award winning" structure. This group is part of the Management Development Project at the University of Alabama.

Solving Problems Creatively

When you are unable to think of a creative idea, consider these five suggestions:

1. *Trigger your unconscious:* Take a rest from consciously thinking about the problem you're trying to solve. You can get insights while you're working out, walking, playing cards, or taking a shower.

2. *Loosen your mind:* Let your mind wander a little. You'll go back to the task at hand relaxed and refreshed.

3. *Break down the problem into a series of doable tasks:* The problem can be broken down into either a set of questions to be answered or a series of small problems that can be solved one at a time.

4. *Do some research:* Look for other examples of the same type of problem somewhere else. Most problems have been faced in some way by someone else somewhere. As we have heard time and again, "there is nothing new under the sun." Search for alternative solutions by looking in other locations.

5. *Ask yourself questions:*
    A. What are the different parts of the problem?
    B. Does one part hold the key to other parts?
    C. Can I apply knowledge from other situations to this one?
    D. Would exaggerating the problem make the solution more apparent?
    E. What is the normal situation? Are there alternatives?

A Creative Group Climate

We have now examined the issues surrounding creativity, in general. Group creativity, however, frequently depends on the climate of the group process itself. A supportive climate increases the probability that individuals and groups will be creative and successful in reaching their goals. The cornerstones of a creative climate are mutual trust, respect, and commitment. Group leaders, facilitators, and members must address the fundamental issues of openness and sharing, if a creative group climate is to be cultivated.

Openness

Maintaining an open, supportive communication climate during the problem-solving process is vital for creativity. People have similar emotional and safety concerns, which usually include: How open and honest can I be in this situation? Will anyone use what I say against me? Will others be honest about their feelings and opinions? Are my goals compatible with the others? Can I freely express my wishes and fears?

Sharing

Being willing to share relevant information, resources, and responsibility is a cornerstone of a creative climate. Information and responsibility must be shared in order to trust that we will not be manipulated. Without trust, we can become defensive and ruin the possibilities for creative interaction. We generally want to know how we fit in, what is acceptable behavior, what our roles and responsibilities are, how we can contribute, and what others expect from us.

Some groups feel good, and we are happy to be members of them. Other groups feel tense or hostile, and being a member of the group is distasteful and hard work. These feelings are based on the dynamics of supportive and defensive climates generated in the group. Jack Gibb (1961) defined strategies that create a supportive group climate versus those that create a defensive one. The difference between these two types of climate lies in how we communicate, not the content, goal, or purpose of what we communicate.

We discuss the six comparisons Gibb made to help explain the difference between defensive and supportive communication. These comparisons are: evaluation versus description; control versus problem orientation; strategy versus spontaneity; neutrality versus empathy; superiority versus equality; and certainty versus provisionalism. In the last category, we discuss the effects of group climate through reciprocity.

Gibb's Communication Climate Comparisons

Evaluation versus Description.   Evaluation places us in a hierarchic relationship, with the evaluator assuming a position of superiority. This immediately throws off the balance of communication and sets up a backdrop for tension.

When someone is blaming us or letting us know he or she is judging what we say or do, we become defensive. Comments such as, "If it weren't for your lack of interest, we'd be doing much better" make most of us defend ourselves rather than listen. At their best, evaluation and judgment teach us to avoid future criticism. At their worst, they lead us to avoid the situation, person, or problem. What evaluation usually does not do is cause us to voluntarily alter our behavior. When such evaluation is delivered in front of the rest of the group, it is face threatening and may cause us to become even more defensive. In addition, the rest of the group is likely to respond by becoming uncomfortable and defensive.

Fortunately, we can avoid that response by describing the same situation with neutral statements of fact. By doing so, we have a very good chance of gaining the support of the other group members. If it really is my fault that the group is not progressing, a simple description without demanding that I accept guilt will allow me to hear the message. Stick to the observable facts. Since our goal should be to make the group work effectively as a unit, little can be gained by ostracizing individual members through evaluation.

To guarantee that our comments are seen as supportive, rather than as simply critical, we need to "own" the statements and take responsibility. "I think we should end the meeting now, so we can go watch the game; we can finish the report later when we don't have other distractions," is vastly different from "None of you seem to care about this report, since all you want to do is watch the game." As with feedback, it is important to be specific in our comments and avoid making value judgments. Saying, "I wouldn't have to repeat myself time and again if you would just pay attention like any adult" is not as likely to make someone listen more closely to my message as saying something like, "Apparently I am not being clear. What can I do to make the process work better?" Clearly, the real issue is our own perception regarding the other group members. Do we see them as needing our judgment, or do we see them as colleagues for whom we have respect and compassion?

Control versus Problem Orientation.   Issuing orders or making it clear that we have the power to control others' behavior creates defensiveness. When we attempt to change the attitudes of other group members or to restrict their freedom, we will likely encounter some resistance. Group members are well aware of where power lies and will resist our claiming it.

In the case of small groups, the point is to solve a problem using the input of all members. It is not intended as a forum for a power play. Orienting the group discussion toward the problem allows a "we" orientation rather than an "us versus them" orientation. In many organizations, there is a great deal of discussion regarding empowering employees through creating a team spirit and a group orientation (Phillips & Wallace, 1992). Unfortunately, many managers and supervisors still believe that telling others what to do is the best way to achieve results (Daniels & Spiker, 1991). In small groups, there is frequently pressure to "cut to the chase" and produce results. Rather than one individual's succumbing to the temptation to take charge and orchestrate the process, however, the end results are better served by describing the problem and letting the group take responsibility for the outcome.

Strategy versus Spontaneity.   The use of gimmicks or manipulation to get what we want may seem strategic in assuring a particular outcome from the group process, but it rarely sets the tone for a cooperative, supportive group climate. Our natural resistance to high-pressure sales comes from our dislike of being manipulated. If the gimmicks do work and we feel we have been manipulated, we are not likely to forgive or forget. At that point the game is on, and the only issue is who wins which round. Missing from this game is the goal of the group!

Spontaneity, on the other hand, is a willingness to be honest and direct. Gibb is proposing that we remain open and responsive to the group process as it unfolds. Rather than trying to plan how we are going to achieve our own goals (strategy), we should be open to the fresh ideas that evolve in the context of the ongoing group process (spontaneity).

Neutrality versus Empathy.   If we come to our group meeting feeling distraught because our apartment caught fire, our computer was ruined, and we lost all our possessions, and our group's only response is, "Too bad," or "That is a problem. Now let's get on with our important group work," we don't feel supported. We are looking for empathy, and we are receiving neutrality. When people are detached from our needs or seem indifferent, they are expressing neutrality.

The opposite of neutrality is empathy. Empathy expresses a concern for group members as people, not just as other group participants. Empathy acknowledges others as worthwhile, and involves a sensitivity toward others, a willingness to suspend judgment, and an attempt to respond to their needs. Simple supportive statements such as, "I'm really sorry. Is there anything we can do? If you are unable to fully participate today, we understand" express interest, show concern, and assure the best possible continued participation of each member in the group process.

Superiority versus Equality.   In any group, there are bound to be discrepancies in experience, training, particular knowledge, status, or power. Although these may be apparent on the surface, for the group to work effectively, as we have discussed earlier, we need the input of all members. When some members perceive themselves or others to be superior in some way, they may shut those with less power, influence, or expertise out of the process, to the detriment of all.

A sense of equality, on the other hand, sets the stage for an effective group process. A simple question such as: "What do you think?" indicates our interest in the other member's perspective. In addition, as we have noted above, it is sometimes the most unlikely person who offers the most creative insights. To have shut that person out of the discussion robs us of the value of her or his input. To the extent that we are all vested in the outcome of the group process, we should encourage equal participation from each of the members.

Certainty versus Provisionalism.   Many of us have areas in which we feel we have particular knowledge or expertise. However, in a group process, we need to be aware that others may hold their own quite different understandings with equal assurance. As we have discussed under "Active Listening," arrogance and disrespect most often serve the opposite purpose from what we have in mind, creating defensiveness in the other group members and undermining the group process. Labeling other group members as wrong, foolish, or naive is clearly counterproductive to achieving the group's task or social-facilitation goals. To the extent that we refuse to listen to others and are unwavering in our positions, there is little hope for productive group discussion.

On the other hand, if we state our positions provisionally, admitting a willingness to hear the views of others, we are more likely to be heard by them, as well. It is important to keep in mind that if the object was for us to come up with the solution on our own, we would not need to bother convening a group.

Summary

The six dichotomous categories allow us to see the difference between defensive and supportive communication. Supportive communication fosters a climate for creative problem solving. When people feel defensive, they are likely to respond in kind. If my contributions or personal attributes come under attack, I am likely to respond in kind. On the other hand, if I feel valued and appreciated for my contributions and for who I am, I am likely to respond in positive ways and support the other members of my group. Ultimately, membership in a small group should bring us joy, make us feel worthwhile, and open us to new challenges and opportunities. Positive group climates benefit all members and foster creativity.

All of these issues impact on group climate. When group members listen attentively and supportively, group climate and the potential for creativity is enhanced. When group members show disrespect and lack of interest, members become defensive, and creativity is discouraged.

DISCUSSION QUESTIONS

1. Provide an example of creativity from your own experience. How does it fit with the chapter's discussion of creativity?

2. What guidelines exist for creative problem solving?

3. What is meant by thinking outside the box? Getting outside our paradigm?

4. Name five cultural barriers to creativity. Why do you think these would keep a group from being creative?

5. Individually, or as a group, find examples of emotional barriers limiting creativity.

6. Identify five metaphors that are used to describe five different majors or concentrations of study on your campus. For example, being a premed is a "bear." Why are metaphors useful in creativity?

7. What are some ways of solving problems creatively?

8. What actions can be taken to develop a creative group climate?

9. What central issues or themes are present across Gibb's six group climate comparisons? What characteristics do the six dichotomous categories share? How do they differ?

10. Individually, or as a group, develop a scenario in which defensive communication occurs. Develop a second scenario in which the same goals are sought but supportive communication is used.

EXERCISES

1. Competitive team creativity; 2. Using creativity tools: The Styrofoam cup; 3. Seeing alternative answers; 4. Using metaphors; 5. Metaphors: Application; 6. Speculate: What if?; 7. Getting Outside limitations; 8. Seeing

1. COMPETITIVE TEAM CREATIVITY

Form small group teams to compete with each other in the following exercise. Each team should write down on a sheet of paper to be handed in: (a) the seven words they identify, and (b) their statement of the three rules used in creating these letter sequences. Points can be given to the groups for the speed with which they complete the task (or group order in which they complete the task), for accuracy in correctly identifying the words, and for correctly stating the three rules used in the creation of these letter sequences.

Find the word in each of the following seven-letter sequences. All seven words are related or similar to each other in some way. Identify three rules that make this exercise relatively easy to accomplish (once you become aware of them).

FRAIPUPLET
BIARNUAFNATS
TCRAFNBREURIRY
IDURAFTTES
UEILDERRBEFRTRIES
RUFIITGFS
TGRRFAIPUES

How does working in a group make completing this exercise faster or more effective? How do the concepts of creative problem solving, such as keeping an open mind, looking at problems in new ways, overcoming perceptual and emotional barriers, use of association, loosening your mind, and triggering your unconscious help to solve this problem?

How does the pressure of feeling a time constraint imposed by being in competition with other teams distract from your ability to solve the problem? Kelly and Karau (1993) suggest that speed and creativity of responses are inversely related (faster responses are less creative) but that, with practice, creativity increases in responses made in shorter amounts of time.

When the solution does come, is there a sudden "pop" of "being able to see the answer" or a slow, methodical, continuous development of the answer? What does this say about how creativity works?

2. USING CREATIVITY TOOLS—THE STYROFOAM CUP

1. Form small groups. You will be given a Styrofoam cup. Your group is to come up with as many uses as possible for this cup. Use the idea needlers and manipulative verbs.
2. Appoint a recorder who will keep track, including the number, of your answers. Most groups can reach 100 uses in about 15 minutes—your allotted time for this exercise.
3. At the end of the 15 minutes, your instructor will declare a numerical winner—the group with the most uses.
4. Return to your list and pick the 5 most creative uses and share these with the other groups. What uses did your group miss?
5. The vast majority of problems can be successfully examined by increasing our own abilities to get outside of our preconceived ideas. In this case that the Styrofoam cup is designed to hold hot liquids.

3. SEEING ALTERNATIVE ANSWERS

1. Solve the following problems—both can be solved:

   Number 1. A man looks at a portrait and says: "Sons and brothers, I have none, but this person's father is my father's son." At which portrait is he looking?

   Number 2. You have 15 matches. Take away six so that you have ten left.

2. Form a small group and reach consensus on the solutions.
3. If you believe it is appropriate, try applying the idea needlers or manipulative verbs.
4. Compare your answers with the solutions provided by your instructor.

4. USING METAPHORS

Directions

Metaphors, comparing unrelated concepts, allow us to develop insights. We talk and think in metaphors all the time as we pore over the class material for a test, jog our memories, go on a diet, juggle our busy schedules, march to different drummers, or fight a cold.

Try developing some metaphorical thinking on the issue or problem being discussed by your group or team. Or, pick a topic important to the group. For example, compare team members and cats on leadership issues and motivation; war and four years of college on challenges and successes; conducting an orchestra and preparing a presentation; raising a child and dealing with a noisy neighbor; river flows and your cash flow; and so on. Most important is to enjoy the process of adding new insights.

Your group issue _____

Metaphors _____

Insights from the comparisons _____

5 . METAPHORS: APPLICATION

1. Pick a problem. Perhaps the group cannot find enough information on a topic, parking on campus is impossible, or the like.
2. Write down a problem statement—be specific.
3. Reduce the problem statement to a word or short phrase.

   WORD: _____

   PHRASE: _____

4. Insert your word to create appropriate analogies—hint, develop several.

   (Your word) is like a:

   (Your phrase) is like a:

5. From these analogies, decide which one(s) is most useful, cleverest, appropriate, or unexpected from these analogies and proceed to solve the problem metaphorically (remember Pringles).
6. Look at your metaphorical solutions. Identify two ideas that can help your group solve the problem.

6 . SPECULATE: WHAT IF?

Directions

Choose a topic that everyone in the group agrees should be addressed. Examples would be how can everyone in this group get full financial assistance to go to college; how can everyone in this group cut study time and get better grades; how can we eliminate antisocial activities; how can we change the Electoral College; how can we take positive actions to eliminate discrimination, and so on.

Now apply the concept "What if?" Ask. For example, what if there was a means to finance everyone's education. What would it need to look like? What do we now have that provides an example or metaphor? Even wilder speculation could include eliminating universities, reducing the four-year degree to a two-year degree, allowing life experiences to be accredited, and so on.

1. Speculate wildly on the topic of your choice. 2. Try applying the idea needlers and manipulative verbs discussed in the chapter. 3. Develop as many alternative solutions as possible. 4. Return and see what can be done to turn these speculative ideas into possible solutions.

7. GETTING OUTSIDE LIMITATIONS

In many situations, we limit ourselves because of our own backgrounds. Two stories can illustrate this point. First a hungry northern pike, when placed in one-half of a large aquarium divided by a glass partition with numerous minnows on the other side, will attempt to obtain the minnows. After battering itself against the glass repeatedly, it learns that obtaining the minnows will be an impossible task. When the glass partition is removed, the pike will not attack the minnows. The same pattern of behavior can be observed when a cat jumps onto a hot stove. Both behaviors exhibit the Pike Syndrome, which is characterized by:

1. Ignoring differences.
2. Assuming complete knowledge based on limited experience.
3. Letting past failures determine future decisions.
4. Failing to consider alternative means for solving the problem.
5. Overgeneralized reactions.

As a group, consider an important campus issue where the solutions now being offered show the Pike Syndrome. Refer to the five characteristics listed. Can you develop additional characteristics?

As a group, develop strategies based on this chapter that will help people break out of the limitations

REFERENCES

Anderson, J. V. (1992). Weirder than fiction: The reality and myths of creativity. *Academy of Management Executive, 6*(4), 40–47.

Benson, J. A. (1988). Crisis revisited: An analysis of strategies used by Tylenol in the second tampering episode. *Central States Speech Journal, 39*(1), 49–66.

Bowers, B., & Gupta, U. (1994, October 19). New entrepreneurs offer simple lesson in building a fortune. *The Wall Street Journal*, pp. A1, A13.

Cummings, T. G., & Worley, C. G. (2001). *Organizational development and change.* Mason, OH: South-Western.

Daniels, T. D., & Spiker, B. K. (1991). *Perspectives on organizational communication* (2nd ed.). Dubuque, IA: Brown.

Davenport, T. H., Prusak, L., & Wilson, H. J. (2003). *What's the big idea: Creating and capitalizing on the best management thinking.* Boston: Harvard Business School Press.

Davis, S., & Davidson, B. (1991). *2020 vision*. New York: Simon & Schuster.

de Janasz, S. C., Dowd, K. O., & Schneider, B. Z. (2002). *Interpersonal skills in organizations*. Boston: McGraw-Hill.

French, J. R. P., & Raven, B. (1968). The bases of social power. In D. Cartwright & A. Zander (Eds.), *Group Dynamics*. New York: Harper & Row.

Gibb, J. (1961). Defensive communication. *Journal of Communication, 11*, 141–148.

Goman, C. K. (2000). *Creativity in business: A practical guide for creative thinking*. Menlo Park, CA: Crisp Publications.

Johnson, C. E., & Hackman, M. Z. (1995). *Creative communication*. Prospect Heights, IL: Waveland.

Kelly, J. R., & Karau, S. J. (1993). Entrainment of creativity in small groups. *Small Group Research, 24*(2), 179–198.

Kuhn, T. S. (1962). *The structure of scientific revolutions*. Chicago: The University of Chicago Press.

Leonard-Barton, D., & Sensiper, S. (1998, Spring). The role of tacit knowledge in group innovation. *California Management Review, 40*, pp. 112–132.

Mattimore, B. W. (1994). *99 percent inspiration: Tips, tales & techniques for liberating your business creativity*. New York: AMACOM.

Morgan, G. (1993). *Imaginization*. Newbury Park, CA: Sage.

Oech, R. V. (1992). *A whack on the side of the head*. Menlo Park, CA: Creative Think.

Osborne, A. F. (1963). *Applied imagination* (3rd ed.). New York: Charles Scribner's Sons.

Phillips, D., & Wallace, L. (1992). *Influence in the workplace: Maximizing personal empowerment*. Dubuque, IA: Kendall/Hunt.

Robinson, A. G., & Stern, S. (1997). *Corporate creativity: How innovation and improvement actually happen*. San Francisco: Berrett-Koelhler.

Sacks, O. (1995). *An anthropologist on mars*. New York: Alfred A. Knopf.

Senge, P., Keliner, A., Roberts, C., & Smith, B. (1999). *The dance of change: The challenges of sustaining momentum in learning organizations*. New York: Doubleday/Currency.

Thompson, C. C. (1992). *What a great idea!: Key steps creative people take*. New York: Harper Perennial.

11

Group Process and Presentation Techniques

CHAPTER OUTLINE

Brainstorming

Creative Decision-Making Techniques
    Focus Groups
    Nominal Group Technique
    Delphi Technique
    Synectics
    Buzz Sessions
    Idea Writing
    Role Playing
    Listening Teams

Problem-Solving Tools
    Flowcharts
    Fishbone Diagrams
    Pareto's Principle

The RISK Procedure

PERT (Program Evaluation and Review Technique)

How These Techniques Are Used

Small Group Presentational Formats
    The Forum
    The Panel
    The Colloquium
    The Symposium

Summary

Discussion Questions

Exercises

References

CHAPTER OBJECTIVES

- Describe the goals and uses of brainstorming.
- Explain focus groups and their uses.
- Outline the nominal group technique.
- Illustrate why and how to use the Delphi technique.
- Clarify by example the use of synectics.
- Explain the use of buzz sessions.
- Provide an example of idea writing.

218

- Taking a single issue, show how to use role playing or listening teams.
- Use a solution to a problem and apply the RISK procedure or PERT.
- Utilize flowcharts, fishbone diagrams, and Pareto's principle.
- How these techniques are used.
- Suggest small group presentation formats.

KEY TERMS

Brainstorming	Forum	Prioritizing
Buzz sessions	Idea writing	RISK procedure
Colloquium	Listening teams	Role playing
Delphi technique	Nominal group technique	Six Sigma
Fishbone diagrams	Panel	Symposium
Flowcharts	Pareto's principle	Synectics
Focus groups	PERT	Total Quality Management

Along automobile row it was said of him that he could sell anything. . . . There was the time he latched on to the old General Sherman tank. Bought it off a junk dealer for twenty-five dollars. Harvey put it on a big wooden platform in front of his lot and offered it as the "Week's Special." Now, you may well ask who in their right mind would buy a fifty-three-ton General Sherman tank, complete with cannon. Most of the scoffers along the row posed the same question. But Harvey had picked up the vehicle on Thursday, and by Friday morning, at 9:12, he had sold it for three hundred and eighty-six dollars! (*From the Twilight Zone*, Serling, 1962, p. 117).

Maybe your group's goal does not include finding a buyer for a General Sherman tank, but whatever your group goal, there are a number of techniques that can enhance your group's creativity, facilitate its problem-solving process, and provide a method by which the group can present that information to a larger audience in a persuasive manner. To solve problems effectively requires an appropriate mind set—viewing problems as opportunities or challenges and looking for solutions. A disciplined approach to defining the problem through a variety of tools and identifying and implementing appropriate solutions is critical (Thompson, 1999). Brainstorming is a productive group creativity enhancer. Specific group techniques for gathering information, developing insights within the group, and working through sticking places in the group discussion process include focus groups, nominal group technique, Delphi technique, synectics, buzz sessions, idea writing, and listening teams. Flowcharts, fishbone diagrams, and use of the Pareto principle are additional techniques that can help groups organize the problem-solving process. RISK and PERT are processes that help groups systematically go through a complex implementation procedure to meet a goal. These are not just hypothetical approaches. Instead, they are used widely in organizations to increase the quality of the products we purchase. In the same vein, they can help your group find better solutions. Finally, the forum, panel, colloquium, or symposium formats can help organize a group's presentation to, and interactive discussion with, a larger audience.

Brainstorming

Brainstorming is one of the most popular and useful techniques for creative problem solving. If you have a concept and are trying to develop as many insights as possible during a group meeting, brainstorming can help. There are four guidelines that are helpful in facilitating brainstorming:

1. The more ideas the better. Quantity is desirable.
2. All ideas are welcome. The wilder the idea the better.
3. No criticism of ideas at this stage. "Free-wheeling" is welcome.
4. Hitchhiking on ideas, using someone else's idea as a springboard for additional thoughts, and combining and improving on ideas are encouraged.

If done well, brainstorming can produce a large number of original ideas. When the creative brainstorming process is complete, we need to sort through these ideas to discover which ones are usable and which are creative but perhaps not very practical. One method for sorting, as presented in Chapter 9, is to assign ideas equally to one of three piles labeled: A, C, and B.

ACB Idea Sorting Method

1. Assign an *A to the best one-third* of the ideas.
2. Assign a *C to the least usable one-third* of the ideas.
3. The *middle one-third automatically receive a B.*
4. Go back to the Bs and separate them into the A or C category.
5. Store the C category ideas for later use.
6. Prioritize the As in terms of their importance, urgency, or applicability to the problem at hand.

The ideas are now organized and the brainstorming session put to use. It is important that the prioritizing step follow the brainstorming session, in order not to stifle the free flow of ideas. Brainstorming can be fun, and we can all enjoy the process of being creative. If the group is critical and nonsupportive, however, the process will not work. The key to successful brainstorming is establishing a climate that encourages individuals to act in an open manner. Brainstorming is one of many ways to enhance creativity in the group process.

Research in organizations demonstrates that the shared feelings of optimism and excitement experienced by removing some barriers encourages a more creative climate (Paulus & Dzindolet, 1993). At SmithKline Beecham, a pharmaceutical firm, brainstorming has been used successfully to help project teams think of innovative actions to existing action plans (Keelin, 1998).

Creative Decision-Making Techniques

Using different types of formats and approaches to deal with different types of issues and different group contexts can enhance the creativity of small group discussions, decisions, and solutions. Focus groups, nominal group technique, Delphi technique, synectics, buzz sessions, idea writing, role playing, and listening teams each have applicability to different settings and for solving different types of problems.

The secret to being an effective group is to use the approaches and techniques most appropriate to the particular circumstances facing the group at that time. We are unlikely to use all of these techniques in the same group, but being aware of a number of strategies provides us with a repertoire from which to choose an appropriate one when needed. If group discussion and decision-making and problem-solving processes have become stalled, more and more of the same process can only give you more and more of the same result. If two meetings a week do not move the group toward solving the problem, why would three or four? If the discussion or decision-making format you are using as a group has reached an impasse, continued discussion using the same format is probably not useful. The following techniques offer different approaches to dealing with particular group circumstances.

Focus Groups

There is an old axiom regarding problems. If you want to know the answer, ask the people involved. They may not know the answer, but, they know what matters to them and can provide valuable insights regarding the possible success of any solution. When you are attempting to find detailed, thorough, and unstructured answers to problems, a focus group can be the vehicle for understanding people's values, interests, and attitudes.

In a focus group, a facilitator introduces an issue or topic and asks the group to discuss it. Later, the responses are carefully examined to identify major themes. Often, the meeting is tape recorded so the entire discussion can be replayed and analyzed later. The facilitator asks questions and helps the group explore issues through their discussion.

Focus groups have been used in advertising and marketing for years as a way to ask a cross section of potential users how they feel about a product, packaging, promotion, or service. Now, they have been extended to include morale problems in organizations, menus for cafeterias and vending machines, arguments to be used by lawyers when approaching a jury, customer responses to products or campaigns, and political campaign issues. The focus group is a highly adaptive technique that encourages a freewheeling discussion on a particular issue. A small group can use the focus group technique to explore the major issues surrounding a problem, decision, or concern and to then organize those issues by theme in an explicit and useful manner. Focus groups can yield impressive results since they provide an additional avenue to creativity. (Yartnoff, 1999). To obtain the best results, ask open ended questions that elicit thoughtful responses, do not try to force the focus group toward a particular solution or allowing the group to focus on a particular solution instead of the problems, or listen to all the possible answers. In essence, focus groups allow you to understand what individuals actually involved the issues think. As with most group processes, structure makes the focus group more effective. A focus group should pay attention to the seven steps outlined in Figure 11.1 (Simon, 1999).

Nominal Group Technique

Research indicates that we produce better ideas when we work in the presence of others. In addition, the group setting allows for a more balanced participation than simply asking for individual input. However, participation by group members is frequently not equal. Some members are quiet while others talk a lot. If the participants have different opinions and goals, not all perspectives and concerns may be heard with equal results. When the input of all parties is needed, the nominal group technique offers a viable method for obtaining it. The nominal group technique is a highly structured meeting agenda that allows everyone to contribute in a relatively equal manner and without having that contribution interrupted by evaluative comments from others. This approach allows controversial issues to be

FIGURE 11.1   Focus Groups—The Seven Key Steps

1. Define the purpose of the focus group. Ask questions such as "what do we want to achieve?"
2. Plan ahead for the session. Why are you having this meeting and when will it occur?
3. Identify and invite the participants. If you have an intact group, then this is fairly easy. Otherwise, choosing the right participants often will decide your success.
4. Provide an overview to your participants so they know why they are attending. Once again, if this is an intact group, provide a reason for the focus group.
5. Generate the questions to be asked. This is not an open-ended forum. Instead, you are trying to determine specific information.
6. Develop a script or a plan of action so you are certain you obtain the necessary information in the time available.
7. Interpret and report the results.

Note: In many situations, professional facilitators are used.

examined and provides a numerical rating of assigned priorities to the ideas and alternatives suggested by members (McShane & Von Glinow, 2000). The nominal group technique typically includes four steps:

1. Participants work alone and respond in writing with possible solutions to a stated problem. This silent, independent generation of ideas in writing is a key to the process for airing a broad range of ideas on the topic.

2. Each member reads his or her ideas aloud in a round-robin fashion without any criticism or discussion. This round-robin sharing of ideas means that each participant contributes a single idea at a time, which is then recorded on a large flip chart. Discussion of the ideas is not permitted until all have been read and the idea sheets taped to the wall so that they can be seen by the whole group. The group facilitator continues to request ideas from participants until all ideas have been recorded or the group reaches a consensus that they have produced a sufficient number of ideas to discuss.

3. The ideas on the list are now discussed and clarified as to their meanings, but with no evaluative comments allowed. The participants discuss each idea on the list until they are clear about the meaning of all suggestions. This can be done in a serial manner. If there are too many ideas to be effectively covered, the facilitator can instead identify and suggest key issues or themes running through the ideas that need to be clarified. During this step, members may also discover that two or more ideas listed on the chart mean essentially the same thing and decide to combine them.

4. Members then rank-order the ideas in order of importance, which is done by individual, secret ballot. The results of this ballot are tabulated and recorded on the flip chart. The results and any follow-up discussion of the voting pattern suggest the group's orientation and possible solutions to the problem.

When issues are too controversial or too complex for a full and open verbal group discussion, the nominal group technique can be useful. For example, if everyone in a group wants to install a computer system but no one can agree on the brand, the nominal group technique can provide an efficient means for involving all interested parties and can facilitate a faster solution. The phrasing of the question or problem to be addressed, however, is important. For this computer system example, for instance, a question of "which computer system should we purchase?" is not an appropriate nominal group technique question. A more worthwhile question would be to ask: "What functions must the new computer system perform?" or "What software must the new computer system run?" The nominal group technique could be an efficient and useful means of obtaining a group-prioritized comprehensive list of the computer functions or software. Because the nominal group is highly structured, there is a greater likelihood that there will be a strong orientation to accomplishing the group's task and a lessened chance for conflict. This task orientation also means that there will be less group cohesiveness because the technique minimizes social interaction (McShane & von Glinow, 2000).

Nominal group technique is a highly structured format that provides a guarantee that everyone can participate. It makes public, in a written form, the choices of the group, and all interested parties are allowed to watch the decision-making process as it unfolds.

Delphi Technique

Sometimes, a group does not need to meet face to face. At other times, it is simply not practical to have everyone get together. The Delphi technique is a written survey method for gathering opinions without holding a group meeting. It is a method that was designed by the Rand Corporation to aid in their ability to predict technological innovations, and it has since been used by groups for many purposes (DeWine, 2001). A large number of people can be included, and distance is not a factor. When you want to solicit a variety of inputs, and especially when you need input from people who are at a distance, the Delphi technique offers a solution.

An initial survey is distributed and the written results are tabulated. These results are then sent back to the original respondents along with additional follow-up questions. A Delphi procedure might start with the formulation of the issues, asking participants to describe and clarify the issue that should be under consideration and how it should be stated. Second, it can solicit options. Given the issue, what options are available? Third, it can help determine initial positions on the issue—which issues everyone agrees are important and should be pursued and which are unimportant and should be dropped from discussion. A focus can then be placed on those issues that show disagreement among the respondents. Fourth, the reasons for these disagreements can be explored and the underlying assumptions, views, or facts being used by individuals to support their respective positions made clear. Fifth, the underlying reasons can be evaluated and the arguments that are used to defend positions can be compared to each other on a relative basis by the group. Finally, the group can reevaluate the options based on their views of the underlying evidence and assessment of each position. The process is summarized in Figure 11.2.

On the negative side, the technique can be cumbersome. Mailings, analysis, rankings, reporting, and follow-ups must all occur at each step, but the technique offers a means to incorporate the ideas of various individuals without having a

FIGURE 11.2   Delphi Technique—Basic Steps

1. Deciding to administer a questionnaire
2. Selecting a group to respond—normally experts or highly involved individuals
3. Formulating the questions
4. Producing the questionnaire
5. Setting a deadline for returning the questionnaires
6. Receiving and analyzing the questionnaires

meeting. The best use for the Delphi Technique is "for complex issues and questions that require much thoughtful consideration" (DeWine, 2001, p. 180). A positive aspect is that it incorporates the value of a nominal group technique, allowing equal participation from all individuals. And the process requires good organization and highly motivated participants, or little participation will occur.

Synectics

Synectics is a formalized technique for group process design that helps groups tackle difficult problems creatively. It asks group members to use analogies to break their existing patterns of thinking and to develop analogies regarding particular concepts in order to see another aspect of a problem (Gordon, 1961). This process requires a skilled facilitator, since the group is attempting to use analogy, metaphor, and fantasy chaining to deal with a real issue, but the goal is to generate new, creative ideas.

The process begins with a review of the "problem as given" as stated by the client or agency for whom the group is trying to solve the problem. An analysis episode follows in which group members ask "how" and "what" questions of the client such as "How is the problem as given a problem for you?"; "What have you done to try to solve it?"; "What is desired from this group?" (Chilberg, 1989). While listening to the client's responses, group members engage in idea writing based on their perceptions of the client's explicit and implied desires, goals, and problems. Next the group lists these ideas on a flip chart or board in the form of "how to" statements (such as, "The problem is *how to* provide easy yet restricted access to particular areas of the building") and the client is asked to offer a solution to each. For those ideas, representing aspects of the problem for which the client is unable to provide a solution, participants are asked to think metaphorically about the problem or to build analogies from other processes. These are listed for the group and are built on through a process of group fantasy chaining by the client and group members in a brainstorming session.

The object is to use analogy and metaphor to create new ways of approaching and thinking about a problem. For example, imagine you are trying to design a car's interior. What possible insights to that design could be offered by thinking of it as a living room, a bedroom, a park, a football stadium, a glass jar, or other type of space? Once an analogy is developed, the group can brainstorm the attributes of the space and develop them through group fantasy themes. (Perhaps it should be thought of as a multifunction sports arena rather than a football stadium and useful for baseball as well as football.) This step of visual analogy begins the process of redesigning the car interior. Synectics is a useful technique when a group has run out of creative ideas, become mired in controversy over how to view something, or just stuck in its problem-solving processes. It can provide a useful energizing (and fun) interlude to reinvigorate the problem-solving process and a creative approach to finding a solution to an otherwise seemingly impenetrable problem. In organizations, it has been used for process improvements by reducing the number of steps the employees must take to complete tasks. Delphi

Group participants are asked to imagine they are part of a manufacturing process. As they go through the daily routines, they discover innovative solutions to creating a more effective process (Weitz, 1995). Because the Delphi Group members are not actually engaging in the work routine, the group members are more likely to see unnecessary working habits that make the job harder for the employees and reduce effectiveness because their imagining the process provides a unique perspective.

Buzz Sessions

When you have a large number of participants and want to encourage participation by each member, breaking them into groups of approximately six members each can be a solution. These groups, called buzz sessions, are designed to create spontaneous small group discussions of a specific problem or question. The groups are given the topic for their discussion and a time limit is announced. After the time is up, a spokesperson from each group reports to the larger group. The responses are summarized on a master list, and the key issues can then be identified and discussed by the larger group.

Because you are dealing with a large number of individuals, careful design is necessary. First, identify the issue and frame it as a target question (for example, "What should be done to reduce the number of accidents that have occurred?"). Second, designate leaders who will facilitate the discussion and place the group responses on flip charts. Provide a time limit for the groups to buzz and discuss the issues. Usually five to ten minutes per issue is adequate. Finally, ask the designated leaders to make reports and present the results to the larger group of the whole. Given the dynamics of those meetings that do not allow long-term group process, buzz session groups open the door to a variety of ideas and invite input from all participants while limiting the time required for the process of generating and discussing them.

Idea Writing

Idea writing also typically divides a large group into small working groups but differs from buzz sessions in that it provides those smaller groups with a written task, rather than an oral discussion. Each participant in the small group responds in writing to a stimulus question and then places his or her response on a pad in the center of the group. These pads are then passed to the right around the group and each participant reacts, in writing, to what is written on each of the other pads. When the pads travel around the circle and reach their authors once again, the participants read the comments made in reaction to their initial statements, and the small group discusses the principal ideas that emerged through the written interaction. The group then summarizes the discussion and can report conclusions, points of agreement, points of disagreement, and those points needing further discussion to the larger group. Idea writing can provide more balanced input from group members than oral discussions sometimes do and may work better than buzz sessions if there are dominant and quiet members in the groups or if the topic for discussion is an emotional or controversial one.

Role Playing

Role playing allows participants to experience and discuss dimensions of a problem or a sensitive issue that they may not normally experience. Then group members can present, analyze, and suggest solutions. The role-playing technique is most useful for a problem involving human relationships and generally involves a five-step process. First, the problem must be identified. Second, members of the group need to come up with a plot, setting, and characters to participate in the problem situation. Third, members choose or are assigned roles to play; nonplayers are involved as observers. Fourth, players present their interpretation of the problem. Fifth, players and nonplayers discuss what occurred during the role playing and analyze alternative approaches to the same situation.

Listening Teams

Listening teams are used to encourage active participation in the process of listening to difficult or challenging information. Listening teams are formed when a moderator or leader divides a group into teams prior to a lecture or presentation. Each team is then assigned a specific listening task. After the presentation, members of each team are given time to take notes, discuss, and organize their thoughts. The team members then serve as resources for the larger discussion of issues that follows.

Problem-Solving Tools

Three problem-solving tools may help the group process by clarifying the goals and the problems to be solved and by analyzing the information gathered, in order to develop alternatives. These are: flowcharts, fishbone diagrams, and Pareto's principle.

Flowcharts

Flowcharts give a visual description of a process across time or transactions, showing the actual ordering of the steps of the process in an ongoing situation. The flowchart can then be compared to a more ideal order or sequence. In a proposed scenario, for example, flowcharts can be used to compare different ways of accomplishing a given task.

There are several different types of flowcharts, depending on the process to be mapped. Deployment flowcharts show who does what, when, in the process. They can be used in small groups for assigning group roles and responsibilities as a way of assuring that each member knows what is expected of her or him, when it is expected, and by whom. Top-down flowcharts are designed to show the major steps in a work process, showing those steps ordered across the top, with the substeps within each of them connected with sequence arrows underneath the major steps. Detailed flowcharts show the sequential order of occurrences and decisions in a work setting, such as the flow of people, products, services, or paperwork. Two examples of detailed flowcharts are shown in Figures 11.3 and 11.4.

Fishbone Diagrams

Fishbone diagrams are also called *cause-and-effect diagrams* or *Ishikawa diagrams* after Kaoru Ishikawa (1982), who first developed this tool. The diagram takes its name from its resemblance to a fishbone, with the problem, or effect, defined as the "head" and shown on the right-hand side of the diagram. On the "bones" growing out of the "spine" (the arrow pointing to the head), the group lists the major possible causes of the problem in their order of probable occurrence or importance. With Ishikawa's original approach, there are four major cause categories: machinery, methods, materials, and people. Depending on the problem to be addressed, however, different categories might be more relevant. To these four main lines (bones), the group adds the subcauses as smaller bones, diagonals, or shorter lines that contribute to the major cause. These are subordinate causes that contribute to the larger causes of the problem. The fishbone diagram may be filled in either by brainstorming or by data gathering. Brainstorming produces possible causes that must be verified by data gathering and analysis. Figure 11.5 shows a simple fishbone diagram depicting a problem with ball bearings. Figure 11.6 on page 232 goes further and presents an extended fishbone diagram showing how order-picking errors can be examined.

Pareto's Principle

Vilfred Pareto's fifteenth-century study of crime in Italy led to a popular concept called the *Pareto principle*. Pareto found that a small percentage of Italy's populace was responsible for a large percentage of the crime. The Pareto principle states that roughly 80 percent of all problems can be traced to approximately 20 percent of all possible causes. In general, around 80 percent of all positive results are produced by 20 percent of the efforts. Approximately 80 percent of a company's profits come from 20 percent of its products. For example, companies have found that "20% of customers often generate 150% of the company's total economic profit, while the worst 20% can lose 75% of the profits" (Selden & Colvin, 2003, p. 123). The 80/20 rule holds for a number of issues. For example, research indicates that approximately 80 percent of sales comes from 20 percent of customers; 80 percent of washing comes from 20 percent of our wardrobe; 80 percent of file usage comes from 20 percent of files; 80 percent of complaints comes from 20 percent of customers; 80 percent of sick leave is taken by 20 percent of employees; 80% of dirt is on the 20 percent of the most used floor area; 20 percent of car parts will cause 80 percent of problems; 20 percent of people in volunteer groups do 80 percent of the work.

FIGURE 11.3 **Flow Chart: Seeking Employment**

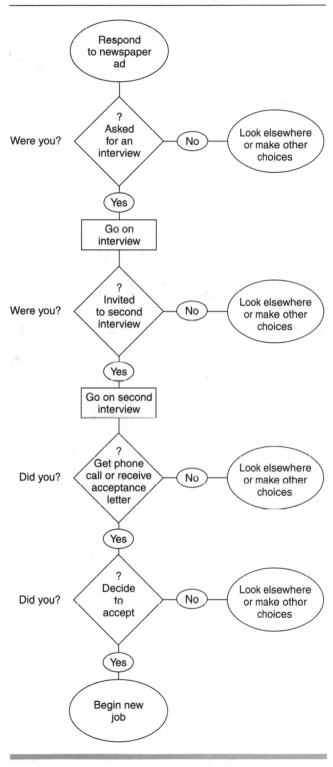

FIGURE 11.4   Flow Chart: From Bed to Work

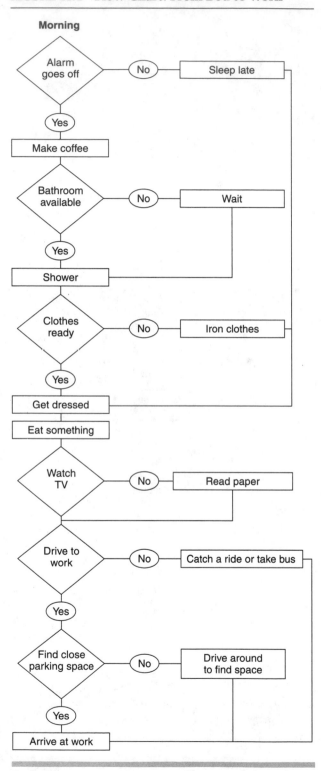

FIGURE 11.5   Fishbone Diagram of Ball Bearing Defects

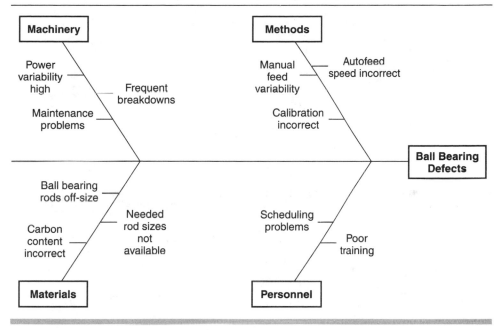

Pareto's principle provides a useful tool for setting priorities in our decision-making process. The complexity of the small group process makes it easy to be sidetracked by issues that can be expected to make little, if any, appreciable difference in the outcome. It is useful to remember that our focus should be on the 20 percent of information that will provide 80 percent of the expected benefit and the 20% of the apparent problem that is critical to be solved.

Pareto charts are bar charts that reflect the relative frequency of a phenomenon, whether it be costs, frequency of occurrence, weights, number of responses to items on a list, or any other measure decision makers might find useful. For example, Pareto charts might be used to show the comparative costs of the various components of a problem. In general, they provide a way of documenting the 80/20 relationships and help focus a group's attention on the most frequently occurring or most important problems. In our community group, a Pareto chart could be used to chart the tonnage of different categories of waste to find out which of those that are amenable to removing from the waste stream for recycling also contribute most to the weight of the stream and which bring in the most value on the market.

Each of these three tools helps a group define and visualize the problem. A flowchart provides a visual description of an ordered chain of relationships. The fishbone clarifies the cause-and-effect relationships. Pareto charts are a useful way of organizing data to help us make effective decisions and to set priorities for our investigation. Thus, these methods help us separate and analyze the individual elements of a problem.

FIGURE 11.6 Fishbone Diagram of Order-Picking Errors

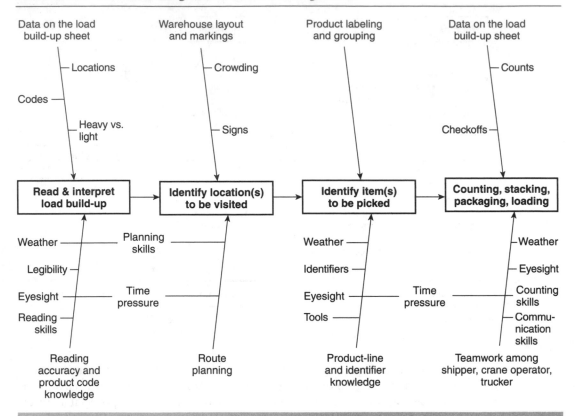

The RISK Procedure

Once you have a solution to a problem, you need to consider the consequences of putting your plan into effect. If your group decided to reschedule classes, for example, there could be some unexpected results that might prove to be negative.

The RISK procedure is a combination of buzz groups and the nominal group technique. The meeting leader presents a solution in detail and the meeting participants are encouraged to think of any risks or problems that might be created by the change. These concerns are compiled on a flip chart. As with brainstorming, all ideas should be welcomed, since the most obscure ones may generate the most serious consequences or spur someone else in the meeting to identify another problem.

The list is compiled and presented later in the meeting or at the next meeting. Using the A, B, C identification of items approach used in brainstorming (or some other means of differentiating the important from the less important problems) a final list of problems that represent potential roadblocks is compiled and prioritized. The A, B, C method assigns ideas equally to one of three piles. If there are 45 items, assign an A to the 15 best ideas. Put a C on the 15 least usable. The remaining 15 ideas are assigned Bs, since these fall in the middle. Now go back and separate the Bs into the A or C category. Store the C category ideas for later use. Go back to the A category and prioritize the ideas in terms of their importance, urgency, or applicability to the problem at hand. The ideas are now organized, and possible resolutions can be discussed by the group.

PERT (Program Evaluation and Review Technique)

Once the solution has been identified, there remains the actual implementation. Program evaluation and review technique, PERT, is a systematic approach for designing the solution steps. This planning system involves eight steps.

1. Identify the final goal of the decision-making process. How will the solution look when it is implemented?
2. List all the events that must occur before the final goal is achieved. Brainstorm to develop this list.
3. Put the steps in chronological order.
4. Use a flow diagram to show how the events will occur.
5. Determine the specific activities that must occur to accomplish each step or stage.
6. Specify the time needed for each event and the end product.
7. Decide whether the deadlines are feasible and if the goals can be met in the time specified.
8. Determine a critical path for the events that must occur and assign responsibility for accomplishment of each step and event within that path to a particular individual or group.

Once responsibilities have been assigned, write down a full timetable with specific deadlines and follow up. A program is only as good as its actual implementation.

How These Techniques Are Used

Total Quality Management (TQM) and Six Sigma are two examples of how these creative decision-making techniques are used in organizations. For example, almost all consumer products in the twenty-first century have a higher quality than their counterparts made 10 or 15 years ago (Cummings & Worley, 2001). When faced with quality issues, organizations began to understand that using the traditional problem solving approaches were inadequate for achieving quality. A popular phrase in organizations is that "more and more of the same can only give you more and more of the same"—freely interpreted, inadequate quality cannot be fixed by using the same approaches. We will examine two of the most successful uses of the techniques we just covered in this chapter.

Total quality management (TQM) involves a comprehensive intervention that focuses all the organization systems on the continuous improvement of quality (Cohen, Fink, Gadon, & Willis, 2001, p. 43). In many cases, teams are used to focus on the needs of internal (other departments and interacting units) and external customers to guarantee quality. When TQM was first introduced, teams would examine past problems and use these creative approaches to find solutions. Now, in those companies experiencing the greatest successes, the emphasis has shifted from fixing problems to looking toward proactive problem anticipation and prevention (Cummings & Worley, 2001). TQM involves training in brainstorming, flowcharts, fishbone diagrams, and other problem-solving procedures as the first step in the long-term process of continuous improvement. In a study of 54 firms of different sizes, TQM adopters outperformed those that did not utilize TQM (Powell, 1995). The most important finding, however, was those successful firms focused more on changing the culture by increasing the use of teams, empowerment and commitment rather than concentrating on the techniques themselves (Powell, 1995). Without the increased use of individuals and teams involved in the actual problem solving, the techniques simply are not as effective.

In addition, organizations are turning to *Six Sigma* which is a process that aims to reduce deviations (e.g., quality errors) to 3.4 defects per 1 million opportunities which translates to a 99.9997% level of perfection. If applied to brewing coffee, this would mean there would only be 3.4 sour pots of coffee per 1 million brewed. If applied to your college experience, it would essentially eliminate all typo's for all your papers—except 3.4 times (3.4 words) per 1 million.

Sigma is a letter of the Greek alphabet used as a symbol by statisticians to mark a bell curve showing that likelihood that something, like the pot of coffee, will deviate from the norm. "The Six Sigma movement attempts to insert the science of hard-nosed statistics into the foggy philosophy of quality" (Jones, 1998, p. 2B). "Getting Six Sigma started begins with the formation of Six Sigma teams" (Defeo, 1999, p. 11). Is it important? Clearly, it depends on how much impact this level of quality will have on the organization's effectiveness. Figure 11.7 shows why increasing quality is important.

Some of the results are impressive. At Dow Chemical Company each "Six Sigma project has freed up an average of $500,000 in the first year" (Ardnt, 2002, p. 72). Allied Signal discovered a way to recycle 200 million pounds of stained carpet a year translating into $30 to $50 million a year. The list of successes is extensive. At the same time, it is a complicated process involving training in the group process, creative problem solving techniques, and statistical analysis. Currently, "the best organizations operate at about Three to Four Sigma, which translates into about 6,200 defects per million" (Defeo, 1999, p. 12) which are the differences demonstrated in Figure 11.7. The benefits of Six Sigma include increased motivation, morale, pride, production, and profitability (Defeo, 1999). But, without proper training in the techniques included in this chapter plus a strong emphasis on statistical analysis, Six Sigma probably will not realize its full value.

FIGURE 11.7 Does Six Sigma Matter?

99% effective means three or four Sigma. If that goal is achieved versus Six Sigma (99.999%) the following would occur.

✓ 20,000 lost articles of mail per hour

✓ 5,000 incorrect surgical operations per week

✓ Two short or long landings per day at each major airport

✓ 200,000 wrong drug prescriptions each year

✓ No electricity for almost seven hours each month

Small Group Presentational Formats

A group often finds that it needs to present its conclusions, findings, recommendations, or a summary of its discussion to a larger audience. There are several formats that are conducive to group discussions and presentations. Forum, panel, colloquium, and symposium formats can help organize a group's discussion and facilitate a group's interaction with a larger audience.

The Forum

The forum provides a small group presentational format in which the group can interact with—speaking and listening to—a larger audience. The forum is a form of public discussion in which the full audience participates, examining a topic or problem by giving short presentations. These presentations are often impromptu speeches given one at a time in an orderly fashion. They may be structured by a moderator who selects the speakers, or they may be ordered by speakers lining up at a microphone located in front of the audience. Sometimes time limits are imposed on the speakers and, on occasion, a moderator who feels that one view has been overly represented by a series of speakers—while another view has been left silent—may call for a representative of the opposing view to speak. Speakers present and support arguments, take positions, take issue with what has been said, ask and answer questions, and respond to comments. An open town meeting and a public "hearing" represent forums. Often a forum is used in conjunction with other public discussion formats, such as a panel–forum or symposium–forum format, with the purpose of presenting information or a proposal and then soliciting public reaction to the proposal. A forum can provide an audience with diverse perspectives from experts as well as an opportunity to obtain additional information from knowledgeable and interested stakeholders. It provides an important opportunity for an audience to give verbal expression to their thinking and provides an opportunity for correcting intentional or inadvertent bias, distortion, or misunderstanding surrounding an issue. A good forum ensures that all parties, opinions, objections, views, preferences, and perspectives can be heard.

The Panel

A panel is a public format in which a group of four to eight experts discusses a problem or decision in front of an audience. This discussion often follows the problem-solving format but uses an informal, sometimes humorous, style of interaction to keep the audience's attention and to effectively share information that may be technical in nature. The moderator starts the meeting; explains the format to the audience; orients the audience to the topic or problem to be discussed; introduces the speakers, perhaps mentioning their expertise and perspective (for example, if they represent a particular group, cause, or company); keeps time; and sometimes summarizes the speakers' positions. The panel format provides no direct interaction between the panel of experts and the audience, but it is often followed by a moderated question and answer or a forum session. The panel should not normally run longer than an hour and may provide another half hour to an hour for questions or for a forum discussion.

Planning a panel is important. The panel must agree on basic definitions, parameters of the problem to be discussed, the questions or issues to be considered, speaker time limits, and the order of the speakers. There should be no big surprises for the speakers on the day of the presentation, and the presentation should not turn into a debate. An effective panel is collaboratively informational to the audience rather than argumentatively confrontational among the speakers.

The Colloquium

A colloquium is a form of public discussion in which a group of three to six experts, usually chosen for their divergent views, discuss a problem, following the problem-solving format, in front of an audience with a moderator facilitating their interaction. The purpose of a colloquium is to identify, develop, and work through possible solutions to a problem for the benefit and with the participation of the audience. The moderator should open the colloquium, introduce the problem, introduce the discussion group, describe the format for the discussion, and moderate the interactions throughout the session. The moderator may have to explicitly encourage audience participation by inviting the audience to ask questions or make comments at points in the discussion. The moderator must also work to keep the discussion focused and moving.

A colloquium frequently opens with short position or opinion statements by the experts and then shifts to a more interactive public discussion of the issues with audience participation, shifting back to comments by one or more of the experts, and returning again to audience comments, so that the discussion is carried on both in front of, and with the participation of, audience members.

A colloquium will probably last at least an hour but not more than two hours. A good moderator must sense the flow of the discussion to ensure not cutting it off too soon, allowing all parties, perspectives, and opinions, to be heard but also not allowing it to drag on repetitiously and become tedious or boring. Achieving a sense of closure is important.

The Symposium

A symposium provides a format for a series of two to six brief speeches made on different aspects of a complex and difficult problem. The speakers are typically experts in different areas related to a problem, and the purpose of the symposium is to present complex technical information to the audience about the problem. The speeches are well prepared, practiced, and polished presentations that are uninterrupted by the audience and presented by skilled public speakers. The symposium should not run longer than an hour and is often followed by a half-hour forum to allow audience questions and discussion of the issue.

Planning prior to the symposium determines how the speakers will divide the topic, the order in which they will speak, and the time allocated for each speech. The speakers and moderator are often seated on a platform, or behind a table and lectern, providing a more formal public-presentation setting. The moderator introduces the session, addresses the important issues surrounding the topic, introduces the speakers, outlines how the topic will be approached by the speakers, and provides a summary at the conclusion of the symposium. If a forum discussion follows the symposium, the moderator moderates that session as well.

Summary

We have discussed brainstorming, ten group decision-making techniques that are useful in the appropriate circumstances, and three problem-solving tools. In line with our goal to increase creativity in decision making and problem solving, changing the way we approach a decision, a problem, or a solution can enhance the outcome quality, moving beyond standard ways of looking at issues, and overcoming creativity blocks and seeking new insights. Brainstorming and the specialized approaches outlined here offer ways to make a group more effective. Creative group structuring and processing can bring different answers and understanding to many issues. The forum, panel, colloquium, and symposium provide different formats for presenting and discussing those understandings. Figure 11.8 provides an audience evaluation form for those group presentations.

DISCUSSION QUESTIONS

1. What is a focus group? How does it differ from a standard group? What topics on your campus would benefit from a focus group discussion?

2. Outline the nominal group technique. Why should it be considered a tool in small group decision making and problem solving?

3. What do you see as the benefits and weaknesses of the Delphi procedure?

4. Handling large groups can be difficult. What are buzz groups and how can they be used? How can idea writing be used with large groups?

FIGURE 11.8   Audience Evaluation Form for Group Forum, Panel, Colloquium, or Symposium Presentations

Group Name

Ratings

CONTENT

New, interesting information	5	4	3	2	1	Old, monotonous, boring
Relevant coherent information	5	4	3	2	1	Extraneous, irrelevant
Practical information	5	4	3	2	1	Useless

PRESENTATION

Clear objectives	5	4	3	2	1	Confused objectives
Well organized	5	4	3	2	1	Scattered
Involving	5	4	3	2	1	Noninvolving

GROUP PRESENTERS

Informed, consistent	5	4	3	2	1	Unsure or unclear
Articulate	5	4	3	2	1	Unexpressive, inarticulate
Stimulating	5	4	3	2	1	Dull

What was the group's main objective or point?

What did you like BEST about the presentation?

Any suggestions for improvements?

5. Design a role play of a difficult small group interaction. Present and discuss it.

6. Discuss the issue of course registration and textbook purchasing. Define the problem.
   A. Develop a flowchart of the problem.
   B. Develop a fishbone diagram of the cause-effect relationships.
   C. Apply Pareto's principle to the problem.
   D. How have these techniques assisted in understanding the problem and possible solutions?

7. Distinguish between a forum, panel, colloquium, and symposium as a means for making a public presentation. Which one would you prefer? Why?

EXERCISES

1. Brainstorming; 2. Practicing technique: Choosing a specific technique; 3. Comparing two techniques; 4. Problem-solving tools; 5. Choosing the best presentational format

1. BRAINSTORMING

Form a small group. Following the brainstorming guidelines in this chapter, brainstorm better ways to use the space of the room you are in right now. Your goal is to develop as many options as possible. After you have completed this exercise, be prepared to report your uses to the rest of the class. As a follow-up or as an alternative, brainstorm to create ideas for one of the following:

1. A better grading system.
2. Introducing a new line of gourmet frozen foods.
3. Fundraising for a community service organization for the elderly. (A foundation will give you $10,000 if you can raise a matching amount in two months.)
4. There is a large empty room on campus that you would like to be able to make multipurpose. At times, you would like to use it for one or two large meetings and at other times you would like to be able to hold a number of small group meetings. The dividing system you will devise should be easily changed, inexpensive, and attractive.

Discussion

1. How creative were your responses? 2. Did you have any difficulty in brainstorming? What were the difficulties? 3. Were some members more active than others? 4. How can you overcome this type of reticence by some group members? 5. As a final opportunity to develop your group's brainstorming abilities, try brainstorming the answer to question 4—overcoming resistance.

2. PRACTICING TECHNIQUE: CHOOSING A SPECIFIC TECHNIQUE

Choose one of the decision-making techniques and use it to organize a group discussion topic. The following example uses a two-step nominal group technique, but an alternative technique can be used in place of it. Choose a question or issue to be addressed. Possible questions include: What are the positive aspects of living in this state, going to this school, or graduating with this major? Alternative questions could be: What can be done to enhance: (a) the image of this community, (b) shopping in this town, (c) driving in this town, (d) the experience of attending this school or of majoring in this department, or (e) attracting tourists to this town or students to this school? The key is that each of these addresses a specific issue, but in the form of a broad open-ended question.

Procedure

Each participant works for 10 to 15 minutes to independently generate a written list of as many ideas to address the stated issue as possible. Next, participants are formed into small groups of approximately six participants, with each participant contributing ideas to a common group list in a round-robin fashion (with each participant contributing one idea) until all ideas are listed on the group's list. Then the group discusses the ideas, combining those that might be stated differently but are essentially the same, and developing those that build on each other. Finally, each of the small groups of six participants presents its list to the group of the whole, and at that level the lists are again combined to eliminate overlapping statements of the same idea, to present the best statement of each idea, and to combine and build on similar ideas. The group now should have a comprehensive list of ideas that involves every member's input to suggested solutions.

3. COMPARING TWO TECHNIQUES

Compare and contrast the use of two different techniques (for example, one verbal group technique such as buzz sessions and one written group technique such as idea writing), and then discuss the outcome of each technique for a particular topic and for the group experience. Both buzz sessions and idea writing are designed to obtain input from all participants, can be performed in relatively similar amounts of time, and work well with "What should be done about" types of questions or issues. Choose two topics of comparable interest and relevance (such as, "What should be done about violence in cartoons shown on television?" and "What should be done about protecting minors from viewing explicit sexual materials in magazines, movies or on the Internet?"). Address one issue through the use of buzz sessions and the other through the use of idea writing, then discuss the productivity and social emotional experience of using each technique to address the issues. Which produced the most ideas? What was the overall quality of the ideas produced using each of the techniques? Which was the more enjoyable experience and why?

4. PROBLEM-SOLVING TOOLS

You have been offered five choices for solving problems: flowcharts, fishbone diagrams, Pareto's principle, the RISK procedure, and PERT. Your group has been asked to analyze the current traffic flow problems on your campus. Pick at least two of the problem-solving tools and analyze the issue. Feel free to "guess" some of the specific details since you are attempting to develop the group's ability to use these tools.

As an alternative, pick an important topic, such as the 2000 Presidential election, the digital divide, violence in the media, quality of high school education as a preparation for higher education, or some other topic of interest to the group, and decide which tool(s) would be most useful for understanding and analysis.

5. CHOOSING THE BEST PRESENTATIONAL FORMAT

Your group has been asked to discuss with the rest of the class your semester-long topic. As an alternative, your instructor might provide you with a topic. Since you are very interested in the success of the presentation, you have decided to examine possible presentational formats in order to pick the best one.

Using a T chart (Chapter 9), develop the advantages and disadvantages of using each of the four formats discussed—forum, panel, colloquium, and symposium—for this particular topic. Be prepared to explain why your team or group believes the format you have chosen has the greatest likelihood for success. Your team or group may also choose to develop an alternative means for presenting that borrows the best attributes of each of the standard formats while overcoming some of the limitations. If so, be prepared to explain your revised approach.

REFERENCES

Arndt, M. (2002, July 22). Quality isn't just for widgets. *Business Week*, pp. 72–73.

Chilberg, J. C. (1989). A review of group process designs for facilitating communication in problem-solving groups. *Management Communication Quarterly, 3*(1), 51–70.

Cohen, A. R., Fink, S. L., Gadon, H., & Willis, R. D. (2001). *Effective behavior in organizations* (7th ed.). Boston: McGraw-Hill Irwin.

Cummings, T. G., & Worley, C. G. (2001). *Organizational development and change* (7th ed.). U.S.: Southwestern.

Defeo, J. A. (1999, July). Six Sigma: Road map for survival. *HRFocus*, pp. 11–12.

DeWine, S. (2001). *The consultant's craft: Improving organizational communication.* Boston: Bedford/St. Martin's.

Gordon, W. J. J. (1961). *Synectics.* New York: Harper & Row.

Ishikawa, K. (1982). *Guide to quality control* (2nd rev. ed.). Tokyo: Asian Productivity Organization.

Jones, D. (1998, July 21). Firms aim for Six Sigma efficiency. *USA Today*, pp. 1B-2B.

Keelin, T. (1998, March–April). How SmithKline Beecham makes better resource-allocation decisions. *Harvard Business Review, 76*, 45–57.

Paulus, P. B., & Dzindolet, M. T. (1993). Social influence processes in group brainstorming. *Journal of Personality and Social Psychology, 64*, 575–586.

Powell, T. (1995). Total quality management as a competitive advantage: A review and empirical study. *Strategic Management Journal, 16*, 15–37.

McShane, S. L., & von Glinow, M. A. (2000). *Organizational behavior.* Boston: Irwin McGraw-Hill.

Selden, L., & Colvin, G. (2003, July). Increasing innovations: What customers want. *Fortune*, pp. 122ff.

Serling, R. (1962). *From the twilight zone.* Garden City, NY: Doubleday.

Simon, J. S. (1999, Sep/Oct). How to conduct focus groups. *Nonprofit World*, pp. 40–44.

Spitzer, Q., & Evans, R. (1997, April). New problems in problem solving. *Across the Board,* pp. 36–37.

Sweeney, P. D., & McFarlin, D. B. (2002). *Organizational behavior: Solutions for management.* Boston: McGraw-Hill.

Thompson, C. B. (1999, Sept.). Problem solving tools to improve productivity. *Journal of Property Management,* pp. 11–16.

Weitz, A. J. (1995). Change: How to remove the fear, resentment, and resistance. *Hospital Management Quarterly, 17*(2), 75–79.

Yartnoff, L. B. (1999, July). Focusing in: How to use focus groups to find out what customers want. *International Banking,* pp. 46–49.

12

Productive Conflict Management

CHAPTER OUTLINE

CHAPTER OBJECTIVES

- Define conflict as a communication event.
- Explain how conflict is a consequence of actions.
- Differentiate between destructive and constructive conflict.
- Illustrate the sources of conflict.
- Elucidate the five styles of conflict resolution.
- Demonstrate negotiation as a strategy.
- Provide examples of the types of power.
- Explain how to make conflict strategies work.

KEY TERMS

Accommodation
Avoidance
Avoidance power
Charismatic power
Collaboration
Competition
Compromise
Conflict management style
Consensus
Constructive conflicts
Destructive conflicts
Diverse backgrounds

Expert power
Flashpoint
Forcing/destructive
   competition
Interdependence
Interpersonal linkage power
Legitimate power
Morphogenic systems
Morphostatic systems
Negotiation
Pattern of interactive
   communication

Personal power
Positional power
Problem solving/collaboration
Referent power
Reward and punishment
   power
Scarce resources
Smoothing
Varying orientations to task
Withdrawal/avoidance

I observed two large ants . . . fiercely contending with one another. Having once got hold they never let go, but struggled and wrestled and rolled on the chips incessantly. Looking farther, I was surprised to find that the chips were covered with such combatants, . . . all the hills and vales in my wood-yard, and the ground was already strewn with the dead and dying. . . . I never learned which party was victorious, nor the cause of the war; but I felt for the rest of the day as if I had had my feelings excited and harrowed by witnessing the struggle, the ferocity and carnage, of a human battle before my door. (*Walden,* Thoreau, 1965, pp. 191–194)

For most of us, conflict evokes images of winning and losing, with one or both of the parties ending up frustrated and demoralized by the situation. Conflict, however, is inevitable in decision-making groups, and many scholars have moved from a perspective that emphasized the negative aspects of conflict to one focusing on encouraging more constructive outcomes and benefits (O'Connor, Gruenfeld, & McGrath, 1993; Witteman, 1991). When handled skillfully within a group's communication processes, conflict can be constructive and beneficial, leading to high-quality outcomes, increased group morale, better perspective-taking skills, and enhanced relationships. The Chinese character for conflict consists of two superimposed symbols graphically showing its two sides: opportunity and danger (Hocker & Wilmot, 1991).

Constructively engaging in conflict can be the key to creating the energy needed in small groups to develop new and creative ideas. For conflict to be constructive, however, both parties must emphasize a mutual respect and collaborative orientation, rather than showing aggressive behavior, lack of respect, or a competitive orientation.

We have all experienced conflict as the result of some interference with the achievement of our personal goals, needs, or expectations. The very nature of being human, with separate bodies and minds, and our own particular sets of needs and desires, brings us into conflict with other people, laws, morals, or other obstacles that prevent us from reaching our individual goals. Conflict happens at all levels of our lives—intrapersonal, interpersonal, group, organizational, and political. Intrapersonally, we may feel torn between our own internal opposing goals or affinities. Interpersonally, we may feel blocked from achieving our goals by another individual. Conflict also occurs within and between groups (intragroup or intergroup). This chapter explores the nature of conflict as a communication event within the interactions of small groups. It examines both constructive and destructive conflict, suggests strategies for conflict resolution, and investigates the power dynamics that underlie the expression of conflict. The objective is to explore the positive expression of dissent within group decision-making processes and the development of more functional and less contentious problem-solving conflict management tactics and strategies.

Defining Conflict within a Communication Context

Conflict can be defined as "an expressed struggle between at least two interdependent parties who perceive incompatible goals, scarce rewards, and interference from the other party in achieving their goals" (Hocker & Wilmot, 1991, p. 12). For a conflict to be a communication event, it must be expressed in some way, verbally or nonverbally. In addition, for a conflict to take place, the parties must be interdependent. If one party does not depend in some way on the other, that party will not necessarily become engaged in the conflict. Conflict is painful and costly in terms of emotional energy, and if there is nothing to be gained by engaging in it or lost by avoiding it, people are likely to not engage in it. On the other hand, those who have the most to gain or lose are the most likely to want to engage in the conflict. Each of the parties to the conflict perceives that the other interferes with her or his ability to achieve what he or she wants, needs, or expects, whether that be a physical item, the affection of another person, honor and respect, freedom to do something, or some other desirable goal or avoidance of loss. Thus, most often conflict happens in a context between people with mutually incompatible goals, who see themselves as entwined with and interdependent upon each other in some way.

Conflict within Systems

Conflict consists of the *substance* of the issue around which the disagreement takes place and the *pattern* of interactive communication between the participants engaged in the dispute. As in any system, the substance and pattern of the conflict are inextricably interrelated through the process. It is the pattern that gives meaning to the substance and the substance that manifests the pattern. In small group conflict, however, it is the pattern of the conflict that determines the quality of the outcome for the group, rather than the substance of the matter over which the conflict is engaged. Regardless of the issue under dispute, if the participants are open to new perspectives and are committed to maintaining their relationships and to resolving their disputes, they are likely to find a satisfactory solution. On the other hand, if they feel little or no relational concern and are afraid of giving up any of their position for fear that, if they don't win, they lose, they are less likely to achieve a satisfactory outcome. To the extent that the pattern itself becomes an issue, however, it can be addressed and resolved when all parties commit to working on it.

Through this process, each action sets in motion a series of counteractions, which create patterns of thinking, behaving, and treating each other. When no new patterns or ways of thinking and interacting are introduced, the group can stagnate. Groups in which new input is not accepted and used are known as *morphostatic* systems. They are nonchanging, simply maintaining the status quo, or expending energy to avoid conflict. Those groups that are open to change, in terms of new ideas and ways of interacting, are called *morphogenic* systems. Constructive conflict can happen only in morphogenic systems, where members are willing to examine their assumptions and perspectives, and to offer new patterns of response. This openness fosters creativity and synergy within the group and within the conflict.

Conflict within Small Groups

As members of a group, we are interdependent. Our group process is intended to result in an outcome we all help to create. To the extent that we all are invested in the group and participate in it, though, we may find ourselves in conflict. Conflict happens at all levels of the group process from organizing the group and deciding procedural mechanisms through the definition of the problem to the smallest details of the specific tasks and issues. If there is no conflict, the group may either be so homogeneous that few, if any, new and creative ideas can emerge, or it may be suffering from unhealthy pressure for conformity and a tendency toward groupthink.

Whether conflict is constructive or destructive depends on several factors, including the origin, or *flashpoint,* of the conflict, as well as the orientation of the group members toward the patterns of conflict resolution. When the flashpoint for the conflict resides in the substance of the particular issues under consideration, it has one of the essential ingredients for engaging in constructive conflict management. On the other hand, when the flashpoint resides in the interactive pattern itself, such as when some members are less vested in the process than others or when the group has developed a history of conflictual patterns regardless of the substance of the issue, then it has the potential of being destructive conflict. Group members who do not feel they have as much to gain as others do can use avoidance or other destructive strategies. Likewise, unresolved "personality clashes" can hinder any attempts at constructive conflict management. Although the issues in conflict may vary, a satisfactory resolution depends on seeking to understand and address the origins of the conflict and on defining the issues, while simultaneously engaging in other appropriate conflict-resolution strategies.

The Substance of Conflict

Assuming that the members are invested in the group, that they feel empowered, and that there is a diversity of viewpoints and experiences, we have the ground for issue-based conflict. If we do not agree with other group members about the particular issues of concern, and if we are reasonably invested in our own perspectives, we are likely to come into conflict with those who oppose us or see things differently (Putnam & Poole, 1987). In constructive issue-based conflict, the causes, or substance, of the conflict should be sought in the present issues under dispute, rather than dismissing the conflict as due to inherent personality problems or to preexisting, and currently irrelevant, issues. For example, Toyota credits "lots of conflict" over how they produce their cars as a major contributor to their enviable position as a quality producer of vehicles (Ward, 1998). Substantive causes that can lead to constructive conflict may be found in at least three sources and their influences on the issue under discussion.

One source is perceived *scarce resources,* including lack of time; insufficient information; inadequate space or place; limited rewards; limited access to financial, informational, or other resources; competition for leadership positions; or any number of other perceived limitations to the full and fair treatment of the group process or of the issues under consideration.

A second source is the *diverse backgrounds* or orientations of group members, including conflicts in values (such as religious, political, or socioeconomic perspectives), differing interests or abilities, varying amounts or types of knowledge or experience related to the subject at hand, different information or opinions about the subject, differing perceptions of one's own or others' relative status or power (including unresolved rivalries for status or power), or other differences in orientations, knowledge, and relationships to the group process and goals or to the issue under discussion.

Our cultural background, perhaps the most apparent example of individual diversity, can affect how we approach conflicts. Group members from collectivist cultures, where individual goals are not as important as the group goals, are more likely to avoid conflict with other group members (Rahim & Blum, 1995). Even if two individuals from different cultural backgrounds perceive the same conflict, their conflict management styles may differ (Rabie, 1994). At the same time, individuals from collectivist cultures can be just as competitive as individualist cultures with people outside the group (Chen, Chen, & Meindl, 1998). Earlier in this text we discussed the different generations at work as possible sources for differing values and perceptions (Zemke, Raines, & Filipczak, 2000). In groups or teams, at work or in other group settings, understanding the importance of diverse backgrounds is critical.

A third source is *varying orientations to task accomplishment,* including divergent definitions or understandings of the breadth or depth of the subject at hand or of the group process to be used; differing levels of commitment to the process and to the project; differing degrees of importance placed on the timeliness for completion of the task; divergent values regarding the level of optimization of a solution; or other differences in understanding, attitude, and approach to the group process and to the task.

As these points demonstrate, the interaction patterns themselves can become the substance of the conflict. There may be a number of other sources of conflict in a particular group as well, but to the extent that they are acknowledged and addressed as issue-based conflicts, they can be managed productively, with everyone feeling they have won something and with the overall outcome the best possible one under a given set of circumstances.

Whether conflict is managed constructively or destructively, however, depends on several additional factors, including members' levels of commitment to the process, their attitudes toward conflict in general and toward the specific conflict in which they are engaged, the amount of time and energy they are willing and able to commit to it, their degree of respect for the other parties in the conflict and the value they place on their interpersonal relationships with those parties, and their level of skill in communicating their way through the conflict.

Patterns of Conflict Management

There is no one right pattern of conflict management suitable for all conflicts on all occasions, at all times, or in all contexts. Some conflicts are simply worth more than others, and we need to use our time and energy resources carefully and productively to resolve them. However, when we see conflict as a dance, rather than as a war, we are all better served (Hocker & Wilmot, 1991). Constructive conflicts share the elements of mutual interpersonal concern, interdependence, and an assumption of *equifinality.* Mutual interpersonal concern means that productive conflict focuses on the critical evaluation of ideas. Conflicts are seen as an opportunity for dialogue rather than as a debate (Zornoza, Ripoll, & Peiro, 2002).

Dysfunctional conflict either refuses, avoids, or suspends that evaluation of ideas and often focuses attention, instead, upon a group member's behavior, abilities, or personality (Witteman, 1991). Interdependence means working together, as a team, in this evaluation of the ideas rather than working separately or at cross-purposes. As previously stated, equifinality means recognizing that there is more than one valid way to reach a successful resolution. Destructive conflicts, on the other hand, are based on a lack of concern for the relational elements in the interaction, a feeling of individual independence and rightness, and an assumption of a zero-sum game of winners and losers that is coupled with limited possibilities for winning so that, when one participant wins, the other must lose.

Many of us use a limited number of conflict management styles or orientations to respond to conflict (Shockley-Zalabak, 2002). Our styles are based on the degree to which we maintain underlying sets of assumptions about the need to maintain our relationships through cooperation with others and the importance of accomplishing the task. As shown in Figure 12.1, a two-dimensional conflict management style grid can be developed that shows the impact of various degrees of emphasis on how we view cooperation with others and task accomplishment.

Problem solving (or collaboration) as its name implies, is the style that seeks to maximize gain for all participants. It is high on both relationship and task orientations. *Smoothing (or accommodation)* is the style that gives in to others in order to avoid conflict. It is high on the relationship orientation, but low on task. *Compromise* is the style that assumes that each side gives in enough to resolve the issue and move on. It is at the middle of the continuum on both orientations, with some concern with relationships and some with task, but overall with a more practical and less idealistic orientation to conflict. *Forcing (or competition)* is a style dedicated to winning and can become *destructive competition* when it means winning at any cost. It is low on relationship orientation and high on task. *Withdrawal (or avoidance)* is the style that concedes before the conflict is even engaged. It is low on both relationship and task orientations. Those orientations that value both relationship and task set the stage for constructive conflict and the potential for a satisfactory resolution. Those orientations that do not value either relationship or task sometimes lead to destructive conflict patterns within the group and a resolution that is unsatisfactory for at least one or more of the participants. Avoiding controversy by acting to smooth over difficulties by accommodating, engaging in too much competition, or

FIGURE 12.1   Five Styles of Conflict Management

Compete		**Collaborate**
Tough battler		*Problem Solver*
Power—We/they		Integrator—Us
Win/Lose		**Win/Win**
	Compromise	
	Conciliator	
	Lose/Lose	
Avoid		**Accommodate**
Impersonal complier		*Friendly helper*
Avoider—Withdraw		Suppressor—Harmony
Lose/Win		**Lose/Win**

*Low—Assertiveness—High
Concern for self
Get the task done*

*Low—Cooperativeness—High
Satisfy others
Prosocial*

too quickly compromising can all develop into dysfunctional conflict patterns within the group.

However, because small groups are interactive systems, understanding how conflict management takes place in them is more complicated than simply understanding the conflict management styles of the individual members. Superimposed on these individual styles are five comparable group conflict resolution strategies. Each of these has both constructive and destructive applications, depending upon the overall orientation of the group and of each of the individuals to the conflict. Thus, conflict management takes place in a complex environment, rarely as straightforward and easy to accomplish as it sounds in discussing it. We will consider these in the order in which they were presented for the individual styles: collaboration (as either consensus or negotiation), accommodation, compromise, competition, and avoidance (Harris, 2002).

Collaboration (and Consensus)

The ideal conflict resolution strategy for any group is one of win-win, or collaboration (consensus). However, consensus takes time, energy, and commitment. It is appropriate for the most important conflicts, but it may not be worth the effort for side issues or matters of relatively small consequence. Consensus requires carefully defining the issues, discussing group process strategies for communication, agreeing on the parameters of a good solution, being open, careful, and considerate, listening to all perspectives, and being willing to take the time and energy needed to forge solutions from the best parts of the perspectives offered. This strategy assumes that "none of us is as smart as all of us are together." While the collaborative style is commonly referred to as "win-win," that does not mean the absence of conflict. In fact, collaboration can involve strong disagreements, but they focus on the problem solving issues not personalities or positions (McNary, 2003).

Collaborative communication entails the participation of all members, with each stating his or her point of view as clearly and concisely as possible, while listening attentively to those of others. Once all initial perspectives have been presented and understood, the conflicting viewpoints are engaged, with each side presenting the rational basis of its point of view. Each party remains open to being convinced by the more compelling aspects of another's argument. The ultimate resolution will most likely combine elements of all or most perspectives, mixing and reshaping the best parts of each to form a new and more creative whole than any individual original part. The resolution should reflect the process itself, as well as the substance of the ideas discussed, with each member contributing to the forging of a final solution. That solution will ideally satisfy all participants, with each having been heard and feeling validated by the process, whether or not his or her own initial ideas were ultimately used. In fact, cooperative team experiences "reduce prejudice, increase acceptance of others, and heighten morale" (Tjosvold, 1995, p. 89). While competition has been assumed to increase productivity, collaboration leads to "higher achievement and productivity, especially on more complex tasks and problems that benefit from the sharing of information and ideas" (Tjosvold,

1995, p. 89). Collaboration is not likely to result in destructive conflict when it is done fairly and when all members feel empowered through the process, but collaboration may involve some negotiation as described in the next section.

Negotiation

Negotiation, as a conflict resolution strategy, involves forging a resolution between opposing points of view, assuring that each side "wins" and gets the benefits most important to its overall goals. As a strategy, it is frequently associated with a more formal determination to enter into the bargaining than is collaboration. It usually follows an impasse in discussion, where disagreements may seem unresolvable, and when neither side seems willing or able to make enough concessions to reach a satisfactory resolution. Depending on the depth of the impasse, an impartial mediator may be necessary to help the parties find areas of mutual agreement. This mediator may be another member of the group who understands the issue and the different perspectives on it, and who can help the parties better understand each other.

Negotiation in this case is not a binding arbitration, where a resolution is imposed by a third party. In this negotiation, the parties must resolve their differences and arrive at a solution themselves. Negotiation implies a commitment to the process and that both sides will bargain with openness and fairness in a good-faith effort to reach a mutually acceptable agreement.

Successful negotiation depends on planning and strategy. It may entail choosing one member from each side to represent that point of view in the presentation of the arguments. Negotiating also requires a thorough acquaintance with all sides of the issues under consideration; a strong rationale for one's own particular point of view, including appropriate documentation; a list of those parts of the issue that can be conceded without harming the essence of one's desired benefit; a good understanding of the other's point of view, how they are likely to argue it, and what they might be willing to concede without losing the essence of their benefit; and a respect for the other party and their viewpoint. A successful outcome will leave all parties satisfied that they got what they most needed or wanted and that the resolution is fair to all parties.

Negotiation, however, can also be handled destructively when members use manipulative strategies, such as starting from the extreme end of one's own conflict continuum; denigrating the other's perspective; refusing to listen carefully; exaggerating the value of one's own concessions, while minimizing those of the other; concealing pertinent information; arguing forcefully, right or wrong; and stonewalling, or being willing to take as long as necessary to win (Hocker & Wilmot, 1991).

Adopting a strategy of negotiation represents a new level of seriousness in the discussion. The important part of negotiation, as with all aspects of constructive conflict management, is to achieve what is best for the overall group effort, without sacrificing the personal relationships that bind the group together (Fisher, Ury, & Patton, 1991).

Defining mutual interests leads to successful negotiations.

Accommodation

Accommodation as a strategy implies giving up all or most of one's own position (or benefit) for the sake of others. It involves a primarily one-sided concession and is most constructively used within a context of collaborative conflict management, with the intention being to reduce interpersonal tension and conflict for the sake of the overall task and the group process. When used to move beyond insignificant or superficial conflicts to save energy and group harmony for the more important issues, accommodation has a positive effect and can be considered constructive. For example, if most members of the group want to meet in the evening and one member prefers days, that member might be willing to go along with the evening time, if she or he possibly can, in order not to derail the group process over a relatively minor point. If, however, this member gives in on most of the important issues that involve conflicting points of view just for the sake of group harmony, that member may eventually end up feeling resentful and angry and may withdraw altogether from the group discussion process. In that case, the group loses the value of that member's unique perspective.

Trading accommodation on one point in order to win favor for another may have positive or negative consequences on the group process. If done in the spirit of constructive compromise, it may enhance the group effort. If, however, it is done in such a way that it pits one issue against another and builds coalitions that divide the group, it may have a long-term negative impact. For accommodation to work well, it needs to be used for the benefit of the overall process. It should not result in the group's losing the benefit of opposing points of view and the synergy that results from constructive conflict. The effect of destructive accommodation is similar to that of destructive avoidance, in that it assumes a limited "pie" that must be divided and forfeits the value of unique perspectives that might add to creative problem solving and enhanced solutions.

Compromise

Compromise, too, can be used as a conflict management strategy within either a constructive, collaborative orientation or a destructive, competitive one. When we decide to split the difference, we are using compromise. This strategy is appropriate when there is insufficient time or energy to work toward consensus and when it is generally agreed that the issue is not worth the use of that time or energy. Compromise can also be used when there are no realistic ways of "expanding the pie" and no easy agreement about its division. When each participant is oriented to the common good, each may be willing to concede some of his or her potential gain, in order to move ahead with the group process. In the example of the waste management community group, those members who would prefer to send all the refuse to the waste-to-energy plant and save the town the difficulty of storing and managing recyclable goods may have to compromise with those who would prefer to recycle everything but the most useless parts of the wastestream. Realistically, the group may decide to send all but a few categories of recyclable goods to the energy plant. In that way, each side may give up part of its perceived ideal solution, in order to meet the larger and more realistic group goals of staying within funding limits and making the solution as easy as possible for the town to administer. Neither group gets all that it wants, but both get some of it, and the solution may, in its implementation, be an optimal one. It is constructive compromise if the process has been handled fairly and with respect for the losses felt by those who have offered some of their own perceived benefit for the common good.

As with competition, however, compromise can be destructive if some members feel railroaded. When power is used irresponsibly to force some members to give up part of their positions in the name of compromise, those who feel they have not willingly participated in the choice are apt to feel disempowered and resentful. Regardless of how "efficient" this kind of power use may appear at the time, it can often backfire at a later point when cooperation and agreement are most needed among group members. Thus, compromise should truly be compromise, with each member feeling empowered in the concession to benefit what all have agreed is the larger good.

Competition

Competition is evidenced by its win-lose orientation. It is marked by self-interest, rather than mutual interest, and by an assumption of a limited resource and limited possibilities for gain. Although it can be associated with destructive conflict management, there are many times and places where "healthy competition" can be seen as constructive and productive. Competition, embedded in an overall orientation of mutual respect and interdependence, when the limits on the competitive forum are clear, and when everyone can agree on playing by the rules of the game, can lead to an efficient allocation of scarce time and other resources. It can also be fun and invigorating, much like when we become involved in playing or watching a football game, a vigorous debate, or games. A decision to use competitive strategies in a small group is appropriate when there is limited time or resources and when the larger goals of the group are enhanced by its use. It is a decision best made by mutual consent, whether implicit or explicit.

Constructive competitive communication in small groups includes making careful rationales for disagreements based on the substance of the issue at hand, while refraining from personal attacks. Using competition to assign leadership roles may be the most efficient way of allowing a group to assess the suitability of one or another person for particular responsibilities. When candidates debate their points of view on the relevant issues and maintain civility and respect for each other, the competitive process can energize discussion around group issues and can assure a measure of group cohesiveness. The group's assumption is that one candidate will win in the final vote or by consensus. The other candidate has, however, been able to state a position and be heard. That member will, as a likely consequence, assume more authority within the group. The competition is also expected to be bounded by the "rules of the game" and not expected to spill over into the subsequent group process. In another example, if there is a limited pot of money to be distributed among various intragroup projects, that allocation may be best decided through a competitive process, with each party putting forth its most convincing arguments for its need for a portion of the money. It may then be discussed until a decision is reached as to which parties should receive what portions of the funding. Depending on the importance of the distribution scheme to the overall goals of the group, the decision may be made by a vote (competition), by compromise, by accommodation, or by consensus (collaboration), thereby embedding the competitive strategy within another overall strategy. However it is decided, some parties may "win" and others "lose," but when the process is working as it should, the larger goals of the group are served. The key to constructive resolution of conflict resides, finally, in maintaining mutual respect among the group members themselves regardless of the immediate issues in conflict.

In its destructive guise, enmeshed within a context of lack of relational concern, the competitive communication style may ignore the rules of fair play and may include personal attacks involving any of the following tactics: confrontational remarks (such as pointing out another individual's errors in thinking or logic, rather than focusing on the issue); personal criticism (such as criticism of the other's characteristics or behaviors); personal rejection (such as antagonism toward the person, rather than toward the substance of the issue); hostile imperatives (such as demands, threats, assignment of blame); hostile questions (such as asking leading or rhetorical questions); presumptive remarks (such as attributions of thoughts or feelings to the other); or denial of one's own responsibility in the area of the conflict (Hocker & Wilmot, 1991).

Therefore, in a small group, where members are interdependent and mutual respect and trust are essential to optimizing solutions, competition needs to be handled carefully and with full awareness of the dangers it can pose. The rules of the competitive strategy, as well as the value of the personal relationships, may need to be made explicit.

Avoidance

The avoidance strategy entails withdrawing from the conflict. If avoidance is due to lack of information, understanding, or any particular opinion on the substance of the conflict, it can be a constructive strategy. The group process is rarely well served when conflict is not constructively engaged in an informed way. On the other hand, when avoidance is the result of feeling disempowered or disengaged, it can negatively impact the group process.

Destructive avoidance in the form of missing group meetings or refusing to participate in the discussion and work robs the group of individual perspectives and energy and impoverishes the decision-making process. When it leads to festering resentments on the parts of the avoiding member, or among the other group members, and to members expressing dissatisfaction with the group process, within or outside the group, it can hamper or actually derail the entire group effort. This aspect of avoidance is discussed further in the section on avoidance power.

When avoidance takes the guise of moving the subject of discussion off the point of conflict, it may temporarily ease some tension, but at best, it keeps the group from working through its disagreements and arriving at a constructive resolution. Conflict is usually resolved only by working through it, rather than by suppressing, avoiding, or exploding it. If it is not satisfactorily resolved, it may fester beneath the surface of any resolution and may later disrupt the outcome.

Groups will develop their own norms (see Chapter 3) on how to handle disputes (Kuhn & Poole, 2000). As you can well imagine, these norms can be quite complex since they are dependent on the combination of the individual styles that are being used to influence the other group members. Some groups tend to avoid issues or disagreements while others distribute the rewards in a manner similar to the competitive style with winners and losers. Groups seeking to effectively manage conflict with an integrative approach, which utilizes collaboration, make more effective decisions than those groups using the avoidance or distributive approaches (Kuhn & Poole, 2000). But, not all issues deserve the time and energy required for collaboration.

Conflict is healthiest when group members face it directly and choose an appropriate strategy for dealing with it. In that way, it serves the larger purposes for which groups are convened—the creative solutions resulting from synergy.

Power in Group Conflict

Although power dynamics are integral to group process at all levels, they are frequently most apparent at points of conflict. As power assures each of us access to the resources needed to maintain life and well-being, it is an essential tool for our survival. To the extent that it is exercised in a social context, we recognize it, respond to it, accept it, and use it through communication. We grant power to others and, in turn, are granted power by others in the groups in which we interact (McShane & Von Glinow, 2000). Although we all hold power in many different forms, we translate it into different currencies, or values, when we trade, spend, or use it in groups. Because groups are systems of interdependent relationships and every part affects every other part, even those who withdraw and refuse to participate are exercising power and influencing the group interaction. When I "take my marbles and go home," I change the possibilities for the group interaction. Power, therefore, underlies most of our group communication patterns and, by extension, our conflicts.

There are at least seven types of power available for use in groups: expert power, interpersonal linkage power, reward and punishment power, positional power (sometimes called legitimate power), referent power, charismatic (or personal) power, and avoidance power (French & Raven, 1968; Raven, 1993).

Expert Power

Expertise is generated by having a particular ability or access to particular information that is valued. To the extent that a group has a problem to solve that involves an understanding of technical, regulatory, political, or other specialized information, those with that information will be in a position to exercise their power to guide and influence the group discussion and decision making. For example, in the community group looking for solutions to their solid waste disposal problem, a trash hauler for the community may have expert power. That person knows the amount and content of the trash that needs to be disposed of. His or her information becomes a vital element in the decision-making process. As with any type of power, however, it is important for the group and person to keep that expertise in perspective and not let it override the larger goals of the group process. It frequently is easier than we realize for those who hold expert power to abuse it by directing it, consciously or unconsciously, toward some measure of personal gain. It is also easy for less informed group members to enhance expert power by putting more stock than is warranted in the expert's opinions.

Interpersonal Linkage Power

Those members in a group who have personal access to people or information sources that can be useful to the group bring a particular power to the group process. Their ability to engage the services of individuals, other groups, and organizations, or to gain access to resources not generally available to others in the group but that may enhance the group's ability to achieve its goals, enhances the power and influence of the member who has that access. In the community group, a member who knows someone in a neighboring community group engaged in a similar task may be in a position to help forge an intercommunity agreement on trash hauling or recycling. If such an agreement potentially reduces the waste disposal costs for both communities by increasing overall volumes and thereby giving added "weight" to the communities' negotiations with their markets, the person responsible for this possibility holds substantial interpersonal linkage power within the group. An office secretary may have interpersonal linkage power in a group when he or she can prevail upon office contacts to do mailings or research for the group. This power, as with any of the other types of power, can have multiple levels of influence and strength.

Reward and Punishment Power

Those who can effectively reward or punish other members of the group hold another type of power. To the extent that we can effectively praise or humiliate fellow group members, we all hold this power. However, we usually think of this as the ability to materially affect another's well-being in terms of a job, financial rewards or punishments, personal relationship rewards or punishments, or other rewards or punishments that we consider particularly meaningful. If one of the drivers for the trash hauler is also a member of the group, she or he may feel intimidated about disagreeing with the trash-hauling boss, for fear of losing his or her job. Additionally, this person may go out of her or his way to support the boss in the hope of getting a raise. In an organizational small group, the administrative assistant or secretary may hold this power. To the extent that person controls the flow of information and access to needed administrative services in the office, maintaining good relations with him or her may be key to doing one's job effectively on a day-to-day basis. When participation in groups is based on regard for reward and punishment power, effective group process may be sacrificed. This type of power, therefore, must be used with great care and with a sense of responsibility.

Positional (Legitimate) Power

Those granted power by others for specific purposes or because of the responsibilities of their position within the group may be said to have positional, or legitimate, power. Their authority may be limited to particular aspects of the group process, or it may be broader. Somewhat like expert power, this may translate into leading discussions and making or contributing to particular types of decisions. Its use can move group process in particular directions and can substantively shape the outcome. If the head of the organization is also a member of the small group, the other members may defer to that person because of his or her position, regardless of how well she or he understands the particular issues being discussed. This represents an unfortunate use of positional power. For example, in the community group, the town accountant knows the condition of the town's finances and may be able to offer insight into current financial arrangements and obligations. Although this is a more legitimate use of positional power, because this person may know what has been done and how it has been accounted for, he or she may not be the best person for anticipating new ways of raising money or reallocating existing funds. Administrative assistants and secretaries also often have positional power due to their valuable knowledge and access to particular information. The elected chair of the group holds positional power as well. As with all types of power, positional power is legitimized by others' perceptions of its value and worth.

Referent Power

The power conferred by affiliation with respected groups or people can be used in certain contexts to enhance personal power in a group situation. It may be used to add to credibility and, therefore, provide those members more influence in the overall group process. In the community group, a member who is a personal friend of the head of the state environmental regulatory commission has referent power, which may appear to be more influential than it actually is or should be. In a group of executives, a person who holds a degree from a prestigious school may hold referent power, if the other group members assume that this person has superior knowledge, whether or not that particular knowledge bears on the issues under discussion.

Charismatic (or Personal) Power

Charismatic power is that which resides in particular personalities and to which others are attracted. It is elusive in that it is difficult to define, but we recognize it when we see it or feel it. There are those who become "opinion leaders" by virtue of their personal charm and characteristics, rather than principally because of their knowledge or expertise. Charismatic power is resident in many individuals in everyday life, and we sometimes refer to them as "natural leaders." Well-known charismatic personalities are the Reverends Martin Luther King, Jr., and Jesse Jackson. President Ronald Reagan is also considered by many to have been a charismatic leader. When used responsibly, charismatic power can be beneficial to group process, ensuring that all members are respected and heard and that fairness prevails. When used irresponsibly, it can further disempower weaker members of a group.

Avoidance Power

Avoidance power may be used when members feel themselves to have little or no power in a group or when they feel they have little to gain from group membership and participation. They may refuse to participate in the process, while at the same time resenting their exclusion from it. Avoidance power may be manifest by these members being late for or absent from meetings, not fulfilling group obligations, refusing to share information or ideas, or sniping at others' ideas within the group. This power may also translate into denial and equivocation (such as refusing to take responsibility for actions or statements); topic management (such as shifting the topic to one with which the person feels more comfortable); noncommittal remarks (such as irrelevant or abstract comments); or irreverent remarks (such as making joking comments at inappropriate times). By engaging in any of these behaviors, these members may effectively keep the group from optimizing its creativity (Hocker & Wilmot, 1991).

Avoidance power in a small group may be felt in numerous more subtle ways, including draining group energy from the task at hand through the group's ongoing attempts to engage and involve the member in the process; draining energy by requiring other members to do larger portions of the work; losing the benefit of that member's contributions to the group effort; and causing resentment among other members, thereby weighing down their own creative energy and preventing them from optimizing solutions.

In the community group, if the trash hauler feels she is not fully appreciated, she may subtly or directly refuse to share information about the quantity and quality of the community's trash, leaving the group to scramble for indirect ways of estimating this information. If the avoiding members take their resentment out by criticizing the group effort outside the group, they may derail the results of the group process when it comes to adopting proposals the group puts forth. If, for example, members talk to other community residents about the negative aspects of the process, it might sabotage the community support necessary to implement the proposals. Avoidance power can be highly destructive and insidious in its effects upon the group and upon its achievements.

On the other hand, avoidance power should not be attributed to members who simply choose not to participate in some aspect of the discussion or process. They may feel they have nothing of substance to offer on a particular point. Lack of full participation may have roots in something other than avoidance power.

Power in Context

It is frequently tempting to criticize participants for their abuse of the power they hold. However, as members of small groups, we must take responsibility for the power we grant to or permit others to have, as well as for that we take ourselves. Expert power is only as forceful as those members who believe in it allow it to be. Avoidance power may be the only perceived route left to a member others have effectively shut out of the process. We are agents of and respondents to power, and we have power and choices in both guises. As such, we are each responsible for the part we play in the use and abuse of power in our groups.

Too often, power is seen as a pie with a limited number of slices, but power is not finite. All people have power, and any individual may simultaneously employ several types of power in any particular group. Power resides in relationships, rather than in individuals. It is relative to the group. The trash hauler in the community group has expert power in that group, but his or her expertise in that area may have little value to a group setting up a children's day care center. Each individual brings a set of experiences, habits, knowledge, and other value to every interaction. The interaction and the context in which it takes place determines the relative power and value of the individuals' participation. A person who feels disempowered in one group may be highly valued and empowered in another. For example, an artist may feel out of her or his element in a meeting of industry executives discussing plant and equipment investment but may be a highly valued member of a creative design team. Thus, power is resident in relationships and relational contexts. In effective groups, members pursue *mutual influence* which leads to a higher level of success because there is a synergetic process occurring (Murrell & Meredith, 2000).

In groups, effective leadership can help ensure the empowerment of all group members. Empowerment may take many forms, but first and foremost it assures a sense of worth and dignity for each individual. A group leader may empower members to make decisions and act on their own, taking responsibility for various parts of the group process (Scott & Jaffe, 1991), or that leader may exercise more hierarchical power, but for the group process to be effective, all members must feel empowered to contribute, whether they agree or disagree with the group leader or with each other. When a group is based on mutual respect, with all members feeling empowered, conflict can be handled constructively, enhancing the overall creative process.

Summary

Conflict is an important part of the group process. When we perceive incompatible goals, scarce rewards, or interference from another party, we have conflict. Conflict can be seen as the key, in some cases, to achieving the best possible solution in a group decision-making process. To the extent that it enlivens us and sharpens our focus on the issue, it can expand the possibilities for creative solutions to problems. For conflict to work constructively, however, we need to focus on issues and carefully delimit goals and expectations. Conflict should be considered part of the decision-making process, with its explicit and implicit parameters. When conflict is engaged constructively, it can enhance group cohesion, while reducing tension.

Essential to making any conflict management strategy work is consensus among group members as to which strategies are appropriate for which conflicts. This means the group must make initial decisions about the overall priorities of the decision-making process, including an explicit understanding of the constraints on the process itself.

Each group must wrestle with conflicts, small and large. The members must determine which issues are the most important and most worthy of the time and energy it takes to achieve consensus. Some will need to be handled quickly and efficiently, in order to save the time and energy required for the more important ones. If it is critical to the group's ongoing mission that consensus be achieved around particular issues, it might be worthwhile for the group to allow the extra time needed to build that consensus.

Underlying successful conflict management, regardless of the particular strategy used, is the honoring of interpersonal relationships and mutual respect, as well as the responsible use of power. Both of these prerequisites take intention and focus, along with an awareness of the cost of disregarding them. Resolving differences can be difficult and fraught with pitfalls. It is not necessarily easy or natural but is, rather, a learned skill. It is frequently easy to succumb to anger, frustration, resentment, hurt feelings, or any number of other personal emotional reactions in the heat of conflict. It is in these instances that practice and learned conflict management behavior can be most useful. Several particular communication strategies help assure constructive conflict management.

Constructive Conflict Management

1. Maintain a commitment to the importance of positive group relationships.
2. State positions directly and honestly.
3. Listen attentively to diverse opinions.
4. Accept responsibility for one's own thoughts and feelings.
5. Address the issues, not the personalities.
6. Communicate understanding of the other persons and their perspectives.
7. Use supportive, rather than defensive, communication strategies.
8. Look for areas of agreement that underlie the disagreement.
9. Focus on particular aspects of the issues, rather than on hardened positions.
10. Generate as many alternatives as feasible before coming to final resolution.
11. Insist that solutions be based on predetermined objective standards.

Difficult as the process of managing conflict may be, the only way around it is through it. Like a fire burning a pile of refuse, if it is doused before the refuse is thoroughly burned, the pile may smolder and reignite later. If the fire is allowed to burn unchecked or is fueled with gasoline, it may leap out of its boundaries and cause unintended harm. On the other hand, if it is allowed to burn within the allowable perimeters, the refuse is consumed, and the problem is satisfactorily resolved. Keeping the fire under control takes planning and a certain amount of time, energy, and focus. It means staying with the heat until it has run its course. So, too, when conflict is engaged constructively, it resolves the issues under dispute and leaves the process further ahead. When all the parties to a conflict adopt positive communication strategies, the outcome has a good chance of being a successful one, with a satisfactory outcome for all participants.

Conflict plays a key role in the functioning or lack of functioning of groups. When it is handled constructively, with careful attention to the patterns of communication interaction, it contributes to the creativity and synergy of group process; and when handled destructively, it undermines the group's best efforts.

DISCUSSION QUESTIONS

1. Define conflict. What do you feel are the key factors or characteristics?

2. Distinguish between substance and pattern in a conflict.

3. What is the difference between a morphostatic and morphogenic system? Provide an example of each from your own experience. Which group would be easier to work with in problem solving? Why?

4. Why are flashpoints occurring in the interactive pattern more difficult to resolve or deal with than those that occur in the substance of the issue?

5. How do scarce resources, diverse backgrounds, and varying orientations to task accomplishments influence the substance of conflict?

6. What are the two dimensions used in determining conflict style? Outline how they create the five conflict managing styles discussed in this chapter.

7. Briefly outline an example of collaborative conflict resolution that you have engaged in. Contrast that with a competitive conflict. Which was more satisfying to you? To the other party?

8. What are important elements in a successful negotiation strategy?

9. Distinguish between accommodation and avoidance. Provide an example of how to utilize each strategy effectively in a small group discussion.

10. What should be the key factors in deciding to use compromise?

11. What are some examples of constructive competitive communication in small groups?

12. Provide an example of the seven types of power in small groups.

EXERCISES

1. Mediating disputes; 2. Recognizing and dealing with conflict; 3. Proverbs as conflict management guides; 4. Personal awareness as a guide to conflict management; 5. Case studies in conflict resolution; 6. Discovering information power; 7. Discovering your own power

1. MEDIATING DISPUTES

Mediation is a process of attempting to resolve conflict through joint decision making and mutual agreement among the parties. Small group team members often participate in the role of mediator to facilitate group discussions. This exercise focuses attention on the skills of a mediator and allows observation, discussion, and practice of those skills (see Table 12.1).

TABLE 12.1   Mediation Evaluation Form

Assign Ratings: 5 = Outstanding; 4 = Effective; 3 = Partly Effective; 2 = Weak; 1 = Inadequate

General Behaviors of Mediator during Mediation Process   **Provide Examples**

_____ Personal and interpersonal behaviors

_____ Managerial and procedural behaviors

_____ Persuasive and tactical behaviors

Specific Accomplishments with Disputing Parties   **Provide Examples**

_____ Elicited trust from the disputing parties

_____ Clarified role of mediation and of mediator
for disputing parties

_____ Stimulated the parties to discuss their
difficulties freely

_____ Facilitated discussion and clarification
of the issues

_____ Identified conflicts

_____ Dealt with anger appropriately

_____ Built a realistic agenda for mediation

_____ Questioned disputing parties appropriately

_____ Helped parties to explore alternatives
cooperatively

_____ Empowered disputing parties to make
mutual decisions

_____ Provided new alternatives parties had not
thought of, but accepted

_____ Clarified the final decision

_____ Obtained satisfactory agreement from both
disputing parties

Comments about the Mediation Process and Suggestions for Improvements:

A mediator becomes an intermediary for the disputing parties but does not have the power to resolve their differences, only to facilitate their reduction of hostility and tension by helping them to listen to each other's perspectives and achieve a mutual agreement through joint decision making. The mediator is not adversarial, is not an advocate for either side, and has no preferential interest in either side of the issue or either party's perspective.

A useful conflict management exercise is to role-play a peer mediation session with team members role-playing the opposing parties and one playing the role of a mediator who facilitates their discussion. The mediator should try to first identify areas on which the parties can agree and then help them negotiate their areas of dispute. The mediation is largely accomplished through helping the parties to engage in active, empathic listening. Two sample mediation exercises follow. An alternative or follow-up exercise is to have teams develop their own mediation scenarios and then resolve them through a role play. The mediation evaluation form can help focus attention on important mediator skills. What types of power does the mediator have to draw upon?

Mediation Exercise One—The Roommates: Four friends moved into an apartment near campus and signed a one-year lease on it. After four months, Sara moved out of the apartment, but assured Jen and her other two roommates that she would continue to pay her share of the rent for the remainder of the lease. Jen is responsible for writing the check each month to pay the rent bill and has covered Sara's portion for the past two months. Each month she has sent Sara a reminder note but has received nothing from her. Yesterday she called Sara and asked for the rent money. Sara indicated that she has had second thoughts about her obligation to pay rent on the apartment since she is no longer receiving the benefit of it, that she has other financial obligations and has to pay rent on her current apartment, and that she feels that she was really forced out of the apartment by her treatment from the other two roommates. Jen took a deep breath and suggested that they try mediation to resolve their differences, and Sara agreed.

Mediation Exercise Two—The Couch: When Pam and Jason moved in two years ago, there was a large sectional couch in the apartment. Neither of them legally owned the couch, but both used it during the year that they lived together in the apartment. Jason moved out three months ago for a job in another state. Pam moved to a new apartment across town last weekend. Beth assumed the remainder of the lease on the apartment and moved in. Yesterday Dave, a friend of Jason who happens to live in an apartment across the street, came over to take the couch to his apartment. He claimed that Jason had given it to him. Beth refused to let him take the couch or even to let him into the apartment. Last night Jason called Beth to tell her that the couch now belongs to Dave and that she should let him have it. When Beth told Jason that she was not going to give the couch to Dave, Jason threatened to come by and pick up not only the couch but the shower curtain, dish drainer, and several other items that he purchased and left in the apartment for Pam's use as long as she was living there. Beth hung up on him and at first didn't know what to do, but finally called Dave and suggested that they try mediation. Dave agreed.

2. RECOGNIZING AND DEALING WITH CONFLICT

Conflict is an inevitable part of the group process. Answer the following questions using your current group, or past group, experiences as a basis.

1. What are the primary causes of conflict in the group?
2. What are the major issues over which conflict occurs?
3. Using the five styles of dealing with conflict, which style is the most prevalent among members? Do some members avoid while others compete? Try to be specific. Do group members accommodate effectively or are there potentially serious compromises?
4. Create a conflict management plan of action. List at least four types of conflict that now exist that the group should avoid in the future. List at least four ways the group members could assist each other in being more effective in dealing with conflict.

3. PROVERBS AS CONFLICT MANAGEMENT GUIDES

Directions
1. Proverbs provide traditional wisdom for resolving conflicts. Identify each of the proverbs below as an example of (a) compete, (b) compromise, (c) collaborate, (d) avoid, or (e) accommodate.

_____ 1. Kind words are worth more and cost little.
_____ 2. The person who fights and runs away lives to fight another day.
_____ 3. You scratch my back; I'll scratch yours.
_____ 4. Might overcomes right.
_____ 5. Only the person who is willing to give up his or her monopoly on truth can ever profit from the truths others hold.

2. Form a group and come to an agreement on the conflict management strategy reflected in each proverb.
3. What are the major premises behind each of the five strategies?
4. How can your group develop effective conflict management techniques that respect the timeworn advice of the proverbs while maintaining an excellent group climate?
5. The answers to the strategies reflected by the proverbs are: (1) accommodate; (2) avoid; (3) compromise; (4) compete; (5) collaborate.

4. PERSONAL AWARENESS AS A GUIDE TO CONFLICT MANAGEMENT

Directions
    Individually, respond to the following questions:

1. Think of the last disagreement you had with someone. How did you handle it?
2. Think of the last time you were certain someone was trying to achieve goals or meet his or her needs without any apparent or sufficient concern for your needs. How did you handle it?
3. You are most likely to get into an argument over what aspects of your group activities?
4. You are most open to criticism from other group members when they. . . ?
5. You are least open to criticism from other group members when they. . . ?

You have identified some of the potential "hot buttons" you might respond to in conflict situations. Now that you are aware of these issues, what type of communication is necessary with the other group members to make certain your hot buttons are not pushed?

5. CASE STUDIES IN CONFLICT RESOLUTION

Below are three case studies. In your group, suggest five approaches to resolving each of these conflicts reflecting compete, compromise, collaborate, avoid, or accommodate. Finally, would negotiation be a better alternative?

1. Two college students share an apartment and all the expenses. It is the end of the year and both students are broke. Unknown to the other, each has invited a friend over for a meal, aware of the fact that there are two potatoes left in the cupboard. Both want potatoes to form the basis of the meal.
2. A local charitable group applied for a grant from a major local authority. They were thrilled when a substantial amount was granted. The new slate of officers wants the money to be spent on entering the new millenium through the purchase of a PC, fax, and photocopier. None of this equipment is now available to the charity. The longtime office manager feels that the money would be better spent as seed money to start a publicity launch and additional fund-raising events.
3. Two parents, one a teacher and the other a lawyer, have one small child. Before starting their family, they had agreed that they would continue working and share household responsibilities including any child care needs. Normally, one of them takes their child to day care in the morning before driving to work, and they take turns picking their child up later in the day. On Sunday evening they called the family doctor because their child had developed a rash. Chickenpox was diagnosed. The teacher has three parent discussions

on Monday and can't take the time off to stay home with their child. The lawyer is due in court.

Compare the advantages and disadvantages of the five different strategies in each situation. Did adding negotiation to the choices assist in dealing with the conflict?

6. DISCOVERING INFORMATION POWER

As a group, answer the following question: Why is a manhole round? Allow each group member to express an opinion. Reach consensus.

Questions: 1. In your past group experiences, what efforts were taken to make certain that all potential information and other types of power were used to the benefit of the group?

2. How can your group make certain that everyone has the opportunity to express his or her opinions and insights? The answer is that if the manhole cover were any other shape, it could fall through the opening. The round design means no hinges, places for clothing or equipment to get caught, or unfortunate accidents because the cover fell on someone's head.

7. DISCOVERING YOUR OWN POWER

No one is powerless. In fact, most of us have some of each type of power. Review your last or current job, your work with groups, or a current relationship and determine your exercise of expert, interpersonal linkage, reward and punishment, positional, referent, charismatic or personal, and avoidance power.

Which type of power has proved to be most successful? Which type of power has created the most difficulties? What choices do you need to make in terms of how you exercise power in a group? How can you improve your exercise of power?

REFERENCES

Benson, J. A. (1988). Crisis revisited: An analysis of strategies used by Tylenol in the second tampering episode. *Central States Speech Journal, 39*(1), 49–66.

Chen, C. C., Chen, X. P., & Meindl, J. R. (1998). How can cooperation be fostered? The cultural effects of individualism-collectivism. *Academy of Management Review, 23*(3), 285–304.

Fisher, R., Ury, W., & Patton, B. (1991). *Getting to yes: Negotiating agreement without giving in* (2nd ed.). Boston: Houghton Mifflin.

French, J. R. P., & Raven, B. (1968). The bases of social power. In D. Cartwright & A. Zander (Eds.), *Group Dynamics.* New York: Harper & Row.

Harris, T. E. (2002). *Applied organizational communication: Principles and pragmatics for future success.* Mahwah, NJ: Lawrence Erlbaum.

Hocker, J. L., & Wilmot, W. W. (1991). *Interpersonal conflict* (3rd ed.). Dubuque, IA: William C. Brown.

Kuhn, T., & Poole, M. (2002). Do conflict management styles affect group decision making? *Human Communication Research, 26*(4), 558–590.

McNary, L. D. (2003, April). The term "win-win" in conflict management: A classic case of misuse and overuse. *The Journal of Business Communication, 40,* 144–159.

McShane, S. L., & von Glinow, M. A. (2000). *Organizational behavior.* Boston: Irwin McGraw-Hill.

Murrell, K. L., & Meredith, M. (2000). *Empowering employees.* New York: McGraw-Hill

O'Connor, K. M., Gruenfeld, D. H., & McGrath, J. E. (1993). The experience and effects of conflict in continuing work groups. *Small Group Research, 24*(3), 362–382.

Putnam, L. L., & Poole, M. S. (1987). Conflict and negotiation. In F. M. Jablin, L. L. Putnam, K. H. Roberts, & L. W. Porter (Eds.), *Handbook of organizational communication* (pp. 549–599). Newbury Park, CA: Sage.

Rabie, M. (1994). *Conflict resolution and ethnicity.* Westport, CT: Praeger.

Rahim, M. A., & Blum, A. A. (1995). *Global perspectives on organizational conflict.* Westport, CT: Praeger.

Raven, B. H. (1993). The bases of power: Origins and recent developments. *Journal of Social Issues, 49*(4), 227–251.

Scott, C. D., & Jaffe, D. T. (1991). *Empowerment.* Menlo Park, CA: Crisp.

Shockley-Zalabak, P. (2002). *Fundamentals of organizational communication: Knowledge, sensitivity, skills, values* (5th ed.). Boston: Allyn & Bacon.

Thoreau, H. D. (1965). *Walden.* New York: Holt, Rinehart, and Winston.

Tjosvold, D. (1995). Cooperation theory, constructive controversy, and effectiveness: Learning from crisis. In R. A. Guzzo, E. Salas, & Associates (Eds.), *Team effectiveness and decision making in organizations* (pp. 79–112). San Francisco: Jossey-Bass.

Ward, A. C. (1998, July-August). Another look at how Toyota integrates product development. *Harvard Business Review,* pp. 36–49.

Witteman, H. (1991). Group member satisfaction. *Small Group Research, 22*(1), 24–58.

Yalom, I. (1985). *The theory and practice of group psychology.* New York: Basic Books.

Zemke, R., Raines, C., & Filipczak, B. (2000). *Generations at work: Managing the clash of veterans, xers, and nexters in your workplace.* New York: AMACOM.

Zornoza, A., Ripoll, P., & Peiro, J. M. (2002). Conflict management in groups that work in two different communication contexts: Face-to-face and computer-mediated communication. *Small Group Research, 33*(5), 481–508.

13

Leadership in Small Groups

CHAPTER OUTLINE

CHAPTER OBJECTIVES

- Explain the characteristics of leadership.
- Identify the varying attributes of leaders.
- Differentiate between theories of leadership.
- Outline the premises behind the leadership style theories.
- Explain the Managerial Grid and its applications.

- Describe transactional and transformational leadership.
- Discuss leadership by adaptation.
- Explain the three characteristics of leaders.
- Spell out the different processes for becoming a leader.
- Illustrate the tasks of group leaders.
- Discuss the influences of leaders on group structure.
- Identify leadership snags.

KEY TERMS

Adaptation leadership
Appointed group leaders
Authority–compliance
Autocratic system
Communication competence
Country club management
Credibility
Democratic system
Effective leaders
Elected group leaders
Emergent group leaders
Empowering group members

Facilitating meetings
Impoverished management
Interdependence
Laissez-faire system
Leader-as-coach
Leader-as-conductor
Leader-as-technician
Managerial Grid theory
Middle of the road
Nature of task
Object and action mediation
Opportunism

Paternalism
Shared facilitative leadership
Situational theories
Systems and leaders
Style theories
Team management
Trait theories
Transformational leaders
Transactional leaders
Universal theories
Vision

In the legendary cycles of the Blackfoot Indians there is an account of the early people, who were poor and naked and did not know how to live. Old Man, their maker, said: "Go to sleep and get power. Whatever animals appear in your dream, pray and listen." And, the story concludes, that was how the first people got through the world, by the power of their dreams. (*The Unexpected Universe*, Eiseley, 1969, p. 113)

Leadership, whether expressed by an individual or engaged in collectively by the members of a group, is about developing dreams, visions, goals, and objectives that help focus a group's energy to engage in its task and accomplish its mission. Leadership is often associated with the symbols, speeches, and insights presented at critical turning points in the thinking of a group, movement, or larger community and that make their goals and objectives real and achievable; but the essence of leadership itself is the conception and articulation of the group's vision (Northhouse, 2001).

Recognizing Leaders

A good leader serves as a catalyst for the group process. Effective leaders listen well and are sensitive to the diverse and subtle influences on a group's ability to work together productively (Bennis & Nanus, 1997). An effective leader may be the one who helps focus and give shape to the discussion, who is able to make sense of apparently disparate ideas, or who encourages group members to express their contradictory viewpoints to stimulate the benefits of conflict among diverse perspectives. An effective leader enables and motivates the group to stay on track, to remain energized and empowered, to resolve conflicts constructively, and to make creative decisions, in order to reach desirable outcomes. Finally, a leader is the person or persons the group looks to when it has reached an impasse, needs guidance in setting a new direction or staying on course, or needs order restored to an unruly group process. An effective leader may be autocratic or democratic and collaborative in making decisions, but she or he elicits respect from group members and, in turn, gives respect to those members (Miller, 1997).

A leader may be the coach who leads the debate team to a successful outcome, the captain of a winning sports team, the person who keeps a group of stranded hikers from panicking and hiking around in circles, or the person who holds a small group together until they have completed the task for which they were convened. "A leader's effectiveness is often measured by the performance of his or her team" (Kolb, 1996, p. 173); and leaders are the ones who usually shoulder the largest burden of blame when their group or team fails to meet its goals or has unfortunate outcomes.

Because leaders are a part of the systems in which they participate, however, their leadership abilities both influence and are influenced by the groups they lead. Many different types of people have been highly effective leaders in different types of situations and contexts. Like power, leadership exists in the context and in the relationships among people, as well as in the abilities of individuals. Most of us recognize a good leader when we see or work with one in a given context, but that same person might not be equally effective with another group or in another situation. A person who understands the ways of the wilderness and how to survive for days in the wild with little or no food or other supplies may be the perfect leader for a group of stranded hikers. Those same skills would probably not be as useful for the leader of a group planning a strategy for putting together a bid on a prime industrial development site. Although we can frequently point to particular individuals as leaders, it is not always as easy to define leadership in such a way that we can anticipate who will make a good leader and who will not, under any and all sets of circumstances.

In general, we can say that a good leader is one who is successful in helping the group accomplish the goals it set out to accomplish, and a poor leader is one who fails to do that. In other words, "Leaders deserve to be so called only when they have been key players in acts of leadership" (Clark & Clark, 1990, p. 20). Since leadership is defined in the context in which it is enacted, it is in the doing of leadership that a leader is recognized, rather than in any particular abstract definition.

Leadership as a Function in a System

Leaders play key roles in the systems in which they participate. Their effect on the patterns of interaction within their groups and between their groups and the external environments in which they are located are often influential in determining the outcome of the group process.

As we have noted in previous chapters, groups as systems are as successful as their ability to bring in and process new information and new ways of approaching problems—their ability to be *morphogenic* (take in, process, and transform information and procedures), rather than *morphostatic* (resisting change and maintaining the status quo). This entails responding to the substance of the internal and external environments within which the group operates, the facts and issues around and within which the group is convened, and the complex interactions between the people, the issues, the multiple environments, and the group's own dynamics.

Leaders act as arbiters of these interfaces, serving as communication links between the group and its external environment and between group members and the process in which they are engaged. The leader must have the skills and knowledge to gather from the environment and decode those factors that are helpful and relevant to the group process, as well as the ability to translate and encode that information into forms that are useful to the group. Effective leaders must mediate both objects and actions. In *object* mediation, the leader "must collect and form detailed impressions about the environment" (Barge, 1994, p. 12); and in *action* mediation the leader must remove environmental obstacles through appropriate behaviors (Barge, 1994). The wilderness leader mediates between the wilderness and the group who is unfamiliar with it. She or he assesses the situation (object mediation) and develops strategies for ameliorating the possible negative effects on the group, helping them understand the situation and behave in appropriate ways (action mediation). For the leader to be effective in this role, however, he or she depends on the group's cooperation and trust in his or her ability. Good leadership in an interactive system requires a "reciprocal relationship between leaders and followers" (Barge, 1994, p. 19).

Theories of Leadership

Whereas the traditional approach to leadership relied on mechanistic metaphors by breaking it down into its component parts, current theories encompass a much broader and more continuous scope of attributes, behaviors, and patterns of interaction. Early theories were based on hierarchic models from industrial organizations. In these contexts, leaders oversaw production employees and were expected to maintain efficiency and discipline against what were assumed to be the natural instincts of the employees to avoid work. Leaders gave orders, and workers were expected to follow them. Workers were not expected to be creative in their thinking or to have ideas for improving their methods of working. The leaders of these groups of workers were expected to be rigid and authoritarian

(Barge, 1994). Changes in organizational expectations, however, have brought comparable changes in leadership expectations.

When we examine leadership today, it appears to be more art than science. It is useful, nonetheless, to try to describe the traits and behaviors that effective leaders share. Although leadership has been the subject of a great deal of communication research, no one theory has fully explained it. On the other hand, although no one leadership theory fully explains the subject, several perspectives taken together can contribute a great deal to our understanding of it.

Most traditional leadership theories define leadership according to either *traits*, personal characteristics associated with an individual person, or *styles*, the behaviors a person manifests. The trait theories assume that certain physical and psychological characteristics predispose some people to leadership (Hackman & Johnson, 2000). The style theories assume that particular kinds of behavior (e.g., task-oriented or relationship-oriented behaviors) underlie leadership ability.

In terms of leadership styles, Gastil (1994) argues that neither a democratic nor an autocratic leadership style is necessarily more efficient or productive. However, he suggests that some benefits of a democratic style of leadership are in giving group members responsibility, which improves the general abilities and leadership skills of group members, assists the group in its decision-making process, and helps group members share important leadership functions.

Superimposed on these two types of theories are the two dimensions of universality and situational dependence. *Universal* theories posit that particular traits or styles characterize leaders across most situations; and *situational* theories posit that any given traits or styles are unique to specific situations (Barge, 1994). The four resulting categories defined by traits, styles, universal, and situational yield a grid that encompasses most of the leadership theories: universal trait theories, universal style or behavior theories, contingency trait theories, and situational behavior theories (Barge, 1994). *Universal trait theories* posit particular personal characteristics that leaders in most circumstances share. *Universal style theories* posit particular behaviors in which effective leaders generally engage. *Contingency trait theories* posit the idea that different personal characteristics are appropriate to leaders in different types of situations, and *situational behavior theories* suggest the idea that leaders adapt behaviors to the requirements of particular circumstances.

Managerial Leadership Grid Theory

Of particular interest among the style (or behavior) theories are those based on results of leadership studies conducted at Ohio State University during the 1950s. These studies found that a concern for task (substance, object mediation) and a concern for relationships (pattern, action mediation) were often associated with leadership and formed the basis for many follow-up studies, including those by Robert Blake and Jane Mouton, who developed the now well-known Managerial Grid (Blake & Mouton, first published in 1964). This grid places a concern for people on a vertical axis and a concern for task on a horizontal axis, defining a two-dimensional space.

The Managerial Grid characterizes seven (1991) leadership styles—team management, authority–compliance, middle of the road, country club management, and impoverished management—according to the point along each of the axes at which a leader's behavior falls (Blake and Mouton, 1985; Blake and McCanse, 1991). These dimensions also correspond to those of the conflict management styles grid, as shown in the parenthetical names associated with each of the grid styles. When considering teams, these researchers added two additional positions, identified as paternalism and opportunism (Blake, Mouton, & Allen, 1987). Each of these seven leadership styles is located on the grid and assigned a value of 1 (least) to 9 (most) on each of the two axes of concern for people and concern for task, as indicated on Figure 13.1.

1. *9,9 Team Management* (Collaboration). The leader demonstrates a high degree of concern for both people (9) and task (9). The group works together with mutual respect and a strong goal orientation. The group has a good chance for a successful outcome. This orientation takes time and commitment from both the leader and the group members, but when time and energy permit, it is clearly a superior group decision-making mode.

2. *9,1 Authority–Compliance* (Competition). The leader is concerned with completing the task (9) but shows little interest or regard for relationships (1). Group members are not expected to participate in the decision making. Depending on the overall context of the group and the task at hand, this may be highly efficient and productive or may lead to feelings of disenfranchisement by the group, causing the group not to support the decisions. In either case, it does not allow for the creative decision making that results from group synergy.

3. *5,5 Middle of the Road* (Compromise). Although not strongly committed in either direction, the leader shows a moderate concern for interpersonal relationships (5) and a moderate concern for the task at hand (5). Without a strong commitment to results, the outcome is not likely to be optimal, but it may satisfy everyone somewhat. If time and energy constraints are the deciding factor, this may be the most practical course.

4. *1,9 Country Club Management* (Accommodation). The group leader is more concerned about interpersonal relationships (9) than about accomplishing the task (1). When the group is convened for the sake of enjoyment or personal contact, this is an appropriate style. If, however, they are trying to find a solution to a problem, this is an inefficient way to go about it. On the other hand, if the group and the leader prefer to feel good about each other, while agreeing that the leader should take sole responsibility for making decisions, this style may work well.

5. *1,1 Impoverished Management* (Avoidance). With a low concern for both people (1) and task (1), the leader does not try to influence group members and cares little for whether or not they achieve their goals. This style is used by leaders who are overworked, don't care about this particular project, or who have "retired on the job." This style is not helpful to the group's interpersonal relationships or goal accomplishments.

6. *9+9 Paternalism/Maternalism.* As in the team management style, the leader shows a high level of concern for both people (9) and task (9). However, rather than assuming the group has its own stake in the outcome and is working for

FIGURE 13.1   Managerial Leadership Grid

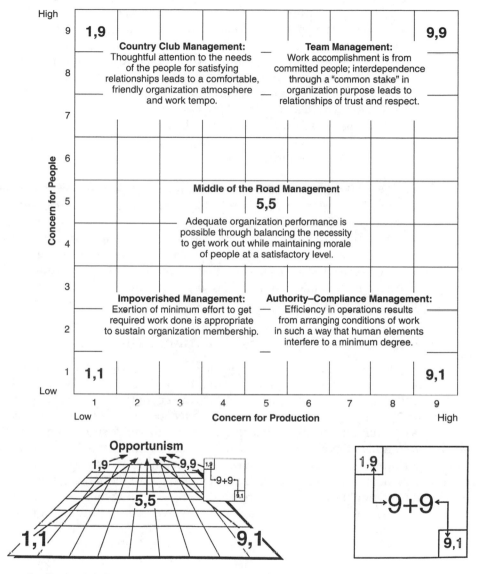

People adapt and shift to any Grid style needed to gain the maximum advantage. Performance occurs according to selfish gain. Effort is given for advantage or personal gain.

9+9: Paternalism/Maternalism
Reward and approval gain loyalty and obedience to work requirement. Failure leads to punishment.

Source: The Leadership Grid® figure, Paternalism Figure and Opportunism from *Leadership Dilemmas— Grid Solutions,* by Robert R. Blake and Anne Adams McCanse (Formerly the Managerial Grid by Robert R. Blake and Jane S. Mouton). Houston: Gulf Publishing Company, (Grid Figure: P. 29, Paternalism Figure: p. 30, Opportunism Figure: p. 31). Copyright 1991 by Scientific Methods, Inc. Reproduced by permission of the owners.

intrinsic rewards, the leader assumes the group is burdened by the task and requires extrinsic rewards. In this case, the leader pushes the group to get the job done, and then rewards the members in ways she or he has available, through salaries, benefits, or working conditions, if they are employees; or through some other benefit, if he or she has a different relationship with the group. Drawbacks are that group members may simply work for a price and never develop loyalty or commitment and pride in the project.

7. *Opportunism.* Several styles are used simultaneously, depending on the people involved. The leader has a 5,5 style toward those group members seen as equals, a 9,1 style toward those seen as less important, and a 1,9 behavior toward those in authority. This is seen as self-serving, with no overall concern for the good of the group and its efforts.

The Managerial Leadership Grid has a subtle bias toward "one best way" of running a group or team, as a 9,9 Team Management of collaboration, and one criticism of this theory is that it is too simplistic in its assumption of universality (Hughes, Ginnett, & Curphy, 1998). However, it is a valuable starting point in understanding different leadership styles and may be useful as a guide to thinking about where and when each can be used appropriately. The various styles the grid mentions have application to different groups and to the same groups at different times, depending on the task and the constraints of time and energy.

Transactional and Transformational Theories

In addition to the trait and style theories, researchers have developed transactional and transformational theories to account for the relationships between leaders and the groups they lead. Moving beyond traits and styles, they focus on the patterns of interaction. A *transactional* approach refers to those leaders who are task-oriented and able to direct their groups in focused and specific ways to accomplish finite goals. They work at gaining their group's compliance through various approaches: offering rewards, threatening punishment, appealing to group members' sense of altruism, or appealing to their rational judgment (Barge, 1994). Transactional leaders intervene in the process only when group members get off the track. Otherwise, they have little involvement with the group. These leaders are similar to the 9,1 (authority–compliance) leaders, except that they use various appeals to motivate team members, rather than relying solely on the authority of their position of power. In this way, they are also similar to the 9+9 (paternalistic) leaders. Transactional leaders are interpersonally distanced from group members and may suffer the same deficit as the 9,1 and 9+9 leaders, in that their members may never be truly involved in the process or its outcomes.

On the other hand, *transformational* leaders have a strong sense of mission and an ability to attract a loyal and committed following. They are those leaders whose groups would "follow them anywhere." These leaders are able to motivate their followers through their charismatic power—their inspirational vision, their ability to express complex ideas in easily understood ways, and their individ-

Dr. Martin Luther King, a transformational leader, at the front of a voting rights march from Selma, Alabama, to the state capital in Montgomery.

ualized attention to followers. These leaders rely on their ability to shape group members' perceptions of the task or mission and to motivate them to aspire to a set of goals, rather than relying on explicit instructions or extrinsic rewards and punishments (Barge, 1994; Hackman & Johnson, 2000). In contrast with those leaders who simply manage a group process by administering, depending on systems, and following the rules, the transformational leader empowers the group to accomplish the tasks through proactive communication and mutual trust (Bennis, 1990). Transformational leaders include some political and religious leaders, as well as some who lead dynamic organizations.

Leadership by Adaptation

Despite the appeal of many theories of leadership, defining leadership in a way that encompasses all situations remains elusive. "Implicit within all leadership theories is the notion that leaders are most effective when they can dissect the demands and constraints of a situation and perform the required actions to take advantage of a situation's opportunities and overcome its constraints" (Barge, 1994, p. 57). Because groups are dynamic systems, leaders need to be able to adapt their styles and behaviors to the needs of the particular group within a context. Ellis and Cronshaw (1992) suggest that leaders are more effective when they develop a social intelligence that allows them to monitor situations and adapt their leadership behaviors as required.

Leadership, therefore, is more often found in the interactions of the group and in its process than solely in the traits and qualities of the individuals enacting it. This is true in multiple senses of leadership, from the formal leadership that emerges or is imposed on the group to the intuitive "dance" the leader engages in to maintain the group dynamic. "Effective leadership, research suggests, is remarkably chameleonlike . . . [it] is a function of the situation in which it is found" (Kotter, 1988, p. 21). There is no "single comprehensive list of leadership qualities and . . . no single path to leadership" but adaptability is a key characteristic of effective leadership (Clark & Clark, 1990, p. 70). Thus, despite the plethora of theories on leadership, the actual manifestation of it is frequently hard to predict but highly evident when we experience it. It happens within the context of the group and is dependent on their responses to it.

A Leader

Lao Tsu is credited with the saying:

> The wicked leader is he whom the people despise.
> The good leader is he whom the people revere.
> The great leader is he about whom the people say, "We did it ourselves."

Leaderless Groups

Leaderless groups, defined as "groups that do not have a designated person with continuing authority over the other members and responsibility for maintaining the group" have existed for decades (Counselman, 1991, p. 243). Many experts, however, have expressed skepticism over the viability and productivity of truly leaderless groups. Yalom (1985) suggested that most so-called leaderless groups in fact have unofficial leaders, frequently more experienced or expert group members, who informally fulfill the leadership functions. Others have cautioned that leaderless groups soon become leadershipless, lack a clear focus or structure, and find it difficult to develop or maintain group norms. Without a clearly defined, shared sense of purpose and a consistent, commonly agreed upon set of working norms, a group may find itself constantly negotiating how it will do things rather than engaging in an efficient performance of its tasks. Leaderless groups have been known to dissolve in disappointment when members' behaviors such as lateness to meetings, absences, and the expression of hostile feelings, coupled with the refusal by one or two group members to discuss group dynamics, have gone unchecked (Counselman, 1991). This is not to say that leaderless groups cannot work. To be effective, however, members must cooperatively take on the leadership functions of (1) continuing to reaffirm the group's task, process, and vision; (2) repeatedly emphasizing the need for a safe group climate in which to engage in their work; and (3) maintaining the group's norms and boundaries between permissible and impermissible behaviors. Whether one person fulfills them or the group as a whole shares them, leadership functions are necessary to effective group processes.

Three Characteristics of Leaders

Regardless of the particulars of any one theory of leadership, there are generally at least three characteristics we expect leaders to manifest. These are vision, credibility, and communication competence. *Vision* provides the direction for the group process, *credibility,* the reason for the group to follow that direction, and *communication competence*, the means for communicating that direction to the group. Each of these contributes to the ability of a leader to influence the group process.

Vision

True leaders are expected to do more than simply conduct meetings, control agendas, and keep track of events. A key piece of leadership is the ability to hold onto an overall vision while moving a group through the process necessary to achieve that vision. Leaders need to set long- and short-term goals, focus attention on relevant activities, manage conflict, and empower other group members to contribute to the creative process (Bennis & Nanus, 1997).

The wilderness leader sets the goal of getting the group safely out of the wilderness. To achieve that goal, she or he must keep the group safe and healthy for as long as it takes to find their way out. This may mean he or she will need to find sources of potable water and ways of feeding and sheltering the group within the constraints of the natural environment, while maintaining the group's morale. Keeping the goal in sight, while keeping the group on track toward accomplishing it, is a complex task.

Credibility

Effective leadership depends on the group's willingness to follow. This willingness is generally based on the group's perception of the leader's abilities and credibility (Hackman & Johnson, 2000). Without the group's trust and confidence, the most visionary leader is paralyzed in her or his attempts to direct the group toward the stated goals and visions. The wilderness leader would be powerless to help the group if they didn't participate in the process. If the group doesn't believe in the leader's ability to help them find their way to safety, or if they don't trust him or her to keep the group's welfare as a priority, they are not likely to follow her or his advice and instructions. Thus, vision without credibility may prevent the most insightful and creative leader from being effective.

Credibility is a complex phenomenon, however, which derives from several sources: competence (knowledge and expertise in a topic); character (honesty and trustworthiness); composure (ability to remain calm under stress); sociability (likableness); and extroversion (degree of interest in others) (Barge, 1994). Each of these builds a base of power and is activated by the perceptions of the value of that power by the members of the group. Those leaders who are perceived to have a relevant power base, as well as the best interests of their group at heart, will have influence in their groups. Leaders who are perceived to lack such a power base or who are perceived to be manipulative or dishonest will have a harder time gaining compliance from their group.

Communication Competence

Another important piece of group leadership is communication competence (Drucker, 1997). For a leader to be effective, she or he must be able to translate his or her relevant knowledge, skills, and situationally appropriate behavior to group members in ways they can understand and trust. Communication competence includes the ability to decode and understand messages coming from the environment—both within the group and from outside of it—and to encode and interpret that information for the group members or for those relevant others outside the group. A leader must be able to communicate in a way that "upholds and 'fits into' the existing cultural value system or transcends that system by articulating an alternative value system" (Barge, 1994, p. 238). As such, leaders must be able to understand their environment and interpret it in a way that makes sense to group members (Buckingham & Coffman, 1999).

Before going on a white-water rafting trip, the river guide explains to the rafters what to expect and how to respond to a given set of commands that the guide will issue when they reach the white water. Before they get in the raft and follow the instructions, though, they need to believe that the guide knows the river and how to interpret the currents, eddies, and falls; that she or he is able to maneuver the raft safely through or around the rapids, cares about the rafters' well-being, and is able to tell them what, when, and how to do things in a way they can understand. In addition, regardless of how well the guide knows the river and techniques for paddling it, if they are out on a treacherous stretch of the river and the guide tells the rafters to do something they have not been told to expect, the guide will need to be able to communicate the rationale for that different command, either verbally or nonverbally, in a way that makes sense to the rafters. Thus, leaders must be able to communicate their overall vision, the credibility of their power base, and their trustworthiness in the situation at hand.

Communication competence also frequently includes an ability to manage ambiguity and uncertainty. A leader must be able to "read" the group, as well as the environment in which it operates, and know when to reduce and when to heighten uncertainty. On the river, the raft guide needs to reduce uncertainty enough to allay the fears of the rafters and keep them calm, so that they are able to enjoy the trip and not panic or cause harm to themselves or fellow rafters. However, the rafters must also understand the dangers of the river, not become too relaxed and casual in the raft, and be prepared for the unexpected. A mix of certainty and uncertainty is required for a fun and safe trip.

The leader of a real estate development group preparing a bid on a prime piece of land balances certainty and uncertainty in the process of putting together a successful bid, as well. Although it is certain that the group needs to offer enough money to outbid the competitors, while keeping their bid low enough to assure that they can make a profit from their development, there is some uncertainty about the exact dollar amount that will accomplish both ends. The leader may want to reduce uncertainty and streamline group discussion by relying on parallels with prior development to the extent possible, but he or she may also want the group to struggle with the unknown aspects of this particular case, to make sure they are not overlooking something crucial and expensive. The leader thus needs to balance the efficiency and comfort associated with reducing uncertainty with the risks of conflict and time-consuming discussion associated with raising the levels of uncertainty. Managing the mix of certainty and uncertainty appropriately in a group is the task of a good leader and a test of his or her communication competence.

Choosing a Leader

Because small groups are convened for a variety of purposes, within diverse contexts, and with a variety of people, talents, time, energy, and tasks, many factors influence the quality and type of leadership needed for an effective group process. Some small groups are formed for a limited purpose, for a limited period of time, with limited resources, and expecting limited commitment from members. Such a group may simply need a leader who can keep the process on track. It may want to leave most of the decision making to one person, with only a nod of approval from the other members. Other groups have broader tasks and more complex goals. Those may benefit from a more collaborative decision-making and leadership style. Leaders may be *appointed* or *elected,* or they may *emerge* during the group process. Leadership may also be *shared* among group members.

Appointed Leaders

For many groups formed within an organizational context, the leader is appointed by a manager in the larger organization. An individual may be appointed to set up the group, call the first meeting, set the agenda, establish group norms and expectations, establish relationships with outside sources of power, and act as an arbiter of the group process. This may be someone with position or referent power in an organization or someone with particular expertise in the area under investigation. An appointed leader with a respected base of power can be beneficial in setting a positive tone to the group process. In addition, a well-connected leader with interpersonal linkages or positional power may make it easier for the group to obtain information and resources needed for the task (Harris, 2002). A leader who commands respect based on the group's perceptions of her or his power may be able to empower group members and manage conflict more effectively than someone not as well perceived.

One drawback to an appointed leader is the tendency such leaders may have to exert their power and overcontrol the group process, thus diminishing the potential contributions of other members. When members feel barred from participating fully, they may use their own avoidance power, with the adverse impact associated with a loss of their input. Even when a leader is benevolent and caring in his or her assertion of power and control, the group may feel disempowered and lose motivation and a sense of shared responsibility for the outcome. Control of group process is a difficult balance to hold. Any leader may be tempted to exert more control than is warranted, but those who are appointed may be more inclined to move in that direction than those who are more democratically chosen.

Elected Leaders

Elected leaders are those the group chooses through its own formal processes. The group may choose them based on their expertise with the task at hand, on their known ability to lead a group process, or because of their perceived power in some other area. Elected leaders share some characteristics with appointed leaders, in that their position within the group is formalized, and their relationship to other members is as the "first among equals." Even when leaders are chosen simply for the convenience of having someone call the meetings and set the agenda with no other formal power in the group, the position itself frequently enhances the perceived power of the person who is chosen. An elected leader is inherently more accountable to the group members than is an appointed one and may be less likely to abuse that power, but most of us can probably cite instances in which democratically elected leaders have taken inappropriate liberties with the exercise of power.

Emergent Leaders

An emergent leader is one who "starts out as any other member of a group of peers, but . . . gradually emerges as leader in the perceptions of the other members by providing leadership services" that the group values (Brilhart & Galanes, 1995, p. 161). There are two types of emergent leaders: those who emerge from a leaderless group of peers and those who emerge alongside an existing leader to meet particular needs.

In studying leaders who emerge from leaderless groups, researchers at the University of Minnesota found that certain actions make some members of a leaderless group more likely than others to become the group leaders (Bormann, 1975; Geier, 1967). Group members who are reticent or lack information or those who are bossy and dogmatic are eliminated as candidates for leadership early in the process. Those members who speak frequently, are well informed, and support democratic group process remain in consideration. It is from this group that the leader will likely emerge. "The Minnesota Studies show that leaders emerge through a method of residues in which group members are rejected until only one remains" (Beebe & Masterson, 1990, p. 253).

On the other hand, in a group with an appointed or elected leader, a member with expertise in the particular area under consideration may emerge as her or his skills are increasingly called upon during the group process. If a small group has been convened to develop a marketing strategy for electronic parts, an executive from the marketing group might be appointed the initial group leader. As the discussion develops, another individual may emerge as especially knowledgeable about the market niche for these particular component parts. If that person gains the respect and trust of the group, the members may turn increasingly to her or him to take over the group process (Cummings & Worley, 2001). This latter type of emergent leadership is similar to the type associated with shared, or facilitative, leadership.

Shared (Facilitative) Leadership

As its name implies, shared, or facilitative, leadership is based on a collaborative group effort, with members sharing power as the task dictates. As the group members become increasingly empowered, leaders become facilitators, rather than directors or managers. Increasing numbers of organizations have turned to self-managing work teams and problem-solving groups (Harris, 1992–1993). In these cases, a team is put together with the empowerment of group members as a primary goal (Cummings & Worley, 2001). As the group progresses toward greater empowerment, the leader's role shifts from direct to indirect involvement. Rather than being in charge, the leader becomes a facilitator who empowers other members to carry out the responsibilities and functions. The facilitative leader regards power as something to be shared with group members. This empowerment of group members often leads to better long-term results. Rather than the leader's eliciting responses from group members, or trying to instill motivation in each person, individuals contribute freely, because each person has some ownership in the group process.

As Table 13.1 indicates, there are advantages and disadvantages to this type of group leadership. To the extent that group members are committed to the process and share in the responsibility, as well as in the power, the process is well-served. Two principal disadvantages to this type of leadership are that conflicts may be more difficult and time-consuming to resolve, if no one member is

TABLE 13.1   Advantages and Disadvantages of Shared Facilitative Leadership

Advantages	Disadvantages
1. Provides a broader range of information on the problem, alternatives, and recommended solution.	1. Less personal accountability for group's decision. A bad group decision is still a bad decision.
2. Lends a more creative approach to problem solving. Uses expertise, information, and member knowledge.	2. Takes group's energy and focus away from task. If getting the job done is the only issue, not worth the time.
3. Group members gain an increasing awareness of leader's problems and hurdles.	3. Increases opportunity for disagreement over issues.
4. Increases commitment to issues and solution.	4. Takes more time.
5. Enhances morale.	5. Allows strong voices to dominate.

empowered to mediate them and that chaos might ensue if there is no one person overseeing the accomplishment of specific tasks and coordinating overall results. However, with a cohesive group and a well-defined task and set of goals, this type of leadership may work well.

Tasks of Group Leaders

In a small group, someone needs to facilitate the calling and planning of the meetings. In addition to calling meetings and setting the initial agenda, there are at least three tasks that usually fall to group leaders: facilitating the meetings, empowering members to ensure full participation, and managing conflicts.

Facilitating Meetings

While a highly motivated team or group might be able to proceed effectively toward their goals during meetings, one person usually needs to accept the primary responsibility for making certain the ball gets rolling, that issues are engaged and resolved in satisfactory ways, and that the larger goals are kept in view. During lively discussion, it may fall to a leader to keep the group on task. While the leader may want to see the group explore as many relevant side issues as possible in specific areas, it is important to balance the time and energy the group spends on individual discussion points against the available time and resources the group has at its disposal. Some issues will warrant a larger share of the group's resources than others, and it becomes the leader's task to make sure that time and energy are appropriately allocated. To increase your effectiveness in facilitating meetings, you will want to review the "Guide to Meeting Effectiveness" (Figure 1.4) presented in Chapter 1.

Empowering Group Members

In complex problem-solving tasks, leaders play crucial roles in empowering group members and encouraging full participation and consideration of all points of view. In other words, they play key roles in developing the synergy needed for creative problem solving. In any group, there are usually those who feel entitled to expressing their opinions and contributing their perspectives and those who hang back and feel their viewpoints may not be as valuable as those of others. For a group to gain the benefit of each member's unique contribution, it may be incumbent on the leader to encourage those who feel disempowered and estranged from the process to become involved. Engaging them, while avoiding making them or others uncomfortable, is the hallmark of a skillful leader.

Managing Conflict

Intrinsic to open discussion is the management of conflict. Conflict is an inevitable part of full participation by diverse participants. Knowing when to relieve and when to stimulate conflict is a key to creative problem solving. On the one hand, when group members become so vested in ownership of their viewpoints that they dig in their heels and refuse to listen to others, a leader may need to back the group away from the point of conflict and search for common ground. On the other hand, if group members are reluctant to speak their minds for fear of causing disharmony or being thought foolish or uninformed, a leader may need to probe the divergent views to begin a full and open discussion of all aspects of an issue. Only through exploring as many perspectives as possible can the group forge an optimum solution. Thus, it is the leader who must orchestrate the group process, knowing when to soothe and when to challenge group members.

Influences on Group Leadership

External Context

The system within which a group is formed is one of the factors that determines the style of leadership appropriate to that group. A group may be formed within the context of a *democratic,* an *autocratic,* or a *laissez-faire* system. A cooperative art gallery or natural foods store is frequently formed as a democratic organization. A small group formed within such a context would be influenced by that type of interaction and is likely to expect collaborative decision making and leadership. On the other hand, many traditional manufacturing organizations are autocratic. They are based on hierarchic, top-down management, and a small group formed within that context may be influenced in its own interactions by that larger system, with an assumption of formal leadership roles and the final authority to make decisions resting with the group leader. In another context, a farmers' market might take place within a laissez-faire system, where a municipality sets aside a given area on certain days of the week for farmers to come and sell their produce. The farmers may not have any formal relationship to the system or to each other, aside from coming when they have something to sell. A small group formed to decide where certain booths should be set up might have very little structure for organizing their decision-making and leadership process, yet they may be efficient in their decision making.

Nature of Task

Although groups are influenced by the context in which they are formed, they are also influenced by the nature of the task for which they are convened. If the task is a straightforward one with an obvious best choice or with a choice that requires more administrative work than decision making, it might fall to a designated leader to come up with an answer with very little group input. For example, a small group from the food co-op convened to find the best prices and sources for oats and wheat might ask one person to do the research and come back to the group with a proposal for them to accept or reject. On the other hand, a group of automobile workers convened to decide how best to form work teams to accomplish a new task may need creative thinking from each member and may choose to develop a collaborative solution. In these cases, the task may override the orientation of the larger system in the group's decision-making format. An example of this can be seen in many American industries' attempts to increase quality in the production process (Caroselli, 1992). Traditionally, industry management has dictated how quality is to be obtained and has told employees what they must do to achieve the goal (Jablonski, 1992). Missing from this formula has been the involvement of the employees who do the actual work. For many employees, these quality mandates have been no different than any other management exhortations, such as cost cutting, reorganizing, safety rules, and summer schedules. However, once organizations began involving employees in deciding how best to resolve quality issues, listening to the employees and taking into account their experience, knowledge, and perceptions through group meetings, they experienced an immediate increase in quality. When employees' input was sought and incorporated into the development of a quality improvement strategy, they felt a sense of ownership and a resulting commitment to implement their solutions (Kearns, 1990).

Interdependence of Group Members

Another factor in the type of leadership that groups need or want is the degree of interdependence between members. The more invested individual members are in the outcome of the group process, the more democratic they are likely to want the process to be. The less invested the members are, the more willing they are to let the leader make the decisions or to make no decisions at all. If the farmers at the market decide the location is not working for them, they might form a group to find a new location. Because they are each invested in the outcome, they may impose a structure on the group to assure that all options are considered and that the needs of each farmer are taken into account.

"Leadership becomes more relevant and important to people in times of perceived crisis and turmoil" (Barge, 1994, p. 181) than at times when things are going relatively smoothly. In addition, within any group, certain tasks may require quick and decisive attention, while others warrant longer time for thoughtful consideration. An effective group leader helps the group make those distinctions and saves valuable time and energy for the important group issues. In general, the leader's task is to coordinate and communicate. This involves listening and responding, allowing for creative discussion and conflict, keeping the group on track, and maintaining civility throughout the process.

Leadership Styles

As in any human endeavor, maintaining balance within a dynamic, morphogenic environment is a challenge not always successfully met. Although small groups are often best served by various participatory styles of leadership, research indicates that American leaders often tend to be a cross between John Wayne and the Lone Ranger (Bradford & Cohen, 1984; Harris, 2002). Americans frequently tend to take as a leadership model that of the heroic, autocratic leadership in a hierarchic system. We often look to the leader to solve problems or to oversee group efforts and to solve them. The leader becomes the center of attention and is expected to run the show. Two specific types of heroic, autocratic leadership behaviors often prevail—the leader-as-technician and leader-as-conductor. An alternative is the leader-as-coach approach.

Leader-as-Technician

In a group set up to solve a problem with technical issues underlying it or with requirements for specialized knowledge or experience, we are apt to look to someone with expertise in that area to lead the process. It becomes the tendency of the group to defer to that person whenever a difficult decision of judgment comes to the fore. If, for example, a group is convened to examine alternatives to traditional and expensive health care options for an organization's employees, the group may look to a health care provider to lead the discussion. When the topics under consideration move toward a discussion of the merits of various options for treatment of specific types of physical or psychological impairment, group members may turn to this leader for insight and direction. Soon it becomes apparent that it is easier and more efficient to simply ask the leader to determine the best course of treatment for various anticipated ills. As we have discussed in earlier sections, this may be efficient for technical concerns or for issues having little consequence, but when the issues involved are broad ranging and of relatively high importance to a number of people, the larger, less specifically technical aspects of these issues need to be considered.

It must be remembered that those with technical expertise, regardless of how deep or broad, are likely to be biased toward a particular point of view. It is easy to forget that most group members probably have some health experience of their own and may be able to offer insights from the perspective of a consumer that the health care provider is apt to overlook. However, when group members feel they don't have particular knowledge of the immediate issues under discussion, they may feel disempowered and become increasingly disengaged from the process. It is easy to see how the "expert" as leader of this discussion could take the acknowledgment of her or his expertise as a cue to control the discussion and the eventual outcome of the decision-making process. As in any group process, the responsibility for leadership and the results of decision making are shared by group members, whether or not they acknowledge their part in it. Each member has the power and responsibility to participate in the leadership of the group.

Leader-as-Conductor

As part of the U.S. western orientation toward hierarchic leadership models, we often assume that the leader should orchestrate the entire group process. While it is important and necessary to coordinate group efforts, the balance between micro-management on the one side and laissez-faire nonmanagement on the other is difficult to attain and maintain. Too often, in the U.S. model, leaders tend to err on the side of micromanagement of the group process. An obvious example is the designated leader who spends all his or her time looking over the shoulders of the group members, checking on every detail. More subtly, high-control managers may so closely define the group process that members are not free to pursue leads they find interesting or promising in unanticipated ways. In either case, jobs or other aspects of the group process that might have engaged individual creativity and commitment become routine and predictable, and group members may lose their motivation.

Our responses as group members and group leaders are embedded in our cultural paradigms and are, therefore, frequently difficult to see. Consequently, groups are often poorly formed and lack the training to take responsibility for the group process. Although it takes time, when groups are carefully formed and initiated with a view toward the goals expected to be achieved, and when group members are empowered by effective leaders, the result produces a positive effect on the decision-making processes.

Leader-as-Coach

Effective coaches use problems as opportunities to build skills, morale, and experience (Harris, 2002). Coaches explain, demonstrate, and lead, rather than order or cajole. They focus on the positive aspects of accomplishments while providing open and honest critical feedback. A coach relates one-on-one, person-to-person, to negotiate values, develop opportunities, facilitate change, stimulate innovation, and encourage trust. Peters and Austin (1985) identify at least five coaching roles. The first is to orient and educate when goals, roles, or conditions change and new skills are needed. The second is to sponsor and encourage when an individual has an outstanding skill and can make a special contribution. The third is to offer special encouragement and to make simple brief corrections. The fourth is to counsel when problems interfere with work or damage performance, or to respond to setbacks. The fifth is to confront recurring problems and issues that are not resolved and that can have a long-term negative impact on the individual, the group, and the task. Coaches take a positive approach, focus on possible solutions rather than problems, treat others as equals, are supportive rather than judgmental, and help set realistic goals.

Summary

Effective leadership of small groups is as varied as the groups themselves and the contexts in which they are formed. Transformational or collaborative leadership styles have an appeal, but there are times and places where other types of leaders may be more effective or efficient. When at sea, a ship is necessarily run as a hierarchic system. During a storm or in the midst of a tight docking maneuver, for example, there is no time to sit and collaborate on a course of action. On the other hand, a democratically run food co-op would not so readily tolerate a leader who took on the authority of the captain of a ship.

The leaders of small groups have as their principal task that of assuring that the group process moves toward a solution to the problem for which the group was convened. The more complex the problem and the more diverse the group, the more difficult and complex the role of the leader. If the task is a routine one or one on which little depends, the leader's role may be minimal. If the task is large, complex, and has possible far-reaching consequences, the role of the leader may be critical to assuring the best outcome.

Although our underlying bias throughout this book is toward collaborative group work, there are contexts and tasks for which other decision-making strategies are more appropriate. Group leaders must be alert to these distinctions and guide the group toward the most efficient use of their time and energy. Some groups look to leadership for direction; others expect to be self-directed; and still others are ambivalent and unsure of their role in the process. Whether leaders are appointed, elected, or emerge, they become responsible for managing and defining, or helping the group define, the process, the goals, the tasks, and the patterns of interaction.

DISCUSSION QUESTIONS

1. What is the relationship between being a leader and the system in which a leader participates?

2. Provide an example from your own experience of a good leader. Does your example fit with the definition of a good leader? How does it fit and how does it differ?

3. How do leaders act as arbiters of the interfaces between the group and the system?

4. Explain the dimensions of universality and situational dependence.

5. Outline the seven options for leadership provided by the Managerial Grid. What elements determine each of these options?

6. Distinguish between transactional and transformational leaders. Provide an example of each type of leader.

7. How can leaders be similar to chameleons? Explain.

8. Define vision and credibility as important characteristics for leaders.

9. Explain communication competence.

10. Leaders can be chosen, can be appointed, can be elected, can emerge, and may share responsibility. Provide an example of each type of leader from your own experience.

11. What are the three primary influences on group structure?

12. Why do leaders become technicians or conductors?

EXERCISES

1. Shared leadership roles; 2. Leadership in an observed meeting; 3. Effective leaders: An analysis; 4. Leadership quotes as guides; 5. Your personal leadership qualities; 6. Androcentrism and leadership

1. SHARED LEADERSHIP ROLES

Shared leadership can come from members of a group taking on specific roles and contributing to the overall group process in ways that allow a group consensus and solution to emerge. The following exercise is a modification of one developed by Rainbow Hawk and Wind Eagle of the Ehama Institute ("Managing, American," 1996). Choose a local problem for discussion with which most everyone has some experience, understanding, or an opinion (for example, campus parking, final exam scheduling, restaurant and dining facilities, and on- or off-campus living conditions are often good topics). Assign each member of a small group a role or perspective from which to contribute comments. These role perspectives can be: (a) the present condition, (b) a history of the problem, (c) a statement of the need for change, (d) the danger that might proceed from a given course of action, (e) the creative possibilities of a given course of action, (f) strategies that might be employed, and (g) possible future solutions. Each person engaging in the discussion should make a "name tag" to sit in front of him or her that identifies the assigned perspective (for example, "present condition," "history of problem," "need for change") and should contribute comments to the discussion only from that one perspective. How does leadership in the discussion evolve? How is that leadership shared and influenced by the roles people take on? Does a solution and a group consensus emerge?

2. LEADERSHIP IN AN OBSERVED MEETING

Observe a group meeting. Who convenes the meeting? How are the leadership functions shared among the members? Who initiates a new topic, asks for more information, or offers support for an idea? Does one person perform all of the leadership roles, or do other members participate in these? What type of managerial orientation is engaged in—task versus people—and how successful is it?

3. EFFECTIVE LEADERS: AN ANALYSIS

We all have examples of effective leaders. Well-known leaders such as Mother Teresa or Secretary of State Colin Powell are often referenced when someone asked who we think is an effective leader. For this exercise, name at least two individuals you feel are effective leaders in the following categories of education, government, religion, and business. These do not have to be leaders everyone will recognize—they merely need to be leaders you believe are effective. Write down the traits and actions that you feel make your leaders effective.

	Traits	**Actions**
Education Leaders		
_____	_____	_____
_____	_____	_____
Government Leaders		
_____	_____	_____
_____	_____	_____
Religious Leaders		
_____	_____	_____
_____	_____	_____
Business Leaders		
_____	_____	_____
_____	_____	_____

Compare your list and the traits and actions with other members of your group or class. Which leaders are listed by more than one individual? Were the traits and actions justifying the listing the same or different? What do we learn about leadership by listening to other individuals explain their choices? Are there specific traits that are most important to being effective? Are there specific actions that seem to characterize effective leaders? How can you use this information to develop your group leadership skills?

4. LEADERSHIP QUOTES AS GUIDES

As a group, determine the underlying direction suggested in each of the following quotes.

1. Of the best leaders, when their task is accomplished, their work done, the people will remark, "We have done it ourselves."–Lao-Tzu
2. Leadership is liberating people to do what is required of them in the most effective and most human way possible.–Max DePree
3. A good leader takes a little more of his or her share of the blame, a little less of his or her share of the credit.–Arnold Glasow
4. The horse never knows I'm there until he needs me.–Willie Shoemaker
5. Whoever wishes to be great among you must be your servant, and whoever wishes to be first among you must be slave to all.–Jesus Christ.

What common themes emerge from these observations? How should we function as team leaders—technician, conductor, or coach?

5. YOUR PERSONAL LEADERSHIP QUALITIES

"Leaders aren't born—at least not full blown. Neither are they made like instant coffee. Instead, they are slow brewed" (Boyett & Boyett, 1998, p. 43). To enhance your personal development as a leader, it is useful to return to the basic skills you bring to a leadership situation. You can proceed from taking this personal inventory to developing a personal action plan for further development.

1. What early childhood experiences did you have that encouraged you to stand in front of class, be the team leader, or perform?
2. What education experiences have you had that added to your leadership abilities?
3. What volunteer or extracurricular activities have you been involved in that developed your leadership abilities?
4. What additional leadership training have you had?
5. When have you failed as a leader?
6. When have you succeeded as a leader?
7. Have you varied your leadership approaches depending on the situation?
8. Based on this inventory, what issues in Chapter 13 deserve a reexamination?

6. ANDROCENTRISM AND LEADERSHIP

Directions
1. List five individuals you consider to be good leaders. For each of your choices, list the characteristics you believe make them good leaders. 2. In your small group compare your lists of characteristics and develop a master list of leadership characteristics. 3. In your group, determine which of these characteristics seem to be primarily male or female. 4. How many females did the group members identify as good leaders? 5. Consider the following issues:

One predominate model for leadership is based on *androcentrism*. Androcentrism means that the male experience is the norm by which all other behavior is measured. This has led to the ". . . privileging of male experience and the 'otherizing' of female experience; that is males and male experience are treated as a neutral standard norm for the culture . . . , and females and female experience are treated as a sex-specific deviation from that allegedly universal standard" (Bem, 1993, p. 41).

Follow-up Questions
1. Did your group tend toward utilizing androcentrism? 2. What are the implications when we exclude or diminish the input of certain group members or

overendorse the input from other members? 3. What steps can be taken to change the impact of androcentrism? 4. If your group did not practice androcentrism, determine what backgrounds or experiences influenced the group and be prepared to report these to the rest of the class.

REFERENCES

Barge, J. K. (1994). *Leadership.* New York: St. Martin's Press.

Beebe, S. A., & Masterson, J. T. (1990). *Communicating in small groups: Principles and practices* (2nd ed.). Glenview, IL: Scott, Foresman.

Bem, S. L. (1993). *The lenses of gender.* New Haven: Yale University Press.

Bennis, W., & Nanus, G. (1997). Toward the new millennium. In G. R. Hichman (Ed.). *Leading organizations: Perspectives for a new era* (pp. 5–7). Thousand Oaks, CA: Sage.

Blake, R. R., & McCanse, A. A. (1991). *Leadership dilemmas—Grid solutions.* Houston: Gulf.

Blake, R. R., & Mouton, R. R. (1985). *The managerial grid III: The key to leadership excellence.* Houston: Gulf.

Blake, R. R., Mouton, J. S., & Allen, R. L. (1987). *Spectacular teamwork.* New York: John Wiley & Sons.

Bormann, E. G. (1975). *Discussion and group methods: Theory and practice* (2nd ed.). New York: Harper & Row.

Boyett, J., & Boyett, J. (1998). *The guru guide.* New York: John Wiley.

Bradford, D. L., & Cohen, C. J. (1984). *Managing for excellence: The guide for developing high performance in contemporary organizations.* New York: John Wiley & Sons.

Brilhart, J. K., & Galanes, G. J. (1995). *Effective group discussion* (8th ed.). Madison, WI: WCB Brown & Benchmark.

Buckingham, M., & Coffman, C. (1999). *First break all the rules: What the world's greatest managers do differently.* New York: Simon & Schuster.

Caroselli, M. (1992). *Quality-driven designs.* San Diego: Pfeiffer.

Clark, K. E., & Clark, M. B. (1990). *Measures of leadership.* West Orange, NJ: Leadership Library of America.

Counselman, E. F. (1991). Leadership in a long-term leaderless women's group. *Small Group Research, 22*(2), 240–257.

Cummings, T. G., & Worley, C. G. (2001). *Organizational development and change* (7th ed.). United States: South-Western.

Cybert, R. M. (1990). Defining leadership and explicating the process. *Nonprofit Management and Leadership, 1*(1), 29–38.

Drucker, P. F. (1998). *Peter Drucker on the profession of management.* Boston: Harvard Business School Press.

Eiseley, L. (1969). *The unexpected universe.* New York: Harcourt, Brace, Jovanovich.

Ellis, R. J., & Cronshaw, S. F. (1992). Self-monitoring and leader emergence. *Small Group Research, 23*(1), 113–129.

French, J. R. P., & Raven, B. (1968). The bases of social power. In D. Cartwright & A. Zander (eds.) *Group Dynamics.* New York: Harper & Row.

Gastil, J. (1994). A meta-analytic review of the productivity and satisfaction of democratic and autocratic leadership. *Small Group Research, 25*(3), 384–410.

Geier, J. C. (1967). A trait approach to the study of leadership in small groups. *Journal of Communication, 17,* 316–323.

Gibb, J. (1961). Defensive communication. *Journal of Communication, 11,* 141–148.

Hackman, M. Z., & Johnson, C. E. (2000). *Leadership: A communication perspective.* (3rd ed.). Prospect Heights, IL: Waveland.

Harris, T. E. (1992–1993). Toward effective employee involvement: An analysis of parallel and self-managing teams. *The Journal of Applied Business Research, 9*(1), 25–33.

Harris, T. E. (2002). *Applied organizational communication: Principles and pragmatics for future success.* Mahwah, NJ: Lawrence Erlbaum.

Hughes, R. L., Ginnett, R. C., & Curphy, G. J. (1998). Contingency theories of leadership. In G. R. Hichman (Ed.), *Leading organizations: Perspectives for a new era* (pp. 141–157). Thousand Oaks, CA: Sage.

Jablonski, J. R. (1992). *Implementing TQP* (2nd ed.). San Diego: Pfeiffer.

Kearns, D. T. (1990). Leadership through quality. *The Academy of Management Executive, 4*(2), 86–89.

Kolb, J. A. (1996). A comparison of leadership behaviors and competencies in high- and average-performance teams. *Communication Reports, 9*(2), 173–183.

Kotter, J. P. (1988). *The leadership factor.* New York: Free Press.

Managing, American Indian–style, (1996, October 14). *Fortune,* p. 130.

Miller, W. (1997, August 18). Leadership's common denominator. *Industry Week,* pp. 96–100.

Northhouse, P. G. (2001). *Leadership theory and practice* (2nd ed.). Thousand Oaks, CA: Sage.

Peters, T., & Austin, T. (1985). *A passion for excellence: The leadership difference.* New York: Random House.

Yalom, I. (1985). *The theory and practice of group psychotherapy.* New York: Basic Books.

14

Observing and Evaluating a Small Group

CHAPTER OUTLINE

CHAPTER OBJECTIVES

- Explain the four ways of learning how to make small groups successful.
- Discuss the design, types, and uses of rating scales.
- Outline the postmeeting reaction form approach.
- Explain the key question regarding information usefulness.
- Describe the observer feedback guidelines.
- Elucidate the evaluation of verbal interactions and content analysis.

KEY TERMS

Barnlund-Haiman Leadership
    rating scale
Brilhart's Postmeeting
    Reaction Questionnaire
Change
Content analysis

Informal roles
Likert scales
Maintenance-oriented roles
Observer feedback
Observer/member scales
Postmeeting reaction forms

Rating scales
Self-centered roles
Systematic feedback
Task-oriented roles
Verbal interaction

"Success" and "Failure" are also partly social constructions. Late in the history of the involvement of the United States in the Vietnam War, one U.S. Senator proposed that the army "declare a victory and come home." The response to the proposal demonstrated that there are limits to arbitrary unilateral evaluations of outcomes, but "success" and "failure" are not uniquely defined by the outcomes. (*A Primer on Decision Making*, March, 1994, p. 88)

For small groups to know that they are effective, they must have some means of evaluating their success or failure. During the group process, members must decide what specific activities should be continued, stopped, or altered. Just completing a project on time does not make a group successful. The process of the group must be evaluated, as well as the short- and long-term consequences of implementing its solutions.

This chapter examines the value of systematic feedback, offers several techniques for evaluating small groups, and engages in some future forecasting by looking at the next 10 years.

Systematic Feedback

There are four ways of learning about how to make small groups successful. The first is to read a great deal about groups and teams. While reading and research can provide theories and insights, they offer no practical experience. We can discover why groups and teams are important and what made a particular team successful, but we may lack a clear understanding of what we should do in a new situation.

The second method is participation in small groups. By using intuition and a gut feeling about effectiveness, we can evaluate and adjust during and after the group process. Although we learn by doing, our abilities to observe our actions while we are simultaneously engaging in them are limited. We may also be engaged in counterproductive small group behaviors and never realize it, because the group continues to be successful, in spite of them. When new demands are placed on our small group abilities, our old behaviors, such as leadership and empowerment behaviors, may no longer suffice. Since we need theories and principles to guide our behaviors, combining steps one and two can be helpful, but even then, we may not know how well we are doing.

A third approach is to obtain external evaluation and advice. This is a useful addition to the first two approaches, if the observer is equipped with tools and knowledge to effectively provide feedback. An observer must provide more than an overall evaluation that it "went pretty well."

A final source of feedback is our own reflection and analysis. In some cases, the straightest route to finding out how well a group did is to ask the members. The group is in the best position to know if goals and objectives have been completed. As a group member, we can give and receive feedback to and from other group participants. A combination of all these techniques can provide the most comprehensive view for the evaluation.

Success and Failure

While being less than perfect is failure to some individuals, and not "getting by" is failure to others, in either case, improvement can occur only if we are aware of the causes and cures. One sage observer stated that the person who makes no mistakes usually makes nothing. Another concluded: Failure is a success if we learn from it. Recognizing failure is one of the surest routes to success, if we examine why we failed.

Since successful small group behaviors are not the norm, we probably will not be resounding successes all of the time. Sound, well-targeted feedback can both help the process and provide some guidelines that focus on improvement efforts.

To become an effective group member and leader, we need to maximize the amount of input we receive. Individual and group feedback can provide valuable information and opportunities for growth.

Observer–Members Scales

Group members can act as participant observers, or outside observers can be used. In general, members should not evaluate a meeting, each other, or themselves while participating. If you are directly involved in the work, you will probably not be a dispassionate observer, and you may not be able to concentrate on the team's work. Two very different skills are involved here—participation and evaluation. Not only is it difficult to concentrate on the group process while we are evaluating (it is difficult to do two things very well at once), but while evaluating, we may give off nonverbal signals that lead other members to think we are not interested or are critical of them, the group, or the process.

When appropriate, consultant observers not directly involved with the group work can provide excellent insights. Recognizing this as an important source of growth and development, corporations systematically offer evaluations of a specific team's process by outside observers in order to help the team develop.

When outside observers are not available, many team development programs suggest appointing a group member to be an observer. This task is handed around among the group members. We learn about a process when we are asked to evaluate it, so the group or team can benefit, and each member becomes more insightful.

Long-standing groups can also set aside specific times to periodically analyze their group process. Increasingly, professional teams earmark the last 10 minutes of any team meeting for reflecting time, giving the group a chance to review their process. This ongoing team development facilitates continued growth.

The quality of any of these approaches to evaluation will be enhanced with specific tools, and the list of items that can be analyzed is limited only by the time available.

Rating Scales

When we ask "how well did we do?" we are setting the stage for the effective use of rating scales. With our small group, we can ask questions ranging from "How well did the group analyze the topic?" to "How fully did all members participate?" Responses may be "very well," "adequately," or "poorly." Depending on the degree of specificity desired, you can make the scale more precise, such as using a Likert scale with a one-to-five or a one-to-seven rating, equating the numbers with terms such as very adequate, moderately adequate, unsure, moderately inadequate, and inadequate. Likert scales are popular and easy to use.

Likert Scale Example

"The group worked well together" (check one):

Strongly agree	_____
Moderately agree	_____
Agree somewhat	_____
Unsure	_____
Disagree somewhat	_____
Moderately disagree	_____
Strongly disagree	_____

The list of questions should be adapted to the particular activity you wish to evaluate and may include leadership, group climate, nonverbal communication, or organization of the problem and solution analysis. A simple, quick, and all-purpose rating scale could include issues such as clarity of problem analysis, equality of participation, listening to each other, and willingness to engage in dialogue and closure.

A scale allows observers and members to provide feedback that can be translated into some definable measure. The results, if gathered from a variety of sources, can also be tabulated to obtain a total score.

The topics included in the rating scale should be relevant to the expected behaviors for a group or team. Each group will have specific concerns that can be included in the rating scale. Possible topic areas are provided in Table 14.1. In fact, any of the issues covered in the preceding chapters can be highly appropriate for a rating scale. To be most effective, the rating scale should cover a variety of topics. It could also include a Likert Scale approach with the seven categories of strongly agree, moderately agree, agree somewhat, unsure, disagree somewhat, moderately disagree, and strongly disagree.

The Barnlund-Haiman Leadership rating scale is a good example of how we can hone in on a particular set of behaviors. As Figure 14.1 on pages 300–302 shows, influence in procedure, creative and critical thinking, and interpersonal relations are considered on a scale of –3 to +3 with –3 meaning the group needed more of some behavior and +3 meaning the group needed less of some behavior.

TABLE 14.1   Rating Scale Topics—Possible Areas of Concern

Amount of participation by the members

Role acceptance by members—Do members do what needs to be done?

Leadership qualities and their abilities to handle disagreements and conflicts

Appropriateness of leadership

Quality of research

Shared research activities and their success

Communication skills including listening, feedback and clarity

Internal process issues such as clarifying and summarizing

Creative processes and actions

Willingness and ability to confront issues

Civilized disagreement that took advantages of diversity of ideas

Appropriate decision-making approaches such as consensus

Quality of climate

Balancing of participation to allow all members to take part

Shared leadership and/or responsibility

Other issues

FIGURE 14.1   Barnlund-Haiman Leadership Scale

Instructions: This rating scale may be used to evaluate leadership in groups with or without official leaders. In the latter case (the leaderless group), use part A of each item only. When evaluating the actions of an official leader, use parts A and B of each item on the scale.

Influence in Procedure

Initiating Discussion

A. 3   2   1   0   1   2   3

Group needed more help in getting started	Group got right amount of help	Group needed less help in getting started

B.   The quality of the introductory remarks was:

Excellent	Good	Adequate	Fair	Poor

Organizing Group Thinking

A. 3   2   1   0   1   2   3

Group needed more direction in thinking	Group got right amount of help	Group needed less direction in thinking

B.   If and when attempts were made to organize group thinking, they were:

Excellent	Good	Adequate	Fair	Poor

Clarifying Communication

A. 3   2   1   0   1   2   3

Group needed more help in clarifying communication	Group got right amount of help	Group needed less help in clarifying communication

B.   If and when attempts were made to clarify communication, they were:

Excellent	Good	Adequate	Fair	Poor

Summarizing and Verbalizing Agreements

A. 3   2   1   0   1   2   3

Group needed more help in summarizing and verbalizing agreements	Group got right amount of help	Group needed less help in summarizing and verbalizing agreements

B.   If and when attempts were made to summarize and verbalize, they were:

Excellent	Good	Adequate	Fair	Poor

FIGURE 14.1 Continued

Resolving Conflict

A. | 3 | 2 | 1 | 0 | 1 | 2 | 3 |

Group needed more
help in resolving
conflict

Group got right
amount of help

Group needed less
help in resolving
conflict

B. If and when attempts were made to resolve conflict, they were:

Excellent   Good   Adequate   Fair   Poor

Influence in Creative and Critical Thinking

Stimulating Critical Thinking

A. | 3 | 2 | 1 | 0 | 1 | 2 | 3 |

Group needed more
stimulation in creative
thinking

Group got right
amount of help

Group needed less
stimulation in
creative thinking

B. If and when attempts were made to stimulate ideas, they were:

Excellent   Good   Adequate   Fair   Poor

Encouraging Criticism

A. | 3 | 2 | 1 | 0 | 1 | 2 | 3 |

Group needed more
encouragement to be
critical

Group got right
amount of help

Group needed less
encouragement to
be critical

B. If and when attempts were made to encourage criticism, they were:

Excellent   Good   Adequate   Fair   Poor

Balancing Abstract and Concrete Thought

A. | 3 | 2 | 1 | 0 | 1 | 2 | 3 |

Group needed to be
more concrete

Group achieved
proper balance

Group needed to
be more abstract

B. If and when attempts were made to balance abstract and concrete, they were:

Excellent   Good   Adequate   Fair   Poor

(continued)

FIGURE 14.1   Continued

Influence in Interpersonal Relations

Climate-Making

A.	3	2	1	0	1	2	3

Group needed more help in securing a permissive atmosphere

Group got right amount of help

Group needed less help in securing a permissive atmosphere

B. If and when attempts were made to establish a permissive atmosphere, they were:

Excellent	Good	Adequate	Fair	Poor

Regulating Participation

A.	3	2	1	0	1	2	3

Group needed more regulation of participation

Group got right amount of help

Group needed less regulation of participation

B. If and when attempts were made to regulate participation, they were:

Excellent	Good	Adequate	Fair	Poor

Overall Leadership

A.	3	2	1	0	1	2	3

Group needed more control

Group got right amount of control

Group needed less control

B. If and when attempts were made to control the group, they were:

Excellent	Good	Adequate	Fair	Poor

Source: Barnlund-Haiman Leadership Rating Scale, from Dean C. Barnlund and Franklyn S. Haiman, *The Dynamics of Discussion* (Boston: Houghton Mifflin Co., 1960, 401–404).

With this scale, 0 is the best score. The leader's "influence in procedure" is evaluated by examining five dimensions (i.e., initiating discussion, organizing group thinking, clarifying communication, summarizing and verbalizing agreements, and resolving conflicts). This scaling device lets a leader and a group know if they are doing too little or too much of a particular activity. This rating scale can also be used with leader or leaderless groups.

Rating scales used by the group members, or outside observers, offer a systematic feedback mechanism. The value of ratings lies in the specificity of the information they provide. Rather than just saying something was good or bad, a scaling device provides a relative comparison. When we combine several forms together, we have a broad-based set of information.

Postmeeting Reaction Forms

Postmeeting reaction forms are questionnaires that seek specific feedback from participants about a particular activity or meeting. This feedback is intended for internal group consumption as an effort to improve the quality of the group process. Rather than finding out at the end of the process that no one thought the meetings were useful, the reaction forms offer immediate opportunities to improve. Specific issues such as leadership, listening, nonverbal interactions, member participation, and climate can be analyzed.

The most important characteristic is that the forms are completed anonymously by members. The results are tallied and reported to the group as soon as possible. As with the individual rating scales, the postmeeting response forms should be tailor-made to the group's needs. A group might spend a great deal of time on e-mail. In that case, the group forms could include questions regarding the format of the e-mail, such as, "Was there timely response by other members?" or "Were messages clear?" Two other examples of questions follow.

Group Response Question Example

Check one response for each question regarding e-mail.

1. Did you feel you were part of the process?
   _____ Really a part
   _____ Included most of the time
   _____ Included occasionally
   _____ Did not feel included
   _____ Felt left out entirely
   _____ Not really ascertained

2. Would you use e-mail again based on this experience?
   _____ Would gladly participate
   _____ Would be willing
   _____ Makes no difference
   _____ Not sure
   _____ No

There are few limits to the types of questions that can be asked. Your goal is to provide a scale that allows tabulation. If all but two group members "felt left out entirely" using e-mail, you have discovered valuable information. You can decide not to use e-mail again, or can further investigate the reasons for the feelings of exclusion.

A more general process would be to use a *postmeeting reaction form*. These questions can be very general in nature, or quite specific.

Postmeeting Reaction Form

1. How would you rate the group's final decision?
   Excellent _____ Good _____ OK _____ Adequate _____ Poor _____
2. What are the highlights of the decision?
3. What are the weaknesses?
4. What changes could be made in the process?

Do not sign your name.

Numerous issues can be examined, including the results, goals of the group, climate, leadership, participation, knowledge and preparation, clarity, cohesiveness, and satisfaction with the group itself. The group decision-making process can be evaluated by asking specific questions using a scale from 1 to 7, with 1 being not at all and 7 being a great deal.

1. How clearly did the group analyze the problem?
2. How well did the group analyze its goal or objective?
3. How clearly was the problem articulated?
4. Was creativity encouraged?
5. Did the group take time to let the analysis develop?
6. Did the group consider all possible solutions?
7. Were the positive consequences outlined?
8. Were the negative consequences outlined?
9. Was sufficient information used in the process?

A team effectiveness critique could include specific interaction issues.

The most important characteristic of any evaluation form is: *How useful is the information to your group or team?* The nine items on the team evaluation form, for example, might be relatively meaningless in a different context. Remember that some of the issues in an effective team that can be rated are goals and objectives, high standards of performance, broad-based participation by all members, conflict

FIGURE 14.2   Sample Feedback Form

Team _____   Date _____

This is a feedback instrument designed to help your team. Circle one of the numbers from 1 to 7 for each of the nine areas of concern.

Instructions: Indicate your assessment of your team.

1. Goals and Objectives

There is a lack of commonly understood goals and objectives.

Team members understand and agree on goals and objectives.

| 1 | 2 | 3 | 4 | 5 | 6 | 7 |

2. Utilization of Resources

All member resources are not recognized and/or utilized.

Member resources are fully recognized and utilized.

| 1 | 2 | 3 | 4 | 5 | 6 | 7 |

3. Trust and Conflict

There is little trust among members and conflict is evident.

There is a high degree of trust among members and conflict is dealt with openly and worked through.

| 1 | 2 | 3 | 4 | 5 | 6 | 7 |

4. Leadership

One person dominates and leadership roles are not carried out or shared.

There is full participation in leadership; leadership roles are shared by members.

| 1 | 2 | 3 | 4 | 5 | 6 | 7 |

5. Control and Procedures

There is little control, and there is a lack of procedures to guide team functioning.

There are effective procedures to guide team functioning; team members support these procedures.

| 1 | 2 | 3 | 4 | 5 | 6 | 7 |

6. Interpersonal Communication

Communication among members is open and participative.

Communication among members is guarded and closed.

| 1 | 2 | 3 | 4 | 5 | 6 | 7 |

(*continued*)

FIGURE 14.2   Continued

7. Problem Solving/Decision Making

The team has no agreed-on approaches to problem solving and decision making.

The team has well-established and agreed-on approaches to problem solving and decision making.

| 1 | 2 | 3 | 4 | 5 | 6 | 7 |

8. Experimentation/Creativity

The team is rigid and does not experiment with how things are done.

The team experiments with different ways of doing things and is creative in its approach.

| 1 | 2 | 3 | 4 | 5 | 6 | 7 |

9. Evaluation

The group never evaluates its functioning or process.

The group often evaluates its functioning and process

| 1 | 2 | 3 | 4 | 5 | 6 | 7 |

management skills, problem recognition, decision making by consensus, climate, synergy, cohesiveness, positive working atmosphere, constructive criticism, individual recognition, no hidden agendas, valuing others, clarity of roles by members, and flexibility. Figure 14.2 on pages 305–306 shows a sample feedback form.

Brilhart's Postmeeting Reaction Questionnaire evaluates eight different characteristics, as shown in Figure 14.3 on page 307 (Brilhart & Galanes, 1992).

Also, an excellent team or group exercise is to develop your own set of criteria. Few activities can be as educational as a group discussion regarding what factors are most important to your particular group, and the resulting feedback is customized and, therefore, immediately useful to the group (Beatty & Haas, 1996). As a starting place, take any combination of the standard feedback instruments provided throughout this chapter and pick the items most salient to your group or team. If you are involved in a semester long project, consider using *formative* evaluations which are done during the process in addition to *summative* evaluations which are done at the end. Your goal should be to continually improve how the group is functioning as well as completing your tasks. How we view the group process at the end can be quite subjective so it is important to provide continual feedback so that the group can modify its activities to increase success (Crews & North, 2000). Often, open ended questions such as "how effective is the group?", "how can the group improve?", and "what needs to change to improve the group?" keep the group on track.

FIGURE 14.3 Brilhart Postmeeting Reaction Questionnaire

Instruction: Circle the number that best indicates your reaction to the following questions about the discussion in which you participated.

1. *Adequacy of Communication:* To what extent do you feel members were understanding each other's statements and positions?

0	1	2	3	4	5	6	7	8	9	10

Much talking past each other, misunderstanding — Communicated directly with each other, with understanding

2. *Opportunity to Speak:* To what extent did you feel free to speak?

0	1	2	3	4	5	6	7	8	9	10

Never had a chance to speak — All the opportunity to talk that I wanted

3. *Climate of Acceptance:* How well did members support each other, show acceptance of individuals?

0	1	2	3	4	5	6	7	8	9	10

Highly critical and punishing — Supportive and receptive

4. *Interpersonal Relations:* How pleasant were members, how concerned with interpersonal relations?

0	1	2	3	4	5	6	7	8	9	10

Quarrelsome, status differences emphasized — Pleasant, empathic, concerned with persons

5. *Leadership:* How adequate was the leader (or leadership) of the group?

0	1	2	3	4	5	6	7	8	9	10

Too weak or dominating — Shared, group-centered, and sufficient

6. *Satisfaction with Role:* How satisfied are you with your personal participation in the discussion?

0	1	2	3	4	5	6	7	8	9	10

Very dissatisfied — Very satisfied

7. *Quality of Product:* How satisfied are you with the discussion, solutions, or learnings that came out of this discussion?

0	1	2	3	4	5	6	7	8	9	10

Very dissatisfied — Very satisfied

8. *Overall:* How do you rate the discussion as a whole apart from any specific aspect of it?

0	1	2	3	4	5	6	7	8	9	10

Awful, waste of time — Superb, time went well

Source: John K. Brilhart and Gloria J. Galanes, *Effective Group Discussion,* 7th ed.

Observer Feedback Guidelines

Obtaining individual observer feedback on the group process is also useful. When you are asked to provide individual written or oral feedback, observe the following guidelines.

1. Avoid generalizations such as "well done." The more *specific* the feedback, the better.

2. Focus on *behaviors* that can be changed.

3. *Don't debate or argue* with the group you are evaluating. Your evaluation is meant to be useful to the group. This is not a forum for your ideas or analysis. Provide your observations, insights, or opinions, but do not demand that the group accept them.

4. *Don't micromanage* the group process. As an observer, your job is not to go over every detail of the process. Choose specific areas and develop them well. In general, a full analysis of two or three items will be much more useful than covering everything.

5. *Remember your role.* An evaluator should function as a facilitator and developer. What will your comments do to enhance the group process? How can the individuals utilize the comments? Avoid statements that say "I didn't like" without providing specific explanations regarding the value of the "liking."

6. *Accentuate the positive aspects.* Always start with the positive and try to spend most of your time finding things the group did right.

7. End with *specific suggestions* for improvement.

8. Be *clear and concise* if you present your ideas orally or in writing.

9. *Compliment in public and criticize in private* is an accepted practice in almost all professional settings. This rule of thumb definitely applies to small group settings.

10. In an organizational setting, developing positive relationships during the feedback process will repay itself time and again. The goal is not to find fault, blame individuals, or criticize the effort. Your job is to help the group or team develop.

Individual Role Behavior

As discussed earlier, our group role behavior falls into three broad classifications—task, maintenance, and self-centered. Task-oriented roles assist the group in accomplishing its goal. Maintenance-oriented roles focus on the social aspects. Self-centered roles are concerned with individual needs. These are *informal roles* that develop *during* the group transactions.

You can use these categories in a single evaluation sheet or let the group decide which ones need to be highlighted. Some honest questioning, looking out for alternative concerns, and reminding the group of past events can be quite useful. In the end, avoid a cookie cutter approach to group evaluation.

Bales's interaction categories offer a specific orientation toward individual role behavior (Bales, 1950). As Figure 14.4 shows, Bales was concerned with twelve issues.

FIGURE 14.4   Bales's Interaction Categories

1. *Seems friendly:* Raises others' status; provides assistance and rewards

2. *Dramatizes:* Jokes; tells stories; gives indirect suggestion

3. *Agrees:* Head nodding; verbal suggestions of commitment about information, opinion, or suggestion

4. *Gives suggestion:* Takes the lead; tries to assume leadership for the task

5. *Gives opinion:* Provides evaluation, analysis, expression of feeling or wish

6. *Gives information:* Provides orientation, repetition, clarification, confirmation

7. *Asks for information:* Requests orientation, repetition, clarification, confirmation

8. *Asks for opinion:* Requests evaluation, analysis, expression of feeling or wish

9. *Asks for suggestion:* Requests direction while maintaining a submissive position; questions designed to call for initiative of others

10. *Disagrees:* Gives passive rejection, mild disagreement; failure to respond

11. *Shows tension:* Laughter, signs of emotional anxiety; holding back

12. *Seems unfriendly:* Reduces others' status: defends or asserts self; conveys negative feelings

Source: R. F. Bales, *Interaction Process Analysis: A Method for the Study of Small Groups.* Published by Allyn & Bacon. Copyright © 1950 by Pearson Education. Reprinted by permission of the publisher.

Once again, the most effective device for your team or group might be a combination of the standard forms and your own group's interests.

Verbal Interaction and Content Analyses

Two additional devices which can be useful are the Verbal Interaction Analysis and Content Analysis Procedures. The Verbal Interaction Analysis traces the number of times members address each other. If a group has five members, you would put the names in a starlike diagram reflecting the same seating pattern used in the discussion. The first time Tom speaks to Sheila, for example, you would draw an arrow from Tom to Sheila. As everyone begins participating, you draw the arrows as they apply. When Tom speaks to Sheila a second time, you mark the arrow. As Figure 14.5 demonstrates, the markings begin to show the interaction patterns. Not only does this analysis indicate who might not be participating, it also shows who has emerged as the leader during this particular discussion. We can also decide if someone is dominating the discussion.

Content analysis is used to analyze the type of comments made. You also can keep track of how often they are made. Any form we have examined can be used for a content analysis evaluation. If you want to know who displayed the most leadership behaviors, develop a list of desired leadership activities and then keep track of how often each group member engages in these activities. The list of individual behaviors would also work for content analysis. Verbal interaction and

FIGURE 14.5   **Verbal Interaction Talk Patterns**

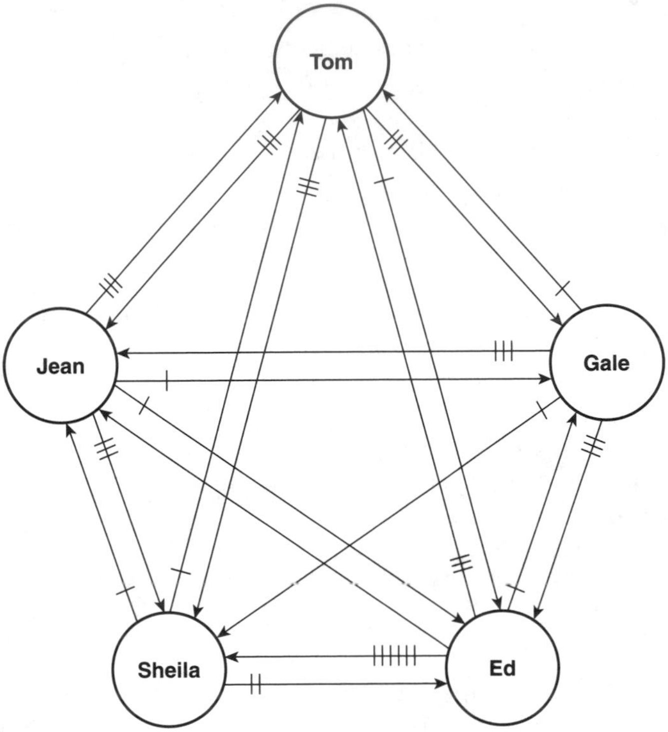

content analysis processes allow observers to be very specific regarding particular behaviors.

Finally, you can keep a journal of the group process. The value of an ongoing journal of activities derives from the fact that we tend to forget important milestones as the process moves forward. When we go back to earlier records, we can recover important insights regarding missed opportunities.

Summary

Anything worth doing is worth doing well. Systematic feedback is the key to successful group processes. Observer/member scales are an excellent means of focusing on specific areas for improvement. Rating scales allow a broad range of analysis of concepts ranging from individual actions to leadership. Individual role behaviors can be the basis for feedback. Verbal interaction and content analysis can hone in on particular behaviors.

We all hope our groups will be successful, but to get the most from our group experiences, we need to incorporate learning. Elbert Hubbard, an American writer, is credited with saying: A failure is a person who has blundered but is not capable of cashing in on the experience. Current quality leaders put it another way: There are no mistakes, only opportunities. The only difference between ability and luck may be the ability to avoid a mistake and repeat a success a second time. All of these comments suggest the importance of feedback and learning as we develop small group skills.

DISCUSSION QUESTIONS

1. What are the four ways of learning about how to make small groups successful? Which ones have you used? Were they successful in teaching general group effectiveness concepts?

2. Why use a consultant or an observer for a small group?

3. How can a rating scale be used to evaluate a small group?

4. What issues would be useful to include on a rating scale?

5. How can postmeeting reaction forms be used? What are their most important characteristics?

6. Outline and discuss the guidelines for providing observer feedback to a group.

7. How can an observer utilize interaction between group members to provide feedback?

EXERCISES

1. Evaluating ourselves; 2. Evaluation of a group or team project; 3. Individual papers; 4. Team evaluation

1. EVALUATING OURSELVES

Use the sample feedback form presented in Figure 14.2 to evaluate your group or team.

Procedure

Each member of the team should perform this evaluation individually and in writing. Next, the group or team should complete a single self-evaluation form that combines all the rating scores of the individual members on one form. Then the group should discuss each scale item on the form, paying particular attention to those items with the least favorable overall ratings and those items showing the greatest discrepancy in ratings among the group members. Finally, the team should discuss ways with which to deal with any potential problems, issues, or concerns raised during this self-evaluation process.

2. EVALUATION OF A GROUP OR TEAM PROJECT

If your group worked on a project, respond to the following questions as a means for providing internal group feedback.

1. Did the final project represent a group effort? Were some group members more involved and did they contribute more than others?
2. Did the project represent a good research effort? Were the goals well defined? Was adequate research using a variety of methods employed?
3. Did the group use a systematic approach to problem solving?
4. Did the group approach the topic creatively? Were various approaches utilized?
5. Did the group develop a unified team that valued diverse opinions, cooperated in problem analysis?
6. Were excellent communication skills used to assist in understanding the problem and developing a positive group climate?

3. INDIVIDUAL PAPERS

The goal of this paper is not to provide a history of the group process. Instead, you are writing to share your observations and to explain what you have learned through the project or group process.

1. Start with Chapter 14 to provide you with some standard evaluation approaches. Adapt this material, if appropriate, to include information in the previous 13 chapters and class experiences. As you evaluate the group experience, choose the most salient topics rather than trying to cover all the materials. For example, one of the most important issues in your group may have been the unequal effort by the members. Explain why you believe this happened, the efforts by the group to resolve the issue, and suggestions— now that you have completed the process—on how to deal with the issue if it occurs in other groups. You should cover at least five major topics.
2. Rank each group member, including yourself, 1, 2, 3, and so forth. The ranking should be your assessment of the quality and quantity of each member's contributions to the team or group process. Explain how you define "contribution."
   a. There is no reason why you cannot be ranked 1 if you believe you made the greatest contribution.

b. You only use 1 one time, 2 one time, and so forth. There can be no ties.

c. Justify your ranking for each individual. This feedback is not meant to encourage a popularity contest.

d. Remember that someone can receive the lowest ranking and still receive a good grade. One member might be ranked fifth by everyone in the group even though everyone believes he or she did A work.

e. Your instructor will let you know if the final ranking will be shared with the rest of the group. Your individual reasons and ranking will not. So, you should be candid.

3. What would you do differently if you could start this group process over?

4. What will you do differently the next time you are in a group?

4 . TEAM EVALUATION

INDIVIDUAL RESPONSE TO TEAM/GROUP—YOUR NAME:

TEAM/GROUP TOPIC:

Thinking back over the last semester, please rank your teammates. A ranking of 1 indicates that this individual was the most productive and "best" team member. You can assign only one "1." Rank the rest of the team, INCLUDING YOURSELF, with a 1, 2, 3, 4, 5. You can ONLY USE EACH NUMBER ONCE.

RANK (FIRST AND LAST NAME!)

1. _____
2. _____
3. _____
4. _____
5. _____

Analysis:

1. Specifically justify your ranking of the team members; why is one person #1, and the like?
2. What were the highlights of the process?
3. What were the low points of the process?
4. Where did the team succeed?
5. Where did the team have less than success?

Critically, what would you do differently the next time you are in a team/group project? Use the textbook and class materials if appropriate.

REFERENCES

Bales, R. G. (1950). *Interaction process analysis: A method for the study of small groups.* Cambridge, MA: Addison-Wesley.

Barnlund, D. C., & Haiman, F. S. (1960). *The dynamics of discussion.* Boston: Houghton Mifflin.

Beatty, J. R., & Haas, R. W. (1996). Using peer evaluations to assess individual performance in group class projects. *Journal of Marketing Education, 18*(2), 17–28.

Brilhart, J. K., & Galanes, G. J. (1992). *Effective group discussion* (7th ed.). Dubuque, IA: Wm C. Brown.

Crews, T. B., & North, A. B. (2000). Team evaluation (Part 2 of 2). *Instructional Strategies, 16*(2), 1–4.

March, J. G. (1994). *A primer on decision making.* New York: The Free Press.

15

Computer Mediated Group Communication

CHAPTER OUTLINE

CHAPTER OBJECTIVES

- Define Computer Mediated Communication (CMC).
- Describe the electronic meeting system characteristics of group support systems (GSS) and of audio- and videoconferencing.

- Discuss the effects of CMC undercurrents on group processes.
- Explain social presence and the effects of media richness, synchronous communication, and other influences of the medium upon it.
- Describe methods for choosing an appropriate communication medium using the communication task, the language demand-technology fit, and the communication function techniques.
- Discuss group process and leadership responsibilities for effective small group CMC.

KEY TERMS

Asynchronous
   communication
Audioconferencing
Audio clipping
Audio delay
CMC: Computer mediated
   communication
Communication functions

Electronic meeting systems
FTF: Face-to-face
   communication
Groupware
GDSS: *Group Decision
   Support Systems*
GPSS: *Group Performance
   Support Systems*

GSS: *Group Support Systems*
Media richness
Language demand-
   technology fit
Social presence
Synchronous communication
Task-technology fit
Videoconferencing

For a few thousand years, they shared their Universe with their machine children; then, realizing that it was folly to linger when their task was done, they passed into history without regret. Not one of them ever looked through his own eyes upon the planet Earth again. But even the age of the Machine Entities passed swiftly. In their ceaseless experimenting, they had learned to store knowledge in the structure of space itself, and to preserve their thoughts for eternity in frozen lattices of light. They could become creatures of radiation, free at last from the tyranny of matter. Now, they were Lords of the galaxy, and beyond the reach of time. They could rove at will among the stars, and sink like a subtle mist through the very interstices of space. (*2001: A Space Odyssey*, original screenplay)

Understanding the Technology and Its Influences on Small Group Communication

Technology affects our communication, our relationships, and our lives. It's *not* a question of *if* we will use technology to communicate with each other; it's a question of *when, how,* and *how well.* Computer mediated communication (CMC) moves communication a step beyond time and space, allowing it to be "instantaneously asynchronous" and geographically prolific, seemingly co-occurring in multiple geographical locations at once. From a human communication perspective, CMC is a social and psychological phenomenon; not just a technological one (Shedletsky & Aitken, 2004).

I now e-mail my mother more often than I call her on the phone and I stay in touch with family, friends, and colleagues who live all over the country by using a variety of Computer Mediated Communication (CMC). Increasingly, I participate in groups that use technology in their communication, decision-making, and problem-solving processes as well. The technologies they use vary from sharing documents as e-mail attachments, to posting general information on the web, using electronic bulletin boards, sharing videotapes of informational presentations, and using on-line computer chat sessions, telephone audioconferences and internet videoconferences to carry on group discussions.

Millions of people are currently using these communication technologies in more than 1,500 organizations that have geographically dispersed group members (Scott, 1999). To stay competitive in today's electronically connected economy, corporations share information at hyperfast speeds using Internets, Intranets, and other forms of CMC (Meyers & Davis, 1998). Sooner or later almost all of us will use CMC in our small groups as well. To be effective in that communication we must understand something about the technology and its multiple influences on small group communication. We must plan for its use and adopt strategies for being effective in our communication (Rogers, 1999). Hacker and Steiner (2001) suggest that users need more than access to the Internet to become successful users of it. They need the opportunity to develop their skills and comfort level with the medium, overcoming their anxieties and developing a positive motivation for use based on their perception of the tangible benefits to be gained by them in their interpersonal, work-related, financial, and political or social interests. In this chapter we explore some of the ways groups use communication technologies, the communication challenges they must overcome, and the ways in which those technologies influence their communication.

The Importance of Understanding Influential Undercurrents

When I was 14 my cousins came to visit one summer and we went swimming. I had just gone through a growth spurt so was taller and stronger than the summer before, and could swim out farther into the ocean and still touch the sandy bottom. Unfortunately, this also meant that, for the first time in my life, I was able to swim out far enough to experience the strong undercurrent. I discovered that when I tried to stand that I could not keep my feet planted in the sand. The ocean kept sweeping my legs out from under me, picking me up, and carrying me farther out to sea. I started swimming toward shore as fast as I could, only to discover that the ocean was stronger than I was, and it carried me out to sea even as I swam against it. At first I panicked and tried swimming even harder, straight for shore, but I made no progress against the ocean's current. Then, fortunately, I remembered that the undercurrent at this beach rushed in on one side of the bay and ran out the other, depositing sand along a point as it receded. For a moment I rested, floated, and looked around. I remembered that my goal was to swim to shore (rather than be rescued by the lifeguard and embarrassed in front of my cousins, or worse, drown at sea) and resumed my swimming with a calm steady stride in a direction away from the beach where I had entered the water. I made progress by swimming across the current to the sandy point and, after a while, the current even seemed to help me achieve my goal. When I reached shallow water I was able to walk back to where my cousins were lying on the beach in the sun. I was exhausted but had reached my goal. I was successful because I knew something about the medium in which I was swimming and was able to use that knowledge in crafting a strategy for negotiating my way through the undercurrents of that medium.

Communicating through a computer medium is much like swimming in the ocean. Understanding the undercurrents of the technology and their influences is helpful to planning a strategy for achieving our goal of effective small group communication. Ignoring the undercurrents of the medium may mean that we find ourselves out to sea.

In this chapter we define computer mediated communication (CMC), discuss the technologies through which it is mediated, and describe the major influential undercurrents within it. We describe computer mediated communication systems and their influences on group processes and communication. We explain ways in which a group can plan to use computer mediated communication, and we suggest methods for crafting effective small group communication strategies for using the technology.

Computer Mediated Communication (CMC)

Computer mediated communication (CMC) describes communication that takes place through a variety of media and provides distributed group members with video, audio, and text-based messaging capabilities (Graetz, Boyle, Kimble, Thompson, & Garloch, 1998). These facilities include computer, audio, and video conferencing systems, computer chat rooms, electronic mail, bulletin boards, list-servers, and newsgroups (Huang, 1999). Many of these CMC systems have software, called "groupware," specifically designed to help groups discuss issues, make decisions, and communicate effectively.

Although some authors limit the use of CMC to describe only text-based computer mediated message systems (for example, Walther, 1996), we include audio- and videoconferencing systems in our discussion of CMC because these systems are becoming increasingly available and useful to groups in their decision-making and problem-solving communication, and because they are increasingly used in combination with text-based systems.

CMC, whether text-based, audiolinked, or video-interactive, generates some common influential undercurrents within the group communication. CMC group members tend to focus more on the task and instrumental aspects of the process than on the personal and social aspects of the group. Thus, they tend to be more content oriented and less social-emotional in their communication style than face-to-face groups are (Walther, 1996). Individuals in CMC groups tend to feel themselves to be more anonymous in their participation and to detect less individual personality in the other group members. They participate more equally, and low-status members often contribute more freely. They also communicate more uninhibitedly, sometimes generating more negative messages and experiencing more difficulty in attaining a group consensus. While CMC groups sometimes have a higher level of conflict, they can also display positive affect and frequently engage in less argumentation. They are less likely to have an emergent leader, and are more likely to have a decentralized and less permanent leadership. CMC groups also tend to de-emphasize personal relationships and experience less interpersonal attraction (McGrath & Hollingshead, 1994). However, they can develop interpersonally positive relationships when groups continue to meet over time (Walther, 1994).

Metzger and Flanagan (2002) report that people, in general, are more active and instrumental in their use of CMC than they are when using more traditional communication media such as books, magazines, newspapers, telephones, and television. People report their computer-mediated-communication through e-mail, chat rooms, and the world-wide-web, to be more active, goal directed, and intentional. They use CMC to purposely seek out specific types of information and entertainment rather than to casually browse or "surf the web" just to pass the time.

Cai (in press) reports that computer use serves different functions than more traditional media. In support of this argument, his research showed that volunteers who gave up the use of the computer for a day did not increase the amount of time they watched television or used other media. Voluntarily giving up television viewing, however, significantly increased the time they spent using other, more traditional, media such as the radio, VCR, and telephone, during the day. Warren and Bluma (2002) report that the average grade-school child, in their study of 180 children, logged on less than three times a week from home, but only a small minority of the parents they surveyed used an Internet filter. Most reported making rules about Internet surfing, and more than 70% of the computers the children used at home were located in an open family area such as the kitchen, dining room, or living room. College and university students use computer mediated communication in the form of chat, instant messaging, and e-mail largely to develop and maintain their personal relationships. Of almost 1,000 university students surveyed, Rumbough (2001) reports that 44% of them used CMC to help maintain long-distance relationships. However, less than 4% admitted to using an electronic dating service. Collectively, these findings suggest that computer use, with its qualities of interactivity, hyper-textuality, synchronous multimedia, and relative lack of gate-keeping, serves a different function than other, more traditional media for users. Groups also use CMC in different ways and to fulfill different communication functions.

Performance Outcomes of CMC Groups

CMC groups take longer to reach consensus even though they generate more unique ideas than face-to-face (FTF) groups (Olaniran, 1994). This is because CMC appears to reduce group members' attempts to criticize and informally pressure each other to conform to a particular idea or way of thinking during the group discussion. CMC groups are less likely to reach consensus than FTF groups and may be less likely to discuss some of the important attributes of problem-solving cases, but, given time, can arrive at quality decisions (McGrath & Hollingshead, 1994).

Bordia (1997) reviewed the ways in which CMC groups differ from FTF groups. CMC groups generally take longer to complete a task, and in the same time period CMC groups produce fewer remarks than FTF groups do. However, CMC groups usually perform better than FTF groups on idea-generation tasks, and there is greater equality of participation in CMC groups. When time is limited, CMC groups perform better than FTF groups on tasks that are less involving but worse on tasks requiring more social-emotional interaction. Given enough time, CMC groups can perform as well as FTF groups in developing social-emotional relationships. There is reduced normative social pressure in CMC groups, and the perception and understanding of other group members is often poorer in CMC groups. When time is limited, other group members are less charitably perceived. CMC groups have a higher incidence of uninhibited comments, which appears induced by a sense of anonymous de-individuation. CMC group members generally show less attitude change resulting from their discussions. These differences are listed in Table 15.1.

Electronic Meeting Systems

Some traditional CMC software systems (groupware) have been specifically designed to facilitate small group communication and meeting processes. These systems, called *Electronic Meeting Systems* (EMS), enhance the group's decision-making abilities and facilitates the communication through the computer medium. Electronic meeting systems that provide electronic support for group-meeting and decision-making processes are called *Group Support Systems* or GSS (also known as *Group Decision Support Systems*, GDSS, and *Group Performance Support Systems*, GPSS). Electronic meeting systems that provide a structured communication medium for group communication are known as conferencing systems. The medium through which this conferencing takes place may provide computer mediated text-based, audiolinked, or digital video communication.

These EMS decision-making and communication conferencing functions are not incompatible with each other and are, in fact, increasingly blended together into groupware packages that provide both GSS and communication conferencing capabilities in a single electronic meeting package. However, discussing EMS

TABLE 15.1   Computer Mediated Communication (CMC) Compared with Face-to-Face (FTF) Groups (Bordia, 1997)

1. CMC groups take longer to complete a task.
2. In a given time period CMC groups produce fewer remarks than FTF groups.
3. CMC groups perform better than FTF groups on idea-generation tasks.
4. There is greater equality of participation in CMC groups.
5. When time is limited, CMC groups perform better than FTF groups on tasks that are less involving.
6. When time is limited, CMC groups perform worse on tasks requiring more social-emotional interaction, but given enough time CMC groups perform as well as FTF groups.
7. There is reduced normative social pressure in CMC groups.
8. Perception (understanding) of other participants and task is poorer in CMC groups.
9. In CMC, when time is limited, the communication partner is perceived less charitably.
10. CMC groups have a higher incidence of uninhibited behavior induced by a sense of anonymous de-individuation.
11. CMC group members evidence less attitude change.

decision-making and communication support functions separately provides some clarity for analyzing the specific influences of each on the decision-making and communication processes of a group meeting.

GSS: Group Support Systems.   GSS combines computer technology, group meeting procedures, and the use of decision-making techniques, to facilitate the decision making and problem solving of a group (Miranda, 1994). GSS generally uses networked computers to provide computer conferencing capabilities. This CMC medium can be configured to provide identifiable or anonymous participant communication; allows simultaneous input from multiple participants, and facilitates a structured group meeting process (Valacich, Dennis, & Nunamaker, 1992). Individual group members can simultaneously type their input into their own computers, and it is displayed on everyone's computer screen at the same time, or posted to a common electronic area for all to view. Their input can be made anonymous by the system's removing all identifying sender information from each message or by the system's assigning an anonymous pseudonym to each participant for the duration of the discussion session. The system can also structure and organize the messages, summarizing the discussion and facilitating such decision-making functions as voting.

The goal of GSS is to make the group meeting process more productive, to increase the speed of group decision making, and to improve the quality of the decisions that are made by the group (Broome & Chen, 1992). GSS is designed to help a group deal with problems of information loss or distortion that can occur during discussion and to facilitate the exploration of alternative issues and approaches to problems and solutions.

By automating the group communication, information processing, and decision-making tasks, GSS has the potential to enhance a group's ability to structure and manage its work while promoting vigilant group information processing, efficient group decision-making procedures, and a commitment to full participation and consideration of diverse views within the group (Poole & Holmes, 1995). However, in comparison to face-to-face groups, GSS groups generally focus more on the organization of the decision-making process, repeatedly returning to the group orientation phase, spending more time on the problem orientation and solution development stages described in Chapter 9, and engaging in more discussion of group procedures; they spend less time on problem analysis and solution criteria development, show no improvement in the depth of their critical thinking or problem analysis, and have no more equal participation among their group members (Poole & Holmes, 1995; Poole, Holmes, Watson, & DeSanctis, 1993). They do not generate more ideas or engage in more critical examination of those ideas, and they do appear to generate higher-quality ideas, but they also take longer to make decisions than face-to-face groups (Scott, 1999).

Following the electronic group meeting procedures that have been explicitly defined by GSS often becomes a major part of their group task, and group members are frequently attentive to these procedures and satisfied with the resulting group process. Their satisfaction drops off, however, if they feel the discussion becomes too structured by the technology. While happy to follow clearly defined procedures, they prefer discussions in which the influence of the technology is less visible.

In addition to this explicit attention focused on group procedure, much of the influence of GSS on group processes can be attributed to the system's ability to provide participant anonymity. Anonymous group members participate more and are more verbose in their expressions than are members in nonanonymous groups. When GSS allows anonymous discussion, however, participants sometimes have difficulty identifying the source of a message. Although this reduces the influence of participant personality, status, and hierarchical position within the group, it also makes it more difficult to recognize a stream of messages coming from the same person across the course of a conversation and can make individual messages more ambiguous and difficult to interpret (Graetz et al., 1998). Groups using anonymous member input often generate more solutions, engage in more critical communication, and develop a higher degree of consensus (McGrath & Hollingshead, 1994). They also produce more critical comments than groups in which the participants' comments are identified (Valacich, Dennis, & Nunamaker, 1992). Anonymity facilitates less inhibited participation, increases the productivity of idea generation, enhances the evaluation of idea quality, and reduces the influence of markers of personal status and power (Miranda, 1994). Groups allowing anonymous input, whether meeting face-to-face with anonymous written comments or meeting through a computer mediated communication medium such as GSS, produce more ideas than nonanonymous groups (Cooper, Gallupe, Pollard, & Cadsby, 1998).

GSS brainstorming groups also produce more nonredundant ideas than do verbal face-to-face brainstorming groups, and are at least as productive as groups using the nominal group technique described in Chapter 11 (Cooper, Gallupe, Pollard, & Cadsby, 1998). GSS technology eliminates the blocking of idea production created by the turn-taking necessities of face-to-face group conversation and reduces the evaluation apprehension of participants. However, this also means that GSS groups may generate more controversial ideas. Although this can produce a positive result when what starts out as an outrageous idea becomes a creative solution, sometimes participants can become so offended by the controversial comments other group members make that they stop participating and withdraw from the group discussion (Cooper, Gallupe, Pollard, & Cadsby, 1998). This withdrawal reduces the social integration of the group and creates a loss in the group's productivity and commitment to goals.

On the positive side, GSS group members are less likely to influence one another than are face-to-face group members, particularly in the early phases of their group meetings. This means that groups are able to progress through the early phases described in Chapter 4 of forming, engaging in conflict, and emerging with some group consensus, with less likelihood of groupthink. Groupthink occurs when pressures for group cohesion and conformity lead to a deterioration in the decision-making process of a group. As discussed in Chapter 3, a group suffering from groupthink may be predisposed to a restrictive mode of thinking that emphasizes apparent consensus, group cohesiveness, a predominant focus on internal group opinions, an isolation from external inputs, and a group homogeneity in ideas and vision. GSS technology provides structural features that mitigate against a group's tendency to succumb to groupthink and encourage a careful analysis of multiple options (Miranda, 1994).

Along with the GSS characteristics of attention to process and participant anonymity, its facility for simultaneous input enhances a group member's freedom to disagree. Simultaneous input reduces turn-taking restrictions, encourages broader and more active participation, speeds up the process of idea exchange, and reduces time pressure on that idea exchange. GSS's structuring of the discussion process—by using an electronically displayed meeting agenda, a sequencing of meeting activities, and the facilitating practices of brainstorming and nominal group technique—helps focus a group on relevant issues and their evaluation. The use of the computer screen as an explicit public forum enhances the group's attention to the information and ideas displayed on it and disassociates those ideas from the individual personalities who express them. Thus, ideas are evaluated more on their own merits than on the merits of their spokesperson.

These GSS features facilitate effective small group decision-making task processes. When these characteristics are removed, GSS groups often perform no better, and sometimes even more poorly, than face-to-face groups (Gallupe et al., 1994).

Audio- and Videoconferencing. In addition to providing GSS capabilities a number of electronic meeting systems also provide audio- and videoconferencing facilities. When provided through the Internet the audio products are sometimes called web-phones, net-phones, or net-to-phone programs and allow a personal computer with an attached microphone and speakers to function much like a telephone. Videoconferencing systems, such as Microsoft's NetMeeting® and White Pine's CU-SeeMe®, allow users of computers with attached microphones, speakers, and video cameras, to simultaneously communicate verbally through an audio connection, participate nonverbally through transmitted video images of the participants, and exchange text and graphic informational documents.

In these systems the quality of the audio is important. Poor audio quality, whether due to a lack of vocal intelligibility, audio delay, or audio clipping, is distracting to participants and problematic to holding an effective group meeting. Some systems can make speaker *vocal intelligibility* difficult if all participants are not equally well heard from different parts of the room. Some speakers' voices may be too soft to be adequately carried by the system or may become garbled because of their distance from the system's microphone. *Audio delays* can occur when an audio signal must travel over a long distance from one meeting site to another. In face-to-face meetings we anticipate simultaneous verbal and nonverbal responses to our comments and are accustomed to very short pause intervals between conversational utterances (100 milliseconds). In audio- and video-conference meetings, when the geographical locations of groups are distant from each other, even a fast communication medium may not provide this instantaneous response (McGrath & Hollingshead, 1994). Relatively short audio delays can interfere with the smooth flow of a meeting, causing participants to become impatient and ill at ease. They can also create a perception that participants at the distant location are not well-prepared for the meeting or that they are cognitively slow and verbally inarticulate. *Audio clipping* occurs when a participant's microphone fails to pick up the beginning of an utterance or drops the end of the utterance. This can happen in systems using voice-activated microphones that turn on and off with the presence of sound. In these systems single-word responses may be lost. Participants interrupting each other, talking over each other, coughing, moving chairs, or even attempting to provide vocalized support for an idea or comment may make it impossible to hear a speaker's complete utterance. Each of these audio problems can create a challenge to holding a productive CMC meeting as they distract participant attention and make concentration on the meeting topic difficult.

In addition to poor audio quality, video image is a communication challenge for videoconferencing. The video picture of participants' faces may not be large enough, refined enough, or updated by the technology quickly enough to accurately provide the subtle facial cues participants need for smooth turn-taking. A lack of clarity in this nonverbal communication can make videoconferencing susceptible to pragmatic conversational difficulties such as determining a speaking order or identifying who is speaking, when someone is almost finished speaking, who is waiting to speak, or who would like to speak next. Frustration with these conversational pragmatics can lead participants to become less involved in the group discussion or to stop participating all together even though they remain physically connected through the medium. In addition to being large enough to be seen, all participants must be visible on the screen during the discussion. Even then a spatial relationship among participants may be missing, eye contact may be difficult to achieve, and facial expressions can be hard to interpret.

Due to the audio delay and visual-spatial relationship difficulties, groups sometimes find the nonverbal communication regulators—such as back-channel utterances ("uh huh," "yeah," "I see"), subtle facial expressions, and other non-verbal cues—difficult to interpret. The utterances may be spoken too softly to transmit through the medium or, when they do transmit, they may become annoying or interrupt the communication interaction. The result is sometimes awkward turn-taking and a lack of spontaneity present in the conversation. Group discussion patterns may develop that are different from those occurring in face-to-face meetings. These differences occur in the frequency and duration of participant speaking turns, participant influence, and the power relationships within the group. Videoconferencing groups also engage in less elaborate discussions, incur fewer conversational digressions, and experience a reduced amount of synergy in the group's planning activities. In general, videoconferencing groups experience a decrease in the amount of informal social communication that occurs (Scott, 1999). Face-to-face group meetings allow participants to chat before the meeting begins; to exchange glances, comments, and nonverbal communication during the meeting; and to discuss other topics afterwards. These multiple conversations facilitate a social richness in the group and produce a sense of personal involvement that is not easily achieved through either audio- or videoconferencing. While this loss in the social-emotional content may have a task benefit as fewer conversational digressions keep a meeting shorter and more focused, it comes at an interpersonal relationship cost (McGrath & Hollingshead, 1994; Sherblom, 1994).

When we meet face-to-face, I simultaneously perceive your nonverbal cues and respond to them while I am speaking. I watch your eyes, your face, and your body posture, listen for your back-channel vocal utterances, and attend to your nonverbal cues of agreement or disagreement. I may alter what I say and how I say it even as I am uttering my words, and before I complete a full sentence. Thus I may end my sentence with a different informational content, vocal inflection, affective mood, and meaning than I might originally have intended. In this sense our small group communication is dynamically co-constructed because you have a direct influence on what I am saying and how I am saying it. In a communication medium other than face-to-face, your feedback is not as readily available to me and is not as immediately influential on my communication. Even in audio- and videoconferencing, because of transmission delays and the audio and video characteristics of the medium discussed earlier, I receive less immediate feedback, less diverse types of feedback, and less total feedback in the same amount of time. This reduction in the immediacy, variety, and amount of simultaneous communication and feedback leads to a reduction in how dynamically co-constructed our communication is and results in a loss of social presence.

Undercurrents of
the Communication Medium

Social Presence

In Chapter 1 we defined small group communication as a "transactional process of using symbolic behavior to achieve shared meaning among group members over a period of time." Some degree of dynamically shared feedback and co-constructed communication is necessary to achieve this sense of shared meaning among group members. Social presence is the perception that participants have that the communication medium facilitates the development of social-emotional-relational communication and shared meaning development among group members. Social presence is associated with the amount and diversity of task and social communication that is facilitated by a medium and describes a participant's feeling that other human participants are really involved in the group communication (Short, Williams, & Christie, 1976).

A rich communication medium through which participants can engage in multiple simultaneous communication with verbal and nonverbal cues, synchronous feedback, a variety of language and inflection, and a personal focus that conveys feelings and emotion along with the informational content produces a greater sense of social presence (Trevino, Daft, & Lengel, 1990). In a face-to-face (FTF) meeting participants simultaneously exchange more types of information—emotional, attitudinal, relational, and contextual—along with the informational content. A text-based communication medium, however, provides less opportunity for the communication of these simultaneous cues, feedback, subtlety of inflection, and emotional-relational content. Text-based messaging systems, such as e-mail, bulletin board systems, and electronic chat have a relatively narrow informational bandwidth compared to FTF communication and provide relatively low levels of media richness (Graetz et al., 1998). This is because text-based CMC is a one-code system, consisting only of the written message through which both verbal and nonverbal contextual meanings must be communicated (Walther, 1996). It lacks the multiple simultaneous channels of FTF communication through which to simultaneously carry vocal (pitch, loudness, rhythm, inflection, pauses, and hesitations), facial (eye contact, gaze, apparent interest level, and facial responses), and physical body (attentiveness, posture, gestures, and relaxation) nonverbal cues. The absence of these simultaneous channels means that fewer nonverbal cues are expressed and less social information is communicated in each message. So deciphering the whole of the relational message takes more time (Walther, 1996).

Media Richness.   Perceptions of social presence vary with the communication medium, and communication scholars have arranged communication media along a rough continuum known as the media richness continuum (Daft & Lengel, 1986). Media that do not carry all types of information simultaneously are considered leaner media as their informational capacities don't facilitate the development of the social-emotional-relational dimensions of communication at as fast a rate.

Face-to-face group meetings provide the greatest opportunity for experiencing rich communication and social presence. Videoconferencing, then audioconferencing, and finally text-based computer conferencing systems are considered leaner communication media. Given time and continuous communication effort, however, even text-only CMC groups can share rich personal, social, emotional, relational information, and get to know each other as fully human participants, thus experiencing a large degree of social presence. In fact, at times this characteristic of a slower relational development through a leaner medium may even be an asset to the growth of greater depths in personal intimacy, trust, co-orientation, and affection among group members (Walther, 1996).

Synchronous-Asynchronous Communication. Another contributor to this experience of social presence is the extent to which a CMC medium provides synchronous or asynchronous communication among participants. This distinction is a recognition that communication is a process engaged in by participants that involves interactive feedback and simultaneous speaking and listening rather than a one-way conveying of information.

One can distinguish between the synchronous and asynchronous means of communication provided by each medium. For example, while videoconferencing is synchronous, playing back a videotape of an earlier conference session is an asynchronous form of communication. Audioconferencing is synchronous, while voice mail is an asynchronous form of audio communication. Computer conferencing systems, "instant messaging," and chat rooms are synchronous, while e-mail, listservers, bulletin boards, and newsgroups provide asynchronous communication.

Yet, even in a synchronous text-based CMC medium, such as "instant messaging" or electronic chat, I complete my whole utterance and push the enter key before I receive your response to any part of that utterance. In asynchronous text-based CMC, such as e-mail and bulletin board messages, I generally complete an entire message containing several utterances or sentences before I receive your response. So, while some forms of communication within each medium are termed synchronous and others are asynchronous, there is really a degree of synchronicity available through the communication in each medium, and these varying degrees of synchronicity influence a group's communication and the experience of social presence.

However, human communication is not technologically determined, and while social presence may be facilitated, enhanced, and potentially constrained by the characteristics of media richness and communication synchronicity, it is not determined by them. Human communicators have the ability to enhance or erode feelings of social presence regardless of the medium they use to communicate. For example, if a face-to-face group meeting is poorly attended or poorly facilitated, or group members are not attentively involved in the group communication, that face-to-face meeting may produce a feeling of little social presence among the group members. However, social presence is more easily facilitated and more commonly experienced in FTF group meetings, whereas an effort must be made to achieve it in CMC group meetings.

One type of CMC group that focuses much of its time and attention on social-emotional-relational communication is the on-line support group. Wright (2002) describes one motive for people to participate in an on-line support group as the ability to transcend geographic distance and time constraints. Participants find it more convenient and flexible to contact other support group members from their home or work computer than to attend a meeting with people at a set time and location. Campbell and Wright (2002) found that once involved in an on-line support group, the key emotional-relational communication dimensions for the group was receptivity, immediacy, and informality. Participants indicated that a benefit to an on-line support group, compared to a face-to-face group, is the ability of the group to ignore turn-taking behaviors and to get numerous simultaneous responses to a question or an issue. Making decisions about a source's credibility and the value of the information received, however, was one of the bigger participant concerns.

A text-based computer bulletin board conferencing group for people with disabilities effectively communicates social support through the CMC medium in the form of verbal and nonverbal communication that reduces uncertainty about the situation, self, other, and relationship, and enhances the perception of personal control (Braithwaite, Waldron, & Finn, 1999; Albrecht & Adelman, 1987). The most common form of social support offered is emotional, with 40% (590) of the 1,472 messages exchanged within the group containing emotional support expressions of empathy and reciprocated emotional expression. These include positive statements of relationship, physical affection, confidentiality, sympathy, understanding, encouragement, and prayer. The second most frequently offered support is conveyed in messages (33%; 461 messages) of instruction, advice, referrals to experts, situation appraisals, and teaching, in ways that reduce uncertainty, make new life situations more predictable, and help people cope with challenges. The third is esteem support (19%; 275 messages) including compliments, self-concept validations, and statements of positive feelings of importance, competence, relief from blame, and rights as a person. Other forms of support include networking (7%; 71 messages) in the expression of similar interests, situations, and concerns, and supportive offers of tangible assistance (2.7%; 41 messages) that involve performing a task or expressing a willingness to help out. Additionally, humor, poetry, nonverbal cues, and signature lines are all used to express support. Humor, while frequently sarcastic or ironic in nature, often includes nonverbal "HAHAHA!" accents in the message. Nonverbal emoticons, such as "(Smile!)," "blush," "grin," "giggle," smiley faces, and sad faces, also play a big role in the messages, as do written expressions for hugs, kisses, shoulder patting, and hand holding (7%; 103 messages). Poetry provides personal self-expression and emotional support for others in ways that promote self-awareness and self-esteem. Finally, signature lines are used to present personally selected axioms and quotations to convey support.

With a desire, and some communication effort, even a text-based CMC group is capable of providing social support communication that develops enduring relationships. A group can communicate in ways that are effective and that support the group's purpose regardless of the technological medium employed.

Table 15.2 summarizes the distinctions made for social presence, media richness, and communication synchronicity available in each medium. Face-to-face offers the richest, most synchronous communication. Videoconferencing provides

TABLE 15.2   Social Presence, Media Richness, and Synchronicity

Communication Medium	Communication Verbal and Nonverbal	Social Presence Media Richness	Synchronous Examples (same time; interactive)	Asynchronous Examples (not at the same time; respond later)
Face-to-Face	**Face-to-face:** Simultaneous verbal content, vocal tone and inflection, facial expressions, hand gestures, bodily posture and angle	Rich media: All nonverbal modalities available	Face-to-face group meeting	Nominal group technique
Video Videoconferencing	**Visual and audio:** Interactive verbal content; nonverbals: vocal tone and inflection, facial expressions, hand gestures, bodily posture, and lean may be present but obscure	Visual and vocal nonverbals available	Videoconferencing	Video recordings: Viewed later
Audioconferencing	**Audio:** Interactive verbal content, nonverbals: vocal tone and inflection, present	Only vocal nonverbals available	Telephone conferences	Voice mail
Text-Based Computer Systems	**Text-based:** Text, graphics: nonverbal "emoticons" used	Lean media: Users create text-based nonverbal expressions	Interactive computer chats GSS	E-mail, bulletin boards, listservs

the next richest medium. Then audio-conferencing and text-based computer conferencing offer the leanest and least synchronous media for communication.

Other Influences of the Medium on Social Presence.   There are several other characteristics of the medium that affect the experience of social presence as well. Typing a message is generally more laborious and time-consuming than speaking in conversation. Thus, when using a text-based CMC system, individuals often use abbreviations, shorten their verbal expression, or omit statements that might be assumed—such as utterances indicating attention, understanding, or agreement (Graetz et al., 1998). While these short cuts speed up the transmission of their message, they can also lead to greater uncertainty among participants as to whether others have agreed with them, understood them, or even read what they had to say. Some synchronous text-based systems, such as electronic chat, allow participants to simultaneously type and send messages to each other, without the conversational turn-taking present in FTF conversation. This means that participants can generate more messages faster. However, when participants are typing their own messages they are likely to be less attentive to the messages posted by others. On the positive side, text-based messages are frequently more carefully composed and edited before they are sent than are spoken conversational comments. This can increase the clarity of the overall group discussion. Also, reticent participants are often less apprehensive and thus contribute more through text-based messaging systems, thereby increasing the overall group participation (Graetz et al., 1998). In addition, Bunz and Campbell (in press) find that participants accommodate and respond to the verbal politeness cues embedded in the body of e-mail messages. Messages structured with a greeting or salutation receive more polite responses than messages that lack these formal politeness cues.

Some Effects of CMC Undercurrents on Group Processes

The Interaction of CMC with Group Size, Diversity, and Proximity.   Group characteristics, such as group size, diversity, and physical proximity of group members to each other when they meet, interact with the communication technology to further influence a group's decision-making process. Large CMC groups appear to benefit the most from using CMC, as they generate more ideas per member than do smaller CMC groups (McGrath & Hollingshead, 1994). Groups having nine members generate more unique ideas per member when using a GSS brainstorming system than do groups having only three participants (Valacich, Dennis, & Nunamaker, 1992). CMC helps reduce the effort required to exchange information, thus facilitating an increase in the amount of group communication and providing a greater sense of group involvement. More diverse groups also experience greater idea generation than homogeneous ones as they bring a greater breadth of knowledge and experience to the discussion. Physical proximity of group members also interacts with the communication medium to influence the group's CMC (Valacich, George, Nunamaker, & Vogel, 1994). CMC groups engaged in discussion through GSS with participants physically separated in different rooms generate more unique ideas, show less idea redundancy, have greater idea originality, and produce higher idea quality overall than groups using GSS with members physically located in the same room. This suggests that it is not just the technology through which the communication is mediated, but the larger physical contextual cues that influence group communication. Members of groups located in the same room, even though they are using CMC as their only medium for communication, are still more conscious of their personal-social identities, experience greater social pressure, and have a greater tendency to conform to the group's expectations and norms than do members of distributed groups.

Gender Swapping.   Past research has estimated that as many as 40 to 60% of Internet users "gender-swap" in their computer-mediated-communication, that is, identify and portray themselves as a person of the opposite gender in their electronic conversations in chat rooms, instant messages, and e-mail. Although Samp, Wittenberg, and Gillett (2003) found the percentage to be somewhat lower with only 233 of their 823 respondents (28%) admitting to having pretended to be the opposite gender on-line; 370 (45%) of those 823 respondents said that they had suspected and questioned the gender of another on-line participant.

Finally, groups that meet and alternately use FTF and CMC demonstrate a greater level of critical thinking in their decision-making process than either FTF or CMC groups. The FTF-CMC combination appears to facilitate a group's ability to develop high-quality decisions (Olaniran, 1994).

Choosing a Medium for the Effective Use of CMC

The challenge for a group is how to utilize an understanding of CMC and its influence on group communication patterns and performance to enhance a group's decision-making, problem-solving, and communication processes. The first step in this process involves planning for the use of CMC by the group. There are several approaches to thinking about the appropriateness of a medium for small group communication. The first is to choose a medium based on the media richness and complexity of the communication task. The second is to think about the language characteristics of the information to be communicated. The third is to consider the communication functions to be used.

Choosing a Medium for the Communication Task

Effectively facilitating a group's decision-making, problem-solving, and communication processes involves choosing an appropriate medium for the communication task (Lengel & Daft, 1988). For efficient communication choose a lean medium. More difficult and nonroutine communication that requires more discussion among group members to achieve a shared meaning demands a richer medium. The development of new plans and strategies also requires a rich medium for a shared group understanding. Use a rich medium to develop social presence and personal relationships and don't let a lack of richness in the communication medium restrict the information shared or implicitly censor the discussion of critical issues. Though communicating through a richer medium may require more time and effort, it is better to endure this loss in efficiency than to inadvertently curtail the group's process by choosing a medium that is too lean to effectively accomplish the communication task. Think about the communication purpose and evaluate the potential use of a new communication technology within the spectrum of available media choices. Table 15.3 lists these recommendations for media selection (Lengel & Daft, 1988).

Finding a Language Demand-Technology Fit

Communication media differ in the type and amount of information they carry. These differences have implications for the group decision-making and communication processes, and groups need to be aware of the fit between the communication demands of their task and the communication medium they use to meet that demand (Farmer & Hyatt, 1994; Bavelas, Hutchinson, Kenwood, & Matheson, 1997; MacDougall, 1999). Three types of language demands are important to communication in a group (Farmer & Hyatt, 1994). These demands are numeric, verbal, and visual symbolizations. Numeric symbolization is the mathematically based aspect of language that requires conveying exact quantities, such as found in numbers and the precise meanings found in mathematical formulas. For business groups these are represented in the numbers used in budgets, the percentages used to calculate sales commissions or profit sharing, and the formulas used to calculate pay increases or health benefits. Verbal symbolization describes the broad array of concepts, ideas, and meanings present in everyday verbal and nonverbal language that provides the rich, multiply layered, and varied interpretation of words. Visual symbolization conveys spatial and geometric information in a pic-

---

TABLE 15.3   Choosing a Communication Medium (Lengel & Daft, 1988)

1. For simple, routine communication choose a lean medium.
2. More difficult and nonroutine communication demands a richer communication medium.
3. Use rich media to develop social presence and personal relationships.
4. Use rich media for implementing new plans and strategies.
5. Don't let a lack of media richness restrict the information shared or censor discussion of critical issues.
6. Evaluate the potential use of a new communication technology within the spectrum of available media choices.

ture, chart, graph, or diagram, and may show two- or three-dimensional representations of a spatial relationship or of a sequence that occurs through time.

Not every CMC medium carries each of these types of information equally well. Text-based computer conferencing systems, for example, carry numeric information with the precision of written language, but have greater difficulty conveying the nuances that distinguish among the multiple possible meanings of language in the expression of a word or phrase. This can lead to misunderstandings in the interpretation of a message. Without the associated vocal inflection, determining whether a person is being open and honest, critical, sarcastic, or humorous, or even whether he or she is asking a question or making an assertion can be difficult. The audio channel provided by the telephone and computer audioconferencing systems carries the verbal and vocal information well, but has greater difficulty expressing the precision of complex numeric equations and the spatial relationships present in visual symbolization. Videoconferencing systems, on the other hand, that are equipped with document-sharing capabilities can more closely approximate FTF communication in their ability to fulfill all three types of language demands. To perform effectively, a group must be concerned with the fit between the symbolization system required for their communication task and the communication medium through which they attempt to accomplish that task (Farmer & Hyatt, 1994).

Matching Media Richness to the Communication Function

Considering the communication function can also help a group choose an appropriate medium. Group communication functions can be divided into eight types: (a) planning functions, such as the development of group agendas, goals, and objectives; (b) engaging in functions requiring creativity and the generation of ideas; (c) intellectual functions such as problem solving; (d) decision-making functions; (e) cognitive-conflict functions such as resolving conflicting points of view; (f) mixed-motive functions that require group conflict resolution; (g) competitive functions that involve issues of power and status; and (h) performance functions when a group undertakes the project. These types of functions have been shown to differ in their demands on the richness of a communication medium (McGrath & Hollingshead, 1994).

Planning and creativity functions require the least amount of media richness and can effectively be accomplished using text-based computer conferencing systems. Text-based computer conferencing systems may even work better for these functions than face-to-face meetings, as text-based computer conferencing systems have a tendency to reduce participant inhibitions, increase more equal participation, and facilitate group generation of a greater number of ideas. Text-based CMC groups also perform better than FTF groups on idea-generation functions, but FTF groups perform better than CMC groups on intellectual ones. Intellectual problem-solving and decision-making functions require more communication richness and are not generally well accomplished using text-based computer conferencing systems but may be undertaken effectively using audio- or videoconferencing systems. CMC groups perform better than FTF groups on decision-making functions, but FTF groups can perform better on negotiation functions. Mixed-motive conflict management functions that require negotiation, coordination, and collaboration are also best accomplished through face-to-face communication (McGrath & Hollingshead, 1994). CMC groups take longer to complete problem-solving functions, but generate more solutions. CMC groups are better suited to achieve quality decisions (Turoff & Hiltz, 1982). When used alone, however, CMC is not a good medium for maintaining group member relationships.

Adopting Effective Group Communication Strategies for CMC

Once a communication medium or media combination has been chosen, a group needs to adopt effective strategies for communicating through that medium (Broome & Chen, 1992). The group must first move beyond their habitual group problem-solving techniques to explore and develop methods that work in the medium they are using to communicate. This may require reframing their problems in new ways and rethinking their group discussion patterns. The group must focus its attention on developing shared group meanings, sequentially building on ideas, and promoting double-loop learning within the group, to clarify and integrate the group's evolving meaning in a way that is less inhibited by the medium. Group members need to explicitly consider the patterns within their shared ideas and the relationships among those ideas, reducing informational loss that might be induced by the medium. They need to balance their use of technology with the needs of group members and avoid the technological trance of having their decisions driven by the technology instead of the larger context of the group's human relationships. They need to emphasize the group's potential for broadening individual perspectives and promoting both individual and collective ownership of ideas. Finally, they need to integrate their use of CMC within the larger context of the group's planning, decision-making, problem-solving, and communication processes (Broome & Chen, 1992).

Facilitating Effective CMC Group Communication

In addition to these strategies, groups using computer mediated communication are most effective when members collaboratively pay attention to and take responsibility for the group's process facilitation. Effective facilitation in CMC groups requires members to competently engage in 13 group facilitation roles in addition to three technology-specific facilitative roles (Clawson, Bostrom, & Anson, 1993).

Just as in face-to-face groups, effective facilitation of CMC groups (a) encourages group member responsibility for and promotes ownership of the group process and results; (b) demonstrates a comfortable level of self-awareness and self-expression; (c) listens to, clarifies, and integrates information and ideas; (d) asks appropriate, well-timed questions to encourage thought and participation; (e) helps keep the group focused on and moving toward its goals; (f) creates and continually reinforces an open, positive, participatory environment; (g) actively builds rapport and relationship; (h) presents clear, concise information and well-developed ideas; (i) demonstrates a flexibility and willingness to adapt to the situation and to other group member needs; (j) helps achieve a clear meeting process and outcome; (k) constructively manages conflict and the expression of negative emotions; (l) encourages and supports the expression of multiple and diverse perspectives; and (m) manages and adheres to meeting time limits and discussion ground rules.

In addition to these traditional face-to-face group roles, members in CMC groups must also (a) have a conceptual understanding of the technology and its capabilities, (b) have an ability to effectively communicate through that technology, and (c) be able to create a comfortable understanding and use of the technology among other group members (Clawson, Bostrom, & Anson, 1993). Table 15.4 lists these roles for effective computer mediated group meeting facilitation.

TABLE 15.4   Effective Computer Mediated Group Meeting Facilitation (Clawson, Bostrom, & Anson, 1993)

As in face-to-face groups, effective computer mediated group meeting facilitation should:

1. Encourage group responsibility and promote member ownership of group process and results.
2. Demonstrate a comfortable level of self-awareness and self-expression.
3. Listen to, clarify, and integrate information and ideas.
4. Ask appropriate, well-timed questions to encourage thought and participation.
5. Help keep group focused on and moving toward its goals.
6. Create and continually reinforce an open, positive, participatory environment.
7. Actively build rapport and relationship.
8. Present clear, concise information and well-developed ideas.
9. Demonstrate flexibility and willingness to adapt to situation and other group member needs.
10. Help achieve a clear meeting process and outcome.
11. Constructively manage conflict and expression of negative emotions.
12. Encourage and support the expression of multiple and diverse perspectives.
13. Manage and adhere to meeting time limits and discussion ground rules.

In addition to these traditional group roles, members in computer conference groups must also:

1. Have a conceptual understanding of the technology and its capabilities.
2. Have an ability to effectively communicate through that technology.
3. Be able to create a comfortable understanding and use of the technology among other group members.

Leading a CMC Group Meeting

CMC group meetings also require a strong discussion leader who can prepare a formal presentation, and then be willing to engage in leading a relaxed, informal group discussion. The group leader should prepare participants for a structured, interactive, electronic meeting and organize that meeting with an agenda, hand-outs, and other materials distributed to all participants before the meeting begins. During the meeting, however, the leader should reduce the formality of the gathering by using a structured but informal communication style and by encouraging members to share in undertaking leadership functions. An effective leader must also be aware of participants' nonverbal communication, as some participants may be nervous and others may be intimidated by the technology and need encouragement to participate. A calm, even-tempered, relaxed leadership style becomes particularly critical when the matters under discussion are important to the group and participants become excited. Adequate preparation and a relaxed communication style are keys to effective CMC meetings (Sherblom, 1997).

Prior to the meeting, an effective leader should: (a) schedule the meeting, (b) confirm the date and time with all participants, (c) plan the meeting for a maximum of two hours, (d) develop an agenda to keep participants focused on the meeting's objectives, and (e) send the agenda and all resource materials to the participants at least 48 hours before the meeting. At the beginning of the session the leader should identify the purpose of the meeting and the person who will facilitate the discussion. The leader should start the meeting on time and end on time. Begin by identifying and individually welcoming each participant and then ask participants to identify themselves when they speak the first time to help facilitate participant interaction. Start the meeting by taking a strong clear leadership role but then relinquish it, encouraging participant interaction as the meeting progresses. Finally, after the meeting, minutes should be prepared and distributed. See Table 15.5.

Summary

Groups increasingly use computer mediated communication (CMC) in their decision-making, problem-solving, and group discussion processes. This CMC is provided through electronic meeting systems having group support system (GSS) capabilities and computer, audio, or videoconferencing facilities. The use of these electronic meeting systems, can influence the communication within the group. Undercurrents of this influence are represented in the concepts of media richness and communication synchronicity that can affect the degree of social presence experienced by group participants. These undercurrents can also impact group performance outcomes and interact with other characteristics of the group (such as group size, diversity, and proximity) to affect the group's productivity and social-relational development.

Groups can manage the effects of CMC through their choice of a communication medium and through the adoption of effective group communication and lead-

TABLE 15.5   CMC Meeting Leadership Functions (O'Rouke, 1993)

1. Prior to the meeting:
   (a) Schedule the meeting.
   (b) Confirm the date and time with all participants.
   (c) Schedule the meeting for a maximum of two hours.
   (d) Plan an agenda to keep participants focused on the meeting's objectives.
   (e) Send the agenda and any resource materials to participants 48 to 72 hours before the meeting.

2. Start the meeting on time and end on time.

3. At the beginning of the meeting:
   (a) Identify the purpose of the meeting.
   (b) Identify the person who will chair the meeting and facilitate the discussion.
   (c) Identify and individually welcome each participant.
   (d) Initially take control with a strong, clear leadership role, then relinquish control and encourage participant interaction as the meeting progresses.
   (e) Ask participants to identify themselves when they speak the first time to help facilitate participant interaction.

4. After the meeting, prepare and distribute minutes.

ership skills. The communication medium used should fit the communication task, the language demands of that task, and the communication functions in which the group intends to participate. Effective group communication strategies include paying attention to group problem-solving techniques and discussion patterns, exploring new ways of sharing ideas and building relationships within the group, and balancing the use of technology with other group member needs. Effective group facilitation promotes a participatory environment for active relational rapport building, a comfortable level of self-expression balanced with active listening, and a constructive management of conflict. CMC requires both a strong discussion leader and group members who will actively take responsibility for the multiple shared leadership functions of maintaining a group focus, a balanced participation, and an eventempered communication process. With these communication abilities a small group can successfully engage in computer mediated communication, accomplishing the groups' tasks while maintaining relationships.

DISCUSSION QUESTIONS

1. What is social presence? What are the important characteristics of it and how can a group effectively increase feelings of social presence in its CMC?

2. What are the three types of language demands? Describe each of them and the technology that provides a best fit for communication to meet that demand.

3. What are the characteristics of computer mediated communication (CMC)?

4. How does CMC differ from FTF communication?

5. Describe the eight communication functions and the media richness characteristics of CMC systems that are best suited to fulfill each function.

6. What are the effects of CMC on groupthink?

7. How do anonymity, group size, and proximity influence participation and communication in CMC groups?

EXERCISES

1. CMC: Mediation and negotiation; 2. Understanding current CMC issues; 3. Experiencing asynchronous communication; 4. Choosing a communication medium

1. CMC: MEDIATION AND NEGOTIATION

Use a couple of the mediation scenarios described at the end of Chapter 12 and in the instructor's resource manual. Divide participants into small groups to negotiate one of these scenarios. One pair of groups will attempt to negotiate the scenario through an available mediated group communication technology (text-based computer chat or discussion group, two telephone speaker-phones, or using video-conferencing software) while another pair of groups will engage in the negotiation face-to-face. After 20 minutes the group pairs switch so that the technology pair of groups meet face-to-face and the face-to-face groups meet through the technology for the negotiation of a second scenario. After the second negotiation the groups should be able to discuss which scenario they found easier to negotiate and why; what difficulties were imposed by the use of the technology; and how their communication style changed during the negotiation through each media.

2. UNDERSTANDING CURRENT CMC ISSUES

Form small research groups to determine the impact of CMC on your college or university. As an alternative, investigate CMC uses in an organization. Obtain permission to conduct interviews of CMC users. Develop a list of current CMC uses such as e-mail or Internet and interview at least five individuals. Ask two specific questions. First, do you feel CMC has helped or hindered your work? Second, what changes would you make in the current CMC to make it more user friendly? Work out a short proposal/presentation with your group's ideas for developing an improved CMC system. Some outside research may be helpful as your ideas evolve.

3. EXPERIENCING ASYNCHRONOUS COMMUNICATION

Your instructor will divide you into groups of two or three. If there are three members, one will be the observer who will provide feedback after the exercise is completed. In the dyad, one of you will be assigned the role of sender and the other the role of receiver. Pick an activity such as folding an airplane or explaining how to eat an unusual meal or how to play a particular card game.

The sender and receiver should sit back-to-back. *Only* the sender is allowed to speak until the exercise is over. The receiver may not ask any questions nor look at the sender. The sender's goal is to describe the concept or activity effectively in the absence of feedback. You have 10 minutes to complete the task.

When finished, the sender and receiver can face each other and the receiver should tell the sender what he or she heard. Compare the receiver's information with the intended message. Now consider what would have happened if the communication had been synchronous. If you have an observer—the third member— receive feedback from this individual regarding the apparent barriers created by asynchronous communication. What are the implications for CMC? For group activities?

Compare your success with other dyads or triads in the class. What actions can be taken to make certain CMC works for your group?

4. CHOOSING A COMMUNICATION MEDIUM

Your small group has been asked to develop a CMC model for a large lecture course. Based on the information provided in this chapter, and in Table 15.2, what recommendations would you make? Make certain your recommendations take into consideration all of the aspects of the large lecture course. Be prepared to discuss your answers with your class.

REFERENCES

2001: A Space Odyssey original screenplay at http://www.palantir.net/2001/script.html viewed 9/1/2003.

Accawi, A. F. (1997, August). The telephone. *The Sun.* 10–13.

Albrecht, T. L., & Adelman, M. B. (1987). *Communicating social support.* Newbury Park, CA: Sage.

Bavelas, J. B., Hutchinson, S., Kenwood, C., & Matheson, D. H. (1997). Using face-to-face dialogue as a standard for other communication systems. *Canadian Journal of Communication 22,* 5–24.

Bordia, P. (1997). Face-to-face versus computer-mediated communication: A synthesis of the experimental literature. *The Journal of Business Communication, 34*(1), 99–120.

Braithwaite, D. O., Waldron, V. R., & Finn, J. (1999). Communication of social support in computer-mediated groups for people with disabilities. *Health Communication, 11*(2), 123–151.

Broome, B. J., & Chen, M. (1992). Guidelines for computer-assisted group problem solving: Meeting the challenges of complex issues. *Small Group Research, 23*(2), 216–236.

Bunz, U., & Campbell, S. W. (in press). Politeness accommodation in electronic mail. *Communication Research Reports, 21.*

Cai, X. (in press). Is the computer a functional alternative to traditional media? *Communication Research Reports, 21.*

Campbell, K., & Wright, K. B. (2002). On-line support groups: An investigation of relationships among source credibility, dimensions of relational communication, and perceptions of emotional support. *Communication Research Reports, 19,* 183–193.

Clawson, V. K., Bostrom, R. P., & Anson, R. (1993). The role of the facilitator in computer-supported meetings. *Small Group Research, 24*(4), 547–565.

Cooper, W. H., Gallupe, R. B., Pollard, S., & Cadsby, J. (1998). Some liberating effects of anonymous electronic brainstorming. *Small Group Research, 29*(2), 147–178.

Daft, R., & Lengel, R. (1986). Organizational information requirements, media richness, and structural design. *Management Science, 32,* 554–571.

Farmer, S. M., & Hyatt, C. W. (1994). Effects of task language demands and task complexity on computer-mediated work groups. *Small Group Research, 25*(3), 331–366.

Gallupe, R. B., Cooper, W. H., Grise, M., & Bastianutti, L. M. (1994). Blocking electronic brainstorms. *Journal of Applied Psychology, 79,* 77–86.

Graetz, K. A., Boyle, E. S., Kimble, C. E., Thompson, P., & Garloch, J. L. (1998). Information sharing in face-to-face, teleconferencing, and electronic chat groups. *Small Group Research, 29*(6), 714–743.

Hacker, K. L., & Steiner, R. (2001). Hurdles of access and benefits of usage for internet communication. *Communication Research Reports, 18,* 399–407.

Huang, L. (1999). The adoption and uses of e-mail among Taiwanese students at an American university. *World Communication, 28*(4), 69–86.

Lengel, R. H., & Daft, R. L. (1988). The selection of communication media as an executive skill. *Executive, 2*(3), 225–232.

MacDougall, R. C. (1999). Subject fields, oral emulation and the spontaneous cultural positioning of Mohawk e-mail users. *World Communication, 28*(4), 5–25.

McGrath, J. E., & Hollingshead, A. B. (1994). *Groups interacting with technology.* Thousand Oaks, CA: Sage.

Metzger, M. J., & Flanagan, A. J. (2002). Audience orientations toward new media. *Communication Research Reports, 19,* 338–351.

Meyers, C., & Davis, S. (1998). *Blur: The speed of change in the connected economy.* Reading, MA: Addison-Wesley.

Miranda, S. M. (1994). Avoidance of groupthink: Meeting management using group support systems. *Small Group Research, 25*(1), 105–136

Olaniran, B. A. (1994). Group performance in computer-mediated and face-to-face communication media. *Management Communication quarterly, 7*(3), 256–281.

O'Rourke, J. S. (1993). Video teleconferencing. A paper presented to the 58th annual convention of the association for business communication, Montreal, Quebec, Canada.

Poole, M. S., & Holmes, M. E. (1995). Decision development in computer-assisted group decision-making. *Human Communication Research, 22*(1), 90–127.

Poole, M. S., Holmes, M. E., Watson, R., & DeSanctis, G. (1995). Group decision support systems and group communication. *Communication Research, 20*(2), 176–213.

Rogers, R. A. (1999). "Is this a great time or what? ☺" Information technology and the erasure of difference. *World Communication, 28*(4), 69–86.

Rumbough, T. (2001). The development and maintenance of interpersonal relationships through computer-mediated communication. *Communication Research Reports, 18,* 223–229.

Samp, J. A., Wittenberg, E. M., & Gillett, D. L. (2003). Presenting and monitoring a gender-defined self on the internet. *Communication Research Reports, 20,* 1–12.

Scott, C. R. (1999). Communication technology and group communication. In L. R. Frey, D. S. Gouran, & M. S. Poole (Eds.), *The handbook of group communication theory & research* (pp. 432–472), Thousand Oaks, CA: Sage.

Shedletsky, L., & Aitken, J. E. (2004). *Human communication on the internet.* Boston: Allyn & Bacon.

Sherblom, J. C. (1994). Teleconferencing. In A. Williams (Ed.), *Communication and technology: Today and tomorrow* (pp. 155–171). Denton, TX: Association for Business Communication.

Sherblom, J. C. (1997). Teleconferencing. In D. C. Reep, *Technical writing: Principles, strategies, and readings* (3rd ed., pp. 556–561). Boston: Allyn & Bacon.

Short, J., Williams, E., & Christie, B. (1976). *The social psychology of telecommunications.* London: Wiley.

Trevino, L. K., Daft, R. L., & Lengel, R. H. (1990). Understanding manager's media choices: A symbolic interactionist perspective. In J. Fulk & C. Steinfield (Eds.), *Organizations and communication technology* (pp. 71–94), Newbury Park, CA: Sage.

Turoff, M., & Hiltz, S. R. (1982). Computer support: Group versus individual decisions. *IEEE Transactions Communications, 30*(1), 82–90.

Valacich, J. S., Dennis, A. R., & Nunamaker, J. F. (1992). Group size and anonymity effects on computer-mediated idea generation. *Small Group Research, 23*(1), 49–73.

Valacich, J. S., George, J. F., Nunamaker, J. F., & Vogel, D. R. (1994). Physical proximity effects on computer-mediated group idea generation. *Small Group Research, 25*(1), 83–104.

Walther, J. B. (1994). Anticipated ongoing interaction versus channel effects on relational communication in computer-mediated interaction. *Human Communication Research, 20*(4), 473–501.

Walther, J. B. (1996). Computer-mediated communication: Impersonal, interpersonal, and hyperpersonal interaction. *Communication Research, 23*(1), 3–43.

Warren, R., & Bluma, A. (2002). Parental mediation of children's internet use: The influence of established media. *Communication Research Reports, 19*, 8–17.

Wright, K. (2002). Motives for communication within on-line support groups and antecedents for interpersonal use. *Communication Research Reports, 19*, 89–98.

APPENDIX

Gathering, Organizing, Processing, and Presenting Information as a Team

I. Choose a Topic

Brainstorm

Start by brainstorming as a group to suggest all the possible topics you might be interested in researching, discussing, and presenting.

Generate a list of these topics. Research each topic for availability of information. At a subsequent group meeting, review this list of topics and make any additions to the list.

Select a Topic

Talk through each item on the list and discuss the positives and negatives of the topic.

Discuss and reach a consensus on a topic that the whole group is interested in investigating.

Discuss

Discuss the topic, expanding upon its multiple aspects, and divide it into sections. Assign sections of the topic to each group member to research, but make sure everyone knows what all the sections are so they can help each other out with the research.

II. Gather Information

Sources of Information:

Popular magazines, television shows, movies: Good for dramatic, attention-getting introductions to a topic and can be profitably used that way, but should not be relied on heavily for strong, factual, supportive information to make your main points.

Library references, books, journal articles: Effective in providing solid support for the main assertions that you want to make about a topic.

Databases, the World Wide Web: Good sources for facts and figures, but they must be interpreted and integrated with other forms of support. They cannot make the case and stand on their own. Use them, but explain to your audience what they mean to you and how they support your argument.

Interviews with experts or people with personal experience: Can add both a human dimension to other types of information and credibility to the argument that you are making. Make sure that the connection between the person's expertise and the evidence provided you is made clear to your audience.

Surveys: Useful for providing evidence on opinion and attitude types of questions and issues. Be careful with the wording of the questions being asked and keep the survey short so that it does not take too much time for people to fill it out. One-page written surveys or oral surveys of three or four questions can be effective for gathering many people's opinions in a short amount of time at busy locations such as a shopping mall, the campus union, or a grocery store. Usually you have to ask permission of the facilities manager before you can survey people on the premises, however.

Quasi-experimental data: Useful for certain topics such as a topic asking whether store owners spend more time with customers who are clean and well-dressed than with those who are dirty and poorly dressed. In this case, two team members could take turns alternately entering stores as well-groomed customers and as poorly groomed customers. A third team member could function as an observer recording observations such as the amount of time before a store clerk waits on each, how long the store clerk spends with each, and how helpful the store clerk is with questions.

III. Process the Information

Organize the Group Meetings and Discussions

Develop a Meeting Agenda

Sample Agenda Format Outline:

Time and place for meeting

   I. Approval of minutes (minutes approved, modified, or corrected)

   II. Subcommittee reports

      A.

      B.

      C.

   III. Old business

     A.

     B.

     C.

   IV. New business

     A.

     B.

     C.

   V. Announcements and other items

     A.

     B.

Keep Minutes of Group Discussions

Minutes should note particularly (a) the information that has been gathered, (b) any decisions that have been made, (c) tasks that have been assigned or volunteered for, (d) duties and roles that have been taken on, and (e) the time and place of the next meeting, and what needs to accomplished before that meeting.

Sample Minutes Outline:

Meeting start time and location

   List of members present

     I. Minutes of last meeting approved, modified, or corrected

     II. Committee reports

       A.

       B.

       C.

   III. Old business

     A.

     B.

     C.

   IV. New business

     A.

     B.

     C.

   V. Announcements, time adjourned, time, date, place of next meeting

Discuss and Present the Information

Distinguish Different Types of Information

Questions of fact are empirically verifiable (dates, statistics, quantities).

Questions of opinion are personal statements that voice a perspective or attitude.

Questions of value are statements about value or worth. They are generally based on cultural values and assumptions and are culturally relative, frequently stated in evaluative terms (that is, good or bad), are not quantifiable, and are not empirically verifiable.

Questions of policy state the way things "should" be or what "should" be done.

Distinguish Types of Reasoning

Inductive reasoning progresses to a general principle from one or more specific facts, instances, or cases. (For example, crime rates are increasing in the community, and pepper spray has been shown to be an effective deterrent to these crimes; therefore carrying pepper spray will increase your safety in the community.)

Deductive reasoning progresses to a specific conclusion or result based on general assumptions, principles, and facts. (For example, reasoning that: [a] generous people give food to the needy at Thanksgiving time; and [b] we are generous people; therefore [c] we should give food to the needy at Thanksgiving.)

IV. Organize the Information for Presentation

Decide on an Appropriate Presentational Format:

Forum, Panel, Colloquium, Symposium

Organize the Presentation:

An effective organizational pattern can be to have sections that follow the decision-making, problem-solving sequence such as: "Defining the Problem," "Analyzing the Problem," "Possible Solutions," "Criteria for a Solution," and "The Best Solution."

Use Informational Supports

Statistics: The judicial use of statistics and other numbers can be effective to make assertions of fact (such as "Seventy-five percent of all drivers exceed the speed limit") when the source of the statistic is identified, the source is credible, and the purpose and meaning of the number to the current topic and presentation are clearly explained.

Personal Stories: These can engender emotional and logical support for the topic, as well as persuasive appeal. They can be effective to introduce a topic or to support a point as long as the story is relatively short, coherent, to the point, and relevant. The reason for telling the story must be obvious to the audience. A poorly told story or one with a vague purpose can leave an audience confused and detract from the rest of the presentation as the audience continues to think about the story instead of listening to the presentation.

Structure the Presentation

Outline Example for a Presentational Structure

Introduction to Topic

Topic Assertion Part One

Support

Support

Topic Assertion Part Two

Support

Support

Conclusion

Example of a Presentational Structure

Topic: The Importance of Daily Exercise

Introduction: Today I will talk about the health benefits of daily exercise. . . .

I will make three points: (1) that daily exercise is easy, (2) that it can help you live healthier today, and (3) that it can help you live a longer, healthier life. My goal is to encourage you to start exercising today.

Assertion: Daily exercise is easy.

Support: Present interview with health specialist reporting that even short amounts of daily exercise time improve health

Support: Present chart from a popular health and fitness magazine showing how easy and fun exercise can be.

Assertion: Daily exercise will help you live healthier today.

Support: Survey of 25 people who jog, play sports, or exercise in the gym responding to questions about how regular exercise makes them feel—positive responses.

Support: Jim's personal story about starting an exercise program and losing 30 pounds, ending with: "I feel great!"

Assertion: Daily exercise will help you live healthier longer.

Support: medical evidence cited from a journal or book showing reduction in cholesterol counts and blood pressure, and other healthful physical characteristics.

Support: Demographic statistics cited from medical journal showing age–death rates among people who exercise regularly and those who do not.

Conclusion: Daily physical exercise is easy and healthier for you today and for the rest of your life. Start exercising today!

V. Practice

Discuss roles with group members.

Divide up duties.

Script out the presentation.

Run through a rehearsal from start to finish.

Time the rehearsal.

Have all the supporting and visual aid materials ready to present.

INDEX